ABORTION: THE

"Abortion: to be or not to be?"

This personal dilemma is being faced
every day by a swiftly-growing
number of people, not least by the
author of this book, who amid the
pressures of a busy NHS practice,
has had to work out his own answer
which would satisfy his duty as
a doctor and also his conscience
as a practising Christian.

The result is this sympathetic and
compassionate book, which ranges
widely over the many aspects of its
challenging and difficult subject.
Nothing of its size and scope has
been attempted before, and it will
be widely welcomed by the very large
group—probably including most
members of society—of thoughtful
people who are deeply concerned by
the moral, ethical, religious,
physical and mental issues involved,
and who are searching for facts
on which to base their judgment.

Rex Gardner is a Consultant
Obstetrician and Gynaecologist in
Sunderland, Co. Durham.

He specializes in the study of the
effects of abortion—performed and
refused; he has lectured in Dutch
and British universities, to professional
societies, and to both Protestant
and Roman Catholic groups, as
well as taking part in debates on TV
and elsewhere.

In 1958 he was ordained as a minister
of the United Free Church of
Scotland, and still preaches, as medical
duties permit, in the pulpits of many
denominations. This combination of
gynaecologist and Christian minister
is possibly unique.

Mr. Gardner wishes to make it clear
that he does not see private patients.

Unto us....

by SPIKE MILLIGAN

Somewhere, at sometime
they committed themselves to me
and so, I was!
Small, but I *was*.
Tiny in shape
lusting to live
I hung in my pulsing cave.
Soon they knew of me
my mother – my father –
I had no say in my being
I lived on trust
and love.
Tho' I couldn't think
each part of me was saying
a silent 'Wait for me,
I will bring you love!'
I was taken
blind, naked, defenceless,
by the hand of one
whose good name
was graven on a brass plate
in Wimpole Street,
and dropped on the sterile floor
of a foot-operated, plastic waste-bucket.
There was no Queen's Counsel
to take my brief.
The cot I might have warmed
stood in Harrods shop window.
When my passing was told
my father smiled.
No grief filled my empty space.
My death was celebrated
with two tickets to see Danny La Rue
who was pretending to be a woman
like my mother was.

Tel Aviv, 8th Feb. 1972

(From *Small Dreams of a Scorpion* published
by Michael Joseph and Jack and Margaret
Hobbs, © 1972. Used by kind permission

ABORTION
THE PERSONAL DILEMMA

A Christian Gynaecologist Examines the
Medical, Social and Spiritual Issues

by

R. F. R. GARDNER, M.R.C.O.G.
Consultant Obstetrician and Gynaecologist, Sunderland Hospitals

with a Foreword by

J. A. STALLWORTHY, M.A., F.R.C.S., F.A.C.S, F.R.C.O.G.
Nuffield Professor of Obstetrics & Gynaecology
in the University of Oxford

EXETER:
THE PATERNOSTER PRESS

ISBN: 0 85364 124 2

AUSTRALIA:
Emu Book Agencies Pty., Ltd.,
1 Lee Street, Sydney, N.S.W.

SOUTH AFRICA:
Oxford University Press
P.O. Box 1141, Oxford House,
11, Buitencingle Street, Cape Town

Made and Printed in Great Britain for
The Paternoster Press Paternoster House
3 Mount Radford Crescent Exeter Devon
by A. Wheaton & Co., Exeter, Devon.

CONTENTS

5

FOREWORD

by Prof. J. A. Stallworthy, M.A., F.R.C.S., F.A.C.S., F.R.C.O.G.
Nuffield Professor of Obstetrics & Gynaecology, University of Oxford

THE BALANCE SHEET OF HEALTH AND DISABILITY FOLLOWING LEGAL abortion has not yet been written in a form to satisfy the critical impartial judgment of an auditor. It may never be written. Delayed sequelae such as infertility, recurrent abortion, and premature labour, with the disappointments and tragedies this can bring, may not become evident until many years after the causative interlude. Their incidence and effect will remain unknown and any accurate assessment of the advantages and disadvantages of abortion will be incomplete unless a carefully planned and supervised long term prospective study is conducted. Moreover the results, some of which will be bad, while others will be good and will contribute to the patient's subsequent happiness, of refusing to terminate pregnancies should be known. This will also require prospective studies involving detailed planning with statistical advice, and thoroughly skilled team-work of high quality.

In the meantime there are two extreme points of view. The one believes that in no circumstances must any pregnancy be terminated, while the other maintains that legal termination of pregnancy is no more than a minor surgical interlude to be regarded as a natural and legitimate extension of contraception. The size of this minority may be overestimated, due to the decibel recording of its protestations. Its declared aim is abortion on demand. Because of this divergence of views, with the emotional reactions which are often associated, it is wise at this stage to avoid using the terms therapeutic and legal abortion as synonyms.

Between these two extremes there is a large cosmopolitan group, probably including most members of society. Some are apathetic until they themselves become personally or indirectly involved with unplanned pregnancy. But a very large group undoubtedly consists of thoughtful people who are deeply concerned by the moral, ethical, religious, physical and mental issues involved. They are searching for facts on which to base their judgment. Though willing to modify their formerly held attitudes to this subject they wish to have some assurance that by doing so they are taking action which is justifiable and right.

Implementation of the Abortion Act of 1967 in England and Wales has been associated with emotional turmoil and confusion of thought.

Very many people are ill informed even on facts which have been established already, either by recorded experience of liberal abortion in other
countries or by the evidence accumulating in these islands. Little publicity
has been given to many of the known delayed sequelae, partly because as
yet information is not precise, while even those intimately involved with
the present Act, either as patients or doctors, are often reluctant or unwilling to consider the long-term view. They have an affinity both with the
ostrich and with Cato and live on the principle of 'Carpe Diem'—let us
live for today, tomorrow may never come!

Readers of this book may not agree with all the views expressed by
its author; in fact it is unlikely that they will, but none can doubt his
integrity and his obvious desire to present a very difficult problem clearly
and honestly. He writes with the double authority of a consultant gynaecologist and an ordained minister. As will be seen from the text his views
are based on a wide personal experience of the problems, anxieties, and
tragedies presented by so many women of all ages when seeking for a way
of escape from an unplanned and unwanted pregnancy. Sympathetic
understanding and compassion which are so evident in this book are
unfortunately absent from much of the publicity currently given to this
challenging and difficult subject of abortion.

Dr. Gardner should be congratulated very warmly on the safe delivery
of this book to his publisher. It has obviously involved a very busy
gynaecological specialist in a great amount of work. There is no doubt
that readers both professional and lay, including those who have to refuse
or perform abortion and those who request or demand it, will find this
volume a most helpful guide. Many of the views expressed in its pages, if
made known to the younger generation now reaching maturity, might
help them to avoid those disillusionments which for many now seem
inevitable.

PREFACE

ALTHOUGH this book is written in the first person, the debt I owe to my friends and colleagues is enormous. As more than a hundred of them helped me with the questionnaire discussed in chapter 16, and many others helped in other ways, it is impossible to list all those who have given their aid.

I am more than fortunate in my friends: among them I must thank for their advice on specific points Professors James Barr, Charles Douglas, Richard Trussell and Donald Wiseman and the Rev. Bill Norman. My colleague Mr. Sydney Cohen has not only made freely available to me his own case records but shared many of the clinical problems, as has Miss Dorothy Watson, Principal Medical Social Worker.

The Rev. Dr. Martyn Lloyd-Jones, and the Rev. Dr. Hugh Trowell have written of their personal experience. My thoughts have to be shaped and reshaped by constant discussion with likeminded colleagues in the Christian Medical Fellowship, and by correspondence with others in the Christian Medical Society of North America. Professors G. A. Lindeboom and J. Janssens did me the honour of inviting me to take part in a conference in the Free University of Amsterdam: I must thank the Dutch doctors and medical students for sharpening my thoughts in discussion; likewise similar groups in Britain.

No such work would be possible without bibliographic assistance. I have been particularly fortunate in the willing and skilful help of the librarians of the Royal College of Obstetricians and Gynaecologists: Miss Patricia Want and her colleagues. Miss Gillian Veitch of the Sunderland Post-Graduate Medical Centre, and Miss Janetta Scurfield of the Sunderland Borough Library have also been most helpful. The Rev. John Cockerton kindly gave me the run of St. John's College Library, Durham. My friend the Rev. Seymour Flinn has kept me supplied with information from the American scene, while Dr. Robert Hall and Miss Jimmye Kimmey of the Association for the Study of Abortion have been generous in supplying reprints.

None, however, of those mentioned have read the manuscript. They are, therefore, in no way responsible for the views expressed, which are solely my own.

My thanks are also due to Mrs Adoline Coburn who patiently typed and retyped the manuscript.

The greatest single influence on my professional life has been that of John Stallworthy, now Nuffield Professor of Obstetrics and Gynaecology in the University of Oxford. In common with a host of my contemporaries in every part of the world, I owe him more than can be expressed. If this work can be found worthy to rank among those which have been stimulated in his department, I shall be content. My debt to him is increased by his agreeing to write the foreword.

Most of all my thanks are due to my wife and family who have allowed me, as soon as I arrived home from hospital, to seclude myself in my study and "get on with the book." As a mother, as a family-planning doctor, and above all as a committed Christian, my wife's advice and comments have been invaluable not only on this manuscript, but on the cases whose burdens I share with her. My son Iain has kindly prepared two of the indices.

It is my prayer that members of the medical, para-medical, and nursing professions involved in these problems, the pastors who are consulted, and above all the families gripped by doubt, may find in these pages some pointer to a decision of peace.

Lastly it is my hope that non-Christians in medicine and in the legislatures may be the better able to understand why sometimes we have to cry with Martin Luther, "Here I stand, I can do no other."

Sunderland, 1971   R. F. R. GARDNER

INTRODUCTION

Here (in abortion) we are confronted with that utmost limit, where the exceptional case lands us, where even theological thought reaches its limit.

HELMUT THIELICKE[1]

ABORTION: TO BE OR NOT TO BE? THE QUESTION IS BEING ASKED BY a number, a swiftly growing number, of people every day.

There are many groups of people involved, each with an individual problem, each requiring particular information. The availability of abortion – how, where and when – is the only question in the mind of the wife who with throbbing head and smarting eyes tries to focus through the cotton-wool masses that seem to fill her mind.

The risks of the operation, and the possible aftermath for his wife's peace of mind, are questions which occur to her husband as he longs to drag his wife back from her despair.

Speed and secrecy are problems which may come to the pregnant student, with every now and then a wave of doubt: what about the child that I carry within me?

To her fiancé, conscious of his own responsibility, the immediate issue may be financial, but in quieter moments he wonders how an abortion would affect their future chance of a child of their own.

To the feminist, the reformer, there is only one question: why is abortion not immediately and freely available as of right to any woman on demand?

Now none of these people are in fact thinking of abortion at all; they are thinking of cessation of pregnancy. To them it is really all so easy. As one psychiatrist has illuminatingly put it "I say that if a pregnancy is regarded as an unfelicitous happenstance, and is aborted, the abortion restores the former state of integrity."[2]

[1] H. Thielicke, *The Ethics of Sex*, London, 1964, Jas. Clarke.
[2] Natalie Shainess, "Abortion and Womankind." In *Abortion in a Changing World* (see p. 34, fn. 2).

The politician wonders how a workable law could be framed, the hospital administrator wonders how the facilities can be found, and, more important, staffed.

The pupil nurse, faced with a training schedule to complete, and aware of the staff shortage on the ward, questions whether the vaunted freedom to opt out on conscientious grounds is a fiction.

The medical social worker, well aware of the pathetic inadequacy of her worn-out patient, and sympathetic to the intolerable burden the woman has to carry, wonders if she is such that she would merely move the burden from the cash column to the conscience.

The minister of Word and Sacraments, facing his trembling visitor, battles with his troubled conscience. Can the destruction of this God-given life be justified?

The psychiatrist, aware that the distressed girl before him has no mental disease, wonders how to act. Should he emulate his professorial colleague who stated "I write letters recommending abortion that are frankly fraudulent, because I am satisfied to be used so that someone may obtain what our society otherwise would deny her."?[3]

The gynaecologist, aware that ultimately the decision lies with him, has his question. He also is thinking of cessation of pregnancy, and the results foreseen and unforeseen by his patient, which may follow. But he, almost alone, is thinking of abortion. Of the act. It is a lonely operation. Although dilatation of the cervix, the neck of the womb, is an operation he performs many times a week, on this occasion it will be different. He takes that first dilator and is tinglingly aware that he is about to seal the fate of a fetus, that he is about to alter history. In other operations the cervix will dilate up readily, but in this operation it will fight, grip the end of the dilator and force it back into his hand. And then at last he will win, and as he does so he will wonder who has lost.

The various groups, and there are others, seeking some help in their questioning, can look long for an answer.

It is true that there is an extensive literature on abortion. Much of it is propagandist, seeking to persuade its readers that abortion is a right to be made more and more widely available, or that it is an evil to be fought tooth and nail. Almost all the remainder is in medical journals, or the printed *Proceedings* of symposia not readily available to the general public, and is too narrow in subject to be of much use in decision-making.

It was in an endeavour to provide such a guide that the present book was planned. It quickly became obvious that it had to cover all aspects of the problem. It is fatuous to leave medical aspects to be dealt with in a work for doctors, for no meaningful decision can be taken by anyone unless they know something of the procedure and its risks. It is dishonest

---

[3] L. Eisenberg, "Abortion and Psychiatry." In *Abortion in a Changing World* (see p. 34, fn. 2)

to encourage anyone to reach a decision without facing the possible aftermath of remorse. Granted that remorse is statistically unlikely, the size of the risk must be examined. It is ingenuous to consider easier abortion without looking at the availability of facilities for the operation. It is meaningless to suggest larger facilities until the availability of willing helpers has been looked into. Above all it is disastrous to consider involvement, whether as helper or patient, until the deepest implications for conscience have been sifted and settled.

For a book covering all factors, it was suggested that experts in theology and philosophy should be called to provide their appropriate chapters. This was rejected for two reasons. There already exists what I have elsewhere described as "the preclinical textbook",[4] in the form of an American symposium on *Birth Control and the Christian*,[5] in which twenty-six participants give their views on allied subjects. It is an indispensable work for the study, but in the actual personal case it is less appropriate. One of the contributors to that work has commented elsewhere, 'Distinguished clerics, psychologists, doctors and lawyers sought to determine what course of action should be followed. They were unable to answer many important questions . . . I ask myself, "Heaven knows: who can tell? Who shall decide when experts disagree?' "[6]

It seems inherent in the nature of the problem that no multiple-author, multi-disciplinary approach can be satisfactory. A theologian or philosopher considering in his study one facet such as the sanctity of life, the relationship of soul to fetus, or the mother's right to wholeness, can relate this to the desirability of abortion. It may seem therefore that to get the whole picture one merely has to add these various contributions together. Unfortunately this does not work. The rights of the fetus, which form the starting point for one argument, conflict with the maternal rights which formed the starting point for the next. As each argument forms a coherent unit, it is impossible to trim it to fit its neighbour, without starting again from the beginning.

The author, as a gynaecologist facing the introduction of the Abortion Act, 1967, had to work out his own approach to the problem. And, like every other person in any way involved in it, he had to reach his conclusions in the light of his moral values. It is amusing to read the frequent articles which appear, castigating medical men for introducing moral values into their abortion practice. Amusing, because the unnoticed motive behind these impassioned diatribes is the writer's own moral judgment as

[4] R. F. R. Gardner, "Birth Control and the Christian." A review article, *In the Service of Medicine*, July 1969.
[5] *Birth Control and the Christian*, Ed. W. O. Spitzer and C. L. Saylor, London, 1969, Coverdale House.
[6] Mr Justice T. S. Clark, "Religion, Morality and Abortion: A Constitutional Appraisal." *Loyala University Law Review*, 1969, **2.**

to what is right.[7] The present author is a committed Christian. As such his answers had to be in full agreement with the Christian faith. The line of reasoning worked out in this volume, then, is that gradually built up by the author himself out of sheer necessity as he faces the practical problem, and it can be considered as an apologia. As Francis Schaeffer has reminded us, we must be able to live consistently with our theory.[8]

It seems to me, therefore, essential that the theological aspects should be dealt with by the clinician. As has been well said by a Professor of Ethics: "The position of personal responsibility that physicians, mothers, and others have, is different from that of a writer of a manual of moral theology, or of the priest who judges the moral rectitude of others . . . . To assume responsibility for an action is quite a different order of experience from ascribing responsibility for an action. Physicians, mothers and others are initiators of action, they are agents in the process of life who determine to a great extent what actually happens."[9] As both a gynaecologist and a minister of the gospel the present author had a unique responsibility to try to relate the various factors involved in the practice of abortion. The Jesuit Father Baum has reminded us: "Theology is of the greatest importance to the life of the Church. But we must clearly understand that theology does not create what we believe: it simply reflects on it."[10]

The Christian is often accused of being intellectually dishonest. It was, therefore, a prerequisite of this enquiry that it should be allowed to lead where it did, with no predetermined conclusions. But such a search must be based on facts, and *facts are the scarcest commodity in the abortion debate*. A survey of the literature will show that certain unsubstantiated statements and figures are quoted over and over again until they assume the validity of accepted fact. In view of this it was decided to tie the argument as closely as possible to the primary literature; hence no excuse is offered for the apparatus of references.

The Plan of the Work

From what has been said it follows that first of all we must try to find out what the abortion situation has been, and what it becomes after the introduction of liberalizing legislation. This in turn depends upon the

[7] This point is made very clearly by one of the leading protagonists of liberal abortion, Madeleine Simms. ("Abortion and the Facts": *World Medicine*, January 27, 1971). In a witty article she suggests there are no crucial facts to be discovered. Each piece of information can be construed as good or bad according to the viewpoint of the observer. 'Not even the simplest and most obvious questions about the effect of the Abortion Act can be answered without at some point coming up against the rocks of value judgement.'

[8] F. Schaeffer, as reported in *Crusade* Magazine, April, 1970.

[9] J. M. Gustafson, In *The Morality of Abortion*, Ed. J. T. Noonan, Harvard University Press, 1970.

[10] G. Baum, "Can the Church Change Her Position on Birth Control?" In *Contraception and Holiness*, Ed. Abp. T. D. Roberts, London, 1965, Collins.

form of legislation, which we cannot therefore overlook. The results of legislation are not always what the legislators intended. We must look into this if future legislation, and there will be much worldwide, is to be wisely worded.

Before becoming involved in considering actual cases it is important to decide whether we should in conscience have anything to do with abortion. This discussion occupies the second part of the book. In view of the author's own position and his own practice this has to be a Christian exposition. Those of other faiths can therefore leave this part aside. They would be wrong, however, to imagine that they can shirk the issue: it is only a consistently suppressed conscience that will lie dormant.

Having faced the general question of the justifiability of abortion, we are confronted next by a specific question: in this particular case is abortion right, and is it wise? Only by weighing all the factors can we hope to reach an answer. And this requires not just a general survey of problems, but notice of how things work out in practice, by considering case-histories.

The illustrative histories entitled "Medical Cases" are all culled from the medical literature, or from the clinical practice of the author or fellow gynaecologists. In the interests of the patient no indication is here given as to the source of the case, and certain non-relevant details have been altered. As the cases have occurred in four continents, any apparent resemblance to a known person can be discounted.

It will, of course, be argued by medical scientists that all this is merely "anecdotal." There is no alternative approach. A doctor who refuses every case, or one who aborts every case, may be able eventually to produce some meaningful figures of long-term results. But immediately he introduces any selection, the end results of his series are as much a reflection of the accuracy of his judgment as of the efficacy of the procedure. The multifactorial nature of the cases seems to rule out any meaningful statistical evaluation of the results.

By the same token the cry will inevitably be raised that the writing is "emotive." Of course it is! How could it be otherwise in a subject where the patient's emotions are, in almost every case, a prime factor? This patient sitting in the chair requesting abortion is not 0.5% of my current series; she is a woman full of fears and doubts, battling against the mentally-clouding effect of a high hormonal blood-level, to come to a decision. Whatever else she needs she needs understanding and emotional rapport.

The person dealing with a woman requesting abortion cannot – or should not – be coldly impersonal. This is not an impersonal subject. There is no agreed solution to be taught. This, then is my personal search, and these my tentative conclusions. I have therefore written this book as I feel from within the problem, in the first person.

Notes on Terminology

Inevitably a few medical terms have had to be used in this volume. For the benefit of those unacquainted with them the following may prove useful.

There are two *ovaries*, one lying on each side of the female pelvis. Each contains several thousand eggs or *ova*. One (or occasionally more) *ovum* is shed each month at the moment of *ovulation*. The *ovum* is swept down a passage, the *fallopian tube*, towards the body of the womb or *uterus*, the neck or *cervix* of which protrudes into the upper end of the birth canal or *vagina*.

The male during intercourse (*coitus*) ejaculates many million *spermatozoa* which swim up through the *cervix* and body of the *uterus* into the *fallopian tubes*. If a *spermatozoon* meets an *ovum* in the tube and penetrates its covering *fertilization* occurs. The fertilized egg becomes in turn an *embryo*, a *fetus*, and a baby. Conception takes place in the tube, the fertilized egg being swept down to implant in the wall of the *uterus* 4–5 days later. If it is trapped in the tube it grows there, giving rise to the dangerous condition of *ectopic gestation*.

The terms *chromosome* and *gene* are discussed in chapter 22, and DNA in chapter 13.

Fetus: It is becoming widely accepted on etymological grounds that this spelling is preferable to *foetus*. It has accordingly being used throughout.

Titles: To provide some guide as to the training of writers quoted, the title "Dr." has been reserved for medically qualified writers, although many others quoted have doctorates in other disciplines. In accordance with customary usage "Mr." and "Miss" refer to British gynaecological specialists. It may well be that some errors have crept into this coding. I trust that any who are wrongly titled will accept this apology, together with my assurance that no discourtesy is intended.

PART I

THE ABORTION SCENE BEFORE AND AFTER
LIBERALIZING LEGISLATION

CHAPTER I

THE GROUNDS FOR REFORM

They can cope with death. It's only living that defeats them.   MORRIS WEST[1]

THERE ARE FOUR GREAT AND COMPELLING REASONS WHY A CHANGE in the laws relating to abortion has been pressed in recent decades. There was first a new awareness of tragedy all round us, previously too often unnoticed.

There is the tragedy of the children of whom it is said that it would have been better had they never been born. Some are deformed in body. The most notable group of these are the children, 300 in Britain, 3,000 in Germany,[2] born following the use by their mothers of the drug thalidomide. Some are deformed in function, such as the spastic, others are deformed in mind. Many feel it an affront to the dignity of Man that such children should have to suffer and grow up, if grow up they do, into a world forever beyond their reach. Only too often the deformity in body or function brings eventually with it a deformity in attitude towards the world. Even the triumphs of pediatric surgery keeping alive the spina bifida patient or the hydrocephalic often prove merely to have increased the number of the unhappy or handicapped.

Even more important are the children born unwanted and unloved. John Stuart Mill witnessed the discovery of the dead bodies of unwanted infants. This made such an impression on him that he took to distributing birth-control handbills in the slums, an activity which earned him a stay in prison.[3] I have, on an afternoon's walk in China, seen the corpses of two newly-born infants whose skulls had been knocked in. While infanticide probably occurs rarely now in the Western world, there are vast numbers of unwanted, uncared for, unloved children growing through a bitter childhood into delinquency.

There is the tragedy of the mothers driven by repeated pregnancy to ill health, or despair, or suicide.   While the last is relatively uncommon, the picture of the woman who has given up and no longer tries to preserve a decent home is an all too frequent reminder of the problem.

[1] M. West, *The Shoes of the Fisherman*, London, 1963, Wm. Heinemann.
[2] J. Peel and M. Potts, *Textbook of Contraceptive Practice*, 1969, Cambridge University Press.
[3] G. L. Williams, *The Sanctity of Life and the Criminal Law*, London, 1958, Faber and Faber.

Then there is the tragedy of the families whose hope of a normal life has been destroyed. This may be because a deformed child so monopolises maternal attention as to leave the remainder of the family, husband and children, to fend for themselves on the periphery of affection. In some the husband's hopes of a satisfying career, with its attendant rewards for the whole family, are dashed because of the help he has to give at home.

The second great reason for reform was the awareness of the extensive practice of illegal abortion going on constantly. This flouts the law, troubles our conscience, and leaves behind a trail of misery. After a "back-street" abortion there are many women who suffer chronic ill-health due to the aftermath of pelvic infection, and many who find themselves sterile, to their life-long regret. Lord Platt, in a House of Lords' debate,[4] hoped that those who were inclined to talk about the sanctity of human life would remember the 50,000 to 100,000 human fetuses which were being destroyed annually in conditions of squalor or dreadful extravagance.

The third problem stimulating abortion law reform was the uneven and uncertain state of medical practice. The legal situation was unsatisfactory. In Britain therapeutic abortion was practised on the strength of one judge having acquitted a gynaecologist. However, an outstanding authority, referring to this case, noted "Mr. Justice Macnaughten's . . . ruling cannot be regarded as binding for the future, and he clearly indicated that the decision lay with the jury, after considering the circumstances. The attitude of juries is not a safe field for prophecy . . ."[5] The American scene was no easier[6] where there was the phenomenon of increasing numbers of technically illegal therapeutic abortions accomplished in defiance of the law because of the pressure of public opinion.[7] As a legal correspondent wrote in the British Medical Journal in 1964: "A grossly heavy burden is put upon the medical profession. In this, as in other matters, the doctors have to bear the conscience of the nation and are liable to suffer for their pains."[8]

From the patient's point of view, all this lead to uncertainty due to the lack of uniformity of medical practice. A request for termination which might be acceded to in one hospital would be rejected out of hand in a

[4] Ld. Platt, Report in the BMJ, 1967, 3, 316.
[5] Sir Sydney Smith, Forensic Medicine (9th Ed. with F. S. Fiddes), London, 1949, J. and A. Churchill.
[6] As a medically qualified lawyer puts it: "Now remember that the doctor here can be a two-time loser with the vague anti-abortion law. If he guesses wrong he can go to jail by way of criminal prosecution. Then in the civil courts he can be sued for not doing it, or he can be sued for doing it under the assault and battery theory: if it is criminal it cannot be consented to, ergo, it is an assault.' (R. J. Gampell, in "Abortion and Constitutionality," in Abortion in a Changing World, vol. 2, see Ch. 3, ref. 2).
[7] E. W. Overstreet, Foreword to Symposium on Therapeutic Abortion and Sterilization, Clinical Obstetrics and Gynecology, 1964, 7, 11.
[8] BMJ, 1964, 1, 188 and 318.

neighbouring one; everything depended on the gynaecologist's interpretation of the law, his sympathies, his judgement, his religious convictions and his courage. In popular opinion the most unsatisfactory feature of all was the feeling that there was one law for the rich, and one for the poor. "These lords and ladies – they can go away and have it done privately. But a working-class woman – what can she do?"[9] "In no other issue in medicine today is there such confusion, emotionalism, sham, hypocrisy and outright flouting of the law as there is in the matter of induced abortions, both 'legal' and 'illegal,' the difference between the two being $300 and knowing the 'right' person."[10]

Great as were the problems so far mentioned, by far the greatest was the constant strain on millions of women throughout their married lives. Sir Dugald Baird, lecturing in 1965, reminded his hearer of President Roosevelt's Four Freedoms: freedom of speech, of worship, from want and from fear; and himself suggested that it was time to consider a fifth freedom – freedom from the tyranny of excessive fertility.[11]

As an individual problem this is probably one of the most constant experienced by married couples once their family is complete. The (American) National Academy of Science reports that in a year 32% of the white and 43% of the non-white couples in the inner city bear unwanted children.[12] With the present pattern of early marriage and very low infant mortality rates it is quite possible, indeed very common, for a couple to have the number of children they want by the time the wife is 22 or 23 years old. She then has more than twenty years more, about 80% of her fertile married life, ahead of her. In the absence of any absolutely certain contraceptive device, free of all fear of possible complications, and acceptable to the emotions and the conscience of the wife, this fear must remain. An ex-nurse, convicted as an abortionist, stated: "Sixty per cent of married women use the Higginson's syringe regular every month, just to be sure they bring the period on".[9] The great majority of married women count, with trepidation, the anxious days until their next period is due. They hail its arrival with undisguised relief.

In the presence of these problems most people felt the need of a reformed abortion law, even if only to protect the conscientious medical practitioner performing a life-saving procedure. The scope and details of any reform, however, were and are the source of much debate, to which we must turn our attention in later chapters.

[9] Moya Woodside, "Attitudes of Women Abortionists," *Howard Journal*, 1963, **11**, 93.

[10] R. B. White, "Induced Abortions: a Survey of their Psychiatric Implications, Complications and Indications." *Texas Reports of Biology and Medicine*, 1966, **24**, 531.

[11] Sir Dugald Baird, "A Fifth Freedom?" *BMJ*, 1965, **2**, 1141

[12] D. H. Bouma, "Population explosion; World and Local Imperatives," *Birth Control and the Christian*, Wheaton, 1969, Tyndale House.

CHAPTER 2

THE ABORTION SCENE IN BRITAIN
PRIOR TO 1967.

Generally humanity is thin on the ground in the matter of abortion.

PAUL FERRIS[1]

FROM THE EARLIEST TIMES, AND IN MOST SOCIETIES, WOMEN HAVE sought abortion for one of four main reasons. The greatest number have been those legitimately pregnant who because of weariness, illness, overcrowding, poverty or the desire at last to become a person rather than merely a breeding-machine, feel they cannot go through with another pregnancy and further years at the sink; or not yet at any rate. In the next group are the single, the separated or divorced, the widowed, for whom this illegitimate pregnancy spells shame and degradation at least, possibly the end of any hope of reconciliation with a separated husband, possibly the end for a teenager of hopes of honourable marriage, or of a career. It might even in some societies mean death, death not only for the girl, but under certain circumstances for her lover (in the Chaga tribe) or even (among the Zulu) for both their families as well.[2] The third group comprises the dilettanti, the Roman matron afraid for her figure, the married woman unprepared to settle down and rear a family, and more justifiably the professional woman whose career – perhaps vital to the family's finances – is in jeopardy. Lastly come the ill and the dying for whom only abortion can offer life.

Such women had the choice of attempting to abort themselves, a difficult and frequently unsuccessful ordeal; or of persuading some medical practitioner to break the law and risk his professional status and livelihood in aborting them; or of seeking out some unqualified person who would help them. At all times the last course has been the most popular; certainly it was so in Britain until 1968.

Back Street Abortion

While the curious can find many lurid tales of terrifying experiences at the hands of obscene and sadistic operators, it is clear that most illegal operations have been performed with some attempt at care, by persons

---

[1] P. Ferris, *The Nameless: Abortion in Britain Today*. London, 1966, Hutchinson.

[2] L. P. Mair, (quoting O. F. Raum for the Chaga; and M. Gluckman for the Zulu) *Survey on African Marriage and Family Life*, Oxford, 1953, O.U.P.

who often have developed no little expertise. The fees charged are often small or in fact are waived, and there is a motive of compassion evident in many operations. It may be doubted, however, whether the title of "Free-lance social worker"[3] is quite appropriate!

Over 80% of convicted abortionists are women.[4] Some 44 convicted women serving their sentence in Holloway Prison were interviewed by Moya Woodside, whose paper[5] gives an authoritative picture of these operators. She found that half of the women were over 60; all but three had children, and one was a great-grandmother. They were mostly from Social Group III (skilled manual worker) with psychological grading of average or dull; only a quarter had been convicted of other crimes. Seventeen of the women had some nursing or midwifery experience; the remaining twenty-seven were completely untrained in medical matters. She comments that it was obvious that some had acquired a good knowledge of anatomy and considerable manual dexterity. Their accounts of the procedure and its hazards could be paralleled in any forensic textbook. One widow said with pride: "I've never lost a case. Never had no trouble, never sent anyone to hospital". She always goes to see her cases the day after to make sure they are all right.

The Holloway women mostly became involved by first succeeding in aborting themselves by use of an enema syringe, and then, as word got round, being begged to help relatives, and later friends. Eventually pressures built up, the threat of suicide if they wouldn't help, the threat that the police would be informed. "So you can't escape. You're caught. You're in a trap." Woodside comments: "There is no doubt that compassion and feminine solidarity were strongly-motivating factors among women who had acquired this skill. They could share the feelings of the supplicant in her plight, or imagine how they would feel if it were their own teen-age daughter or grand-daughter who was 'in trouble'." Financial reward played little part in their activities, the sums changing hands often being of the order of five to forty shillings. They were proud that they had saved marriages and homes when, for instance, they had aborted the wives of servicemen serving abroad.

This rather cosy picture has been countered by another worker who claims that the fee is a main factor, that although the woman may be grateful to the abortionist she has to pay, and pay handsomely.[6] Charitable or not, the results can be disastrous. Woodside's series produced ten fatalities: "She said she'd rather die than have it" (as tragically, she did, from air embolism, within minutes of the operation). It is this train of tragedy which, above everything else, has been the stimulus to abortion law reform.

[3] The phrase is quoted by R. F. Tredgold (see p. 238, fn. 4).
[4] B. M. Dickens, *Abortion and the Law*, London, 1966, MacGibbon and Kee.
[5] Moya Woodside, "Attitudes of Women Abortionists." *Howard Journal* 1963, **11**, 93.
[6] J. G. Weir, "Lay Abortionists." In *Abortion in Britain*, London, 1966, Pitman.

The sequence of events[7] is delay until the second period is missed, then use of a drug "to bring the period on". Despite the fact that these are either inefficient or toxic,[8] women continue to buy them, often at considerable expense. Although inefficient so far as procuring an abortion the drug may yet damage the fetus, or even, if in large enough dosage, kill the woman. The next stage is instrumentation, with the use of something sharp – such as a knitting needle – which may well penetrate the uterine wall and cause intra-abdominal injuries; or the use of slippery elm bark, or an enema syringe. Death is in general due to ignorance of anatomy, unsterile instruments, dangerous techniques, or desperation. There has been a marked fall in certified deaths from abortion in Britain over the past three decades: from 432 in 1930 to 62 in 1960[9]. Of these in all years about two-thirds have been due to infection. The fall is, in fact, surprising because of the increasing number of women in the child-bearing age and because improved autopsy techniques are now uncovering many cases where abortion had not been suspected. While some of the fall may be credited to improved skill on the part of the abortionists, and many cases are transferred to hospital where blood transfusion must play an important part, the advent of ever-improved antibiotics must take the major credit, for infection is the great threat in back-street procedures.

Medical Case 2.1. A woman of 40 was admitted to hospital as a threatened abortion. While in there she was heard to say to other patients that should they 'need help' at any time they should contact her. She was allowed home but readmitted *in extremis* a few days later, dying shortly after admission. Some hours later the mortuary attendant summoned the gynaecological resident who found the whole body grossly distended with the formation of gas-filled blisters on the torso. Death had been due to a very virulent gas-forming organism.

Medical Case 2.2. A charming married woman in her mid-twenties was admitted with a widespread infection which could not be controlled with the then available antibiotics. She had two children, the younger of whom was a hydrocephalic. All her time and energies were devoted to his care. Finding herself pregnant again she sought the help of an abortionist. Her husband sat holding her hand while she lay dying. The gynaecological resident overheard her say 'I'd do the same again for you, darling,' just before she died.

The patient may die from the overwhelming nature of the infection, or from the shock it occasionally produces.[10] Her kidneys may fail; a Hammersmith Hospital series of renal failure cases included 41 occurring after abortion: in the majority there was clear evidence of interference with the pregnancy, and in most of the remainder it was suspected.

[7] A. K. Mant, "The Dangers of Legal and Illegal Abortion." *Proc. Royal Society of Medicine*, 1969, **62**, 827.

[8] *Survey of Abortifacent Drugs*. London, 1965, Abortion Law Reform Association.

[9] Sir George Godber, "Recent Progress and Future Aims in Obstetrics." *Journal of Obstetrics and Gynaecology of the British Commonwealth*, 1971, **78**, 193.

[10] R. P. Pulliam, "Endotoxic Shock." *Bulletin of the Sloane Hospital for Women*, 1965, **11**, 14.

Despite the use of an artificial kidney machine, eleven of these women died.[11]

Air embolism, due usually to air entering the intake of the enema syringe, is a frequent cause of sudden death occurring very shortly after, or during, the abortion. I have, however, seen it occur many hours later, the air having reached vessels in the head.

Not all complications of criminal abortion are fatal. One of the most tragic in single girls, often in their teens, is sterility:

Medical Case 2.3. A 30-year-old educated lady sought specialist advice because she had been married for eight years without conceiving, and was getting desperate. It turned out that her fallopian tubes were blocked by infection, and it was necessary for her to have a tubal reimplantation operation with only a small prospect of success. She told the story of having become pregnant by her present husband but before marriage to him was possible, presumably because a previous marriage of his had not yet come to divorce. She found a back-street abortionist who syringed her out, with the result that she passed tissue which by her description was infected. They married two years later, but never again did she succeed in conceiving. Her distress was marked.

How many criminal abortions have been performed each year? The question is complicated by definition. If one includes every woman who routinely uses a syringe, as suggested by Moya Woodside's informant,[5] then one must get a much larger number than if one includes only those on whom instruments are used illegally by an abortionist. Most would count only the latter, but even so estimates vary widely, one might say wildly. It is here that we encounter the motivation of the writer. Those anxious to influence the legislature towards radical liberalisation of the law tend to quote high figures, those of a more conservative outlook tend to quote low figures.

All figures are guesses: for Britain they vary from 250,000[12] to 10,000 a year, much the most widely quoted being 100,000 per year. In 1964 C. B. Goodhart[13] criticised this and, working on the reported death rates from abortion, showed that (unless the mortality rate from illegal abortion in a back street was only two or three times higher than the mortality rate from childbirth in good hospital conditions) a figure of 10,000, or slightly larger, was likely to be accurate. This statistical method has been criticized by B. M. Dickens,[13a] who preferred the calculations based on the known total of abortions, spontaneous and induced. Just prior to World War II the British Medical Association and Governmental committees, using these figures, had suggested that if 40% of all were criminal then the

[11] K. Smith, J. C. Browne, R. Shackman and O. M. Wrong, "Acute Renal Failure of Obstetric Origin," *Lancet*, 1965, **2**, 351.
[12] E. Chesser, 1950. Quoted by B. M. Dickens, *op. cit.*
[13] C. B. Goodhart, "The Frequency of Illegal Abortion." *Eugenics Review*, 1964, **55**, 197.
[13a] B. M. Dickens, *op. cit.*

total annual figure for criminal abortions was 44,000 – 60,000.[14] Other writers mark this up by accepting a criminal proportion of more than 40%.

C. B. Goodhart in 1969 returned to the fray.[15] He quoted a National Opinion Polls figure of 31,000 induced abortions per year, but as 40% of the questioners did not reply this is not very valuable. He was, however, able to work on Sir Dugald Baird's unique figures and experience in Aberdeen, where under a very liberal abortion policy there were 68 legal abortions per year between 1961–3, for a population of 185,000, and where Sir Dugald believes criminal abortion has been almost eliminated. On this basis Goodhart suggests a rate of not more than 20,000 per year for Britain as a whole. Had this figure been the accepted one at the time of the abortion debates in Parliament, attitudes might well have been different.

Legal Abortion

The history of the development of the law on abortion goes back to Anglo-Saxon times, and has been described in detail by Dickens[15a]. As early as 1846 the Criminal Law Commissioners realised the need to legalize certain abortions and suggested that the then operative law (of 1837) should have added to it the proviso: "Provided that no act specified in the last preceding Article shall be punishable when such act is done in good faith with the intention of saving the life of the mother whose miscarriage is intended to be produced." Unfortunately no action was taken when the Offences against the Person Act was passed in 1861. It remained the abortion law of England until 1967:

Section 58. Every woman, being with child, who, with intent to procure her own miscarriage, shall unlawfully administer to herself any poison or other noxious thing, or shall unlawfully use any instrument or other means whatsoever with the like intent, and whosoever, with the intent to procure the miscarriage of any woman, whether she be or be not with child, shall unlawfully administer to her or cause to be taken by her any poison or other noxious thing, or shall unlawfully use any instrument or other means whatsoever with the like intent, shall be guilty of felony, ...
(Section 59 made it a misdemeanour to supply anything for these purposes.)

Where the woman died the crime became one of murder, although in later years this was reduced in most cases to manslaughter. The position therefore of the medical man faced with the certain death of his patient (e.g. from renal failure, were her pregnancy to continue) was an unenviable one.

[14] Report of the Inter- Departmental Committee on Abortion, 1939. Quoted by B. M. Dickens, see ref. 4 above.
[15] C. B. Goodhart, "Estimation of Illegal Abortions," Journal of Biosocial Science, 1969, I, 235.
[15a] B. M. Dickens, op. cit.

Mr. Aleck Bourne, a senior Obstetrician in London, had for some time thought of challenging the position, and in 1938 the opportunity presented itself. A 14-year-old girl had been walking with friends past the Guards Barracks when they were invited by soldiers to come in and see a horse with a green tail. This particular girl, perhaps out of bravado, accepted, was taken to a room and raped by several guardsmen. She was so physically traumatized by this that she had to be admitted to hospital. Aleck Bourne recounts that having kept her in bed for several days to observe what type of girl she was he formed the impression that she was not a gay girl of the streets. This opinion was confirmed when he had to do a minimal pelvic examination and the girl completely broke down. "At 10 a.m. on the eighth day, I operated. At 6 p.m. two police officers called as they wanted the girl to give evidence against the guardsmen who had been arrested for assault. Chief Inspector B. also said that in no circumstance could he countenance the operation on 'humanitarian grounds.' I made it plain to the Inspector that I could not recognize his right to dictate to me what I, as a surgeon, should or should not decide to do in the best interests of my patient, that I did not understand what he meant by 'humanitarian grounds' as most of medicine is humanitarian, and that in any case I had already operated on the girl and, if he wished, he could arrest me."[16] The trial was to become historic, largely on account of Mr. Justice Macnaughten's summing up. At the start of the trial, counsel pointed out that the indictment alleged that Mr. Bourne had used instruments intended to procure abortion, but failed to allege that he did so "unlawfully," which word created an essential pre-condition to the commission of an offence. The judge held that the word "unlawful" was not meaningless, and implied an alternative "lawful" use. The Infant Life (Preservation) Act of 1929 has included the proviso that "no act shall be punishable when done in good faith with the intention of saving the life of the mother," and this he held must apply to abortion. "I confess I have a great deal of difficulty in understanding what the discussion" (on life and health) "really meant. Life depends on health and it may be that health is so gravely impaired that death results. The Attorney-General suggested to Mr. Bourne that there was a clear line of distinction between danger to health and danger to life . . . . but is there? The Act of 1861 does not permit of the termination of pregnancy except for the purpose of preserving the life of the mother. But I think myself that those words ought to be construed in a reasonable sense: if the doctor is of the opinion, on reasonable grounds and on adequate knowledge, that the probable consequence of the continuation of the pregnancy would indeed make the woman a physical wreck, or a mental wreck, then he operated, in that honest belief, for the purpose of preserving the life of the mother."[16a]

[16] A. Bourne, *A Doctor's Creed: The Memoirs of a Gynaecologist*, London, 1963, Gollancz.
[16a] B. M. Dickens, *op. cit.*

Aleck Bourne's acquittal is the foundation on which therapeutic abortions were performed for the next thirty years. There were, however, several problems. The first of these was the problem of definition: what, legally speaking, is a mental wreck? Then Mr. Justice Macnaughten refrained from putting a close definition on the phrase "for the purpose only of preserving the life of the mother," thus giving the jury in the Bourne case, and future juries, a wide measure of discretion.[17] It appeared too that this judgement did not establish the propriety of an operation to terminate the pregnancy of a woman of below average health when the danger to her well-being arose from having to nurse and rear a child, even had she already a large family and had been medically advised against further pregnancy.[17a]

The second problem was that neither this case, nor any similar, was ever tested at appeal. There was therefore no certainty that another judge, in a like case, would come to the same conclusion.

One further statement of Mr. Justice Macnaughten's has been little quoted, but is of importance to our study: "There are people who, from what are said to be religious reasons, object to the operation being performed under any circumstances . . . A person who holds such an opinion ought not to be an obstetrical surgeon, for if a case arose where the life of the woman could be saved by performing the operation and the doctor refused to perform it because of his religious opinions and the woman died he could be in grave peril of being brought before this Court on a charge of manslaughter by negligence."[17]

Therapeutic abortion became common in the years following. In hospital it was the invariable practice to have two senior opinions, often three, in writing, and to do the operation quite openly. No such case was challenged legally. This system had its drawbacks. In one hospital in which I was house-surgeon one was not permitted to write "For termination of Pregnancy" on the operating list, if the patient had an Irish name. This was to protect the patient from the attention of the priest.

Doctors working in nursing homes, and especially those who performed abortions in their consulting rooms, were in a much more delicate situation. The strain to which this exposes a doctor is suggested by the criminal proceedings taken against Drs. Bergmann and Ferguson, both of high reputation and integrity. Following her acquittal of performing an illegal operation, Dr. Bergmann pleaded guilty to a separate count – attempted suicide. Nevertheless, for doctors working openly and in hospital Mr. Pells Cocks was right in saying "this fear of legal consequences is a myth."[18]

The real issue was one of indication for operation. Was it justified in this case, and what weight was to be given to mental symptoms? In

[17] A Legal Correspondent in the BMJ, 1964, I, 188, 318.
[17a] B. M. Dickens, op. cit.
[18] D. Pells Cocks, letter in the BMJ, 1967, I, 569.

1966 a Cambridge obstetrician listing the last hundred cases reported that ninety-three of them had been performed on the recommendation of one of their psychiatrists.[19] The same year the Simpson Memorial Maternity Pavilion in Edinburgh reviewed its past ten-year abortions: only 39% were performed on psychiatric grounds.[20] The situation has been well described by Dr. K. H. Tooley, a psychiatrist: "At the London Hospital we once looked at the criteria for termination of pregnancy, and we were a little disturbed to find that provided you were 14–16 you always had your pregnancy terminated – if you were 16–20 you were a naughty girl and never had it done (this is for single women); that if you already had a large family you had it done – if you were reaching middle life you had what was considered to be a completed family; you had the greatest possible sympathy. Now, I am sure that when these facts came out we had none of us been aware that we were selecting cases with these criteria. We thought we selected cases with entirely different criteria."[21]

It was the psychiatric angle that was the most difficult. Short of a straightforward serious medical disease, the only way to a legal abortion was by way of a psychiatrist's recommendation. "In countries where the legal restrictions are rigid the physician consciously or unconsciously exaggerates in the formal recommendation for therapeutic abortion the risk of suicide, to meet the legal requirements that the continuation of the pregnancy constitutes a threat to the patient's life and health . . . the threat of suicide is often used to intimidate physicians and others to recommend abortion".[22] Paul Ferris suggested that some psychiatrists were being used as a social convenience because they wanted to be so used for reasons of principle, seeing the woman in her socio-economic situation as a human being in need who required help to preserve her life, using "life" in the widest sense of the word. "There were, however, risks in the financial aspect . . . the fact that a psychiatrist in private practice is charging a fee for his time doesn't make his belief any less honest. Individually there are psychiatrists in private practice, recommending abortion, whose motives are honourable. It is only collectively, when the number of Harley Street recommendations is compared with the handful of recommendations under the National Health Service that you get a whiff of corruption."[1]

Professor Keith Simpson has recalled "A threat to commit suicide was enough for some. Indeed in one case I had, a doctor told the mother to bring her daughter to him again when she found her (that is, her daughter) with her head in the gas oven. It did not matter whether the tap was on, so

[19] O. Lloyd, Reported in the BMJ, 1966, I, 1105.

[20] Simpson Memorial Maternity Pavilion, Edinburgh. Report, 1966. Medical Annual, 1968. Bristol, Wright.

[21] K. H. Tooley, "If All Abortions are Legal, which are Desirable?" In The Abortion Act: A Symposium held by the Medical Protection Society. London, Pitman.

[22] A. Simon, "Psychiatric Indications for Therapeutic Abortion and Sterilization." Clinical Obstetrics and Gynecology, 1964, 7, 67.

long as her head was in the oven. 'And a suicide note', I quote the doctor's words, 'would help'."[23]

The fact remains that it was widely believed that, provided one could somehow discover the right Harley Street door to knock on, any woman who was prepared to pay between one and two hundred guineas would be directed to two accommodating psychiatrists, obtain their consent, and return to the doctor for termination. The poor were naturally incensed about the difference of their lot in having to seek the help of an unskilled abortionist and undergo the operation in conditions of maximum danger to health. It was this, says Norman St. John Stevas,[24] which provided the emotional drive behind reform within the Labour Party, and which was so strong in the Parliamentary Labour group that, Catholics apart, only a handful of individuals within it opposed change.

How many legal abortions were performed? In NHS hospitals in England and Wales, according to the Minister of Health, the figures rose steadily from 2,040 in 1960 to 6,380 in 1966. For the private sector no figures are available but Mr. P. Diggory[25] made careful enquiry among his gynaecological colleagues in 1966 and 1967, arriving at a figure of 15,000 per year in 1964–66, and 17,500 in 1967: this figure we may accept as being as near to accuracy as we shall get. (It is an interesting sidelight on the care with which one has to accept abortion figures that in 1964 the Southwark Coroner was told (by a private practitioner in whose nursing home 400 women were aborted each year) that "about 300,000 of these legal abortions are done annually."[25a] Were that figure only ten times too large one wonders where all the cases went to when notification became compulsory in 1968.)

The position prior to 1968 therefore was difficult. It was difficult for the doctor. It was true (as the judge stated in the Bergmann–Ferguson case) that it was not required that the doctor's opinion be correct, only that it be honest.[1] However, some operations were still performed at the doctor's risk. "Good faith on the part of the doctor, and a concurring opinion by a specialist given in good faith on the desirability of terminating a pregnancy, do not in themselves make the operation lawful; there must be a threat to the woman's life or health which is related to the condition of pregnancy, and is capable of expression in terms of physiology or psychiatry. It may be that miscarriages are procured in hospitals where the child is likely to suffer from a substantial disability . . . in such cases, however, the law does not permit the operation, it may merely refrain from interfering."[25b]

[23] K. Simpson, "Criminal Abortion: A Dying Art?" In *The Abortion Act* (op. cit.).
[24] N. St. John Stevas, "Abortion and the Law." *Dublin Review*, Winter 1967–68, **241**, 274.
[25] P. Diggory, J. Peel, and M. Potts "Preliminary Assessment of the 1967 Abortion Act in Practice." *Lancet*, 1970, **I**, 287.
[25a] B. M. Dickens, *op. cit.*
[25b] B. M. Dickens, *op. cit.*

It was little wonder then, that some in their despair took matters into their own hands. In 1949 a husband killed his wife attempting to abort her and the trial judge sentenced him to five years in prison. On appeal this was reduced to allow immediate release. Lord Goddard said "The appellant, who certainly deserves the description of being a devoted husband, was living with his wife and two children in circumstances which were truly deplorable. They were all living in one small room, and the prospect of another child being added to their number was such as might have moved anyone to the greatest pity . . . The circumstances were that this man and his wife were trying to prevent another little life from being brought into the conditions in which they were living. The offence is a serious one, but there are circumstances which enable the Court to take a merciful view."[26]

Such a situation – unsatisfactory for the women, unsatisfactory for the doctors, unsatisfactory for the law, but richly rewarding for the unscrupulous – could not be allowed to continue.

[26] Rex v. Tate. Reported by B. M. Dickens, *op. cit.*

CHAPTER 3

THE ABORTION SCENE ABROAD

The statistics suggest that the evil dreaded in the Roman Empire has still to be feared in the modern world: the greatest threat to the life of a human being is his own parents.   PROFESSOR JOHN NOONAN[1]

THE CONTEMPORARY PRACTICE OF ABORTION IN VARIOUS PARTS OF THE world has been described by a number of authors.[2] For our purpose we can consider it, not on a geographical basis, but by the degree of strictness or laxity of practice.[3]

Prohibition of Abortion

Possibly the only country where abortion is prohibited completely, and where the law is said to be observed, is the Republic of Ireland. There are a number of other countries which in law are equally strict, but where observance is more lax. In Taiwan[4] despite the illegality of all abortion, a questionnaire to obstetricians suggest that for every thousand births there are 180 abortions, usually to "correct" contraceptive failure.

Abortion Only to Save the Mother's Life

Perhaps the most stringent rule is that introduced in Zanzibar in January 1970 with a mandatory death sentence for anyone performing an abortion, this being deemed as child-destruction and thus murder. Abortions are allowed, however, at the Government hospital if necessary to save the life of the mother.[5]

Many other countries legally permit abortion only on these grounds. The efficiency of such laws may be judged by the fact that it is believed that in France the number of illegal abortions may be from one-third to

---

[1] J. T. Noonan, *Contraception:* A History of its Treatment by the Catholic Theologians and Canonists. 1967, Harvard University Press.
[2] See for example the papers in volume one of *Abortion in a Changing World:* The Proceedings of an International Conference on Abortion Convened by the Association for the Study of Abortion, at Hot Springs, Virginia. November 17-20, 1968. 1970, Columbia University Press. Also C. Tietze and Sarah Lewit, "Abortion." *Scientific American,* Jan 1969, 21.
[3] Ruth Roemer, *American Journal of Public Health,* 1969, **57,** 1906.
[4] L. P. Chow, "Abortion in Taiwan." In *Abortion in a Changing World* (*op. cit.*).
[5] *The Times,* Jan. 20, 1970.

one-and-a-half times that of the number of live births.[6] These are rough estimations and should be treated with reserve. However, for Chile, which has such a law,[3] there are some figures available. There patients who have had illegal terminations occupy 160,000 bed-days a year in hospitals. In Santiago 43% of women seeking contraceptive advice admit to an induced abortion. Reporting these figures, Dr. B. Viel comments "experience shows in all Latin America that neither religious teaching nor punitive legal measures help."[7]

Abortion on Maternal Health Grounds Only

A number of the United States, and European countries such as Switzerland, permit abortion on these grounds.

The main result here is that women seek an illegal practitioner. In some countries these are often qualified doctors. In America a *Dr. X* has dictated his story of 25,000 abortions,[8] and at a recent conference Dr. R. D. Spencer read a paper reporting his own over 30,000 abortions performed on non-legal grounds over the past quarter of a century: "To me, a good and sufficient reason is the simple fact that the person has firmly decided she does not want the baby."[9] In the U.S.A. in 1966, only 9,000 legal abortions were granted, but one million illegal ones were estimated to have been performed. That this frequently-quoted figure, like our British one, may have been grossly inflated is shown by some New Orleans figures.[11]

Similarly in Greece abortions are frequently performed by qualified practitioners on the quasi-legal pretext of menstrual disorders. Over the whole country a third of the women and a quarter of all pregnancies are involved, while in Greater Athens half of all pregnancies are artificially terminated, and more than half the women admit to having had an illegal abortion.[12]

[6] D. V. Glass gave the figures of 31 induced abortions in Lyons, and 42 in Paris, per 100 live births. (*Abortion in Britain:* see, ch. 2, ref. 6). However L. and R. Breitenecker calculated that in Paris, for 95,000 births, there were 150,000 abortions with several thousand deaths, 61% complications, and 25% sterility resulting (*Abortion and the Law* (Ed. D. Smith) Cleveland, 1967, Press of Western Reserve University).

[7] B. Viel, "The Sequelae of Non-Hospital Abortions." In *Abortion in a Changing World* (*op. cit.*).

[8] Dr. X. *The Abortionist*, London, 1962, Gollancz.

[9] R. D. Spencer, "The Performance of Non-Hospital Abortions." In *Abortion in a Changing World* (*op. cit.*).

[10] D. Lowe, *Abortion and the Law*, New York, 1966, Simon and Schuster.

[11] C. L. Harter and J. D. Beasley state: "The rate of illegal abortion in the medically indigent class is indicated by the fact that the ratio of septic abortions to live births in the Charity Hospital was 12 per thousand, none died. Either the women eligible for treatment at the Charity Hospital were not having very many criminally induced abortions or else they were having them performed by highly competent abortionists so there is a low incidence of complications. Because of their low economic status we do not believe the latter to be the case." "A Survey Concerning Induced Abortions in New Orleans." *American Journal of Public Health*, 1967, **57,** 1937.

[12] V. G. Valaoras, and D. Trichopoulos "Abortion in Greece." In *Abortion in a Changing World* (*op. cit.*).

Abortion on Medico-Social Grounds

Starting in the 1930s the Nordic countries introduced legislation permitting abortion on medico-social grounds. Permission usually has to be given by a committee, and the time-lag involved in this procedure may be one reason for the continued high rate of illegal abortions, a rate which falls only when approval is granted very easily indeed.

The Swedish laws are typical. By the 1938 Act abortion could be approved on medical grounds where the advent of the child would entail serious danger to the mother's life or health due to illness, physical defect or weakness of the woman; on humanitarian grounds following rape, incest, or pregnancy under the age of 15; and on eugenic grounds where insanity, mental deficiency, grave defect or serious disease in a child could be expected. If hereditary disposition existed in the woman simultaneous sterilization was required.

In 1946 the socio-medical indication was added: "When in view of the woman's conditions of life and her circumstances in other respects it may be presumed that her physical or mental strength would be seriously impaired by the advent of the child and the care of the child" (i.e. "foreseen weakness"). It is not laid down that illness, physical defect or weakness should exist in the woman at the time of operation. The paragraph thus refers chiefly to a more "gradual wearing down of the woman's strength." The legislators have emphasized, however, that abortion for purely social reasons is not permitted. The vast majority of Swedish abortions are performed under the "foreseen weakness" condition.[13]

In 1965 the legal abortion rates per thousand live births were in Iceland 12, Norway 52, Sweden 56, Denmark 60 and Finland 61. However, in Sweden at any rate there is a growing leniency in interpretation and application of the law, seen by the fact that the percentage of applications terminated rose yearly from 49% in 1963 to 77% in 1967. There is also a growing public desire for further liberalization of the law.[14]

Abortion on Socio-Economic Grounds

The Scandinavian type of legislation moves relentlessly on to abortion's being legalized without any medical indication whatever being required.

In 1947 the Japanese birth rate was 34.3 per thousand; it had halved by 1957,[15] very largely due to the introduction of easy abortion. It is usually said that the Eugenic Protection Law of 1948 was the result of the spectre of over-population, but it was pushed through the legislature on the

[13] P. Arén, and C. Amark "The Prognosis in Cases on Which Legal Abortion has been Granted but not Carried Out." *Acta Psychiatrica et Neurologica Scandinavica*, 1961, **36**, 203.

[14] G. Geijerstam, "Abortion in Scandinavia." In *Abortion in a Changing World* (op. cit.). It was reported in *The Times* on July 8 1971 that a Swedish Government Committee has recommended that abortions should be free, and that the woman alone should make the decision to terminate pregnancy.

[15] M. Muramatsu, "Family Planning Practice among the Japanese." *Eugenics Quarterly*, 1960, **7**, 23.

stimulus of medical members who used arguments very similar to those used in the British Parliament. The law was further liberalized in 1949.

The fact that infanticide and abortion have a long history in Japan[15] probably made acceptable the practice of abortion on demand, even though this is technically illegal. The number of reported abortions rose from 246,000 to a peak of 1,170,143 in 1955, with a slow but steady decline thereafter.[16] Due to tax evasion it is generally assumed that less than half the abortions are notified, so the true total may have reached 2½ million per year at the peak. It is interesting to note that the figure of abortions since 1948 is many times that of all Japanese losses during World War II, including Hiroshima and Nagasaki, and most striking to compare the outcry and shame resulting from those two holocausts.

Only 5% of these abortions were performed on account of medical conditions. In the words of a Japanese gynaecologist, "The general public tends to think of induced abortion in much the same way as constipated patients do of a purgative. Most ... women under 20, in their first pregnancy, desire an induced abortion."[17]

A section of public opinion has revolted against "this massive *antepartum* infanticide."[18] As early as 1951 the Japanese Cabinet, fearing the undesirable results of abortion on the woman's health, decided to replace widespread resort to it by contraception.[19] The task has been slow and difficult.

By 1970 Japan, faced with a shrinking and ageing population, was trying to stimulate an increasing birth rate once more.

The Soviet bloc illustrates the varying combinations of law, and shifting practice.[20] The law of the U.S.S.R. has passed through permissive, restrictive, and further permissive phases. In its towns three out of four pregnancies end in abortion.[21] Nevertheless, termination of a first pregnancy is discouraged, because according to a Soviet professor of obstetrics and gynaecology such terminations are not good medical practice and are socially unwarranted even for the unmarried, since illegitimacy has been abolished and the state cares for a child until the woman can assume responsibility.[3]

[16] Y. Manabe, "Artificial Abortion at Midpregnancy by Mechanical Stimulation of the Uterus." *American Journal of Obstetrics and Gynecology*, 1969, **105**, 132.

[17] M. Ishihara, "Analysis of the Present Situation in Japan." In *The Christian Physician in the Advance of the Science and Practice of Medicine:* Report of the Second International Congress of Christian Physicians, Oxford, July 11–15, 1966. Ed. A. M. Connell and G. A. Lindeboom, The Hague, 1967, Oranje.

[18] S. H. Tow, "The Challenge and Control of the Population Explosion." In *The Christian Physician in the Advance of the Science and Practice of Medicine, op. cit.*

[19] K. Koya, "A Study of Induced Abortion in Japan and its Significance." *Milbank Memorial Fund Quarterly*, 1954, **32**, 282.

[20] M. Potts, "Legal Abortion in Eastern Europe." *Eugenics Review*, 1967, **59**, 232.

[21] K-H. Mehlan, Professor Mehlan is from the Institute of Hygiene, University of Rostock, German Democratic Republic. His article gives full statistics for Eastern Europe from 1957–1966, and is particularly valuable as coming from inside the Eastern Bloc. ("Abortion in Eastern Europe." *Abortion in a Changing World, op. cit.*)

It is interesting to notice the *volte-face* in Eastern Europe. In Rumania, where in 1965 there were four legal abortions for every birth, the law was changed in 1966. Abortion is now available "on demand" only to women over forty-five, except on medical indication. Whereas the earlier legislation started with the view that all women should be free to decide the fate of their pregnancies, the official reasons given for making the change were the serious effects of legalized abortion upon the health and reproductive capacity of women, upon the stability of the family, and upon the morality of the country, especially its youth.[21] In Hungary, where in 1968 there were 130 legal abortions for every 100 births, and in Czechoslovakia there has been in recent times an increase in late sequelae following abortion.[22] Pregnancies after repeated legal abortion are found to be twice as likely to end in spontaneous miscarriage, premature birth, stillbirth, or difficult delivery. As in Russia so in Czechoslovakia there has been a sharp limitation of indications for interruption of the first pregnancy because of its particular dangers.

Proponents of easy abortion in the West are strangely silent on these facts. They also forgot to tell us that in the whole Eastern bloc only in Poland has there been any success in persuading women to adopt contraceptive techniques instead of relying on abortion; and that even in those countries where there is complete legalization of abortion unmarried women resort to illegal rather than legal practitioners.[21]

Abortion on Demand

In March 1970 in the State of Hawaii it became law that provided the operation was performed by a licensed practitioner on a woman who fulfilled certain residential requirements the termination of a non-viable pregnancy was legal. No grounds for operation are enacted, and there appears to be no regulation requiring the reporting of operations.[23]

Withdrawal of all Law on Abortion

In 1970 the States of Alaska and New York deleted all laws on abortion from their statute books. The procedure became a matter for private arrangement between patient and physician, on a par with other medical conditions.

During the first six months of New York's new law the hospitals in New York City performed 69,000 abortions: this means that for every live birth in the city there is one abortion.[24] In one hospital, where the

[22] A. Klinger, "Demographic Consequences of the Legalization of Induced Abortion in Eastern Europe." *International Journal of Gynaecology and Obstetrics*, 1970, **8**, 680.
[23] Act 1, Session Laws of Hawaii. I am indebted to H.M. Miyamoto, Administrative Assistant to the Director of Health State of Hawaii for allowing me to see a copy of this law.
[24] Association for the Study of Abortion, Newsletter, Winter, 1971.

annual abortion rate had increased from two cases to 5,000 cases, resistance on the part of nursing and medical staff had resulted in the setting aside of a special ward and special operators for these cases.

If difficulties exist in a system under which one can approach any gynaecologist at will, and obtain access to hospital beds on payment, it is obvious that further difficulties would arise in a country operating a national health service where a specific doctor is in contract to deal with each person. The doctor who in no circumstances will accede to requests for abortion would be in an impossible position. The shortage of doctors would make it impracticable for families to be transferred wholesale to the lists of the permissive practitioners. Similarly the principle of district hospitals with two to four gynaecologists responsible for the area means that the permissive consultant will find all his beds blocked with such cases and lose all opportunity to practise his speciality. His restrictive colleague will lose the rapport with general practitioners on which his practice depends, and by his conscientious refusal to co-operate will produce a bottleneck for abortion patients. Any country with this type of health service, introducing fully permissive legislation, must inevitably provide abortoria, staffed by willing operators and nurses, for the fit woman. On the other hand the ill patient who requires expert help will always be acceptable in the specialist gynaecological department.

In theory, apart from total and absolute prohibition of abortion the only unequivocal situation is that in which there is no law. Even "abortion on demand" is unrealistic as there must be occasions where the medical state of the woman is so precarious that no doctor, however liberal, would dare risk an operative procedure; and therefore would have to refuse the woman's demand. All intermediate legislation is fraught with uncertainty and with the constant temptation to bend the law or flagrantly to disregard it.[25]

There has been considerable dissatisfaction with the American laws,[26]

[25] Prof. P. O. Hubinot, if I understand him rightly, performs termination of pregnancy in Brussels when he considers it indicated, disregarding Belgian law. (*Abortion in a Changing World, op. cit.*

[26] For the United States scene the following papers may be consulted:

A. Barno, "Criminal Abortion Deaths, Illegitimate Pregnancy Deaths, and Suicides in Pregnancy." *American Journal of Obstetrics and Gynecology*, 1967, **98**, 356.

C. Tietze, "Therapeutic Abortions in the United States." (This paper attempts to estimate the number of legal abortions performed in the U.S.A. in 1963–65). *American Journal of Obstetrics and Gynecology*, 1968, **101**, 784.

E. M. Gold, C. L. Erhardt, H. Jacobziner and F. G. Nelson, "Therapeutic Abortions in New York City: A 20 year Review." *American Journal of Public Health*, 1965, **55**, 964.

J. W. Eliot, R. E. Hall, J. R. Willson and Carolyn Houser, "The Obstetrician's View." (This paper reports results of a questionnaire sent to hospitals approved for residency, revealing their practice of abortion). In *Abortion in a Changing World, op. cit.*

K. R. Niswander, M. Klein and C. L. Randall, "Therapeutic Abortion: Indications and Technics." *Obstetrics and Gynecology*, 1966, **28**, 124.

J. J. Rovinsky and S. B. Gusberg, "Current Trends in Therapeutic Termination of Pregnancy." *American Journal of Obstetrics and Gynecology*, 1967, **98**, 11.

and since 1967 a number of the States have enacted legislation permitting abortion on fairly liberal medical grounds:[27] Colorado,[28] NorthCarolina,[29] California,[30] Georgia, Maryland, New Mexico, Arkansas, Kansas and Oregon being the earliest. But within two years of the introduction of the new legislation there was pressure, for instance in California,[31] for further enactment to liberalize completely.[32] This demand was in part due to the uncertainty inevitable in working any partially restrictive legislation, and partly due to pressure by those who are dissatisfied at any restriction on termination of pregnancy.

It will be interesting to see if and when the example of Rumania has to be followed, and the wheel turns full circle. Meanwhile those who think the Church is the only barrier to unrestricted abortion may care to consider the experience in Israel. Among Jewish women the percentage who have had an induced abortion varies according to religious observance – 19.2% for those who are non-observant of religion, 9.8% for those partially observant, but only 3.2% for those observant.[33] They should ponder also the statement of a Nigerian gynaecologist: "Abortion on demand is against the conscience of the ordinary African; it just would not be acceptable to the people."[34]

E. W. Overstreet, (Ed.) Symposium on Therapeutic Abortion and Sterilization. *Clinical Obstetrics and Gynecology*, 1964, **7**, 11.

The American Medical Association: Statement opposing induced abortion except on certain grounds, adopted by the House of Delegates, June, 1967. *BMJ*, 1967, **3**, 444.

The American College of Obstetricians and Gynecologists: Statement on grounds for abortion will be found reprinted in *Birth Control and the Christian, op. cit.*

See also the publications of the Association for the Study of Abortion, 120 West 57th St., New York 10019.

[27] J. M. Ingram, "Changing Aspects of Abortion Law."*American Journal of Obstetrics and Gynecology*, 1969, **105**, 35.

[28] W. Droegemmuler, E. S. Taylor and Vera E. Drose, "The First Year's Experience in Colorado with the New Abortion Law." *American Journal of Obstetrics and Gynecology*, 1969, **103**, 694.

C. Dafoe, "Colorado's Abortion Law: An Obstetrician's View." *Nebraska Medical Journal*, 1970, **55**, 3.

S. W. Downing, R. Lamm and A. Heller, "Abortion under the New Colorado Law." *Nebraska Medical Journal*, 1970, **55**, 24.

[29] R. T. Parker, reported in discussion printed after Droegemuller's paper—see fn. above.

[30] Phyllis E. Thurstone, "Therapeutic Abortion: The Experience of San Mateo County General Hospital, and the State of California." *Journal of the American Medical Association*, 1969, **209**, 229.

[31] J. M. Kummer, "New Trends in Therapeutic Abortion in California." *Obstetrics and Gynecology*, 1969, **34**, 883.

[32] S. Meyerowitz and J. Romano, "Who May Not Have an Abortion?" Editorial in *Journal of the American Medical Association*, 1969, **209**, 261.

[33] R. Bachi, "Abortion in Israel." *Abortion in a Changing World, op. cit.*

[34] O. Akinla, "Abortion in Africa." *Abortion in a Changing World, op. cit.*

CHAPTER 4

ARGUMENTS FOR AND AGAINST
A LIBERAL ABORTION LAW

Abortion . . . this insoluble problem. I say insoluble because it has bothered mankind for at least 2,500 years.   ALECK BOURNE[1]

IN THE YEARS FOLLOWING WORLD WAR II MANY THOUGHTFUL PEOPLE, considering the situation as it has been outlined in our earlier chapters, felt the time had come to press for an alteration in the law. Abortion was, they were told, "as simple and safe as drawing a tooth." Its easy availability should bring numerous benefits.

Effect on the Previous Practice of Abortion

Back-street abortion, with all its trail of misery and death, would become a thing of the past, or so it was claimed. But was this likely to be so? The Scandinavian experience was not encouraging. Dr. L. Huldt[2] has shown that between 1950 and 1961 the incidence of legal abortions in Stockholm affected the frequency of deliveries, but not that of criminal abortions. Only recently has the number of criminal abortions begun to fall, but simultaneously the rate of legal abortions has been "raised immensely."[3]

Unless no limitations whatever remain on legal abortion some women will have to rely on back-street help. A warning that this would inevitably be so was made by a barrister in 1966[4] and was, in the same year, very clearly spelled out by John Robinson, then Bishop of Woolwich. "We have to realise that even the most liberal law we can conceivably get at this moment will scarcely touch the hard core of the problem. Of the (up to) 100,000 abortions each year in this country and the million-plus in the United States not more than a small proportion could, or should in good faith, be legalized even under a bill as wide as Mr. Steel's. For, in order substantially to alleviate the toll, both mental and physical, of

---

[1] A. Bourne, In discussion reported in *"The Abortion Act"* (see p. 31, fn. 21).
[2] L. Huldt, "Outcome of Pregnancy when Legal Abortion is Readily Available." *Lancet*, 1968, **I**, 467.
[3] L. Huldt, Personal communication, May 1969.
[4] B. M. Dickens, *Abortion and the Law*. London, 1966, MacGibbon and Kee.

illegal terminations, the law would have to be stretched to the point of being discredited."[5]

In fact, rather than reduce the number of illegal abortions it is possible their number might, initially at any rate, go up. "Experience in other countries such as Sweden where the abortion laws have been liberalized showed that the incidence of recourse to criminal abortion was not reduced and might be increased, since criminal abortion seemed less criminal in this situation."[6] It was claimed that the previous expensive, and sometimes suspect, "West End" abortions would become a thing of the past. In the event we were later to see the growth of what Professor Keith Simpson was to call "the new abortion trade (and I use that word with care)."[7] In fact the largest number of requests for legal abortions that follow on the introduction of liberalizing legislation comes from a new source. In a study of women who applied for legal abortion in Sweden it was found that not more than 9% went on to provoke abortion; the other 91%, although prepared to seek a legal one, would not take illegal steps. This confirms the view that legal abortion is largely addressed to an entirely new clientèle of women, who would never have had a criminal abortion, and would give birth to the child if the possibility of legal abortion had not existed.[8] Glanville Williams, a Professor of Law, frankly stated, "Although the social result is rather to add the total of legal abortions to the total of illegal abortions than to reduce the number of illegal abortions, a body of medical opinion refused to regret the legal abortions on this account."[9]

The claim that easier abortion would prevent suicide will be discussed later; suffice for the moment to notice a series of 304 women who were refused abortion. Of these sixty-two threatened to commit suicide if refused, but none did.[10] The threat is, however, very occasionally carried out, often enough to give some slight weight to this argument.

The Woman's Right to Choose

While there can be only a minority of women who, like Moya Woodside's abortionists, consider that men treat women like dustbins,[11] there is very wide support for the battlecry that every woman should have the right to decide whether she should bear her child or not. This claim is

[5] Bishop J. A. T. Robinson, Lecture to the Abortion Law Reform Association, October 22 1966. Reprinted in *Christian Freedom in a Permissive Society*, London, 1970, S.C.M. Press.

[6] P. R. Myerscough, during debate "That the Abortion Act of 1967 was a Disastrous Mistake." *SMJ*, 1968, **13**, 396.

[7] K. Simpson, "Criminal Abortion: A Dying Art?" In *The Abortion Act (op. cit.)*.

[8] P. Arén and C. Amark, "The Prognosis in Cases in which Legal Abortion has been Granted but not Carried Out." *Acta Psychiatrica et Neurologica Scandinavica*, 1961, **36**, 203.

[9] G. L. Williams, *The Sanctity of Life and the Criminal Law*, London, 1958, Faber.

[10] B. J. Lindberg, 1948 (In Swedish) quoted by A. Barno (see p. 39, fn. 26).

[11] Moya Woodside, "Attitudes of Women Abortionists." *Howard Journal*, 1963, **11**, 93.

made to appear so self-evident that one is ashamed of having to point out three difficulties.

The first in my view is that this introduces quite a new theory: that conception and child-bearing are two separate and almost unrelated events; that, in fact, pregnancy is the matriculation without which one could not go on to the next stage of child-bearing, but which does not in itself commit one to that course! This seems to run counter to all female psychology.[12]

The second difficulty is that the woman does not know what, in fact, is involved in such a decision. She cannot know if there will be any operative complications, and whether she will ever again be able to conceive. She cannot be sure how the other members of her family will react. She cannot know what will be the response of her own conscience, post-operatively and in later life. No one can know. Those, however, who deal with these problems day in and day out may, at least, be thought to have an informed and mature judgement worth heeding.

The third snag is that if she is to take this decision she must do so at the time when she is mentally least capable of doing so.[13] Recently I saw a patient at follow-up clinic. Although neither she nor I have grounds so far to regret the abortion I had performed, she said: "Of course I couldn't think straight when I came to you to ask for the operation." Many women find that in each menstrual cycle their mind becomes less alert as their hormone levels increase just prior to the onset of menstruation. In early pregnancy the same thing happens, but to a greater extent, becoming usually maximal in the third month. This is the very time this decision is most frequently taken. Often this mental fog clears in the second trimester, although one woman doctor tells me that for each pregnancy she has a nine-month blank in her memory. To expect a woman at this of all times, to be able to sit down and come to a clear-headed decision is unrealistic.

Aleck Bourne wrote: "Those who plead for an extensive relaxation of the law have no idea of the very many cases where a woman who, during the first three months, makes a most impassioned appeal for her pregnancy to be 'finished', later, when the baby is born, is thankful indeed that it was not killed while still an embryo. During my long years in practice I have had many a letter of the deepest gratitude for refusing to

---

[12] "A woman's body, according to the Christian view, is not the domain and property of others. It is hers to control and she alone is responsible to God and to society for its use. When she yields that control, and through intercourse is involved in intra-personal relationships with a second party, and through conception with a third party, and indeed to human society as a whole, it becomes too late for her to justify abortion on the basis of self-determination." Carl Henry quoted in "Abortion, can an Evangelical consensus be found?" *Eternity* (Philadelphia) Feb. 1971.

[13] M. J. Daly has noted that the legitimately pregnant woman, and often those illegitimately pregnant too, are ambivalent to the pregnancy. This ambivalence is so universal that it may be considered normal in the first trimester. "The Unwanted Pregnancy." *Clinical Obstetrics and Gynecology*, 1970, 13, 713.

accede to an early appeal."[14] In the Swedish series of women who went through with their pregnancy despite abortions having been approved, four gave birth to stillborn children, and four babies died in the neonatal period. Two of the women imagined that the death of the child was a punishment for their having applied for abortion; one still suffered from such ideas even although she had got herself a "substitute child."[15]

Medical Case 4.1. A married woman asked her GP if she could have an abortion. He was not sure that this was warranted, but agreed to send her to the gynaecologist for a second opinion. Prior to the hospital appointment the patient started to bleed, was seen by the doctor on emergency call (who knew nothing of her request) and was sent into hospital as a case of threatened miscarriage. She was carefully treated and sent home with the pregnancy still intact. Her postponed gynaecological appointment (at another hospital) now was obtained, but she was found to be too far advanced for abortion. The pregnancy went to term. On delivery her comment to her GP was: 'Oh, God has been very good.'

The Child's Right to be Wanted and Healthy

A reformed Act would, for the first time, allow consideration to be given to the child. The aim so well stated by Dr. W. H. Finlay must commend itself to everyone: "A child ideally should be born into a home where he or she was conceived in an atmosphere of love, where his or her arrival is contemplated and planned for and where provisions are made for his or her infancy and childhood. This concept is the foundation of the grandeur of the family unit."[16] This surely can only be achieved within marriage and implies the use of an adequate contraceptive technique. If, however, that technique proves less than adequate is there a place for abortion to maintain this ideal?

More important, the Act should permit a reduction in the number of abnormal children born. The matter is discussed in detail in chapter 22; we note here only the magnitude of the problem. In the debate on Lord Silkin's Bill, the Bishop of Southwark (Dr. Mervyn Stockwood) recalled visiting, against medical advice, some closed wards. "I shall never forget," he said, "seeing these children – one did not know what to call them – some with large heads and practically no bodies and others in all sorts of contortions. One child I asked about had had nineteen fits that day. Whether or not they were human is a theological problem beyond my understanding."[17]

The anguish of a parent to whom is born such a child, or even one much less deformed, is beyond words. There is fear for the years ahead with the child, fear for the child after the parents' death. "The frantic rushing to

[14] A. Bourne, *A Doctor's Creed: The Memoirs of a Gynaecologist*, London, 1963, Gollancz
[15] P. Arén and C. Amark, *op. cit.*
[16] W. H. Finlay, "Genetic Reasons for Limiting Conception." *Birth Control and the Christian* (*op. cit.*).
[17] Bishop of Southwark. Quoted by B. M. Dickens (*op. cit.*).

anyone who claims to cure, and the slow death of hope as every honest doctor says that science has no answer."[18]

There were those, on the other hand, who recalled what unexpected joys and blessings an abnormal child could bring into a family. Dale Evans Rogers (wife of Roy Rogers, the American cowboy star) has written, as from her daughter's viewpoint, of her two-year stay on earth as a mongoloid baby, and of the blessing she brought to the home, and indirectly to many others in a like position.[19] There will always be a number of abnormal children born unexpectedly, and one hopes they will bring similar consolations, but this does not appear to be good grounds for permitting the birth of a child known at an early stage in pregnancy to be abnormal.

Effect of Illegitimate Pregnancy

The right of a child to be wanted is one of the factors in this complex problem. B. M. Dickens refers to "the repugnant concept of punishment by child-birth. It may be that those who offend the ethical precepts of a society and cause inconvenience by contravention of its moral code should be denied privilege or prestige. However, to argue that women who become pregnant by immoral relations must be denied legal abortion, and must bear children to indicate their sin and to deter others, is to render the child a stigma and blight to the mother. This may condemn the child to a regrettable inheritance and a precarious future, and such morality as is preserved by this policy may be bought at a high price in terms of in-dividual human happiness and respect for a child's right to be wanted and loved."[20]

On the other hand the official Inter-Departmental Committee of 1937 stated[21]: "There can be no doubt, moreover, that such a measure (the granting of abortion upon request) would prove an added temptation to loose and immoral conduct, and would render all the more difficult the task of educating individuals to a proper appreciation of sexual morality." The Church of England Committee, while recognizing that that statement is open to criticism, goes on: "Nevertheless there is an inherent connexion between a responsible – it is not too much to say a reverential – attitude to sexual relationship and a reverence for life; and it is not unreasonable to suppose that a weakening of the latter, which must accompany a wide-spread resort to induced abortion for no better purpose than the relief of an inconvenience, would find its counterpart in a weakening of the former and a trivializing of the sexual act . . . . We would repudiate (however) all and every 'use' of the illegitimate child as a means of pronouncing a moral

[18] W. E. Sangster, In preface to *Angel Unaware* (*op. cit.*).
[19] Dale E. Rogers, *Angel Unaware*, London, 1953, Marshall, Morgan & Scott.
[20] B. M. Dickens, *op. cit.*
[21] See (p. 28, fn. 14).

judgement upon his parents . . . . We would also maintain that to destroy him in the womb for no other reason than that his presence there is inconvenient is a fundamentally inhuman response to the fact of his existence . . . ."[22]

Very often the girl is confused – should she have the baby? But her mother's mind is clear: "You will ruin your future if you go on with it." She will do anything to help her daughter and in doing so may go further than the girl is willing to go.[23]

Medical Case: 4.2. A 19 year old single girl demanded abortion for social reasons. She had been worried before this but, since securing a privately arranged termination of pregnancy she has become severely depressed, having active suicidal thought and excess guilt feelings. Termination in this instance had tended only to aggravate, if not to produce, a depression of psychotic intensity with a threat to life.

Where the girl herself is anxious for an abortion there are still problems. There is too much publicity in going into hospital. "How can you moti-vate the stay in hospital to your relatives when you are admitted for a legal abortion?" asked a Swedish girl. She did not wait for legal per-mission to come, deciding that criminal abortion was safer and better.[8]

Socio-Economic Factors

"If we are to assume that medical responsibility includes providing the healthiest kind of family situation for the healthiest possible child, the medical indications would cover a much wider range."[24] The concept of "health" has been moving steadily away from the negative aspect of the absence of disease, towards the positive aspect of wholeness, which must include not only a satisfactorily functioning body, but a mind at ease. It is naturally assumed this involves a satisfactory socio-economic situation. Prosperity is not in fact essential, as has been shown repeatedly. For instance Paul of Tarsus wrote, "I have learned to find resources in myself whatever my circumstances. I know what it is to be brought low, and I know what it is to have plenty. I have been very thoroughly initiated into the human lot with all its ups and downs – fullness and hunger, plenty and want. I have strength for anything through him who gives me power."[25] This is, however, no reason for being satisfied with less than the best circumstances obtainable for the family. At what point are we to say that socio-economic circumstances justify abortion? If we say that poverty and a poor economic situation make a further pregnancy insupportable in the 1970s, how much less bearable must another mouth have been among the

[22] Church Assembly Board for Social Responsibility, Abortion: An Ethical Discussion. London, 1965, Church Information Office.
[23] P. Ferris, The Nameless: Abortion in Britain Today, London, 1966, Hutchinson.
[24] D. H. Bouma, "Abortion in a Changing Social Context." Birth Control and the Christian (op. cit.).
[25] Phil. 4: 11–13, NEB.

working classes in the industrial revolution, or the depression of the early 1930s? By these criteria how many of us today should have been disposed of prior to birth? How many of us studying this problem, with our education and measure of prosperity, must have seemed, or our progenitors must have seemed, to be disastrous mistakes?

In Japan, by house-to-house interviews three doctors (two of them gynaecologists) interviewed 1,380 women, all of whom had had their first induced abortion under the article approving abortion when "pregnancy or delivery might markedly injure the health of the mother because of her physical or financial condition." It proved that only 17% stated that their reasons were principally health; all other reasons given were related to the fear of difficulties in household financing in one sense or another.[26] Aleck Bourne states: "In this age the production of the fourth or even the third pregnancy, if not terminated during the early weeks, will seriously and probably successfully compete with the anticipated new car or foreign holiday."[28]

There are occasions when one feels that financial needs are very real, as in the woman I saw recently who said "Things could be worse, grandma pays for the children's shoes, and my two oldest go out to deliver papers before going to school." The difficulty is when the economic problems, perhaps not severe in themselves, weigh so much on the patient that she develops mental strain to such a degree as to indicate termination. One realises that could the financial problems be solved her worries would cease and the need to abort would no longer arise. But how to solve them? Often it is a long-term problem, especially where the woman, whose earnings help to keep the family together, is by this new pregnancy compelled to give up work for a number of years.

World Population

Professor P. J. Huntingford has drawn attention to the shattering calculation that at the present rate of population growth there will be more people alive by 1980 than have died throughout the whole course of history.[27] Conditions today are in direct contrast to the Middle Ages when theologians treated abortion as an offence against fecundity – a thwarting of the divine purpose, by means of marriage, to replenish the earth. With waste lands to cultivate, forests to cut back, armies to be recruited for defence or attack, it was decreed an offence to deprive the tribe, the king, the state, of a single potential subject. Today this very fecundity is probably the world's greatest threat. The President of the World Bank chose

[26] Y. Koya, "A Study of Induced Abortion in Japan and Its Significance." *Milbank Memorial Fund Quarterly*, 1954, **32**, 282.
[27] P. J. Huntingford, "The Right of the Individual to Freedom of Choice and Medical Responsibility." Paper read at the Planned Parenthood Federation Conference at Budapest. September 1969. I am indebted to Prof. Huntingford for allowing me to see his manuscript,
[28] Aleck Bourne, *op. cit.*

a speech at the Catholic University of Nôtre Dame, Illinois, as the occasion to deliver this warning: "Human dignity is threatened by the population explosion, more severely, more completely, more certainly threatened than it has been by any catastrophe the world has yet endured. There is time – just barely time – to escape that threat."[29]

Now in Britain and America the explosion of population has not been used as an argument for abortion, as contraceptives are readily available and are obviously the preferable method. In some areas (Japanese and Eastern European figures have been given in the previous chapter) legal abortion has, in fact, had a very marked demographic effect. These countries have the medical facilities to make this possible. In underdeveloped countries however, and these are the ones where the population growth is the most marked, only "the medicine of poverty"[30] is available. Where an intra-uterine contraceptive device (IUCD – "the coil") is the only realistic method of population limitation, skilled abortion would not be practicable even if desirable.

The Dignity of Life

Protagonists of a liberal abortion policy see this as a step in raising the dignity of Man. Sir Dugald Baird has made the point that abortion should be looked at not in isolation, but against the background of changing society and the status of women. ("That's what I have tried to do, raise the quality of human life – not just materially, I am thinking of something cerebral.") The Abortion Act, he thought, makes an important contribution to raising the quality of human life.[31] Can man rise to his full stature while subject to the tyranny of unrestrained fertility? However, another British professor of obstetrics, sympathetic to a liberalizing abortion policy, admits that "therapeutic abortion . . . . is associated to some extent with human denigration."[32]

What will be the effects on the whole family, especially on thinking children, if they discover that mother has had a termination because of a threat to their comparatively high standard of living? "Psychiatrists have stressed the importance of the family in the development of children's character and personality. If the bill goes through, they will have to reckon increasingly with materialism in the family as a potent dynamic force in a world of social and educational competition."[33]

A less obvious but equally important effect of easy abortion on society is its implication that one person is entitled to judge the value of another's existence. "The chief danger" (and Dr. Margaret White is here discussing

[29] Reported in The Guardian (Manchester) May 1, 1969.
[30] The phrase is Professor Maurice King's in his Medical Care in Developing Countries, Nairobi, 1966, OUP.
[31] Moira Keenan, in an interview with Sir Dugald Baird, The Times, June 18, 1969.
[32] P. J. Huntingford, op. cit.
[33] R. E. Hemphill, Letter in the Lancet, 1967, I, 324.

abortion for possible fetal abnormality) "is that it breaches an important principle by suggesting that the deaf, the blind, and the maimed are disposable. It is only a short step from disposable babies to disposable people."[34] The principle can, of course, immediately be extended. Professor Henry Miller, a supporter of a liberal abortion law has stated: "It is easy to have the feeling that the hopeless psychopath or the imbecile would be better dead. To dispose of such unfortunates out of hand would be entirely reasonable in a society that was biological and nothing more. But this is a political and not a biological society. Once we accept that it is not our duty to try to keep our patients alive, the principle – or lack of it – has an unfortunate habit of proving almost indefinitely extensible, not only to patients but to other members of society. History shows the ease with which it can be extended to one's political opponents or those of a different colour or religious persuasion. The principle must not be conceded. Somebody asked "What use are such people?" To which the only appropriate reply is surely "What use is a baby?"[35]

Where does it stop? In 1962 Madame van de Put having killed her eight-day-old daughter who was suffering from thalidomide deformities was acquitted of murder. St. John Stevas comments " . . . . the Liege verdict is fundamentally uncivilized and dangerous. It invites imitation. Within a few days of the verdict a Belgian housewife was remanded in custody for having killed her 3-year-old mentally-retarded daughter. Over the centuries society has contrived to limit the taking of human life, under rigidly defined circumstances, to the state. The van de Put case in effect confers a licence to kill on the individual citizen, and a licence with no clear limiting terms."[36] The Abortion Act, in a word, puts into one person's power the right to forbid life to another.

The Effect on the Patient

Arguments about the effect of readily available abortion turn largely on the effect on the mother's health, any mental aftereffects, and the effects on her socio-economic circumstances. These are all dealt with at length in Part III of this book and need not detain us. In the general debate one point appears to have escaped notice to a large extent: how will the woman see herself in relation to her husband? Reporting 5,000 abortions performed in Rumania under the old liberal law, a woman doctor noted that 23% of women had had three to four abortions earlier, 36% had had five to ten abortions, 4% had had ten to fifteen, and 2.7% had had more than fifteen abortions already! She commented that most men lost their respect for women, treating them only as sexual partners. On the other hand

[34] Margaret White, *Having it Taken Away*, London (n.d.), Mother's Union.
[35] H. Miller, "Economical and Ethical Considerations." A Symposium on The Cost of Life. *Proceedings of the Royal Society of Medicine*, 1967, **60**, 1216.
[36] N. St. John Stevas, *The Right to Life*, London, 1963, Hodder.

when the law was greatly tightened in 1966 mothers regained their self-respect.[37]

Effect on the Doctor

Many antagonists of the abortion law reform made great play of the Hippocratic Oath. They seemed to imagine that at graduation newly qualified doctors formally swear to observe this. If in fact this is done at all, it can only be in a few places. It contains promises to share one's substance with one's teachers, to teach the art to one's sons and teacher's sons, and the vow that one will not operate for urinary calculus.[38] None of these are now kept. The clause "I will not give to a woman a pessary to procure abortion" is of interest, but not very relevant.

Nevertheless, it is true that the alteration of the law involves a tremendous change. "Superficially the new laws may only codify what is already current practice, but they also spell the end of the code of ethics on which Western medicine has been built. We shall have to find a new code which will include the right to decide on who lives and who dies, and which will be more in keeping with the beliefs of modern scientific man."[39]

While easier abortion is liable to make demands on doctors in several areas of medicine, the brunt must fall on the G.Ps. and gynaecologists. The matter was put bluntly at a symposium in London " . . . . most of those in favour of abortion on demand or easier abortion are those most remote from the performance of the task. I have met very few general practitioners or gynaecologists who like the duty which is imposed upon them in any measure at all; they are very unhappy to be parties to something which they find repugnant."[40] Gynaecologists have felt bitter at the burden placed on them by Parliament. "The same people who think it wrong to ask a man to perform legal homicide at the behest of the State, or for a law-enforcement representative to thrash a young thug, find it justifiable to ask a doctor, traditionally the maintainer of human life, to terminate a potential life for sometimes little more than the convenience of the mother."[41] What was particularly riling was that it was this particular Parliament that passed the Act. "It is passing strange that a Parliament so concerned with saving the life of a convicted murderer should be so willing to destroy life, perhaps because it is so innocent and so small?"[42]

One point that seems to have been overlooked is that gynaecologists

---

[37] A. Panaitescu-Mirescu, "Psychosomatic Aspects of Abortion". Paper read at the Third International Congress of Psychosomatic Medicine in Obstetrics and Gynaecology, London, April, 1971.

[38] Hippocrates. *The Genuine Works of Hippocrates*, Tr. F. Adams. Baltimore, 1939, Williams and Wilkins Co.

[39] H. Z. Liebeschuetz, Letter in the *BMJ*, 1966, 1, 1359.

[40] H. A. Constable, Opening the discussion reported in *The Abortion Act (op. cit.)*.

[41] W. Y. Sinclair, "The Doctor in a Permissive Society." *In the Service of Medicine*, No. 57, April, 1969.

[42] G. W. Theobald, Letter in the *BMJ*, 1966, 1, 977.

are also obstetricians. "A patient struggling for life or to preserve a pregnancy expects the doctor to try, and go on trying beyond reason – and he usually does. But will he try quite as hard if he has just come from destroying a fetus? He may *think* he can keep the two functions separate in his mind, but the unconscious influence will be insidious."[43] Those words were penned before the passing of the Abortion Act 1967; certainly I am aware of their truth today. Whereas earlier we had regular meetings to discuss every unsuccessful pregnancy, and try to pin down any preventable factor with a view to ever-improving results no such meeting has been suggested since 1967. I confess to finding in myself a lessening of enthusiasm. Is there any point in struggling quite so hard to preserve an unborn fetus already at risk and which may well never flourish, when one has just been called upon to terminate healthy pregnancy after healthy pregnancy? It is a temptation one tries to resist: but it would be dishonest to deny its existence. "The gynaecologist has a repugnance to taking life; woe betide us if we get used to it."[44]

Effect on the Nurse and the Hospital

The effect of a liberalized law on the other members of the hospital team, especially on nurses working in the theatre, was foreseen. The Church of England Board of Social Responsibility drew attention to the clause "No person shall be under any duty ... to participate in any treatment authorized by this Act to which he has a conscientious objection." After pointing out that medical practitioners can work according to their own conscience it went on: "The situation of Matrons and Nurses is different. They may have conscientious objections to abortion in any form, in which case it is clearly their duty to seek work in hospitals or branches of hospitals where these questions do not arise or where these conscientious scruples would be sympathetically understood." At the same time it realised the difficulty of those prepared to accept that there are some justifiable operations but felt that they were being ordered to assist in cases not within the spirit of the Act. "It would then be their duty, after reasonable enquiry, to class themselves with the general conscientious objectors."[45] This is, no doubt, all very true, and excellent advice for the senior sister well established in her profession. How is the junior 18-year old pupil nurse going to cope? How can she finish her training if she is not prepared to do gynaecology? Or how is she going to fare if she refuses to deal with certain classes of patients? How could a duty roster, or even meal-breaks, be arranged when one nurse would not look after certain of the patients in the ward, patients perhaps not yet round from the anaesthetic? One's mind boggles at the kind of treatment the pupil nurse might receive at the

[43] D. Le Vay, Letter in the *Lancet*, 1967, I, 510.
[44] R. W. Taylor, Letter in the *BMJ*, 1966, I, 738.
[45] Church Assembly Board for Social Responsibility. *The Abortion Act and its Conscience Clause*, May, 1968.

hands of some senior nurses, and at the report of her conduct which would be entered on her training schedule.

That the physical availability of resources would make any flood of admissions difficult was also foreseen. It was suggested that there was unlikely to be more than a marginal increase in the number of cases as already there were not enough beds or nurses in our hospitals to deal with routine cases. How wrong can you be? It was also naïvely stated that as every abortion meant one delivery less, obstetrical beds could be switched to gynaecological use – ignoring the fact that the units are usually geographically distinct. The alternative of performing abortions within the maternity unit seems to me so cruel to the patient that I cannot believe its supporters had understood the problem.

A Stop-Gap?

Abortion was advocated as a "stop-gap" until such time as improved contraceptive techniques and education took effect. Its need is, in fact, likely to be less when an efficient, safe, readily available, cheap, "hindsight" pill has arrived. That day is not yet; whether or not it is desirable will be discussed later.

Meanwhile this claim has very little foundation in fact. In Hungary, women are not interested in contraceptive means but rely on artificial abortion as a method of family planning.[46] In Japan, Dr. Y. Koya's investigations showed that only 27% of the women practised contraception prior to their abortion; the chief reasons for failing to do so were indifference and lack of knowledge.[47] In Mr. Peter Diggory's British series, 47.8% had used no contraceptive method ("the doctors and nurses in this series seemed little better off than the rest of the sample in this respect"[48]). And he tells me there were a very large number of doctors' wives and daughters.[49] In my experience, the women who have an unwelcome pregnancy have not conceived usually because of ignorance of contraception. If they are married it has happened because of temporary unavailability of the means; if they are single, because passion overtook them unexpectedly.

It is said that in Sweden the thing to do if you are in the young set is to have intercourse without contraception as an act of bravado. The situation in Britain is not altogether different for the Chief Medical Officer has commented that there is plenty of evidence that young people experimenting with sex do not take any action to avoid pregnancy.[50] In some

[46] B. Konstek, 1964. Paper in Hungarian quoted by F. T. MacFarlane in discussion following Droegemuller's paper (see p. 40, fn. 28).
[47] Y. Koya, op. cit.
[48] P. L. C. Diggory, "Some Experience of Therapeutic Abortion." Lancet, 1969, I, 873.
[49] P. L. C. Diggory, Personal communication.
[50] Chief Medical Officer of the Dept. of Health and Social Security. On the State of the Public Health, Annual Report, 1969. London, 1970, H.M.S.O.

cases this is merely fecklessness. There are other single girls who indulge in intercourse yet who are not prepared to take contraceptive precautions for to do so, in their eyes, would be to imply a degree of commitment which they are not willing to make.

The hope that education and improved contraception will solve the problem of the unwanted pregnancy is a mirage. It would be wise to face that fact now.

If this be so, how often are we to be prepared to abort the same woman?

Medical Case 4.3. A twenty-year-old unmarried girl, seen at out-patients, asked for termination because she had had two therapeutic abortions in London privately on psychiatric grounds in the preceding ten months, and could not afford a third.

In Czechoslovakia, 50% of women aborted had a second abortion, and 12% a third abortion, within two years.[6]

Conclusion

We were told that all, however, would be well! The act was to be purely permissive. "Religious objections to abortion based on doctrine cannot be refuted, as ultimately the objection stems from belief incapable of empirical demonstration. A permissive law accommodates both believers and non-believers, and subjects neither to the will of the other; this may indeed be the nature of religious freedom and tolerance."[51] How facile this hope too proved to be will be seen in later chapters.

[51] B. M. Dickens, *op. cit.*

CHAPTER 5

THE PROTAGONISTS

It seems to me that "theologians" on either side of the rationalist-supernaturalist controversy have become mere case-makers, primarily out for proofs .... It looks as if some kinds of argument whatever they appear to be about, can indeed be largely sterile because they are not really aimed at finding a synthesis, they are covert polemic, and they aim at victory. With warfare of all kinds, truth is indeed the first victim. KATHLEEN NOTT[1]

THE DEBATE LEADING TO THE PASSAGE OF THE ABORTION ACT, 1967, is now a matter of history, and therefore need not be considered in detail for our present purpose. It is, however, instructive to look at it briefly, not only in order to provide a bibliographical apparatus for those wishing more details, but more importantly as a salutary warnin to those in other lands. And to us for the next time!

That the 1861 law was unsatisfactory can be noted from the attitude of the law. A learned judge commented that the law should be substantially modified.[2] In 1963, of policemen questioned only 24% thought that abortion should be a criminal offence,[3] and half of Moya Woodside's informants found the police "decent and kind."[4] A full discussion by Bernard Dickens, himself a barrister, has been published.[5]

The Pro-Abortion Lobby

For reasons outlined in our earlier chapters, widespread dissatisfaction with the law grew, and in 1936 the Abortion Law Reform Association (ALRA)[6] was formed by three women. While by 1939 there were 400 members, this had sunk to 200 by the early 1960s. It was largely the advent of new leadership, and in addition the thalidomide tragedy, which gave it the boost to pass the thousand mark by 1966.[7] It was this miniscule

---

[1] Kathleen Nott, in *Objections to Humanism* (Ed. H. J. Blackham), London, 1963, Constable.

[2] J. McCardie. Quoted by B. M. Dickens, *op. cit.*

[3] B. Whitaker. Quoted by B. M. Dickens, *op. cit.*

[4] Moya Woodside, "Attitudes of Women Abortionists," *Howard Journal*, 1963, **11**, 93.

[5] B. M. Dickens, *Abortion and the Law*, London, 1966, MacGiffon and Kee.

[6] The Abortion Law Reform Association (ALRA), 22 Brewhouse Hill, Wheathampstead, Hertfordshire.

[7] K. Hindell and Madelaine Simms. "How the Abortion Lobby Worked," *The Political Quarterly*, 1968, **39**, 269.

proportion of the population which by dedicated work and effort was principally responsible for achieving the change in the law. Seven Bills were introduced into Parliament without success before David Steel, Liberal M.P. for Roxburgh, Selkirk and Peebles, having won the ballot for the right to bring in a private member's bill, espoused the cause of abortion law reform and brought his bill triumphantly on to the Statute Book. Behind all these efforts the ALRA had been working tirelessly. News letters brought stimulus to members, urging them to local endeavour by propaganda in their own groups – women's guilds, local Labour parties, or any group who would listen – and by writing to the press whenever possible. For this, ammunition was provided in the form of abortion deaths, trials before the courts, friendly comments from authorities and pro-abortion medical opinions. The aims of the ALRA were "to secure such changes in the law as will provide that a registered medical practitioner may lawfully terminate a pregnancy at the request of the patient or her guardian:

1. When it is necessary for preserving the physical or mental health of the woman.
2. When there is serious risk of a defective child being born.
3. When the pregnancy results from a sexual offence (such as rape, incest, or intercourse with a girl under sixteen)".

At the 1966 annual meeting a fourth category was added:

4. When the pregnant woman's capacity as a mother will be severely overstrained.[8]

Who were this thousand who changed our civilization? "After the law was eventually reformed ALRA was able to question its members about their beliefs, occupations and personal characteristics. Nearly two-thirds of them turned out to be women, two-thirds had had higher education, and one-fifth were doctors or para-medical. One in three of the women members had required an abortion at some stage in her life, and one in four had obtained one, mostly legally, mostly privately. Although most of the members had been brought up in the conventional religious denominations, the rate of lapse from religious observance was striking. 74% were now atheists or agnostics. Half the members had been born into Anglican homes but only 10% were still Anglicans in 1968. 13% of ALRA's members had been brought up as Nonconformists and 13% as Jews; these figures had fallen to 8% and 5% respectively. 51% were Labour supporters, 21% Conservatives; quite different from the spread of party loyalty in the country as a whole. Membership overlapped heavily with that of the Family Planning Association (39%), the National Trust (31%) and the Fabian Society (21%), but members showed

[8] ALRA Annual Report for 1966–67.

little interest in the other reform groups. Only 39% were satisfied with the 1967 Abortion Act; 57% hoped for further reform."[7]

Agnosticism and Abortion Reform

Unfortunately there is one fact here which we must look at more closely, as its implications run through the whole abortion controversy: "74% were now atheists or agnostics." That this is no coincidence is seen from the close liaison, sometimes affiliation, with the ALRA of the Secular Society[9] and various Humanist associations.[10] The first bill presented to Parliament in 1953 had been introduced by a vice-president of the Rationalist Press Association. Madeleine Simms, one of the foremost ALRA workers, has written "Most of the early ALRA committee were freethinkers who saw organized religion as the main obstacle to the full emancipation of women."[11]

The importance of the agnostic in the abortion debate is that he and the Christian are not talking about the same things. "You cannot have a dialogue with those who are theologically neuter. It is like playing Beethoven's Fifth Symphony to a person who is tone deaf."[12] That was written by a Roman Catholic. Now the present writer would disagree with the Roman Catholic view on abortion, but in debating with the local branch of the Guild of St. Luke, St. Cosmas and St. Damian we were talking about the same thing and building on the same premises. When however he propounded in public debate the Christian implications of abortion, one of the opposing team (a member of the ALRA's medico-legal council) brushed them aside in a sentence, remarking "I am not able to discuss the matter as I am not a theist."

The Christian sees the whole world, and every aspect of his own life, in relation to "A just God, and a Saviour" to whom each of us will one day have to give account and before whom every knee shall bow.

If we look at humanist literature we see quite a different picture. "Humanist" and "agnostic" are not, of course, synonymous terms (after all, John Robinson has said: "Because I am a Christian, I *am* a radical humanist"[13]), but for our present purpose I may be allowed to equate them.

Sir Julian Huxley has written "(Man) is not merely exceedingly young; he is also exceedingly imperfect, an unfinished and often botched product of evolution . . . . Man, in fact, is in urgent need of further improvement." So far the Christian might be in some agreement, although his diagnosis of cause and cure are very different. Sir Julian goes on to

[9] ALRA Annual Report for 1962–63.
[10] ALRA Annual Report for 1963–64.
[11] K. Hindell and Madelaine Simms. *Abortion Law Reformed*, London, 1971, Peter Owen.
[12] N. St. John Stevas, "Abortion and the Law," *Dublin Review*, Winter, 1967–68, **241**, 274.
[13] Bishop J. A. T. Robinson, "On Being a Radical." Reprinted from *The Listener*. In *Christian Freedom in a Permissive Society*, London, 1970, S.C.M. Press.

suggest that man's salvation lies in eugenics: negative eugenics using contraception or sterilization, combined where possible with A.I.D. (artificial insemination by donor) or other methods of vicarious parenthood; all to prevent genetic deterioration. Positive genetics he feels to be the more important and will rely largely on what he calls E.I.D. (eugenic insemination by deliberately preferred donors) an effect multiplied many thousand-fold by deep-freezing superior sperm; and made more efficient when the technique of grafting of deep-frozen ova into women has been mastered.[14] One can readily see how abortion would fit into this programme. But is man's chief end to improve his genetic stock or is it "to glorify God, and enjoy Him forever"?[15] Do suicide figures prove that "genetically superior" folk are in any way happier?

In a very different vein Aldous Huxley wrote "I had motives for not wanting the world to have a meaning; consequently assumed that it had none, and was able without any difficulty to find satisfying reasons for this assumption . . . . The philosopher who finds no meaning in the world is not concerned exclusively with a problem in pure metaphysics; he is also concerned to prove that there is no valid reason why he personally should not do as he wants to do . . . . For myself, as no doubt for most of my contemporaries, the philosophy of meaninglessness was essentially an instrument of liberation. The liberation we desired was simultaneously liberation from a certain political and economic system and liberation from a certain system of morality. We objected to the morality, because it interfered with our sexual freedom; we objected to the political and economic system because it was unjust. The supporters of these systems claimed that in some way they embodied the meaning (a Christian meaning, they insisted) of the world. There was one admirably simple method of confuting these people and at the same time justifying ourselves in our political and erotic revolt; we would deny that the world had any meaning whatsoever."[16] Obviously if the world is meaningless the only course to pursue is the pleasure of the moment.

Now although such a course would be easy it must be said that many agnostics have dedicated their energies, and their often outstanding talents, to the cause of the needy and oppressed. They have shown a concern for the underprivileged and defeated which often puts the Christian to shame. I am honoured to have among my friends agnostics whose concern for social justice is an example one would seek to follow. It is easy to see how, given their views, abortion reform is a cause they would be expected to champion. For one whose horizon is limited to terrestrial existence the Christian with his altogether different focus must seem an infuriatingly obscurantist busybody. The clue lies in the focus.

[14] Sir Julian Huxley, "Eugenics in Evolutionary Perspective." The Galton Lecture for 1962 reprinted in *Essays of a Humanist*. London, 1964, Chatto and Windus.
[15] The Shorter Catechism, 1648.
[16] Aldous Huxley. *Ends and Means*, London, 1937, Chatto.

The apprentice devil Wormwood had to be reminded that ". . . the Church as we see her (is) spread out through all time and space and rooted in eternity, terrible as an army with banners. That, I confess, is a spectacle which makes our boldest tempters uneasy. All your patient sees is the half-finished, sham Gothic section on the new building estate . . . . When he gets to his pew and looks round him he sees just that selection of his neighbours whom he has hitherto avoided . . . . You may know one of them to be a great warrior on the Enemy's side. No matter. Your patient, thanks to Our Father below, is a fool. Provided that any of those neighbours sing out of tune, or have boots that squeak, or double chins, or odd clothes, the patient will quite easily believe that their religion must therefore be somehow ridiculous."[17]

The point must also be made that among the ranks of the ALRA there must be many people of Christian conviction. In fact an early ALRA pamphlet was *A Clergyman's View*.

The Anti-Abortion Lobby

No organized opposition to the ALRA came into being for thirty years until David Steel's bill was well under debate. Then the Society for the Protection of the Unborn Child (SPUC)[18] was organized. A little earlier the ALRA had listed their opponents as generally belonging "to one of three groups: Roman Catholics, elderly and extreme Anglicans, Moral Rearmers (MRA)."[19] Perhaps because of this, SPUC made it clear that there were no Roman Catholics or members of MRA on its Executive Council. Its aims were:

1. To uphold the principle that human life ought not to be taken except in cases of urgent necessity.
2. To reassert the principle laid down in the United Nations "Declaration of the Rights of the Child," that children need "special safeguards and care, including appropriate legal protection, before as well as after birth."
3. To consider how far the Medical Termination of Pregnancy Bill . . . is consistent with these principles, and to oppose it where it is not.
4. To assist as far as possible in spreading knowledge of means which are likely to improve the prospects, as opposed to taking the lives of unborn children.[20]

Despite its lack of Roman Catholic members on its executive it had a good deal of R.C. support, as well as support from many other Christian people. It was able to present a petition with more than half-a-million

[17] C. S. Lewis, *The Screwtape Letters*, London, 1942, Bles.
[18] Society for the Protection of the Unborn Child(SPUC), 47 Eaton Place, London S.W.1
[19] ALRA Newsletter no. 17, Winter, 1966.
[20] SPUC Application Form for Membership.

signatories appealing for a Royal Commission to go into the whole abortion picture, rather than that the law be amended without this information.

It would be possible to include at this point several pages of vituperative quotations from the battle. Holders of the opposite viewpoint not only had their attitudes castigated, but were personally denigrated and their motives impugned. The opposition's efforts were "malicious," and their supporters "captive."

Medical Viewpoints

The medical profession also entered the contest. The journals were full of letters, many of them making assertions which the writers should have known were inaccurate. At a more serious level the medical organizations declared themselves. Psychiatric views tended to be liberal. A questionnaire to members of The Society of Clinical Psychiatrists[21] showed that a quarter of its members favoured termination on request in the first three months; while of a group of general practitioners and public health doctors[22] attending a course in family psychiatry, no less than 62% held this view.

The Royal Medico-Psychological Association issued a Memorandum in 1966 advancing a pragmatic view of medical ethics, suggesting that the individual doctor must be free to follow his own conscience. They felt there were occasions when a shift to health would be promoted by termination, and in the case of a potentially abnormal fetus its removal would make way for the conception of a normal one. On the other hand "we believe we should resist attempts to make the termination of pregnancy lawful merely on the grounds that it is inconvenient to either or both parents."[23]

Among gynaecologists, many of whom saw themselves cast in the role of executioner, there was widespread disapproval. The fellows and members of the Midlands Obstetrical and Gynaecological Society were circulated with a memorandum stating the case against abortion law reform, due to its effect on society, on the public's attitude to doctors, on the sanctity of life, and as a degradation of character, and asserting that the present law was satisfactory. Fifty-five gynaecologists gave this memorandum unqualified support, a further ten supported it with some reservations, and only three did not support it.[25] In the Leeds Region consultant gynaecologists issued a statement: ". . . should the Bill become law, our present practice of terminating a pregnancy where well-established

[21] J. G. Howells, Letter in BMJ, 1967, 2, 53.
[22] J. G. Howells, Letter in BMJ, 1967, 2, 314.
[23] Royal Medico-Psychological Association (RMPA), Memorandum on Therapeutic Abortion, approved by Council, July, 1966. British Journal of Psychiatry, 1966, 112, 1071.
[24] RMPA Lancet, 1967, 1, 1337.
[25] W. Mills, Letter in BMJ, 1966, 1, 355.

medical indications exist will be unchanged, and we do not expect to terminate more pregnancies than before."[26] The Royal College of Obstetricians and Gynaecologists unanimously adopted a report stating that the present situation (i.e. the 1861 Act, plus case law) "commends itself to most gynaecologists in that it leaves them free to act in what they consider to be the best interests of each individual patient." It went on to draw attention to the operative risks: "Non-fatal *serious* complications occur in not less than 3% of cases of legalized abortion induced by experts under modern conditions, and morbidity rates of as high as 15% are reported." They were against the writing into any Act of automatic abortion for any girl under the age of sixteen as this "might give rise to the idea that any girl who is younger than this could risk conceiving in the belief that she could demand therapeutic abortion if the need arose, and could have the effect of encouraging promiscuity in the young." They made the point: "The interpretation of any new Abortion Act and its application to medical practice in this country would be largely the responsibility of obstetricians and gynaecologists. It would therefore seem wise that legislators should be reasonably sure of their co-operation before deciding on any alteration of the Law." Pointing out the importance of preventive medicine, they felt that the need for new legislation to cover sterilization was of far greater urgency than a new abortion law.[27]

The British Medical Association issued a report by a special committee recognizing the need for new legislation. It recommended that therapeutic abortion should only be legal in an approved place, with a second opinion, and with confidential notification. Grounds recommended were the health of the mother, or the risk of serious abnormality of the fetus. They did not mention social considerations. "Whether or not a pregnancy should be terminated is a question which can be decided only in the circumstances of each particular case. The ultimate decision to advise termination of pregnancy rests with the doctors in charge of the case and, subject to the conditions laid down to safeguard the security of the pre-viable foetus, the law should not seek to influence this decision by further defining the degree of risk which must be present before termination can be regarded as lawful."[28]

Later the BMA and RCOG made a further joint statement on the text of Mr. Steel's bill, pressing that one of the two medical practitioners approving the operation should be a consultant and that nursing-homes should be approved. So far as the "social" clauses were concerned they felt these might lead to an excess demand which would be unacceptable to the medical profession, and that the factors, "though only permissive

[26] Leeds Consultant Gynaecologists. Quoted in ALRA Annual Report, 1966–67.
[27] Royal College of Obstetricians and Gynaecologists (RCOG). "Legalised Abortion," Report by the Council. 1966, 1, 850.
[28] BMA, "Therapeutic Abortion," Report by a BMA Special Committee, *BMJ*, 1966, 2, 40.

would inevitably lead the public to believe that termination would automatically be carried out in the instances mentioned." They suggested the inclusion of the phrase (earlier recommended by the Church of England Board of Social Responsibility)[29] that "account may be taken of the patient's total environment, actual or reasonably foreseeable."[30]

A systematic random sample of G.P.s was carried out by National Opinion Polls in May 1967, with a 65.5% response rate from the 1,800 doctors to whom questionnaires were posted. They were asked their opinion of Clause 1(1) of the act (see next chapter) which contains its main provisions. The response showed that:

59% thought it to be generally satisfactory,
6% thought it unsatisfactory as the grounds were too restricted,
21% also thought it unsatisfactory, and that the grounds should be more restricted,
10% unsatisfactory, as they disapproved of all these grounds,
4% were undecided.[32]

Among the plethora of articles, hand-outs, and propaganda of all kinds one must be mentioned. *To be or not to be* was an anonymous pamphlet[33] reportedly written by a Lancashire lawyer, Peter McDonald. "You don't need to believe in God to believe in the sanctity of human life – Then we learnt about Dachau and Belsen . . . . Are we still determined to uphold the sanctity of human life . . . . If the Abortion Bill goes through, Herod will laugh in Hell. There will be perpetrated in our name a Massacre of the Innocents more dreadful in its scope than any Herod could have imagined."

A year after victory David Steel in a speech to the ALRA listed some of the steps to triumph. In particular he felt this to be due to having the right men in the right place at the right time. Roy Jenkins was at the Home Office; the Minister of Health was Kenneth Robinson, one of the earlier, unsuccessful presenters of a Bill to reform the abortion law. John Silkin the Government Chief Whip was the son of the peer whose two bills were the last to fail. Douglas Houghton, Chairman of the Parliamentary Labour Party, was husband of the chairman of the ALRA.[35]

A detailed account of the battle from the Abortion Law Reform

[29] Church Assembly Board for Social Responsibility, *Abortion: An Ethical Discussion*, London, 1965, Church Information Office.
[30] "Medical Termination of Pregnancy Bill: Views of the BMA and RCOG." *BMJ*, 1966, **2**, 1649.
[31] National Opinion Polls Ltd. "Survey of General Practitioner Opinion of the Medica Termination of Pregnancy Bill." May, 1967.
[32] John Barr, "The Abortion Battle," *New Society*, March 9, 1967.
[33] *To Be or Not to Be*, Manchester (n.d.), E. Ainsworth and Son.
[35] D. M. S. Steel, "Abortion Act Vindicates 16 Years of Effort." *Medical Tribune*, Oct. 31, 1968.

Association viewpoint has been published.[11] The authors, unfortunately, have come to believe their own propaganda, and make sweeping generalizations. Perhaps the most staggering is that "medically and legally the embryo and fetus are merely parts of the mother's body, and not yet human." Norman St. John Stevas, commenting on this sentence, remarks "(they) produce not a tittle of evidence for this astonishing assertion, which if true would make nonsense of the entire controversy."[36] David Steel, in his foreword, is also critical, thus: "The authors state 'Abortion on request is a logical concomitant of contraception on demand,' but this is not a proposition which commends itself either to me, to Parliament, or to public opinion."[37]

One last fact is worth noting. It was Aleck Bourne's action, recorded earlier, which had brought the whole subject of abortion alive. He served as a member of ALRA's medico-legal committee[7] in its early days. But, with the founding of SPUC we find him as a member of its executive committee. He believed that his acquittal had had undesirable effects.[32] Later he was to say "I am strongly opposed, and always have been, to anything like indiscriminate abortion."[34] His stance did not endear him to the reformers. "Bourne was a hero of the public of his time because he challenged the law and risked his career for the sake of a young girl. But the hero had the moral outlook of a high-minded Victorian governess and later turned out to have feet of clay."[11] Mr. Bourne's stand has not had the notice it warrants, witness the fact than an American Catholic, writing in 1969, states "If anyone may claim the title of patron saint of the movement for easier abortion it is surely Dr. Aleck Bourne."[38] It would be surprising were he to be the last to change sides in this way.

[34] A. Bourne. In discussion in *The Abortion Act, op. cit.*

[36] N. St. John Stevas, "The Trump Cards of the Abortion Lobby," *The Times*, Feb. 18, 1971.

[37] D. M. S. Steel, Foreword to *Abortion Law Reformed, op. cit.*

[38] R. Shaw, *Abortion on Trial*, London, 1969, Robert Hale.

CHAPTER 6

THE WILL OF THE PEOPLE

The law is that which puts a difference betwixt good and evil, betwixt just and unjust. If you take away the law, all things will fall into confusion. Every man will become a law to himself, which, in the depraved condition of human nature, must needs produce great enormities. Lust will become a law, envy will become a law, covetousness and ambition will become laws .. .
JOHN PYM *to the House of Commons: November* 1640[1]

The Abortion Act, 1967

THE ABORTION ACT EVENTUALLY RECEIVED THE ROYAL ASSENT ON October 27th, 1967, and came into operation six months later. The actual wording makes a fascinating study.

Sir John Peel, President of the Royal College of Obstetricians and Gynaecologists has commented ". . . it is quite clear that what this Act really means largely depends upon what you want it to mean . . . there is clearly a confusion . . . different people and different disciplines are interpreting this Act in different ways . . . . This is one of the sad things, I think, that a great deal of this confusion could have been avoided if only the laymen involved in seeing this particular Bill through the House of Commons had been prepared to take some measure of professional advice."[2]

Writing in *The Times,* Ronald Butt made the following points: "The Act is working badly, chiefly because of the way in which it was passed. It was a badly and loosely drafted Bill." He goes on to quote Hindell and Simm's paper (see below) and continues: "In other words it was a good Act from the point of view of the abortion lobby precisely because it was badly drafted. So much for respect for the law being founded on its certainty and clarity."[3]

Let us now look at the Act,[4] section by section. I express merely my own opinions, but this is the method by which everyone is interpreting and acting upon this law. The legislature having apparently abdicated its responsibility to give clear guidance, we are back in the position that

[1] J. Pym, Quoted by Sir Charles Firth, *Oliver Cromwell,* 1900, OUP.
[2] Sir John Peel, in discussion in *The Abortion Act, op. cit.*
[3] R. Butt, *The Times,* June 20, 1969.
[4] Abortion Act 1967. c. 87.

existed in the twelfth century B.C.: "In those days there was no king in Israel, and every man did what was right in his own eyes."[5]

An Act to amend and clarify the law relating to termination of pregnancy by registered medical practitioners.

Section 1. Subject to the provisions of this section, a person shall not be guilty of an offence under the law relating to abortion when a pregnancy is terminated by a registered medical practitioner if two registered medical practitioners are of the opinion, formed in good faith, that . . . . .

Section 6. In this Act, the following expressions shall have meanings assigned to them; "The law relating to abortion" means sections 58 and 59 of the Offences against the Person Act 1861, and any rule of law relating to the procurement of abortion;

It has been very much emphasized by protagonists of abortion law reform prior to the passing of the Bill that the Act is *permissive*. It does not lay down what the gynaecologist *shall* do; it states what he *may* do. In fact it is less positive than that: it states that it will not be considered a crime should he perform an abortion under the listed conditions. Since the Act became law, however, the tune has changed, and its permissive nature – as we shall see in our next chapter – is being threatened.

Subsection (1), *paragraph* (a): . . . . that the continuance of the pregnancy would involve risk to the life of the pregnant woman, or of injury to the physical or mental health of the pregnant woman or any existing children of her family, greater than if the pregnancy were terminated . . . .

Paragraph (b) In determining whether the continuance of a pregnancy would involve risk of injury to health as is mentioned in paragraph (a) of subsection (1) of this section, account may be taken of the pregnant woman's actual or reasonably foreseeable environment.

The first problem in interpretation is the phrase "greater than if the pregnancy were terminated."

The attitude of the Abortion Law Reform Association, as expressed in their pamphlet distributed to all general practitioners in the United Kingdom, is: "Prior to the Act it was sometimes thought that termination of pregnancy was lawful only when it was necessary to prevent the patient from becoming a 'wreck.' The Act makes it clear that this is not so. It is enough if the continuance of the pregnancy involves a risk greater than if the pregnancy were terminated. Since there is no evidence that the medical termination of pregnancy involves any substantial risk, it follows that a pregnancy may lawfully be terminated in order to secure a relatively small improvement in the woman's medical condition."[6]

There is a natural progression to the argument of a psychiatrist: "Even

[5] Judges 21: 25.
[6] Abortion Law Reform Association. *A Guide to the Abortion Act* 1967 (3rd ed. 1969). This includes the actual Act and also sections 58 and 59 of the 1861 Offences Against the Persons Act, and section 1 of the Infant Life Preservation Act, 1929.

our own figures in this country ... suggest that it is at least twice as dangerous to have a perfectly normal pregnancy as it is to have what I might call a perfectly normal abortion. So it does seem to me that, willynilly, the legislature has provided grounds on which I could – legally-abort any woman who asks me, because in my view it is more dangerous for her to continue with her pregnancy than it is to have an abortion now."[7]

On this point let us leave the last word to David Steel, the Member of Parliament whose Private Bill this was: "The addition of the words, 'greater than if the pregnancy were terminated' was made in the House of Lords on the insistence of the former Lord Chancellor, Lord Dilhorne, who intended them to restrict and define 'risk.' I was not keen on this phrase and doubt whether it can be said to mean anything in practice."[8]

What is involved in the wording "in determining whether or not there is such risk of injury to health account may be taken of the pregnant woman's actual or reasonably foreseeable environment"? Dr. C. P. Wallace makes the point: "If this clause becomes law it would inevitably lead the family doctor into a position where he immediately accepts the carefully-worded argument advanced by the patient herself, in some instances supported by her husband; the result – so-called "abortion on demand." The alternative is that the doctor purports to form a judgement himself, which would, I suggest, require the omniscience of the Deity – i.e., a judgement based on considerations of the patient's total environment actual or reasonably foreseeable. Even few of my esteemed friends the psychiatrists could count on such a degree of second sight ..."[9]

Legal Grounds for Termination

For the purposes of certification the grounds are divided into four clauses. Clause 1 deals with "risk to the life of the pregnant woman" and presents few moral problems, except to Roman Catholics. In the first eighteen months of the Act, of the more than 62,000 abortions performed, only 2,664 were reported under this clause.[10] When the reality of the risk to maternal survival has been substantiated by the appropriate specialist in cardiology, urology, surgery or medicine one operates: and in this case without thought of the maturity of the fetus. Obviously if two to three weeks' delay would bring the fetus to viability, without gravely worsening the prognosis, one waits.

There is provision made in Section 1 (4) for an even more grave group of cases. A special pink form (Certificate B) which does not require two

[7] P. H. Tooley, "If All Abortions are Legal, Which are Desirable?" In *The Abortion Act*, *op. cit.*

[8] D. M. S. Steel, Personal communication.

[9] C. P. Wallace, Letter in the *BMJ*, 1967, **2**, 767.

[10] P. Diggory, J. Peel and M. Potts, "Preliminary Assessment of the 1967 Abortion Act in Practice." *Lancet*, 1970, **I**, 287.

medical opinions, is available for those cases which have to be performed:

> "immediately:
>   1. To save the life of the pregnant woman.
>   2. To prevent grave permanent injury to the physical or mental health of the pregnant woman."

As will be noted below, in these rare cases (and only twenty cases were performed under this "life-saving" clause in the first eighteen months[10]) one is not permitted to opt-out on conscientious grounds.

> Clause 2 deals with "risk of injury to the physical or mental health of the pregnant woman."

So far as the physical health is concerned two problems, neither of them very troublesome, are noted. The first is the "fake" complaint, based on a genuine medical condition in the history, but which has long since cleared up or been cured. It is customary to consult the old clinical notes, and confirm with the consultant previously concerned that all is well. The other is the "trivial" complaint produced to lever one towards compliance with the patient's immediate wish; after all, both indigestion and piles may not take kindly to pregnancy. Fortunately such complaints are made rarely.

On the other hand the phrase "mental health" is the central one of the whole Act. The obvious answer would be to consult the psychiatrist for this, just as one consults the urologist about women with renal failure. A later chapter is devoted to this; it is sufficient to say here that unfortunately the pitch has been queered for two reasons. First, the psychiatrists have allowed themselves to be used as excuses. In many cases the only man who could save a murderer from the noose was the psychiatrist; and with such a responsibility who would blame him for finding some psychiatric "reason" to recommend clemency? Similarly as one of them has said: "Before 1968 the psychiatrist was the horse and cart for driving through the law; he was the person who was generally involved in allowing terminations to occur for what were primarily social reasons . . ."[7]

The second reason is that while in physical matters different specialists will diverge only slightly in their opinions, among psychiatrists there is no consensus of opinion–at any rate in the milder cases. It appears to be the case that one can obtain whatever opinion one wishes by ensuring the patient is referred to the appropriate psychiatrist. The psychiatrist, when dealing with a non-psychotic patient, appears to be in an area without landmarks. However, now that the gynaecologist has become involved in abortion he too finds himself in that position, and can understand the dilemmas.

Where referral to a psychiatric colleague means the apparently automatic return of a green form signed, the gynaecologist finds that his freedom of decision has been compromised. The time inevitably comes when unless he is prepared to abdicate and act merely as a technician he decides to judge "mental health" himself – only to find it is his turn to be manipulated:

Medical Case 6.1. A quiet unsophisticated girl of 16 became pregnant after a single act of intercourse. She was a member of a closely-knit family, and the apple of her grandparents' eyes. The grandfather had already been treated in a mental hospital. Despite the fact that the girl and her mother were devout practising Roman Catholics they requested abortion, in part lest the shock of the pregnancy were to destroy his recovered mental stability. There is no clause to cover this, therefore, "mental health" had to be invoked with the implication that the girl would be grief stricken were her pregnancy to upset her grandparents.

In a word, this is the clause used to cover a multitude of cases where abortion is felt to be justified for reasons which, although conscientious and honourable, are not included in the Act. It is also the clause usually used by those practising "abortion on demand." Having come so far, where is one to draw the line? Part III of this book seeks to provide some data for this problem.

Clause 3 deals with "risk of injury to the physical or mental health of the existing child(ren) of the family of the pregnant woman."

This is the so-called "social clause," the one invoked where financial stringency and inadequate housing are felt to warrant abortion. The Anglican committee noted "this would appear to presuppose the existence for a given family of a circumscribed area or potential of resources and services, the enjoyment of which would be put in jeopardy by the new birth. Is this so? . . . If it is, must not the threat be admitted in the case of *any* expected child above a number arbitrarily determined?"[11] Another writer pinned the difficulty down more specifically: "How can the birth of another child affect the mental health of any existing children? It is more often the only child who is prone to emotional problems than the child of a large family. A mother might perhaps claim that her children always go to winter sports at Christmas and her confinement in January would interfere with this to the detriment of their mental and physical health, or even that the birth of a third son would mean taking the other two away from their expensive public schools and sending them to day schools. It might be very difficult to prove in a court of law that either of these situations would have no effect on the children's mental or physical health. But are these compelling reasons for legalizing an abortion?"[12]

[11] Church Assembly Board for Social Responsibility. *Abortion: An Ethical Discussion*, London, 1965, Church Information Office.
[12] Margaret White, *Having it Taken Away*, op. cit.

A moment's thought will show this clause to be unnecessary, as any such problem, if genuine, would so worry a mother that she could readily be considered under Clause 2.

Section 1 (b) of the Act, and Clause 4 of the Certificate, deal with the opinion

> that there is a substantial risk that if the child were born it would suffer from such physical or mental abnormalities as to be seriously handicapped.

The only real problem that arises here is as to the meaning of "substantial." The deformed child is considered in Chapter 22.

The difficulties arising from the vague wording of the Bill were realized, perhaps not sufficiently, during the debates. A former Under-Secretary at the Home Office, W. F. Deedes, said the dilemma was which course they should select to achieve their object. Should they aim at providing a loose framework within which the medical profession would be given discretion? or should they seek to give directions and define criteria to which members of the medical profession must adhere? They were in some danger of getting the worst of both worlds. If the medical profession was given total discretion – which was not accepted by some – the public would understand that. But with semi-discretion some members of the profession would be exposed to accusations either of acting beyond the letter of the law or of wilfully refusing to act up to the limits prescribed by the law. Widely different interpretations would be made by doctors about how they might act.[13]

Hindell and Simms (the latter was General Secretary of the Abortion Law Reform Association) in their paper *How the Abortion Lobby Worked* have this to say: "The Abortion Lobby did not secure everything it hoped for. It did not achieve an unequivocal statement in law that bad social conditions were in themselves a justification for abortion, or that a girl pregnant under the age of consent, or as a result of rape or incest, had undeniable grounds for abortion. But the vague term of the clauses ... seem to embrace all these circumstances, and sympathetic doctors will probably act upon this assumption."[14]

The Conscience Clause

> Section 4. (1) Subject to subsection (2) of this section, no person shall be under any duty, whether by contract or by any statutory or other legal requirement, to participate in any treatment authorized by this act to which he has a conscientious objection:
> Provided that in any legal proceedings the burden of proof of conscientious objection shall rest on the person claiming to rely on it. [(3) in Scotland a statement on oath is sufficient.]

---

[13] W. F. Deedes, quoted in Parliamentary Report in the *BMJ*, 1967, **I**, 439.
[14] K. Hindell and Madelaine Simms, "How the Abortion Lobby Worked." *The Political Quarterly*, 1968, **39**, 269.

(2). Nothing in subsection (1) of this section shall affect any duty to participate in treatment which is necessary to save the life or prevent grave permanent injury to the physical or mental health of a pregnant woman.

The implications of the conscience clause, as of the phrase "in good faith" will be considered later. Suffice it to say that the conscience of hospital staff does not need prodding.

Medical Case **6.2.** An experienced Registrar was performing an abortion by the vaginal route. As the available senior staff were Roman Catholic he was being assisted, as was usual, by nurses. On applying the vacuum sucker, instead of products of conception he found abdominal contents (omentum). The consultant from the contiguous (twin) theatre was summoned, but before he had time even to change gloves and take over the operation he found senior Roman Catholic trained staff at the table who assisted while the abdomen was opened, the uterus emptied, and the damage repaired. No request for their help had been made, which was quite unexpected, and was not provided for his own abortions.

It seems to me that that case demonstrates the real meaning of conscience.

Certification

Section 2 requires notification of cases to the Minister of Health.

A green certificate bearing the signature of two medical practitioners, and marking the clause, or clauses, under which the operation is to be performed, must be completed prior to abortion, and filed in the patient's notes. A second certificate is forwarded to the Ministry of Health. This requires additional information; the woman's marital status, National Health Service number, maiden name, number of existing children, date of her last menstrual period, and date of her last previous abortion under the Act. The type of operation, whether sterilization was also carried out, and any complications are also to be listed.

There was much debate as to whether any form of certification was justified. This is not called for by law for any other type of operative procedure. What caused greatest alarm, however, was the fact that the giving of this information to the Ministry could be considered a breach of the confidential doctor-patient relationship. The knowledge that (theoretically) the police could have access to these records under certain circumstances caused further dismay. So far these fears do not appear to have been realized.[15] The fact that the forms are posted directly by the gynaecologist (or his secretary) to London, without passing through any intermediary, and to the Chief Medical Officer, not some administrative boffin, has to some extent relieved our consciences.

Secrecy is in any case regrettably very difficult to achieve. In addition

[15] Concern was felt in June 1971 when it was reported in the press that a woman who had had a termination of pregnancy, had been visited by the police. However Sir George Godber (personal communication, July 8, 1971) tells me that police investigations have been made only in instances of suspected failure to notify terminations in approved places.

to the medical, nursing, and clerical staff involved, theatre porters, ward cleaners, sixteen-year-old nursing cadets, and all manner of ancillary and domestic staff are in a position to see the Theatre Operation Lists. In an area where everyone knows everybody's business the patient in a large ward is very likely to be recognized by the visitors at some other patient's bedside, if not by some other patient. More than once at follow-up clinic one of my patients has told me that although she had maintained the strictest secrecy, she was teased about her termination immediately on returning to her place of work. Whilst every attempt is, and should be, made to preserve the patient's secret, with the best will in the world there can be little certainty that this can be achieved, certainly if the operation is to be performed in the patient's home town.

The remainder of the Act is purely of administrative import.

CHAPTER 7

THE CHANGING CLIMATE OF OPINION

Sons are a gift from the Lord, and children a reward from him.   Psa. 127:3
... doubleplusungood refs unpersons, rewrite ...   GEORGE ORWELL[1]

WE CANNOT SAY THAT WE WERE NOT WARNED. IN 1965 THE Church of England study group quoted Dr. Yoshio Koya's paper to the U.N. World Population Congress in Belgrade of the same year, in which he offered a warning to other countries preparing to introduce laws which "would legalize abortion, or enlarge the conditions under which the operation may be permissible.... If people at large were once accustomed to induced abortion, it might be extremely difficult to make them come back to the previous reproductive behaviour."[2] The Anglican group commented "To build up a habit of mind which regards abortion lightly as an easy remedy for any adverse situation, personal or social, might be in fact, to do people and society a grave disservice by addicting them to another social disease."[3]

The influence of climate was also mentioned in the *Sex and Morality* report prepared for the British Council of Churches: "Installation of slot-machines for contraceptives in every university Union ... would imply, wouldn't it, that the community expected intercourse to be the casual and impromptu conclusion to an evening's entertainment? In that climate, once created, abortions do not decrease but increase. For even the ready availability of contraceptives is no guarantee that in the stress of the moment they will be used."[4]

An opinion which will probably carry more weight is that of the outspoken, liberal, anti-Vietnam War leader Dr. Benjamin Spock. In a book published in 1970 he writes: "For decades I was an uncompromising civil libertarian and scorned the hypocrisy involved in the enforcement

[1] G. Orwell, *Nineteen-Eighty-Four*, London, 1949, Secker and Warburg. 1954, Penguin Books.
[2] Y. Koya, "Some Essential Factors for Fertility Control in Japan," quoted in *Abortion: An Ethical Discussion, op. cit.*
[3] Church Assembly Board for Social Responsibility. *Abortion: An Ethical Discussion*, London, 1965, Church Information Office.
[4] *Sex and Morality*. A Report Prepared by a Working Party Under the Chairmanship of the Rev. K. G. Greet, and presented to (but not accepted by) the British Council of Churches 1966. London, 1966, S.C.M. Press.

of obscenity laws, but recent trends in movies, literature, and art toward
which I think of as shock obscenity, and the court's acceptance of it have
made me change my position . . . particularly in view of other brutalizing
trends . . . In our so-called emancipation from our Puritan past I think
we've lost our bearings. Many enlightened parents still have inner convictions but are afraid that they don't have a sure basis for teaching them
to their children. Some of their children are quite bewildered as child
psychiatrists and school counselors report."[5]

It is to be hoped that others may heed our British experience.[6] We
have found that much of what was written about abortion became irrelevant on April 24th, 1968. Just as after Fleming's discovery of penicillin
therapeutics has never been the same again; just as after Hiroshima the
expectations of mankind can never be the same again; so after the passage
of the Abortion Act pregnancy in Britain can never be the same again.

In every unwelcomed pregnancy, abortion is now an option which
may be seriously considered. With each abortion the circle of women
who will consider it gets larger.

Prior to 1968 among married pregnant women it was only the desperate who thought seriously of a furtive visit to the back-street abortionist, only the rich and *avant-garde* who decided to go for a "West End
legal" abortion. The vast majority might hope and even pray for a spontaneous miscarriage, might even take a double dose of castor-oil; beyond
that they gave abortion no thought.

Now all this is completely altered. The decent married woman has
by her planning and toil made a good home, has done the best for her
family, and now perhaps at last sees the end of the tunnel in sight. At last
she is beginning to re-establish her identity as a person in her own right
outside the confines of the home. This woman finding herself pregnant,
saying "Why should I go through with this – back to the washtub, back
to the drudgery, back to the scratching and scraping of twenty years,"
picks up her handbag and makes for her general practitioner's surgery.
One such, when faced by me with the wording of the Act, agreed with a
laugh that she hadn't a leg to stand on. But it was worth a try – and she
had, at least, obtained the promise of a sterilization after delivery.

For many overburdened, stretched to the limit, it is no "try on," but a
cry for help. For such a one the Abortion Act is a life-buoy thrown to a
drowning woman.

The point to grasp is that it is the existence of this life-buoy that makes
all the difference. The mother does not now *have* to bend her back to this
new burden with such strength and courage as she can muster. Were
there no other outlet she would in all probability do just that, and succeed

[5] B. Spock, *Decent and Indecent*, London, 1970, Bodley Head.
[6] R. F. R. Gardner, "Christian Choices in a Liberal Abortion Climate." *Christianity Today*
(Washington), May 22, 1970.

in some measure. But given this new option, that task assumes a terror and a dread dimension it never had before. A dreary trudge across the barren rain-lashed moor is one thing, but if it can be abandoned at any moment, more grit is needed to complete the journey.

Medical Case 7.1. A forty-year-old woman was treated with "the pill" not as a contraceptive, but for a gynaecological disorder. In due course the therapy was stopped. The gynaecologist thought it wise to comment that there would be the risk of pregnancy now that the patient was no longer having hormones, and that she should, therefore, take other precautions. To which she replied "Oh, I don't think I'll bother, there's always the Abortion Act to fall back on."

Among the unmarried the change in climate was even more marked. A popular magazine for young women carried an article in its May 1970 number, with a heading which occupied half a page:[7]

IT'S LEGAL
THEREFORE IT'S RIGHT
THEREFORE IT'S MY RIGHT
AND IT'S ALL RIGHT
BUT IS IT?

The article itself, taking up the last part of the argument "And it's all right – but is it?" gave a wise and well-balanced series of views pointing out many of the dangers and difficulties in abortion. It never, however, challenged the reasoning in the first three lines of its title. It is this type of reasoning, very widely held by women in Britain today, which has made the whole problem so difficult. Recently I refused to abort a young, healthy, married woman merely because she was inconvenienced that the second child was coming earlier than they had wished. Her angry retort was "Does this mean that I have to bear a child neither my husband nor I want? Why, every day we read in the paper of women flying to Britain because they can have an abortion if they want one."

On the doctor this change in climate has as great an effect. In some cases he experiences relief. Relief at his new freedom with easy conscience to help the needy. In other cases he is in a quandary. In this problem case where others bend the law, should he do likewise?

Medical Case 7.2. A thirty-six-year-old single woman had to work full time in a factory and also run the home as her mother was an invalid. Her father and brother did nothing to help in the home, and were unprepared to finance it so that she would not need to earn. Once a month she allowed herself a night out at a club – the only moment of life and colour in her drab existence. There, seduced while under the influence of alcohol by some lover (and such a girl craves love) she was deserted by him as soon as she became pregnant. He left the country without leaving an address. Seen at eight-weeks' pregnancy she nowhere fitted into the categories of the Act.

[7] "What They Don't Tell You about Abortion." *Honey* Magazine, May, 1970.

In such a case, while compassion suggests that a patient's self-reproach could be used to fit her into Clause 2 (mental health), honesty reminds one that such was not the intention of Parliament. To bend or not to bend?

It is, however, in cases where refusal seems indicated, that the effects of our new climate have their most marked effects.

It is true that some refusals are not difficult moral decisions, however the patient may weep or the parents cajole. In their hearts patient and parents know your decision is valid, hate you as they may. The real crunch is in that case where one is aware that many gynaecologists would agree to abort.

"Wot's the good of you, Doctor! Call yerself a Christian and won't help my daughter NOW! Yer know's yer *could;* yer *won't.* Yer as 'ard as the rest of em, frightened of some Council" – so a Cockney mother pleading in a Christian Medical Mission many years ago.[8] Now, without even a Council to be frightened of, what sort of picture do we give?

The woman there in tears is saying to herself, over and over again, "If only, if only, he'll say YES – he'll sterilize me too, I know. In two weeks I'll be home and SAFE; my years of fear will be over; I'll be able to be the kind of wife, and mother, and person I've always longed to be. If only . . ."

The gynaecologist facing this woman is under very considerable tension. He is aware of her problem. He is aware of her emotion. He weighs other factors of which she knows little, and cares – in this crisis – not at all. He is aware too of the crowded waiting-room, and the waiting list for his beds.

Prior to 1968 the expected answer to an abortion request was "NO;" an answer backed by the full weight of the law, of medicine and of the Church, and supported by public opinion. Post-1968 the expected answer is "YES." Not only can that answer almost always be fitted into the loose wording of the Act, but it is now in accord with a good deal of public opinion. It agrees, moreover, with the woman's desires and her lately aroused expectations. If spoken she immediately feels her problems resolved; although whether the future will confirm that is another matter. The grounds, therefore, for "NO" have to be immeasurably more secure in medicine and conscience than would those for a similar decision a few years ago.

It is within this new climate that we must continue our enquiry.

[8] D. Johnson, Personal communication.

Chapter 8

LIFE AND DEATH UNDER A LIBERAL ABORTION LAW

We have power to make you divide the crops, for this is our law, and we will see this is done. But we have no power to make you behave like an upright man.
BAROTSE ELDERS[1]

A citizen has a right to order another double whisky but the publican may refuse to supply it to someone who has been drinking excessively. The ethics of a noble profession should not compare unfavourably with those of a public bar.
PROFESSOR J. A. STALLWORTHY[2]

EIGHT MONTHS AFTER THE 1967 ABORTION ACT BECAME LAW A SENIOR gynaecologist was to say ". . . all in all we did not expect a very great change in practice from that obtaining before the Act. We thought there would be a slightly more liberal attitude to the problem, for that, after all, was the purpose of the new law. How wrong we were."[3]

Just how wrong, and just how great the changes that followed the Act we must now observe.

The great error was in underestimating the flood of applicants for abortion. In the first few weeks abortions were being performed at a rate equivalent to 25,000 per annum. Steadily quarter by quarter the figures go up, and despite suggestions that the demand is levelling off,[4] there is as yet no sign of this. By early 1971 the rate was more than 90,000 a year. There is no knowing where it will stop.[5]

Detailed figures will be found in the Reports of the Chief Medical

---

[1] Barotse Elders, Quoted from M. Gluckman, by Lord Patrick Devlin, *The Enforcement of Morals*, 1968, OUP.

[2] J. A. Stallworthy, "Therapeutic Abortion." *Practitioner*, 1970, **204**, 393.

[3] T. L. T. Lewis, "The Abortion Act." *BMJ*, 1969, **1**, 241.

[4] P. Diggory, J. Peel and M. Potts, "Preliminary Assessment of the 1967 Abortion Act in Practice." *Lancet*, 1970, **1**, 287.

[5] In the absence of restrictive legislation it has been suggested that the demand might be 500 or more abortions per thousand live-births giving a figure of 2.4 millions by 1980 in the U.S.A. (C. W. Tyler and J. Schneider, "The Logistics of Abortion Services in the Absence of Restrictive Criminal Legislation in the United States." *American Journal of Public Health*, 1971, **61**, 489). If one accepts their data a much larger figure could be reached, suggesting that in Britain, in the absence of all legislation, we might face a demand of around 900,000 per year. It must be remembered that abortions are not balanced by an equal fall in births. This is the experience of all countries which liberalize their abortion laws.

Officer.[6] It is by no means certain that all abortions are reported;[7,8] in fact, the numbers are almost certainly larger. During each period the number of single, widowed, divorced or separated women aborted was greater than that of married women.

It may be wondered what was the nature of the health risk, which is far and away the principal cause given for the operation. In one period of women aborted under this clause only 33% were married, the remaining 66% having illegitimate pregnancies (and of these 9 out of 10 were single). It seems obvious that single women are not more likely to have physical disabilities than married ones, especially as 92% were under the age of 30, but only 2.3% under the age of 16.[9] As 60% of all abortions because of "risk to the physical or mental health of the women" were done on single young women in the 16–30 age group, the only reasonable explanation must be that most operations are done on "mental" grounds.

The General Practitioner

The general practitioner is the first person to feel the load. His duties have been well summarized by Dr. Margaret Dudley-Brown as: to know the Act and understand it; to apply the knowledge objectively; and to avoid having to use the Act at all! This last task, she suggests, should be achieved by G.P.s approaching their patients positively, not only on family planning but also on the much broader issue of health education; on how best to lead a full and good life.[10]

There is the constant problem of finding the time to deal adequately with the problem. There are also special ethical problems. What should a G.P. do when a woman, not his own patient, comes to him with her request which she is not prepared to take to her own G.P.? Is it ethical to treat another doctor's patient? Is it not even less ethical to insist she transfer to his list? What is he to do with his own patient when he conscientiously disapproves of abortion? Is he condoning sin in sending her to another doctor? Or again, he may merely feel that this particular request is unjustified. "Few, if any, doctors would claim that in considering a request for therapeutic abortion they are able completely to divorce themselves from their religious, moral and ethical beliefs and attain an objective and detached view point. Inevitably the woman refused abor-

[6] The most useful documents are the Annual Reports of the Chief Medical Officer of the Department of Health and Social Security *On the State of the Public Health*, for 1968 and 1969. London, H.M.S.O. and The Registrar General's Statistical Review of England and Wales *Supplement on Abortion* for 1968 and 1969, London, H.M.S.O.

[7] Royal College of Obstetricians and Gynaecologists. "The Abortion Act 1967. Findings of an Enquiry into the First Year's Working of the Act." *BMJ*, 1970, **2**, 529.

[8] R. G. Bird, "Point of View." *Medical News-Tribune*, Feb. 6, 1969.

[9] *On the State of the Public Health*: 1968, *op. cit.*

[10] Margaret Dudley-Brown, "The Duties of the General Practitioner under the Abortion Act." *The Abortion Act, op. cit.*

tion by her G.P. is likely to believe, if mistakenly, that the refusal is based on such grounds."[11]

Although many general practitioners are able to dissuade patients from proceeding with their request for abortion, a large number of patients are referred for gynaecological opinion. This is either because there is some doubt in the doctor's mind, or at the insistence of the patient.

The Private Sector

In 1968 and in 1969 some 40% of notified abortions were being performed in "approved places," this percentage varying from quarter to quarter. These are the cases where an abortion is performed "privately," that is for a fee, in a nursing home. In 1969 of all private abortions, 90% were performed in the north-west sector of London.[12] It is this area which has given London the unenviable title of "Abortion capital of the world," due largely to the ease with which abortions are said to be obtainable. Patients reach these clinics through several sources. Some merely prefer to be treated in anonymity and arrange their abortion, which would have been readily available in a N.H.S. hospital, via their G.P. with a gynaecologist in private practice. It seems, however, that the majority are girls who realize they are unlikely to get a N.H.S. abortion. These may apply to a Pregnancy Advisory Service, such as those in Birmingham and London. These are registered charities which are efficiently run by workers who go into the problems in detail, and usually manage (70%[4]) to obtain an abortion for their clients. Other less reputable contacts can be made. In 1970 there was a furore over the story of a taxi-drivers' syndicate which picked up girls and had its own contacts with the private sector.[13]

There are those who believe that as even the most normal pregnancy is statistically more dangerous than an early abortion (a view unsupported by the results[7,14]), any abortion, at least in the first trimester, may be carried out on request. One advocate of this opinion is reported as saying: "This may not be what Parliament intended, but they put up the umbrella and we are sheltering under it."[15] In this situation it seems that any woman who can find the fee, usually about £150, can have an abortion at will.

This position has been denounced. "Confusion is aggravated even by responsible newspapers with reports which sometimes create the impression that the Act of 1967 introduced abortion on demand. It did not. The fact that some practitioners, by word or deed, appear to defy the law adds to the confusion, particularly when they are not challenged by

[11] G. J. Davies, Letter in the *BMJ*, 1969, **2**, 118.
[12] *On the State of the Public Health:* 1969, *op. cit.*
[13] "Taxi Abortion Scandal," *News of the World*, March 22, 1970.
[14] J.-O. Ottosson, "Legal Abortion in Sweden," *Journal of the Bio-Social Sciences*, 1971, **3**, 173.
[15] Report in *The Sunday Times*, April 20, 1969.

the law. For example, nowhere in the Act is it stated that a woman can have abortion by right merely because she wants it. Therefore, if a doctor states that he is prepared to evacuate a uterus because his patient requests it he defies the law and performs a criminal abortion, whether he operated in a hospital or a nursing home. The fact that he may honestly believe that a woman *should* have a right to decide is irrelevant so far as the ethics and legality of his action are concerned, with the law as it now stands."[2]

The Act requires that the medical practitioners signing the statutory forms for abortion, form their opinion "in good faith." It is, of course, possible to make light of this. "A recurrent hobby horse is the 'good faith' of the recommending doctors, whatever those weighty words mean."[8] Professor Keith Simpson of the Department of Forensic Medicine at Guy's Hospital points out that "good faith" is absolutely fundamental, and instances some methods in part of the private sector which are "not indications of good faith . . . If therefore, we question the good faith of certain professionally qualified abortionists, for such they undoubtedly are, we must also question the lawfulness of their practice. If it is not lawful, it is unlawful; and this is criminal. There is no alternative. If such practices are rife – and in my view it is quite clear they are – criminal abortion is far from being a dying art. The new Act has legitimized the practice for those who can afford it."[16]

The financial side of private clinics has attracted a good deal of attention. A Christian gynaecologist told me that she had been invited to help in such a clinic with the expectation of fees 400% greater than her present income: it was added that most of these "would be paid in banknotes." The implication of this would not be lost on the Collector of Taxes!

Nevertheless, there can be no doubt that many practitioners operate, because of honestly held convictions that every woman should have a right to an abortion should she so wish. They hope that the practice of "abortion on demand" in the private sector will so alter public opinion as to force the practice on the NHS.

Concern has, however, been expressed at the poor standards of care and equipment in some clinics, with a resulting considerable tightening up of inspection by the health authorities as a result. There can be no doubt that an operator who performs a dozen or more abortions every day necessarily develops a greater degree of expertise than the gynaecologist who perhaps does one or two twice a week. But this expertise is more than counter-balanced by three great disadvantages. All evidence points to the fact that many "private" patients receive a far more cursory medical and gynaecological examination pre-operatively than they would as patients in a normal NHS unit. The equipment in many nursing homes, certainly in the early stages, was far inferior to that available in

[16] K. Simpson, "Criminal Abortion: A Dying Art?" In *The Abortion Act, op. cit.*

a NHS hospital. At an inquest[17] on a patient who died following abortion in a private clinic, the coroner said: "Looking at the nursing home in terms of the Abortion Act, it is self-evident that two necessary criteria are missing – that of having blood and being able to administer it."[18] The third disadvantage is the brevity of the stay in hospital, with the consequence that pre- and post-operative care must usually be less thorough than in a NHS hospital.

A striking first-hand account of the difference between one patient's experience of a NHS and a private abortion was published in a lengthy unsigned letter to *The Guardian*.[19] The writer of this had her first abortion in a NHS hospital in Newcastle, and describes her sympathetic examination by the consultant gynaecologist and another doctor, as well as her interview with a psychiatrist. She details the usual full regime of admission the day before operation, premedication and post-operative care for a further twenty-four hours. She then contrasts with this a second abortion in a London clinic. Her total stay was of five hours' duration, she was not examined pre-operatively, and had to walk upstairs to the operating theatre and climb on to its table; and afterwards walk back downstairs to her bed. Of surgical preparation, rest and quiet, there was little, if any. The difference between the two types of unit, as this correspondent recorded them, is most striking. What is equally striking is the reaction shown by a further correspondent replying a week later. He wrote: "Her guilt-ridden letter does make some sense as a form of public confession . . . . I am not qualified to judge the medical value of the satisfying ritualistic touches which your correspondent evidently cherishes . . . any (undesirable) after-effects are so rare as to be almost non-existent."

Standards in the private sector are, however, rising; partly in consequence of the frequent outcries in Parliament. In Birmingham a virtually non-profit making clinic has been opened especially to deal with these cases at a lower fee and with better facilities; the forerunner, its organizers hope, of many such.[20]

The influx of foreign girls to London to obtain abortions has caused a good deal of concern; by early 1971 they accounted for 11% of the total number. No accurate figures can be available as there is no statutory need for the patient to give her home address, and many from abroad no doubt book in as from their London hotel. However, in the first full year, 2,265 were notified as having their domicile abroad: over a thousand from West Germany, seven hundred from North America, with France, Holland and Scandinavia also represented.

Periodically there has been a stir with the report of "package tours"

---

[17] Report in the *BMJ*, 1969, I, 454.
[18] Report in *The Sunday Mirror*, Feb. 9, 1969.
[19] "An Abortion Factory and The Alternative." *The Guardian*, April 10, 1969.
[20] Report in *The Sunday Times*, December 7, 1969.

to London (abortion included) arranged from Denmark[22] and the United States.[23] Such reports have never been verified.

In the atmosphere of charge and counter-charge it is very difficult to weigh objectively the role of the private sector. At the moment, in the absence of adequate facilities within the N.H.S. the facilities in London which they provide serve as a safety-valve. They have also the benefit of providing anonymity, which may be difficult to obtain in a small centre. To the extent that they provide "abortion on demand" illegally to those able to pay, their existence must be deplored.

The Public Sector

General hospitals provide better facilities, a more prolonged stay in hospital, a full gynaecological team, more adequate numbers of nurses, better theatre facilities, constant staff cover at all grades, unlimited blood, and all this in a general setting without the atmosphere of an "abortion factory"[19] and at no cost to the patient. Such hospitals are the best places for an abortion, the problem for the patient is to get in. There is a 90% chance that she will be interviewed personally by a consultant. As only 4% in this category favour abortion on demand[7] her request is less likely to be granted than by the private operator one of whom told me that he refuses less than 0.5% of applicants. The likelihood of acceptance varies from hospital to hospital. An unpublished review of the practice during 1970 of ten NHS units showed that the percentage of applications granted varied from 50.8% to 85.2%.[24]

Although variations depend partly on the outlook of the various gynae-cologists, a major bottleneck is the pressure on facilities. Few consultants can be so limited as the one who described the chaos caused in her practice by the abortion cases.[25] With a waiting list of seventy patients she had three beds and one operating session. It will immediately be noted that were she to abort three women a week she could do no other operative work. The fact that they only stayed in two days, or that the operating time might be only an hour, is unimportant: her beds would be blocked until the next operating session a week later. Those of us who have a far larger allotment of beds and theatre time still find the pressure of the abortion case considerable. There are at least two instances in which the

[22] Reports in *The Sun*, July 5, 1969, and *The Daily Telegraph*, July 4, 1969.

[23] Report in *The Times*, March 23, 1970.

[24] The practice varies from region to region of the NHS. For instance in 1969 of women domiciled in the Newcastle region 95.6% had their abortion in an NHS hospital in their home region, 0.5% in NHS hospitals elsewhere, 0.9% privately in Newcastle, and 2.6% privately in London. Compare this with women domiciled in the Birmingham region of whom only 45.4% had their abortion in an NHS hospital in their home region, 1.6% in NHS hospitals elsewhere, 6.1% privately in Birmingham and 46.4% privately in London. (*On the State of the Public Health*, 1969, *op. cit.*)

[25] Anne Boutwood, "The Effect of the Act on Gynaecological Practice." In *The Abortion Act, op. cit.*

admission of women who subsequently proved to be suffering from pelvic cancer was delayed for several months because abortion cases had been given priority.[7] At the end of 1969 almost 90,000 women in England and Wales were awaiting a NHS gynaecological bed.[12]

If pressure on beds is severe, pressure on out-patient clinics is worse. A normal practice is to make new patient bookings at ten-minute intervals. In the abortion cases, as well as the normal history and examination, there is a further more detailed history to be taken out of hearing of the nursing staff. The general practitioner has to be tracked down by telephone for amplification of a letter written guardedly as he had had to assume the patient would steam it open and read it before coming to the clinic. Then the medical social worker has to be put in the picture and interviewed again after she had talked to the patient, and one's secretary telephoned to try to find a bed. This takes half-an-hour on average. When, as in the week of writing, one has five requests at one clinic, the chaos can be imagined, not to mention the annoyance of other patients kept waiting, and the frustration of the staff who see their lunch-break having to be abandoned. The upshot on occasion is that the genuine gynaecological case is seen by a junior doctor, as the consultant is bogged down with abortion investigation. At the average gynaecological clinic one patient in seven is requesting abortion.

Worse perhaps than the pressure of the work on the gynaecologist, is the constant barrage of propaganda seeking to prove he is not carrying out his duties. As has been discussed in an earlier chapter, the law is purely permissive. No matter. "The 'lack of good faith' in refusing doctors is not such a popular topic, but there is some evidence of frank lawbreaking (where doctors do not even consider a case and do not invoke the conscience clause) and glib evasion of honest consideration of socio-psychiatric grounds for abortion, which make up the vast majority of cases."[8] Mrs. Renee Short said in Parliament that it was clear that in some parts of the country gynaecologists within the NHS were not carrying out their duties under the Act, and were abusing the conscience clause.[26]

A crop of articles appears in the popular press from time to time in similar vein. A typical one was entitled "Abortion – where the NHS has failed,"[27] and proceeded to give four case histories. While there are factors in the management of these cases, as reported, with which I personally would not agree, there are journalistic aspects which give

[26] Hansard, July 7, 1969. Mrs Renee Short has kindly elaborated on this in a personal communication. Among her grounds for criticism were those cases where applicants for abortion were not examined by the consultant gynaecologist. She further comments, "There is no desire from anybody to force anybody's conscience but I am sure you will agree that from the patient's point of view it is tough luck on her if she lands up with a gynaecologist who generally refuses to give terminations and who gives her a flat 'no' without advising her to seek advice from another consultant."

[27] "Abortion: Where the NHS has Failed." *The Sunday Times,* July 6, 1969.

quite the wrong impression, perhaps because no gynaecologist had any-thing to do with the article, or the psychiatrist and journalist had been misinformed – but the impression left is unfounded. In one case we read: "The termination was performed, but by this time it was so late she had to have the abortion by hysterotomy, which means that she had to have an abdominal operation, and now bears the transverse crescent-shaped scar which reveals that she had had an abortion . . ." Crescentic supra-pubic scars (the Pfannenstiel incision) are used for a wide variety of operations. How many innocent women will suffer from the impression given by this statement we shall never know.

In another case the woman was refused an abortion by her G.P. and the first gynaecologist to whom she was referred. A second gynaecologist who examined her found an ectopic pregnancy (i.e. not in the uterus). "She was immediately given an abortion. Ectopic pregnancies are extremely dangerous and are always fatal unless operated on. The woman's life would have been endangered if she had accepted the original doctor's decision." This is the perfect red herring. The abortion issue is quite irrelevant except as the cause of the ectopic pregnancy's being discovered. The implication is that all early pregnancies must be considered for abortion (even if the child is desired) lest there be an ectopic pregnancy present! As most ectopic pregnancies cause their dangerous effects before the second missed period, this would require that ante-natal examinations be performed six to eight weeks earlier than is at present usual, and that a pelvic examination be always performed. I have seen a wanted preg-nancy lost as a result of such an examination in the early months. The implication that the woman was saved because she was immediately given an abortion is quite unfounded; she was saved because the ectopic pregnancy was removed, presumably by removal of the fallopian tube. Even the Roman Catholic Church, with its absolute refusal to permit abortion, accepts the removal of a tube containing a pregnancy on the grounds that the loss of the latter is merely a secondary effect.[28]

The statement is repeatedly made that "some doctors fail to give any reason for refusal to abort, although they are required to by the Act."[29] There is, of course, no such requirement at all in the Act, nor any require-ment for a doctor to have anything whatever to do with such cases, except where life is in immediate danger. It is difficult to resist the im-pression that there is a deliberate campaign to spread this false impression in an endeavour to intimidate the medical profession.

The pressure is not only directed at doctors. A news sheet distributed free to student nurses carried a feature on abortion. This included an interview with Diane Munday who said ". . . nor should an anti-abortion nurse try

[28] A. Keenan and J. Ryan, *Marriage: A Medical and Sacramental Study*, London, 1955 Sheed and Ward.

[29] Anonymous "Harley Street Psychiatrist" quoted in "Abortion: Where the NHS has failed." *Op. cit.*

to influence others. Nurses have a right to their own opinions but they do not have a right to force their own views on to their colleagues."[30] This surely is an astounding admonition to be made by the General Secretary of the ALRA, a self-confessed pressure group!

Other more practical pressures weigh on the hospital. Theatres are difficult to staff for these operations. In one, 75% of the nursing staff opted out of abortions because of religious objections, or for moral reasons, or because of the unpleasant nature of the work. In others, theatre sisters were trying to protect student nurses from unpleasant duties such as cleaning the apparatus. Student nurse recruitment may suffer.[31] In a Lancashire hospital "Catholic nurses are told that if there is nobody else to do the work it must be done by them whether they have any objections or not."[32] Only 19% of consultants state that they never find reluctance on the part of nursing staff.[7]

This disquiet on the part of staff shows no sign of easing. In June 1970 the theatre staff at one English hospital stated they were no longer prepared to deal with abortions.[33] Later that month the Royal College of Nursing wrote to the new Secretary of State for Social Services pointing out that the working of the Abortion Act "had an adverse effect on staff morale .... If this situation continued it could well have an effect not only on the willingness of nurses to take appointments in operating theatres where large numbers of abortions were performed, and in gynaecological wards in which these patients were nursed but, additionally, in the long term on recruitment to the nursing profession."[34] That same month, one of my regular anaesthetists told me that she was no longer willing to anaesthetize abortion cases.

Junior medical staff find themselves in a very difficult position.[35] It is in the nature of a competitive profession that promotion depends on the good report of one's senior. There is an added factor in British gynaecological training, in that, as a pre-requisite of appearing for the higher examination, the trainee must perform a certain number of operations personally, assisted by his senior. Seniors do not give operations to juniors who are out of favour. In some hospitals the junior is required to provide, unquestioningly, the second signature on the Green Form. In others he is expected to operate on these cases at the bidding of his chief. This I feel to be quite wrong.[36] In fact, 47% of consultants do all, or at least 90% of

[30] "Two views on Abortion." SNAP, November, 1970.
[31] National Association of Theatre Nurses Congress, NAT News, Winter, 1969.
[32] Report in The Times, Oct. 4, 1969.
[33] Report in The Nursing Times, June 25, 1970.
[34] Royal College of Nursing, RCN News, June 24, 1970.
[35] For instance, in California where the number of abortions is doubling every six months, among the reported resulting difficulties is "a revolt of the residents." (A. J. Margolis and E. W. Overstreet, "Legal Abortion Without Hospitalization," Obstetrics and Gynecology, 1970, 36, 479).
[36] R. F. R. Gardner, in discussion in The Abortion Act, op. cit.

their cases themselves; and only 13% hand over more than half of their cases to juniors.[7]

Such are the consequences of the Abortion Act that 58% of gynaecologists consider that it will adversely affect recruitment to their ranks.[7] One told the press "Since the 1967 Act my life as a gynaecologist has become a misery."[37] The result can be more tragic. At the inquest on a senior Manchester gynaecologist, his brother told the coroner that the doctor was in despair because of the Abortion Act. "He was a devout Catholic, and he said that this statute put him and many others with strong religious beliefs on the horns of a terrible dilemma."[37]

In the opinion of many the only way out, under the present law and in the present climate, is the institution of special Abortion Centres staffed by doctors and nurses prepared to do this work, thus relieving hospitals.[8] But while half the gynaecological consultants approved this scheme, only 21% would be prepared to work in one.[7] The answer would obviously be to staff them with doctors less fully trained. This, however would be to put the patient at greater risk when anything went wrong.

Public disquiet at the working of the Act is aroused from time to time by some spectacular incident of which the most famous was the Glasgow case of January 1969. An unmarried student was aborted of a twenty-six-week pregnancy. The fetus was placed in a bag and handed to the incinerator attendant who, half-an-hour later, heard a whimper. Asking the theatre attendant if he knew what the bag contained the latter said it was "a kiddie," that he knew it was alive, and he agreed it was "a bloody shame." The child was then placed in an incubator but died some eight hours later.[38] At the inquiry the Procurator-Fiscal asked: "You are not suggesting that because it was an abortion operation the people in charge just put the baby aside and did not bother with it." To this the professor of medical jurisprudence replied "Yes. I think that is exactly what happened." The purpose of the operation had been to get rid of an unwanted child, therefore the question of resuscitation probably never entered anyone's head.[39] The final word on this macabre case may be left with the Roman Catholic Archbishop of Cardiff who wrote; "The jury recommended that when an infant near or at a viable age is delivered by abortion, all possible resuscitation facilities should be used. If that quotation were not so tragic, what a Gilbertian situation it would reveal! One removes a fetus from a situation in which it will certainly live and places it in a situation in which it will certainly die. To all this no one says 'Nay.' Having done your best to kill it, you must now, by the recommendation of the jury do your best to revive it since, so the jury says, it died not by removal from the womb but because it was not resuscitated! . . . There

[37] Report in *The Times*, April 30, 1970.
[38] Reports in *The Times*, May 22 and 23, 1969.
[39] Report in *The Scotsman*, May 24, 1969.

are two ways of resuscitating a child and one of them is to leave it where it is . . ."[40]

A later storm was caused by the claim that live fetuses were being sold by a private clinic for research. It was suggested that they were to be kept alive on a heart-lung machine to 40 weeks gestation and then "slaughtered."[41] It appears that this was a complete misunderstanding. As a result, however, a committee has been set up to look into the whole question of fetal material for research. So far as dead fetal material is concerned, few of us can see any objection to its use in bona fide research; so far as a living fetus is concerned, this is a very different matter. If a fetus cannot be allowed to live it should at least be allowed to die.

To what extent has the Abortion Act achieved its aim? This can be thought of from various angles. The Minister for Social Services told Parliament in March 1970 that but for the Abortion Act there would have been a further 20,000 illegitimate children now alive. On the other hand, there is no evidence that the number of back-street abortions has lessened. In calculating these, much reliance has been placed on the number of "spontaneous" or incomplete abortions admitted to hospital. But the figure for these (53,128) in the twelve months after the Act is slightly larger than for the twelve months before the Act came into operation, when it was 51,701.[7] Complications from the operation, which it had been said would be negligible, were not infrequent. Of the 199 departments reporting on this in the RCOG report, only eighty had no complications, and eight deaths were mentioned. This report is incomplete; the figure for 1969, given in Parliament, was fifteen deaths.

Two of these fatalities are worthy of especial mention as they cast doubt on much of the case as advanced by the abortion lobby. Two women died of suicide following abortion. Leaving aside for the moment all the other arguments for caution, these cases by themselves entitle – rather demand – the utmost care on the part of the gynaecologist in assessing his patients. The word "care" should perhaps be emphasised. In British medicine every patient in a hospital is "under the care" of a consultant who is responsible, both in conscience and law, for the management of that case. The suggestion that "the gynaecologist is really cast in the role of technician in an abortion case,"[8] is quite unacceptable, because meaningless. However people may agitate, practitioners write, or psychiatrists sign, the patient eventually enters a gynaecological ward, "under the care of Mr. A." We would not have it otherwise. As a psychiatrist has said, "We must never forget that (the gynaecologists) are the final arbiters and must have the last word."[42]

Because of this there have been two attempts to amend the Act so as to

[40] Abp J. A. Murphy, Letter in The Times, May 28, 1969.
[41] Report in The Times, May 16, 1970.
[42] P. H. Tooley, "If All Abortions are Legal, Which are Desirable?" In The Abortion Act, op. cit.

ensure that abortions are done by, or under the supervision of, consultant gynaecologists, or doctors of an equivalent status. One attempt by Norman St. John Stevas was narrowly defeated in July 1969, the other by Gordon Irvine was "talked out" in February 1970. The General Election of 1970 changed the complexion of Parliament and it proved possible to obtain the signatures of 250 members to a motion calling for an investigation into the working of the Act. In February 1971 the Secretary of State for Social Services announced the setting up of a committee of inquiry, under Mrs Justice Lane, to examine the working of the Act. Its task would be "to review the operation of the Abortion Act 1967 and, on the basis that the conditions for legal abortion remain unaltered, to make recommendations." Whether any progress can be made while that condition is retained remains to be seen.

The doctors' surgeries, the hospital out-patient departments, the private clinics, are today thronged with a host of women seeking to get rid of their pregnancies. Some have been brainwashed into equating "unwanted pregnancy" with "unwanted child" and make a journey they will one day regret. Some are careless members of the permissive society with no sense of responsibility either for their behaviour or for their coming child. Some are worn-out women burdened by long years of child-bearing and child-rearing who seek well deserved relief. The majority do not fall neatly into any of these categories. In this chaos the Christian seeks to find God's will. We must now follow him in that search.

PART II

*THE ETHICAL QUESTION: IS ABORTION EVER
JUSTIFIED?*
THE SEARCH FOR A CHRISTIAN ANSWER

CHAPTER 9

WHY INVOLVE CHRISTIANITY WITH ABORTION?

There are circles in which one has to remind people that Jesus is not important primarily because he anticipated Marx.   PETER HEBBLETHWAITE[1]

There are no non-religious activities: only religious and irreligious.

C. S. LEWIS

The Religious Basis of all Viewpoints

ALL DECISIONS ON ABORTION ARE RELIGIOUS DECISIONS. AT ONE END of the spectrum the Roman Catholic can have no part in it because of his religious belief in the sacredness of God's gift of life. At the other end the humanist is irked by the restrictions remaining even after the liberalizing 1967 Act, because of his view that the dignity of the mother as a person must include her right to decide whether to bear her babe or not. While humanists are themselves divided[2] as to whether or not to consider their philosophy as a religion, they certainly approach abortion law liberalization with a motivation and a zeal appropriate to a religious crusade.[3] It follows that the frequently heard demand that religious views must be kept out of the abortion question is naïve, if not dishonest. As it would be impertinent to suggest to a humanist that he should abandon his particular standpoint in approaching abortion, so it is equally inadmissible for that demand to be made of the Christian.

It may seem easy to banish moral considerations. Sir Roger Ormrod has pointed out: "The Western World is changing over from a community or communities based more or less firmly on what is called the Christian Ethic . . . to one based on humanistic or sociological principles. These are even less clearly perceived or defined but have one clear-cut consequence. Decisions as to conduct can no longer be referred to a generally accepted set of principles but have to be taken afresh in each

[1] P. Hebblethwaite, "Objections to Malcolm Muggeridge." *The Times*, June 21, 1969.
[2] H. J. Blackham, *Objections to Humanism*, London, 1963, Constable.
[3] The United States Supreme Court has held that the test whether or not a belief is to be regarded as religious is "whether a given belief that is sincere and meaningful occupies a place in the life of the possessor parallel to that filled by the orthodox belief in God." In 1961 it pronounced as dictum that "Secular Humanism" is a religion, despite the absence of any belief in God. P. Ramsey in *The Morality of Abortion* (Ed. J. T. Noonan), 1970, Harvard University Press.

individual case by each individual practitioner."[4] But decision is possible only in the light of a standard or code. The medical man without this finds himself lost. "The doctor is burdened enough trying to preserve life without getting involved in questions of when to terminate it. Indeed, it is a burden of modern man that so much is to be resolved by conscious choice unguided by ethical code. One may feel at times that whatever gods there may be laugh in their far-off heaven at the dilemma of man who, through seeking to control nature and bring more out of the realm of contingency and under human control, has managed to become increasingly perplexed, confused, and self-destructive."[5] Similarly Dr. C. D. Leake admits to the strain: "To our chagrin we are discovering that there are no comfortable absolutes on which to rely in our moral dilemma but rather that responsible choices have to be made by each of us as individuals as to the appropriate ethic or way of conduct in the evershifting confrontation with the realities of our tension-filled lives."[6]

It is, of course, possible to believe that there are no such things as moral standards. But those agnostics who criticize the introduction of moral values and conscience into the abortion debate, should logically show no interest in the Vietnam war, or race relations: to their credit they are usually utterly inconsistent and do take a live interest in such problems.

At a colloquium on ethical dilemmas from medical advances one of the participants made the point: "When you talk about the greatest good of the greatest number you are still left with the question 'In the name of what is this called a good for anyone?' . . . You are driven back to some interpretation of what it means to be a human being, and what is good for each individual . . . . Medicine is not autonomous . . . science will not generate its own values."[7] The chairman commented "Perhaps the colloquium should have included a theologian and an artist; little cognizance was taken of the contributions to human wisdom that have come from outside the realm of scientific endeavour."[8] Another participant quoting words of the great American atomic scientist Robert J. Oppenheimer, "I believe the strength and soundness of Christian sensibility, the meaning of love and charity, have changed the world at least as much as technological development" added, "If we accept the importance of continuity with the past, Dr. Oppenheimer's words, which sound more like something coming from a theologian than a scientist, should give pause about making any drastic changes or departures from the basic

[4] Sir Roger Ormrod, "Medical Ethics." *BMJ*, 1968, **2,** 7.

[5] T. Lidz, "Reflections of a Psychiatrist." In *Therapeutic Abortion* (Ed. H. Rosen), New York, 1954, Julian Press.

[6] C. D. Leake, "Technical Triumphs and Moral Muddles" (see fn. 8).

[7] S. E. Stumpf, In discussion (see fn. 8).

[8] J. R. Elkington, "The Changing Mores of Biomedical Research: A Colloquium on Ethical Dilemmas from Medical Advances at the American College of Physicians." *Annals of Internal Medicine*, 1967, **67,** Supplement 7.

Judeo-Christian concepts of ethics and morals that are the foundation of all the law of Western civilization."[9] However, in the field of abortion many reformers, no doubt, would agree with Representative Allen B. Spector of Maryland who said "Sound medical practice and religion don't necessarily coincide . . ."[10] Others are quite clear that religion is the main obstacle. In a TV confrontation one of the organizers of the Birmingham Abortion Clinic said to his Christian opponent: "What you are trying to do is to impose a biblical statement on a secular community."[11]

It is, of course, possible to admit the interest of religion in abortion and yet feel it should be discounted. Sir Dugald Baird is reported as saying that he sympathises with his colleagues who hold strong views against abortion: "I myself," he said, "have come full circle from a strong religious background, so I understand their attitude. But I don't think it has got much of a place today."[12]

The Inevitability of Christian Involvement

That the Christian doctor should give thought to the question is inevitable. "The obstetrician with strong religious convictions," a lawyer warns, "is likely to be exposed, at least in theory, to a more dangerously embarrassing choice than in the past. One only hopes that the problem will never arise. But the possibility cannot be excluded."[13] A general practitioner has said: "If we must be proud, let it not be in the inviolability of our consciences but in our openness to our patient's viewpoint. I have, therefore, little sympathy with those who state on religious grounds that they are unable to consider the problems. Indeed I believe on religious grounds that we must all examine these problems with as much of an open mind as we can muster, for how else are we to claim the respect of our patients? And what is there religious about dealing with difficult ethical issues with a rubber stamp?"[14] Many critics of the Church feel that its influence has been almost wholly bad in this field. "The Christian Church has often been praised for the heightened value that it attached to human life: the debit side of the account – the frightful punishments practised by our professedly Christian ancestors, in gross misinterpretation of the plain teachings of the New Testament, must not be overlooked."[15] "Too many (pregnant women) have died because moralistic clergymen and the mercenary underworld have driven them

[9] W. E. Burger (see p. 90, fn. 8).
[10] Report in *The Christian Science Monitor*, July 23, 1969.
[11] M. Cole, in A.T.V. programme "Team at Six," Jan. 8, 1970.
[12] Sir Dugald Baird, Interview in *The Times*, June 18, 1969.
[13] G. Howe, "Abortion Law: Past, Present and Future," in *The Abortion Act, op. cit.*
[14] I. G. Lennox, "Problems of the Abortion Act in General Practice," in *The Abortion Act, op. cit.*
[15] G. L. Williams, *The Sanctity of Life and the Criminal Law*, London, 1958, Faber.

into the hands of unskilled individuals."[16] Such critics would doubtless be delighted if the Church were to withdraw altogether from the field. On the other hand, some believe that the Church could be useful as a tool. "It may be argued, of course, that a change in the theologically induced social climate could relieve a sense of guilt following abortion."[17] And, as we have already seen, clergy have been active members of pro-abortion lobbies, especially in America.

To come to some understanding of the Christian's role in abortion reform we have to recognize there are at least four strands in the Church's mission.

The Worth of the Individual

First, there is the recognition of man's eternal worth and destiny, not as a race, but individually – a value to God so great that He was willing to pay the price of the Cross.

In the words of Lord MacLeod: "The only ultimate reason why man, as man, has individual significance, is because Christ died for him."[18] With the knowledge that Christ so loves this woman that He died for her, the Christian has the supreme motive to help her.

Involvement in the Total Situation

Second, there is the recognition that such help for people involves the whole of their situation. "The trouble with the Christians is not that they have strict morals but that they don't seem to care very much. They don't care about the agonies of unhappy marriages, about the loneliness of the unmarried, about the dilemma of the homosexual."[19] Now that comment hurts. But before we react against it we must search our hearts to see if it be true. While at times, both in history and in our personal lives, it has been true that we have not cared very much, there can be no doubt that no body of people has cared so much as the Church.

Our Lord cared. He was interested in people, in their problems of the here and now, in the sick, the poor, the widowed, the ostracised.[20] He commanded His disciples to heal the sick, to cleanse the lepers.[21] In His parable of the Judgement Day He tells how "The king will say to those on his right hand, 'You have my Father's blessing . . . For when I was hungry

---

[16] R. M. Crawley and R. W. Laidlaw, "Psychiatric Opinion Regarding Abortion: Preliminary Report of a Survey." *American Journal of Psychiatry*, 1967, **124**, 559.

[17] B. Dickens, *Abortion and the Law*, London, 1966, McGibbon and Kee.

[18] Lord George MacLeod, quoted in S. E. Wirt, *The Social Conscience of the Evangelical*, London, 1968, Scripture Union.

[19] M. Thornton, quoted by L. Hodgson in *Sex and Christian Freedom*, London, 1967, S.C.M. Press.

[20] Lk. 8:24; 21:1; 7:12; 17:12.

[21] Matt. 10:8.

you gave me food; when thirsty, you gave me drink: when I was a stranger you took me into your home, when naked you clothed me; when I was ill you came to my help, when in prison you visited me.' When the righteous will ask when they did these things the King will answer 'I tell you this: anything you did for one of my brothers here, however humble, you did for me.' "[22]

In quoting Paul's words, "Only let your manner of life be worthy of the gospel of Christ,"[23] John Robinson makes the important point: "for 'manner of life' it is significant that Paul uses the same word *politeuesthe* which later in the epistle he is to use of the Christian's *politeia*, 'citizenship in heaven', and which we use for 'politics'. Being worthy of the Gospel, evangelization, *includes* the concern for civilization. No definition of 'the spiritual life' of the individual or the community, which leaves out political engagement in the broadest sense of that term can claim to be true to the whole counsel of God."[24]

The Church has always seen this wide implication, and never more so than in times of spiritual awakening. The evangelical revival, sparked off in the 18th century in the lives of John and Charles Wesley and George Whitefield, was the source of the vast majority of the great philanthropic work of the next century, among every kind of need.[25] It would be enough merely to recall the work of William Booth and his Salvation Army.[26] Before anyone yields to the temptation to castigate the Church for a lack of interest in social problems he should dip into the history of 19th century England.[27]

Unfortunately, for the past 100 years there has been a slackening of this concern within the evangelical wing of the Church. In J. N. D. Anderson's view this has been "principally attributable to two factors. First, we have been so conscious that the world as a system lies under the judgement of God, and that it is our duty to win individuals out of that system, that we have failed to appreciate that this is only one side of the biblical doctrine of the Christian in society. Second, we have been so frightened of the 'secularization of theology' that we have seldom really got to grips with a 'theology of the secular'."[28] The result of all this was that, certainly between the world wars, the "social gospel" became taboo in evangelical circles. It seemed an activity indulged in by those who had nothing better to do, an occupation for the nominal Christian who had lost all concern for the salvation of the lost. It was so, too, in America: "From the vantage point of our own day it looks as if something happened to render opaque the

[22] Matt. 25:35,36,40.
[23] Phil. 1:27.
[24] J. A. T. Robinson, *On Being the Church in the World*, London, 1960, S.C.M. Press.
[25] J. W. Bready, *England Before and After Wesley*, London, 1938, Hodder.
[26] R. Collier, *The General Next to God*, London, 1965, Collins.
[27] Kathleen Heasman, *Evangelicals in Action: An Appraisal of Their Social Work*, London, 1962, Bles.
[28] J. N. D. Anderson, "Christian Worldliness." In *Guidelines* (see fn. 31).

social vision of many an evangelist. The desperate, wasting plight of the poor slid out of his purview."[29]

This time of blindness is at last over.[30] In Britain its end was most clearly seen in papers read at the National Evangelical Anglican Congress, at Keele, in April 1967.[31] It was an unequivocally evangelical voice that reminded us: "A church which appears to care for men's souls without caring for their bodies cannot claim to be following the principles laid down by its Founder."[32]

Christians of other theological positions have not suffered from this particular imbalance, and have continued in their, often extensive, works of mercy. Among some Protestants, however, it sometimes appears that the balance has been lost completely between the various functions of the Church, with good works monopolizing attention. The issue is perhaps most clearly seen in Father Hebblethwaite's comments on objections to Malcolm Muggeridge: "The stock clerical objection to Muggeridge's brand of Christianity is that it is too often other-worldly and does not allow for the social and political implications of the Gospel. It was crudely put by someone who asked whether Christian in *Pilgrim's Progress* should not have ceased to gaze at the Heavenly City ahead and concentrated on improving living conditions in the City of Destruction. 'Or perhaps' added Muggeridge, 'lingered on in Vanity Fair and nationalized the brothels' . . . it is the *identification* of the Gospel with its social consequences that he rejects."[1]

This function of the Church can be summed up in the words of our Lord's brother: "The kind of religion which is without stain or fault in the sight of God our Father is this: to go to the help of orphans and widows in their distress and keep oneself untarnished by the world."[33]

The Call for Social Righteousness

The third strand in the Church's mission is its duty to press for social righteousness, and this certainly makes it very, very unpopular today. It always has. The slave owners in the days of Wilberforce, the factory-owners in the days of Shaftesbury, and others whose pockets were hurt by the social zeal of evangelical reformers in the 19th century, cannot have been enthusiastic about the Christian conscience. The Church which exercises this function finds itself not merely unpopular but persecuted. John the Baptist denounced Herod's marital behaviour and it cost him his

[29] S. E. Wirt, *op. cit.*

[30] In Britain the most obvious manifestation of this was the initiation in 1970 of *The Shaftesbury Project on Christian Involvement in Society*. A series of study groups on Christian Social Concern in specific areas has been started. (39 Bedford Square, London WC1B 3EY.)

[31] J. I. Packer (Ed.) *Guidelines: Evangelical Anglicans Face the Future*, London, 1967, Falcon Press.

[32] Sir Frederick Catherwood, *The Christian Citizen*, London, 1969, Hodder.

[33] Jas. 1:27.

head.[34] It was Christ who took a whip to those defiling the temple by their financial practices.[35] This stand against what the Christian sees as immorality has continued right through the centuries. We may not now always agree with our predecessors' understanding or morality, but then we do not stand in their shoes. For instance, John Calvin taught that the civil power had the right and duty to support the Church, and use its authority in establishing religion.[36] But T. M. Lindsay has pointed out: "Every instance quoted by modern historians to prove, as they think, Calvin's despotic interference with the details of private life, can be paralleled by references to the police-books of mediaeval towns in the fifteenth and sixteenth centuries. To make them ground for accusation against Calvin is simply to plead ignorance of the whole municipal police of the later Middle Ages."[37]

But, as Lord Devlin has reminded us, "A State which refuses to enforce Christian beliefs has lost the right to enforce Christian morals."[38] While none of us today would believe it possible or desirable to coerce belief, the situation concerning morals is less easy. That private actions are no concern of the public has been powerfully argued. Devlin counters with the argument that the law exists for the protection of society, and illustrates by considering the murderer who acts only upon the consent, and maybe at the request, of his victim, and is, therefore, no menace to others. Despite this such a murderer does threaten one of the great moral principles upon which society is based, the sanctity of life, and therefore the law must act. He further criticizes the view that there ought not to be a collective judgement about immorality *per se*, by pointing out that if society is not prepared to say that homosexuality is morally wrong, there would be no basis for a law protecting youth from "corruption" or punishing a man for living on the "immoral" earnings of a prostitute.[38]

In a democratic society it is indeed an inescapable responsibility for the Christian to use his influence because, like every other citizen, he bears a measure of personal responsibility for misgovernment, bad laws, or wrong policies, unless he has played his full part in trying to get a better government into power, better laws on the statute books, and better policies adopted.[39] The whole question of the Christian as a citizen has been dealt with by Sir Frederick Catherwood,[32] who, as Director-General of the National Economic Development Council, had an unsurpassed view of the field.

In this field of morals it is fascinating to notice the ambivalent attitude

[34] Matt. 14: 4–10.
[35] Matt. 21: 12–13.
[36] J. Calvin, "Institutes of the Christian Religion." Geneva, 1559, 4:20:3.
[37] T. Lindsay, "History of the Reformation" (vol. 2), Edinburgh, 1907, T. & T. Clark.
[38] Lord Patrick Devlin, *The Enforcement of Morals*, 1965, OUP.
[39] J. N. D. Anderson, *Into the World: the Need and Limits of Christian Involvement*, London 1968, Falcon Books.

of the non-Christian about the great issues of the day. If the Church fails to speak out strongly on, for example, racial injustice, there is justified criticism. In fact it is usually the Church that does so speak. The part played by the Confessional Church in Germany before and during World War II should not be forgotten. When, however, in response to the same conscience, the Church speaks out against wrong-doing in society, it is castigated as an interfering busybody. Dietrich Bonhoeffer as the heroic pacifist who saw it his duty to plot against Hitler's life is widely and deservedly admired: I have not noticed his condemnation of abortion as murder[40] quoted by the same admirers, although both beliefs must have been the result of his informed Christian conscience.

The Church has to be the salt in the world:[41] salt purifies, but it stings!

The Watchman Must be Alert

The fourth strand in the Church's witness to which attention must be drawn, is that of warning. The historian Herbert Butterfield has commented: "It is easy to make plans of quasi-political salvation for the world if we can have human nature as we want it to be, and presume on a general change of heart in our fellow men. And when such plans go wrong, it is easy to find a culprit – easy for the idealist to bring from under his sleeve that doctrine of human sinfulness which it would have been so much better for him to have faced fairly and squarely in the first instance . . . . It is essential not to have faith in human nature. Such faith is a recent heresy and a very disastrous one."[42] Human nature is sinful, and God must deal with sin.

The Christian sees time as linear, and in Oscar Cullmann's picture we are living between D-Day (the Cross and the Resurrection) and V-Day.[43] This planet Earth is not to drag out its long years until, silent, it becomes a mass of metal at a low temperature. The King will return. Even now He watches and demands righteousness. Ever since Old Testament times this has been the cry of the prophet. It still must be.

As the storm clouds gathered over Nigeria in 1966 the Nigerian Provost of Lagos Cathedral preached a series of sermons on social righteousness. He talked of gross social inequalities, of hatred of enemies of one's tribe, of political corruption and of rigged elections, of all the things that blew up his country while he was still preaching. And he did this in the context of "interviews" with the Old Testament prophets[44] – prophets who contrasted the wickedness of the country with the justice of God. Non-believers think of Christians as trying to frighten them with a harsh tyrannical God bent on spoiling the fun, but nothing could be further from

40 D. Bonhoeffer, *Ethics*, London, Fontana.
41 Matt. 5:13.
42 H. Butterfield, *Christianity and History*, London, 1950, Bell.
43 O. Cullmann, *Christ and Time*, London, 1962 (Revised ed.), S.C.M. Press.
44 F. O. Segun, *Cry Justice*, Ibadan, 1966, Daystar Press.

the truth. The prophet Hosea heard God say:

> Yet it was I who taught Ephraim to walk,
> Picking them up in my arms.
> Yet they never knew that it was I who healed their bruises
> I led them with gentle encouragement,
> Their harness was a harness of love.
> How, oh how, can I give you up, Ephraim!
> How, oh how, can I hand you over, Israel!
> How can I turn you into a Sodom!
> How can I treat you like a Gomorrah!
> My heart recoils within me,
> All my compassion is kindled.
> I will not give vent to my fierce anger –
> I will not destroy Ephraim again.
> For I am God and not man,
> I am the Holy One in your very midst,
> And I have not come to destroy.[45]

But even love can be spurned:

> Now they are hemmed in by their own deeds
> And they must face me.[46]

The Christian has no less a love of his country than other men, therefore where he sees evil triumphing he must speak. "One of the paradoxes of the twentieth century is that you are called a pessimist if you question the depressing conventions of the age, and a crazed pessimist if you hold out Christ as the only hope."[1]

The whole of this volume sets out to explore what may be a Christian approach to abortion. This chapter has, I hope, set out why the Church should, or rather must, speak on this question.

[45] Hos. 11: 3,4,8,9. Trans J. B. Phillips, *Four Prophets*, London, 1963, Bles.
[46] Hos. 7: 2 (Phillips).

Chapter 10

THE ATTITUDE OF THE CHURCH

Christian moral decision is a work of unending translation – translating the insights derived from the life and teaching of Christ into the situations in which we find ourselves. This work of translation is not a private activity .... It is done in relation to the whole Church in every age, and particularly in relation to the New Testament.
J. W. Bowker[1]

THE HISTORY OF THE CHURCH'S ATTITUDE TO ABORTION HAS BEEN reviewed recently by both Protestant[2] and Roman Catholic[3] scholars. Professor Noonan's masterly account of the Catholic view of the control of conception from the earliest times must be consulted by all serious students.[4] A mere thumbnail sketch is therefore all that need be provided here.

The Early and Mediaeval Church

The Church's attitude was to forbid abortion – absolutely. It must be remembered that the Early Church came into being in a licentious, pleasure-loving, degenerate empire where abortion was practised on the most trivial of grounds, such as the damage a pregnancy might cause to the woman's figure. Where no one else gave any thought to the rights of the unborn baby it was natural that these should be championed by the Church with its sense of the sanctity of life. Within the first century of its existence it had specifically condemned abortion.[5]

However, partly due to Stoic influence, theologians in later centuries developed a negative attitude towards marriage. Discussion became bogged down in debate on the time when the fetus was ensouled. At one time, for instance, it was held that a male fetus was animated at the 40th day, but a female not until the 80th! Actual human problems seem largely to have been lost sight of.

[1] J. W. Bowker, "The Morality of Personal Relationships." In *Making Moral Decisions* (Ed. D. M. MacKinnon), London, 1969, S.P.C.K.
[2] L. A. Kalland, "Views and Position of the Christian Church." In *Birth Control and the Christian* (op. cit.).
[3] J. T. Noonan, "An Almost Absolute Value in History." In *The Morality of Abortion: Legal and Historical Perspectives*, 1970, Harvard University Press.
[4] J. T. Noonan, *Contraception: A History of its Treatment by the Catholic Theologians and Canonists*, 1965, Harvard University Press.
[5] *Didache* (The Teaching of the Twelve Apostles) 5, 2.

The Roman Catholic Church

The views of the pre-reformation Church have been carried on in Roman Catholicism.[6] For a time there was, in practice at any rate, some relaxation of the absolute ban against abortion in the case of the very early fetus. Recently Roman Catholic liberal scholars have pointed out that the theological basis for this was sound,[7] and that the practice should once again be permitted. Certainly by the late 19th century, however, it was made clear by repeated rulings that under no condition was abortion permissible. Even permission to remove a fetus which could never develop, from a fallopian tube which would certainly rupture and kill the mother, was won only after a hard fight in the teeth of bitter opposition. Now, however, not only is removal of an ectopic pregnancy licit, but so too is the sacrifice of a fetus when this is incidental to, and not the main purpose of, an operation to excise a diseased organ.[8]

As recently as October 1970 the Pope castigated abortion as an act of "barbarism." "Abortion has been considered homicide since the first centuries of the Church and nothing permits it to be considered otherwise today.... Certainly the Church is aware that anguishing cases arise when the life of the mother appears threatened but it cannot admit for this reason 'therapeutical' abortion as it is called."[9]

There are many groups – clerical, medical and lay – within the Roman Catholic community who despair of the official position and are striving for a change.[10] Meanwhile it must be noted that Roman Catholic women frequently request abortion. One Liverpool gynaecologist reported that 45% of his patients for abortion were of this denomination.[11] Subterfuge is common and inevitable. Recently a devout Roman Catholic woman came to me with her problem of hyperfertility. Her conditions were such that were she to become pregnant again it would be a disaster, so she and her husband practised contraception, but at the cost of absenting themselves from the sacraments. I sterilized her and post-operatively sent her to make her peace with her church.

The Anglican Communion

THE CHURCH OF ENGLAND Church Assembly Board for Social Responsibility set up a committee to consider abortion, and its lengthy and

---

[6] See e.g. R. Shaw, *Abortion on Trial*, London, 1969, Hale.

[7] J. F. Donceel, "A Liberal Catholic's View." In *Abortion in a Changing World, op. cit.* He discusses the doctrine of hylomorphism which teaches that the human soul is the substantial form of a man, and can exist only in a real human body, not in a virtual human body.

[8] E. McDonagh, "Ethical Problems in Abortion." *Theology*, 1968, **71**, 393,443,501.

[9] Reported in *The Times*, Oct. 13, 1970.

[10] For a tentative theological attempt see B. Häring, "A Theological Evaluation." In *The Morality of Abortion, op. cit.*

[11] C. L. Moss, In *The Abortion Act 1967, op. cit.*

thoughtful report published in 1965[12] is one of the basic works on the subject. This document was discussed in 1967 by the Archbishop of Canterbury in an address to Convocation. "If we are to remain faithful to the tradition, we have to assert, as normative, the general inviolability of the fetus . . ." said Dr. Ramsey, recalling a key passage, "we shall be right to continue to see as one of Christianity's great gifts to the world the belief that the human fetus is to be reverenced as the embryo of a life capable of coming to reflect the glory of God whatever trials it may be going to face." The archbishop agreed that the following problems should be dealt with under the category of risk to the life or mental or physical health of the mother: the risk of birth of a deformed or defective child; conception after rape; circumstances when the bearing and rearing of the child would prove beyond the total capacity of the mother. "Besides both compassion and justice there are the two Christian convictions of which we must never lose sight. The first is that the eternal destiny with God in heaven possible to every child conceived in the mother's womb matters supremely. The second is that while we must strive to remove suffering we do not foreclose the ways in which in the midst of frustration and handicaps some of the glories of human lives may be seen."[13]

The Board for Social Responsibility also circulated in May 1969 a broadsheet to inform clergy whose advice is sought on the operation of "the conscience clause."[14]

The Reformed Churches

THE CHURCH OF SCOTLAND Social and Moral Welfare Board in 1966 stated "we cannot assert too strongly that the inviolability of the fetus is one of the fundamentals and its right to life must be strongly safeguarded . . . but we recognize that this general right is, in certain circumstances, in conflict with other rights. In the Reformed Church, the paramount concern has been for the mother."[15]

In its report to General Assembly in 1967, commenting on Mr. Steel's Bill, the Board was against the "social clause," and felt unnecessary and undesirable the clause "in determining whether or not there is a risk of injury to the health or well-being, account may be taken of the patient's total environment actual or reasonably foreseeable." The Assembly accepted its Board's report, which could be summarized: "We believed that statutory authority should be given to the termination of a pregnancy in a carefully circumscribed Bill, on the main ground that the continuation of

[12] Church Assembly Board for Social Responsibility. *Abortion: An Ethical Discussion*, London, 1965, Church Information Office.

[13] Abp M. Ramsey, Speech to Church Assembly, Jan. 1967.

[14] Church Assembly Board for Social Responsibility. *The Abortion Act 1967 and Its Conscience Clause*, May, 1969.

[15] Church of Scotland. *Supplementary Report of the Social and Moral Welfare Board*, May, 1966.

the pregnancy would involve 'serious risk' to the life or 'grave injury' to the health whether physical or mental, of the pregnant woman whether before or after the birth of her child. In cases of possible deformity we had strong reservations believing termination only justified in a few certain cases that should be left to the medical practitioner in the light of the above section. We did not think that the pregnant woman being defective, or being under the age of sixteen were sufficient grounds in themselves."[16]

The Kirk's Moral Welfare Committee is re-examining the whole question in the light of recent developments.[17]

THE UNITED FREE CHURCH OF SCOTLAND Committee of Public Questions referred to proposed legislation in its report to General Assembly in 1966. It was not prepared to say that in no circumstances would it support a Bill, but went to some lengths to list the difficulties including: "Is it compassion to allow abortion which may involve the person in a sense of guilt to be borne to the end of her days? Who is to judge whether this child or that, if born, will not find life worth living?"[18]

THE FREE CHURCH OF SCOTLAND. The Committee on Public Questions, Religion and Morals in its report to General Assembly of 1969 referred to medical problems, especially Euthanasia. *Inter alia*, it noted: "The provisions of the Abortion Bill are now in widespread operation and, in addition to the essential and gruesome evil of this matter, namely that the nation is imbruing its hands in the blood of its unborn infants, there is evidence of the emergence of associated abuses. The nation will yet be called to account for the perpetration of this crime against unborn humanity . . . there is the urgent problem of the protection of the doctor's position (which) has already arisen in acute form for many doctors in relation to abortion . . . . There is great need, in view of these and other developments, to sound forth with renewed emphasis the Christian doctrine of man as created in the image of God . . . . And we should also trumpet forth to the people of our own country and of the world that the only secure protection, for themselves and for their children, from the experimentation and exploitation of eugenists, abortionists, euthanasiasts and the rest, is in the private and public application of the doctrines and principles of the Christian Faith. In a society of ever-extending bureaucratic control of our private lives, it is not morbid fancy to envisage the emergence of a totalitarian situation where some of these practices would not be only permissible but compulsory."[19]

[16] Church of Scotland. *These My Brethren* (*Report of the Social and Moral Welfare Board*) May, 1967.

[17] D. A. Allan (Secretary to the Moral Welfare Committee). Personal communication, April, 1969.

[18] United Free Church of Scotland. Extract from the *Report of the Committee on Public Questions*, 1966. Kindly provided by Mrs. W. Bell, Secretary to the Church.

[19] Free Church of Scotland. Extract from the *Report of the Committee on Public Questions, Religion and Morals*. Kindly provided by the General Treasurer of the Free Church.

THE PRESBYTERIAN CHURCH OF ENGLAND Church and Community Committee reported to its General Assembly in 1967 that "it rejected the Roman Catholic view that all abortion is murder, also, the opposite extremely permissive view. There is need for a Reformed Church statement on the moral status of the fetus." It was unconvinced that Mr. Steel's Bill should be supported.[20] In 1969 the Committee issued a broadsheet on Sex and Society written by Mr. Hugh Arthur, a senior gynaecologist, in the light of the Abortion Act.[21]

THE CONGREGATIONAL CHURCH IN ENGLAND AND WALES had this matter constantly under review in its responsible committee during 1965–67, and was engaged in lobbying and discussion on the proposed legislation. It did not, however, make any authoritative statement.[22]

The Baptist Church

THE BAPTIST UNION Christian Citizenship Committee largely agrees with the Church Assembly report already mentioned, "there being no distinctly Baptist point of view on this issue." The chairman of this committee produced a statement as a basis for discussion in which he makes the point that the unborn child is a human being in its own right and that a decision for abortion can only be made on the basis of a life for a life. The so-called social reasons for abortion should be seriously challenged.[23]

(It is interesting to compare this with a policy statement adopted by the American Baptist Convention in 1968: "Because Christ calls us to affirm the freedom of persons and the sanctity of life, we recognize that abortion should be a matter of responsible personal decision. To this end we as American Baptists urge that legislation be enacted to provide . . ." to allow abortion on demand up to the end of the twelfth week, but thereafter only on grounds roughly similar to the British ones.[24])

[20] Presbyterian Church of England. Extract from *Report of the Church and Community Committee*. Kindly provided by the Rev. A. L. Macarthur, General Secretary of the Church.

[21] H. Arthur, *Sex and Society*, 1969, Presbyterian Church of England. Mr Arthur, although not in this paper, distinguishes between *Reproduction:* a function which we share with the animal kingdom, and into which casual conception both inside and outside marriage falls. *Pro-creation:* by which, as human beings, we imperfectly fulfil God's purpose in creation. It may be evinced simply as a stirring of maternal concern for what has been conceived, and is seen in some patients, both single and married, in spite of their requests for termination. If this concern is observed, Mr Arthur believes it is to be encouraged and supported for the sake both of the fetus and of the health of the mother. When it fails to show itself at all then he considers that termination is a much more reasonable option. (Personal communications, February 1969 and October 1970).

[22] A. G. Burnham (Asst. Secy. for Social Responsibility). Personal communication, September, 1970.

[23] D. D. Black, Personal communication, August, 1970.

[24] American Baptist Convention. Quoted in *Birth Control and the Christian, op. cit.*

The Methodist Church

The Methodist Conference in 1966 passed a resolution at the recommendation of its Department of Christian Citizenship advocating reform of the law along the lines later enacted. Particular concern was felt for those who felt unable to cope with a child, or another child. They also suggested that the working of any new legislation should be carefully reviewed at the end of five years.[25]

In its 1970 report the Department commented: "One very real cause for concern is the abuse of the law in certain private establishments where excessive fees are charged.... We believe in the integrity of the (medical) profession as a whole, and we have deep sympathy with those whose consciences are often burdened by the responsibility laid upon them. This makes it all the more reprehensible that a few should make great financial gain out of human misery. Our own view is that the present law should continue to operate for the time being.... We cannot too often reiterate our profound conviction that the answer to the abortion problem lies in sound education in personal relationships and parental responsibility, which is an integral part of the Church's task."[26] Conference passed a resolution noting "with sympathy the increasing concern of many professional people, especially among the nursing and medical professions, at the way in which the Act is being interpreted by some doctors.... Conference calls on the Secretary of State for the Social Services to undertake at an early date a thorough review of the working of the Abortion Act."[27]

Other Churches

THE PENTECOSTAL CHURCHES. In January 1970 the official organ of the Assemblies of God in Great Britain and Ireland carried an article on Abortion by a member of its Executive Council. He commented: "Once life is denied to the unborn fetus as a matter of course on demand, the next logical step is euthanasia; the ending of the life of the unfit, the aged and infirm. Christian conscience demands that all concerned in the drafting and enforcing of legislation have due regard to the sanctity of life and to the rights of incipient life.... The opportunity for free and easy abortion could hardly be greater than that offered by this Act of Parliament. The breadth and latitude of its permissiveness must be an embarrassment to the many doctors whose art is dedicated to the saving and sustaining of life." It ended with an appeal for readers to write to their Member of Parliament supporting attempts to amend the law restrictively.[28]

[25] Methodist Church. *Manifold Witness:* The Report of the Christian Citizenship Department, 1966.
[26] Report for 1969–70.
[27] Personal communication, July, 1970.
[28] A. F. Missen, "Abortion: Comment on Recent Legislation and Further Motions Before Parliament." *Redemption Tidings,* January 29th, 1970.

THE RELIGIOUS SOCIETY OF FRIENDS has not discussed Abortion at its Meeting for Sufferings, or Yearly Meeting.[29] However in 1963 a group of Friends published *Towards a Quaker View of Sex*,[30] a significant, if unofficial, contribution to the wider debate. A highly controversial work, it includes among its "last words" these: "The challenge to each of us is clear: accustom yourself to seeking God's will and to the experience of his love and power, become used in your daily life to the simple but tremendous spiritual fact that what God asks he enables, provided only and always that we will to do his will."[31]

THE CHRISTIAN BRETHREN by the nature of their polity have no corporate view. Of my personal friends among Brethren, many of them doctors, none holds abortion always to be wrong, and none condones abortion on demand. All require adequate grounds for abortion, but vary somewhat in their interpretation of what grounds are adequate.

THE SALVATION ARMY. At the time Mr. Steel's bill was before Parliament, the General of the Army issued a statement making the following points. It would be sufficient to legalize the current medical practice without widening the grounds for abortion. The argument that the bill would put an end to illegal abortions was an unproven assumption. "The humane considerations which have prompted the Bill can be fully recognised, and yet the most serious hesitations be held as to the grounds on which human life, even in embryo, can be destroyed." He recommended that the progress of the Bill be halted and instead a Royal Commission set up to study the matter.[32]

The British Council of Churches

Most British churches are members of this council, and much of the thinking on abortion has been done in its Advisory Group on Sex, Marriage and the Family. While legislation was before Parliament in 1967 the Council supported in some measure public pressure for reform. It held that the medical termination of pregnancy should be permitted in cases where continuance of the pregnancy would involve serious risk to the life or grave injury to the physical or mental health of the woman. The Council, however, expressed serious doubts about the wider grounds for

[29] A. White, Recording Clerk to the Religious Society of Friends. Personal communication, August, 1970.

[30] A. Heron (Ed.) *Towards a Quaker View of Sex*, London, 1963, Friends Home Service Committee.

[31] On the other side of the Atlantic the American Friends Service Committee have issued a booklet *Who Shall Live? Man's Control Over Birth and Death* (New York, 1970, Hill and Wang) in which the view is supported that abortion under proper circumstances is preferable to the birth of an unwanted child, and that the woman should be able to have an abortion legally if she has decided that this is the only solution she can accept and if the physician agrees that it is in the best interest of mother and child. (They do not clarify what, in their opinion, should be done if woman and physician disagree!)

[32] Salvation Army. *Christian Concern*; statement kindly made available to me by Lt. Col. Fenwick, Northern Division, Salvation Army.

abortion then proposed and called for a parliamentary review within five years of any Act passed.[33]

In February 1970 it published a pamphlet on the working of the Act, quoting figures from other countries, outlining some of the problems to be faced, and suggesting points for group discussion.[33]

No doubt it will continue to be the chief agent in bringing the official views of the various Protestant denominations before government in future negotiations.

A great number of other religious groups have taken an interest in the topic. One which merits mention is a Protestant Anti-abortion Group[34] operating chiefly in the Midlands. It has picketed abortion clinics, and distributed literature likening the British practice of abortion to the (American) Pinkville massacre episode in Vietnam. "We would assert that in many ways legalised abortion has become the national sin of this country. And we also believe that 'on account of these things the wrath of God is coming.'" It is interesting to note that the activities of this largely Pentecostalist group have been favourably reported in the Roman Catholic press: an ecumenical serendipity indeed!

Churchmanship and Abortion Stance

It would be impracticable to present a complete survey of the position on abortion taken up by every branch of the Church, if only because attitudes are fluid and constantly under review. We have, however, noted enough from our review of the major denominations in England and Scotland to see the overall spectrum of views.

Not only at denominational but at individual level this spectrum closely follows theological viewpoints.

Inevitably the theologically liberal will feel free to select such biblical concepts as they wish to support their views on abortion. These tend to emphasize mostly, if not wholly, the woman's rights and wishes.

The theologically conservative, on the other hand, see themselves as standing under the Word of God and must needs bring together all biblical insights in building a coherent attitude to abortion. That this need has its value may be seen by the fact that, so far as I am aware, most serious theological discussion and debate on the subject by Christians, as opposed to arguments between Christians, has been done by conservative evangelicals in the medical profession. Among others, the Christian Medical

---

[33] British Council of Churches. Advisory Group on Sex, Marriage and the Family. *The Abortion Act 1967–69: A Factual Review.*

[34] In 1971 this group was organised as SOUL (Sanctity of Unborn Life). Information may be obtained from W. Spring, 67 York Street, Rugby.

Fellowship in Britain,[36] the Christian Medical Society in North America,[37] and the Protestantse Christelijke Artsen Organisatie[38] in the Netherlands, have held conferences, study-groups, meetings of gynaecologists, and in their journals and other publications have dealt in depth with the problem. In 1968 the Christian Medical Society and the journal *Christianity Today* jointly sponsored a consultation in the U.S.A. of Christians working in various specialities, "to study the medical, theological, and legal principles bearing on the problems of contraception, sterilization and induced abortion with a multi-disciplinary approach. To seek to establish moral guidelines for decision which will be medically sound, rooted in a biblical ethic and which will be of pragmatic value to the practising physician and minister." Its published report[39] forms an essential background to the practical study which it is the aim of the present volume to provide.

The Conference adopted a *Protestant Affirmation on the Control of Human Reproduction*. In its theological section it states:

Abortion confronts the Christian with the most perplexing question of all; Is induced abortion permissible and if so, under what conditions? If it is permissible in some instances is the act of intervention still sinful? Can abortion then be justified by the principle of tragic moral choice in which a lesser evil is chosen to avoid a greater one? As to whether or not the performance of an induced abortion is always sinful we are not agreed, but about the necessity and permissibility for it under certain circumstances we are in accord.

The Christian physician who is asked to perform an abortion will seek to discover the will of God in this as in every other area of his life. He needs divine guidance for himself in his practice and for counselling his patients. The physician in making a decision regarding abortion should take into account the following principles:

1) The human fetus is not merely a mass of cells or an organic growth. At the most, it is an actual human life or at the least, a potential and developing human life. For this reason the physician with a regard for the value and sacredness of human life will exercise great caution in advising an abortion.

2) The Christian physician will advise induced abortion only to safeguard greater values sanctioned by Scripture. These values should include individual health, family welfare and social responsibility.

3) From the moment of birth, the infant is a human being with all the rights which Scripture accords to all human beings; therefore infanticide under any circumstances must be condemned.

[36] Christian Medical Fellowship (CMF), 56 Kingsway, London WC2. Journal, *In the Service of Medicine*.

[37] Christian Medical Society. 1122 Westgate, Oak Park, Illinois 60301. *Christian Medical Journal*.

[38] For details of this, and twenty other similar societies in different parts of the world see *A Brief History of the Christian Medical Societies* (2nd ed. 1969). Published for the International Congress of Christian Physicians by the CMF.

[39] *Birth Control and the Christian:* "A Protestant Symposium on the Control of Human Reproduction." (Ed. W. O. Spitzer and C. L. Saylor), Wheaton, 1969, Coverdale House Publishers.

Under "Guidelines for Professional Practice" are the words: "The sanctity of life must be considered when the question of abortion is raised. At whatever stage of gestation one considers the developing embryo or fetus to be human, even at birth, the potential great value of the developing intrauterine life cannot be denied. There may, however, be compelling reasons why abortion must be considered under certain circumstances. Each case should be considered individually, taking into account the various factors involved and using Christian principles of ethics."[39] The whole document is worthy of study.

It is a frequent jibe that committed Christians hold a hard and negative ("puritanical" is the favoured adjective) attitude to abortion far removed from the compassion of Christ. Those who make such a statement cannot have looked at all the evidence.

THE SEARCH FOR A PLUMBLINE

*'He is able to keep you from falling'... This means that our holy religion is
not simply an ambulance which follows in the wake of the battle to deal with
casualties. It has another task much more positive and creative and aggressive: it
is itself the armour which wins victories.*   J. S. STEWART[1]

Is This Quest Meaningful?

WE HAVE SEEN THAT THE CHURCH SPEAKS WITH A VARIETY OF VOICES.
What then is the Christian to do? In the Protestant world pronouncements of the various denominations are seen as guidelines, and therefore to be considered along with other factors. The Roman Catholic, some of whose tensions have been described in our previous chapter, is in a much more difficult position.

If the Church does not provide the standard we need, perhaps we could trust in "sanctified common-sense." This, however, had led to an even wider spectrum of opinions than have church deliberations. At one end there is the prohibitionist. One of my correspondents (a Presbyterian elder) stated succinctly, and in red ink: "All abortion is MEDICAL MURDER, Gal. 5. 21 ('... envy, drunkenness, carousing, and the like. I warn you, as I warned you before, that those who do such things shall not inherit the kingdom of God'), and the logical outcome of earlier works of the flesh. As we are now living 'as in the days of Lot' we will see more and more of this. Only in a case where the Christian is sure that without an abortion we are murdering the mother shall the former operation be prayerfully contemplated." At the other end of the spectrum an unnamed clergyman, writing for the Abortion Law Reform Association, advocates abortion on demand.[2]

Having failed to find any firm ground in the pronouncements of the churches, or in personal judgement, where are we to look?

Are we asking the wrong question? Perhaps there is no plumbline against which to measure our activities. Many are quite clear on this. Aleck Bourne wrote: "Despite the unbreakable claims of the Christians who believe that Christ's moral teaching is absolute, there is no ultimate appeal or norm beside which a system or details of ethics can be compared,

[1] J. S. Stewart, *The Wind of the Spirit*, London, 1968, Hodder and Stoughton.
[2] *A Clergyman's View*: Abortion Law Reform Association.

and therefore we must begin the moral considerations of this subject, abortion, as other problems of morality, by remembering that its rightness or wrongness is the estimate of the race, epoch and civilization of the time."[3]

Much contemporary theology agrees in denying the existence of any objective ethic, although J. W. Bowker has pointed out a danger here. "The collapse of objectivity in ethics means that the individual or the State can, if it wishes, pass beyond judgement; and what that led to was clearly seen in Stalin's Russia. It means also that, on the one hand, morality as a matter of private opinion, and on the other totalitarian contempt for the opinion of private individuals (which at first sight seem so opposed to each other) are, in fact, two streams from the same source, that the end always justifies the means, and that morality is circumstantial."[4]

Be that as it may, much modern theology is clear that the past days of certainty based on objective laws have gone and gone for ever. "The man who has moved beyond tribal culture and its town or bourgeois afterglow knows that he must bear a burden the people of those eras never bore. He must live with the realization that the rules which guide his ethical life will seem just as outmoded to his descendants as some of his ancestors' practices now appear to him. No previous generation has had to live in the glaring light of this realization. Simple ethical certainty, of the sort once available to man, will never be possible again."[5] Those who accept this view of Harvey Cox's must find it depressing, but perhaps it is a burden of the manhood to which modern theology says we have arrived.

"Man come of age."[6] The suggestion that at last we can be really adult and free of divine tutelage may seem an alluring one. It enticed Eve when Satan used it in the primal temptation. The fact that our first parents yielded is no reason why we also should be deceived. When we have the offer of the constant presence, guidance and empowering of our loving Father, who wants to clutch such hollow freedom? It is true we have Paul's picture of growing up out of the bondage of infancy,[7] but the growth is not into self-reliant manhood, but into sonship. Harold St. John has put our relationship very aptly: "I am my Father's child, not His privy counsellor."[8]

"Love" – The Only Standard?

To many, however, it seems there is one standard to which we can cling: the standard of love. Asked which was the greatest commandment in the law, Jesus replied: " 'Love the Lord your God with all your heart,

[3] A. Bourne, *A Doctor's Creed; Memoirs of a Gynaecologist*, London, 1963, Gollancz.
[4] J. W. Bowker, "The Morality of Personal Relationships." In *Making Moral Decisions* (Ed. D. M. MacKinnon), London, 1969, S.P.C.K.
[5] H. Cox, *The Secular City*, London, 1965, S.C.M. Press.
[6] The phrase is Dietrich Bonhoeffer's.
[7] Gal. 4:1.
[8] Patricia St. John, *Harold St. John*. Glasgow, Pickering and Inglis.

with all your soul, with all your mind.' That is the greatest commandment. It comes first. The second is like it: 'Love your neighbour as
yourself.' Everything in the Law and the prophets hangs on these two
commandments."[9] Joseph Fletcher in his classic book[10] writes "Christian
situation ethics has only one norm or principle or law (call it what you
will) that is binding and unexceptionable, always good and right regard-
less of the circumstances. That is 'love' – the *agape* of the summary commandment to love God and the neighbour. Everything else without
exception, all laws and rules and principles and ideals and norms are only
contingent, only valid *if they happen* to serve love in any situation." As his
view has been very widely accepted in liberal theological circles it must
occupy our attention – particularly so as, by 1970, Fletcher was saying:
"I am prepared to argue that Christian obligation calls for lies and adultery
and fornication and theft and promise-breaking and killing, sometimes,
depending on the situation."[11]

The final point to notice in reading situational ethic literature is that,
having quoted our Lord's summary of the law, only the second part
"love of the neighbour" comes under scrutiny. However, staying with
them, we notice first of all the problem of knowing what is, in the actual
situation, the loving action for our neighbour.

To start with we have the difficulty of our ignorance of all the factors.
How can I possibly, in applying situational ethics to an abortion problem,
know enough of the woman's family situation, character, marriage relationship, let alone the economic future of the country as it will affect her
husband's livelihood, and future health or even survival of her husband or
present children? of future marriage-breakup, or of remarriage? How can
I know what the future might hold, for the good or ill of mankind, for
this fetus if it were born? Yet without this foreknowledge, how can I
know what is the "loving decision" to make to her request?

A second difficulty is that of identifying the true nature of the love that
we have for our neighbour. Is it indeed, as our Lord commanded, *agape*
(which William Barclay[12] has translated as "unconquerable benevolence,
undefeatable goodwill"). Or is it *eros*? (Of this he comments: "it always
has a predominantly physical side, and it always involves sexual love.")
For instance in a discussion on *agape* Joseph Fletcher gives the following
example.[10] A young unmarried couple might decide "Christianly" to have
intercourse in order by achieving a pregnancy to force a selfish parent to
relent his overbearing resistance to their marriage. But, as Christians, they
would never say "It is all right if we 'like' each other". He implies that
"loving concern" can make it all right, but that merely "liking" cannot.

[9] Matt. 22:35-39 (NEB).
[10] J. Fletcher, *Situation Ethics*, London, 1966, S.C.M. Press.
[11] Southern Baptist Christian Life Conference, Atlanta, as reported in *Christianity Today* ,
Washington) May 8, 1970.
[12] W. Barclay, *Flesh and Spirit*, London, 1962, S.C.M. Press.

The reader is invited to reject "liking" but approve the insertion of "*agape*". I find it very difficult to believe that "agape" is the appropriate word here. Inevitably *eros* is involved and the example falls to the ground.

There is, indeed, a fruitful source of confusion in the various meanings of "love." C. S. Lewis distinguished at least four.[13] Having started from an apparently biblical base, modern thinkers reach "love is the only thing that matters," and their confusion is made obvious by their dictum that sexual intercourse is only "right" in the presence of love. From this they argue that it follows sexual intercourse may be right outside marriage; and conversely will be wrong inside marriage if the act is not one of love. Ignoring for the moment their slip from *agape* to *eros*, let us look at this statement, as it is widely proclaimed by apostles of situational ethics, and has a bearing on our abortion clientèle. Extra-marital sex will be considered in later chapters; for the moment consider the other side of the coin. "Coitus is only right as an act of love" seems self-evident, but could only be enunciated by those whose vision is limited to the western world of the present era. C. S. Lewis has discussed this in relation to our ancestors: "If all who lay together without being in the state of *Eros* were abominable, we all come of tainted stock .... Most of our ancestors were married off in early youth to partners chosen by their parents on grounds that had nothing to do with *Eros*. They went to the act with no other 'fuel' so to speak, than plain animal desire. And they did right; honest Christian husbands and wives, obeying their fathers and mothers, discharging to one another their 'marriage debt' and bringing up families in the fear of the Lord. Conversely, this act" (and he should, perhaps have added, "as demanded by our 20th century prophets") "done under the influence of a soaring and iridescent *Eros* which reduces the role of the senses to a minor consideration, may yet be plain adultery, may involve breaking a wife's heart, deceiving a husband, betraying a friend, polluting hospitality and deserting your children."[13]

And what of other cultures? More than once I have heard Indian women doctors, disillusioned by their work in British gynaecological units, sing the praise of the "arranged marriage." At present I have a colleague who first met her husband on their betrothal day, and next at the marriage. Such women are often charming, witty, urbane, and cultured. They see the shoddiness of much that passes for "love" in our western society. In their culture divorce and a second marriage are ruled out, therefore this marriage must be made to work. They see love as something to be achieved: this is a realization that should come to us all. From prison Dietrich Bonhoeffer wrote: "It is not your love which sustains the marriage, but from now (the wedding day) the marriage that sustains your love."[14]

---

[13] C. S. Lewis, *The Four Loves*, London, 1960, Bles.
[14] D. Bonhoeffer, *Letters and Papers from Prison*, London, 1953, S.C.M. Press.

No. The present-day equation of "love" with *eros* will not do. It will not do even for marriage. Still less will it help us to fulfil Christ's law. And, towards an understanding of "love to one's neighbour," it helps not at all. We must look elsewhere.

The Primary Object of Our Love

Joseph Fletcher is surely right in reminding us that "God *is* love, He doesn't merely *have* it or *give* it; He gives Himself – to all men, to all sorts and conditions: to believers and unbelievers, high and low, dark and pale, learned and ignorant, Marxists and Christians and Hottentots."[10] As God knows the answer to all questions, surely it must follow that the more closely I can draw to God, and the more I can be moulded to His will, the better and more efficiently will I be able to manifest love for my neighbour.

It seems to me, therefore, that the exponent of situational ethics may be right in suggesting that there is only one law, and is right in leading us to it in Christ's summary of the law. However, at the last moment he fails by placing the weight on the subsidiary clause rather than on the primary one of love to God. If we truly love Him, love to our neighbour must follow.

This, of course, then raises the question, what does it mean to love God? The Prophet Micah said :"What does the Lord require of thee but to love mercy and to do justly and to walk humbly with thy God."[15]

A Christian woman was persuaded to make her first visit to a cinema to see the film version of her favourite book. On taking a seat she bowed her head in prayer. Her embarrassed husband nudged her saying, "You don't do that here," to which she replied as she rose to go home, "If I can't pray here then this is no place for me." A rather antiquated story, no doubt, but it exemplifies our point that the Christian's walk must be one in which every activity, leisure as well as work, is done in fellowship with God. No action, therefore, can be counted loving unless it is in accordance with God's nature, and that nature is Holy. "He is of purer eyes than to behold iniquity."[16]

Bishop John Robinson, explaining the situational approach in its relation to sex, gives the following illustration. To the young man asking in his relations to a girl "Why shouldn't I?" it is relatively easy to say, "Because it's wrong," or "Because it is a sin," and then condemn him when he, or his whole generation, takes no notice. It makes much greater demands to ask and to answer the question "Do you love her?" or "How much do you love her?"[17] If we are following the situationists' own rule then we go back to Christ's summary of the law, and find that we must start by asking this young man "How much do you love the Lord?" This must be the question; Jesus Himself says "It comes first." This is no

[15] Mic. 6: 8.
[16] Hab. 1: 3.
[17] J. A. T. Robinson, *Honest to God*, London, 1962, S.C.M. Press.

bandying of words, as every Christian young man and girl with the normal complement of God-given emotions, knows perfectly well.

Joseph Fletcher writes: "Situationists welcome . . . an attitudinal ethic rather than a legal one. 'Have this mind among yourselves, which you have in Christ Jesus' (Phil. 2:5) and *then* as Augustine says, 'whatever you do will be right!' The mind of him whom Bonhoeffer called 'the Man for others' is to be for others, for neighbours."[10] Now this aphorism of Augustine is translated by John Robinson[17] as "Love God, and do what you like"; we would do well to remember our Lord's own statement of His mind: "My food is to do the will of Him that sent me . . . I seek not my own will but the will of Him that sent me . . . I always do what is pleasing to Him."[18]

Is there then no absolute objective standard? I believe there is, and we can be led to it by a comment of Valerie Pitt's: "The new men would, I suspect, fall back if pushed on the commandment: 'Love is the lesson which the Lord us taught.' They depend, like the old moralists, on the presuppositions of revelation. Like it or not, their absolute is still 'the Bible says.' "[19] We could have reached the same conclusion by noting the word of the Apostle John: "For this is the love of God, that we keep His commandments, for all who keep His commandments abide in Him, and He in them."[20] Inevitably we must turn to the Bible.

The idea that the Bible can in this matter – or any other – speak with authority is frequently discounted. To confine ourselves to quotations from writers dealing with our subject we find Glanville Williams saying: "To a lawyer theological discussion of the fundamentalist type makes fascinating reading . . . . The texts themselves . . . are authorities and not open to dispute . . . . Fortunately there is always sufficient doubt and contradiction in the sacred texts to enable a common-sense result to be reached if the interpreter is willing to do so."[21] The ALRA's anonymous clergyman writes "I have always considered it futile to quote texts from the Bible in support of an argument since precisely opposite texts can usually be found, if you know where to look for them."[2]

Such views are understandable if one looks at the Bible as a multiple-author textbook, comparable in authority and standing to similar works in other disciplines. After all the first step in scholarship is to keep a very critical attitude towards one's authorities. With the church speaking equivocally, with sanctified common-sense producing an infinite variation in views, and with a fallible Bible, one is left bereft of help. The Whiteleys have written, "During a long experience of ethical discussion with university students and a variety of adult education classes, while we have met

[18] Jn. 4: 34; 5: 30; 8: 29.
[19] Valerie Pitt, "A Plea for Chastity." In *Prismatics*, (Ed. C. Martin), London, 1966, Hodder and Stoughton.
[20] I Jn. 5: 3.
[21] G. L. Williams, *The Sanctity of Life and the Criminal Law*, London, 1958, Faber.

people (mostly Catholics) who based their morality on ecclesiastical authority we have found scarcely anyone who tried to settle a disputed point by reference to a matter of religious doctrine, or by quoting the Bible."[22]

The cardinal mistake, which results in such an inadequate view of Scripture, is that one has forgotten the work of the Holy Spirit: which I see as being two-fold in this connection.

First, the Holy Spirit is the sole author of the Bible. Granted it was written over more than a thousand years. Granted He used the personalities of different men through whom to write. However, while the idea of the Bible as a library of books may be useful for teaching purposes it obscures the basic fact that it is a homogeneous, one-author work, whose parts are mutually complementary. Such an understanding of the nature of God's Word results in an approach which is utterly different from that one would employ with the most authoritative human work. Perhaps an illustration will help. I possess a letter written a hundred years ago by my grandfather to his wife. As a social document it is fascinating: the near-slavery of his work-place, the grinding poverty, are most moving. But the sentiments this document arouse in me must be completely different from those that letter aroused in his bride when it reached her Cotswold cottage. To me it is a document from a man I never knew, a voice from a bygone age: to her it was a word from her beloved. So the Christian should pick up his Bible as a message from his living, loving Lord.

The Holy Spirit has, however, a second ministry in relation to the Bible. Perhaps I can make my point by analogy.

So far as the Lord's Supper is concerned there is a low view which sees it as merely a remembrance, an act done out of obedience. In contrast there is a high view in which the believer rightly partaking of the elements is aware of the "Real Presence."

So far as the pulpit is concerned there is the low view: "chaps talking,"[23] or even, in the words of a theological student to me recently, "coward's castle." Then there is the much more worthy view epitomized in J. S. Stewart's challenge that we "mount the pulpit steps in thrilled expectancy that Jesus Christ will come amongst His folk that day, travelling in the greatness of His strength, mighty to save."[24] Describing such a view, Ian Henderson uses the words "A Real Presence in the pulpit."[23]

Just so it seems to me that we would be wise to recognize a Real Presence in the reading of the Bible – as much in our private devotions as in public worship. This is a work of the Holy Spirit. There can be few of us, seeing the Bible in this way, who have not had the experience of finding a well-known verse becoming the special word of God to us, for today, in

[22] C. H. Whiteley and Winifred Whiteley, *The Permissive Morality*, London, 1964, Methuen.
[23] L. Henderson, *Scotland: Kirk and People*, London, 1969, Lutterworth.
[24] J. S. Stewart, *Heralds of God*, London, 1964, Hodder and Stoughton.

our particular circumstances. An example, relevant to our present problem, will be found in Chapter 14.

We, therefore, turn to the Bible as our plumbline, to seek to understand God's mind for us, and for our patients. In doing so we might use the Psalmist's prayer:

> "Open my eyes, that I may behold
> Wondrous things out of thy law."[25]

[25] Ps. 119:18.

CHAPTER 12

OLD TESTAMENT GUIDANCE

Before I became a sociologist I was an ordained minister. When I was in seminary in training I participated in many ethical and theological discussions about abortion and these had great meaning for me. Then when I went out, and did research on the realities of abortion as a sociologist, I suddenly realized that all of the discussion I had had in that prior context were irrelevant to the reality of what was going on. I only wish that I could take some of my former theology and ethical professors with me to show them what I see now. KENNETH R. WHITTEMORE[1]

The Meaning and Marring of Man

ABORTION IS OF MORE THAN MEDICAL IMPORTANCE, PRINCIPALLY because a human life is at stake. The life is only potential, but by the time the woman comes to see her doctor the statistical chances are in favour of the fetus going on to safe delivery, and becoming a living man. What does it mean to be man?

Our ancestors interpreted man as having been "made in God's image," with reference to the body. And, of course, the highest way we can think of Him is in anthropomorphic terms: to try to do otherwise is to end up with thinking of Him as a rather vague cloud, threatening rain. But our anatomy and physiology is demanded by our terrestrial habitat, and quite inappropriate to the One who inhabits eternity.[2] The last generation saw man as a higher animal; the present generation sees him as a highly sophisticated miniaturized computer. Whether animal or machine we are separated by an infinite chasm from God.

Our likeness to God has been identified by Francis Schaeffer as lying in personality. "Within the Trinity, before the creation of anything, there was real love and real communication. This God who is personal created man in His own image; and so personality is intrinsic to his make-up . . . . No one has ever thought of a way of deriving personality from non-personal sources . . . if man has been kicked up out of that which is only impersonal, by chance, then those things that make him man – hope of purpose, beauty, and verbal communication – are ultimately unfulfillable

[1] K. R. Whittemore, "The Availability of Non-Hospital Abortions." In *Abortion in a Changing World, op. cit.*
[2] Isa. 57: 15.

and thus meaningless.... The green moss on the rock is higher than he, for it can be fulfilled in the universe which exists whereas he cannot."[3]

Man, then, is like God in being a person, with self-knowledge, rational, able to think abstractly, and with a moral sense. Without being able to see God he can know His presence, and respond in love to Him. Without these he might be a very efficient tool, a slave, but God had higher plans for him: no less than to make him a son, and "joint heir with Christ."[4] It has been well put by Dr. Douglas Jackson "... the divine image constitutes man's uniqueness: it is this that makes him of such worth in the sight of God. Though man sometimes appears frighteningly frail and small, even to himself – 'What is man, that thou art mindful of him?' – yet as a creation to an artist, as a son to a father, he is of great value to God, of sufficient value for Christ to intervene in the history of mankind, and endure the cross to bring us back into the right relationship to Himself. Christ's death on the cross is the measure of man's worth in His sight."[5]

But why was the Cross necessary? God's high purpose for man required response to Him of his own free will, and man exercised that free will to disobey, and enter the state of rebellion which is the root of all his troubles. Not only has man been contaminated, but all his planet, so that Paul talks of the whole of creation as being in a kind of cosmic labour awaiting deliverance.[6]

The concept of the Fall is central to the whole subject of abortion, and the Christian's involvement, as has been made clear by Helmut Thielicke. "With respect to the medical indications for abortion this break between the original state and the conditions of this aeon becomes acute in that the conflict between life and life does not occur in the original order of creation, and therefore the order of creation cannot provide a direct solution of the conflict. Where there is suffering and sickness, they cannot be interpreted as being the result of God's proper will, but are actually the reverse of this real will of God. It is not possible to trace back directly and indiscriminately to the creative will of God both the birth of children and the crippling of children, both the blossom and the 'frost that blights the springtime blossom,' and thereby transform Him from the Lord of the order of creation into what is basically only a First Cause."[7]

While as individuals we can through the atoning work of Christ upon the Cross abandon our disobedience and regain that fellowship with God which had been His original plan, we still live in a world which no longer represents God's will. Hence disease. Hence poverty. Hence

[3] F. Schaeffer, *The God Who is There*, London, 1969, Hodder and Stoughton.
[4] Rom. 8: 17.
[5] D. M. Jackson, *The Sanctity of Life*, London, 1962, Christian Medical Fellowship.
[6] Rom. 8:22.
[7] H. Thielicke, *The Ethics of Sex*, London, 1964, Jas. Clarke.

disharmony. Hence malformations. Hence each and every cause which brings women to the doctors' consulting rooms, seeking abortion. It is not, in many cases, anything to do with their individual sin, but that the whole world has been disordered by the sin of man, and all its inhabitants, sinners and saints, suffer together.

Abortion in the Old Testament

There is only one clear reference to abortion in the Old Testament, and this refers to accidental miscarriage. In contrast there is an Assyrian Law: "If a woman has cast the fruit of her womb by her own act and charge and proof have been brought against her, she shall be impaled and shall not be buried."[8] It is possible to argue that the absence of a corresponding Israelite law meant that criminal abortion was unknown, or that it was lightly regarded! However, as this law is unique in the Assyrian and Babylonian texts, Professor Wiseman feels this is a specific and therefore rare case.[9]

The passage in Exodus[10] reads, in the Revised Version of 1881:

And if men strive together, and hurt a woman with child, so that her fruit depart, and yet no mischief follow: he shall surely be fined, according as the woman's husband shall lay upon him; and he shall pay as the judges determine. But if any mischief follow, then thou shalt give life for life, eye for eye, tooth for tooth . . . .

However, in the New English Bible of 1970 it reads:

When in the course of a brawl, a man knocks against a pregnant woman so that she has a miscarriage but suffers no further hurt, then the offender must pay whatever fine the woman's husband demands after assessment.
(Then, as a new paragraph, it goes on) Wherever hurt is done, you shall give life for life, eye for eye, tooth for tooth . . . .

There are two divergent schools of interpretation; the source of disagreement turns on the meaning of the Hebrew word for fruit, and a mistranslation in the Septuagint version, which Jerome was later to use.

The common interpretation is that if the woman, as a result of this brawl, goes into labour and has a miscarriage or stillbirth; then a fine is payable, but if harm follow, i.e. if she die, then the full life for life is exacted.[11] The second view is that the fine is payable for the blow,

[8] G. R. Driver and J. C. Miles, *The Assyrian Laws*, Oxford, 1935, Clarendon Press.
[9] D. J. Wiseman, Personal communication.
[10] Exod. 21: 23.
[11] Those taking this view include, among Jewish scholars: I. Jakobovits. Jewish Views on Abortion. *Abortion and the Law* (Ed. D. Smith), Cleveland, 1967, Press of Western Reserve University. I. Klein. Abortion—A Jewish View. *Dublin Review*, Winter, 1967/8 **241**, 382. Protestant scholars whose papers appear in *Birth Control and the Christian* (*op. cit.*) are divided. This view is supported by B. K. Waltke, J. H. Scanzoni and K. Kantzer.

providing that no harm follow to mother or child.[12] (A third depends on the mistranslation of "that no harm follow" by "her child be born imperfectly formed," and leads to the view that a fine would do if the fetus had not been ensouled;[13] but that the crime was murder if it had.[14] The last view does not appear to command support now.)

It would seem fairly obvious that in any case the text implies a difference in the eyes of the law between the fetus and a person.[15]

The Sixth Commandment

"Thou shalt not kill." Surely this rules abortion out of court? Joy Davidman talks of "our terrifying inner confusion over the sixth commandment" from the problems of the atomic bomb to those killers of soul who spend their lives twisting and bullying wives or children or employees out of all human shape.[16] For thus widening the command she has our Lord's own example.[17]

But the command is also narrower. On the very next page of Exodus we have the command to kill those who break certain laws. It is nonsense to suggest God forbids what He also commands. The verb used ("*Rasach*") refers to "illegal killing inimical to the community,"[18] and is rightly rendered by the New English Bible "Thou shalt not murder." It is important to see the Commandments in their perspective;[19] for the first time murder is conceived not as a natural privilege, to be paid for in blood money if necessary, but as a moral transgression.[16]

Biblical Grounds for Taking Life

The Old Testament Scriptures tell us that God commanded the life of members of His covenanted people was to be forfeited on a number of

[12] This view is trenchantly upheld by J. W. Montgomery in "The Christian View of the Fetus," whose bibliography lists other authorities supporting his position (*Birth Control and the Christian: op. cit.*).

[13] For a discussion on the time of "ensoulment" see ch. 10.

[14] Quintus Tertullian, quoted by I. Jakobovits, *op. cit.*

[15] W. F. M. Wallace disagrees. He argues that in this case the abortion was unintentional. The attacker may not even have been aware that the woman was pregnant. In his view the lesser penalty reflected lesser responsibility on the part of the taker of life, but not a less valuable life. ("A Biblical View of Prenatal Life." *In the Service of Medicine*, Jan. 1971.)

[16] Joy Davidman, *Smoke on the Mountain*, London, 1955, Hodder and Stoughton.

[17] Matt. 5: 21-22.

[18] E. McDonagh, "Ethical Problems of Abortion," *Theology*, 1968, **71**, 443.

[19] R. Wallace has written, "The Commandments begin with a reminder of the grace that has liberated the people of God. Because this grace has now to be motive for all their conduct towards God and towards men . . . they have to learn to live not in the hope of attaining salvation by moral or religious striving but in the sheer gladness of a salvation already freely given by a God who knows all their weakness and is aware of all the havoc that their rebellious natures can work in His plans." (*The Ten Commandments: A Study of Ethical Freedom*, Edinburgh, 1965, Oliver and Boyd). For a similar Roman Catholic view see S. E. Kutz in *Contraception and Holiness* (Ed. Abp T. L. Roberts), London, 1965, Collins.

grounds[20] that involved disobedience to His laws. They also tell us that He commanded Israel to acts of genocide,[21] and Himself wiped out all but a faithful handful in the flood.[22] The modern theological attitude is that some of these events, such as the flood, never happened, and that others were due to the misunderstanding of God's will in an early phase of religious development. Orthodox belief, modern as well as ancient, finds this interpretation unacceptable.

Following Sir Frederick Catherwood's dictum that biblical words normally mean what they say and say what they mean,[23] what can we make of the fact that the Bible apparently treats life much more lightly than we do? Can it be that only as modern man has lost any belief in the after-life has death become the ultimate tragedy? It appears from Scripture that there are other matters more important than terrestrial life. The purity of His people is one such matter, so that those within who disobeyed, or those without who might lead His people to worship other gods, must be destroyed. In New Testament times the story of Peter's challenge to Ananias and Sapphira exemplifies the same truth.[24]

It is easy to notice the mistakes which some in the Church down the ages have made by acting on specific commands given by God in other times to other of His servants.[25] Modern man is just as mistaken in imagining that because he partially understands the natural laws by which a fetus is conceived and develops he is entitled to forget the One whose laws they are. The Old Testament reminds us that God is the giver of life,[26] the One by whose power fetal development occurs,[27] and to whom every living soul belongs.[28] This being so, life is no to be taken on one's own initiative, not even for that most inescapable of obligations, the blood feud.[29] Man is not to cause the death of the innocent and guiltless,[30] for the blood of the innocent cries to God from the ground.[31]

Conclusions

What can we learn from the Old Testament germane to our present

[20] See e.g. Exod. 21: 18,19,20.
[21] See e.g. I Sam. 15: 3.
[22] Gen. 7: 23 (also 6: 13).
[23] Sir Frederick Catherwood in his appendix on "Christian Authority" (in *The Christian Citizen*, London, 1969, Hodder and Stoughton) details seven grounds for Biblical interpretation, of which the one here quoted is the sixth.
[24] Acts 5: 1–11.
[25] A typical example of criticism of the Church's action will be found in Glanville Williams (*The Sanctity of Life and the Criminal Law*, London, 1958, Faber). This should be read, however, in the light of a critique by D. W. Vere ("Humanism and the Sanctity of Life." In *In the Service of Medicine*, July, 1960).
[26] Zech. 12: 1.
[27] Ps. 139: 13, and Job 10: 8–12.
[28] Ezek. 18: 4.
[29] Gen. 4: 15, and Num. 35: 15–25.
[30] Exod. 23: 7.
[31] Gen. 4: 10.

study? On the general setting of sexual ethics, guided by Professor Noonan, we notice four propositions: Woman is a person like man; marriage is good; fecundity is good, but human sexual love has a value independent of fertility; sexual acts are not necessarily good.[32]

On the specific topic of abortion we have to rely on inferences. Dr. D. W. Vere has commented: "It is promised that men will be guided if they are meek. To the arrogant and self-willed the Bible yields nothing, and it is the embarrassment and strength of Christian ethics that the quality of the inference drawn from the Bible depends upon the willingness of the person to submit to God."[33] It seems to me that we have learned two things: all life belongs to God; and all God's people must obey Him, even taking life when He wills it, but only when He wills it. As Karl Barth, writing about abortion, has put it: "If God can will that this germinating life should die in some other way, might He not occasionally do so in such a way as to involve the active participation of these other men? How can we deny absolutely that He might have commissioned them to serve Him in this way, and that their action has thus been performed and had to be performed, in this service?"[34]

In one word: obedience. Obedience, not to a tyrant, but to the One who has loved us (patients, ministers and doctors) with an everlasting love.[35]

[32] J. H. Noonan, *Contraception*: "A History of its Treatment by the Catholic Theologians and Canonists." 1965, Harvard University Press.

[33] D. W. Vere, "Why the Preservation of Life?" In *Ethical Responsibility in Medicine* (Ed. V. Edmunds and G. C. Scorer), Edinburgh, 1967, Livingstone.

[34] K. Barth, *Church Dogmatics* Part III, Vol. 4, Edinburgh, 1961, T. & T. Clark.

[35] Jer. 31: 3; 2 Pet. 3: 9.

CHAPTER 13

THE SPIRITUAL STATUS OF THE FETUS

Thus we are men, and we know not how: There is something in us that can be without us, and will be after us; though it is strange that it hath no history what it was before us, nor cannot tell how it entered in us. SIR THOMAS BROWNE[1]

FOR MORE THAN TWO THOUSAND YEARS MEN HAVE ARGUED ABOUT THE fetus, the origin of the soul, the time of its infusion, and the fate of the soul in induced abortion.[2] It has been found difficult to make a moral judgement against killing the newborn baby which would not also apply to the fetus just prior to birth, or a moral statement appropriate to the cell immediately after conception which is inappropriate to it before that event.[3] A case has been made[4] for considering life as a continuum from the present back to the first emergence of the DNA molecule[5] three thousand million years ago.[6]

In this situation of doubt the Roman Catholic Church has played for maximum safety for the soul by absolutely forbidding abortion on any grounds,[7] although never pronouncing on the time of the infusion of the soul. Protestant theologians have avoided stating explicitly that the soul is implanted at conception, but they too are none the less clear as to the implications of abortion. Dietrich Bonhoeffer remarked: "To raise the question whether we are here concerned with a human being or not is merely to confuse the issue. The simple fact is that God certainly intended

[1] Sir Thomas Browne, *Religio Medici*, Norwich, 1642.
[2] A useful review of modest size is that by L. A. Kalland, "Views and Position of the Christian Church—An Historical Review," in *Birth Control and the Christian* (see ch. 1 fn. 12). For fuller treatment see J. Noonan, *Contraception:* "A History of its treatment by the Catholic Theologians and Canonists," 1965, Harvard University Press.
[3] Church Assembly Board for Social Responsibility. *Abortion: An Ethical Discussion.* London, 1965, Church Information Officer.
[4] J. Lederberg, "A Geneticist Looks at Contraception and Abortion," *Annals of Internal Medicine*, 1967, **67**, Suppl. 7, 25.
[5] DNA (deoxyribonucleic acid) carries the genetic information in each cell of the body, and replicates itself in each new daughter cell.
[6] "There are a living human sperm and a living human ova before the moment of fertilization, and all that happens at that moment is that two squads of 23 chromosomes each perform a nimble quadrille on the genetic drill-field and rearrange themselves into a platoon of 46. There is no more human life present after this rearrangement than there was before ... what life there is is the same as before; it is continuous." C. Means, in *Abortion in a Changing World, op. cit.*
[7] Pius XI, Papal Encyclical *Casti Connubii* 1930.

to create a human being, and that this nascent human being has been deliberately deprived of his life. And that is nothing short of murder."[8] Karl Barth inculpates a wide circle: the woman, the operator, the relatives who allow, promote, or assist the act, "and in a wider but no less strict sense the society whose conditions and mentality directly or indirectly call for such acts and whose laws even permit them." He maintains that no pretext can alter the fact that the whole circle of those concerned is in the strict sense engaged in the killing of human life . . . it is a man and not a thing, not a mere part of the mother's body.[9]

Where such intellectual giants have pronounced it may seem presumptuous to reopen the matter, but this we must do, for two reasons.

First, while philosophers meditate we must not only meditate, but act. I who am due to perform an abortion tomorrow must know whether I am to have a murder on my conscience.

Scientific Pointers

Secondly, we have new scientific evidence. Science can say nothing about the soul; it can provide some of the data which has to be considered in reaching our conclusions. There are three recent insights in embryology and obstetrics to be considered.

IDENTICAL TWINS: If the soul is infused at conception what about identical twins who separate from a common cell-mass after conception? Some have sought to solve the problem by dating the beginning of life from the implantation of the embryo into the uterine wall some four to six days later.[10] This argument will not do, for in 4% of identical twins the separation does not take place until well after implantation.[11] Unless we are to agree with the suggestion that the soul splits likewise we are driven to conclude that in some cases at least its infusion is not before the fourth week of intrauterine life.

FETAL WASTAGE: Embryologists now believe that anything up to half of all conceptions end in spontaneous miscarriage, usually very early on.[12] The mother is often completely ignorant of the fact that she had conceived, perhaps merely noticing that she passed a few clots with her normal monthly loss. If all these are possessed of souls the implications for the after-life are formidable.

Protestant theology denies the existence of a limbo, but affirms that the souls of the innocent are received into heaven. We must also recall that free will implies that a certain proportion of men will refuse the

[8] D. Bonhoeffer, Ethics, London, 1963, Fontana.
[9] K. Barth, Church Dogmatics, Part III, Vol. 4, Edinburgh, 1961, T. & T. Clark
[10] P. Ramsey, "The Sanctity of Life," Dublin Review, Spring, 1967, 241, 3.
[11] These are the monochorial monoamniotic type of monozygous twins. See M. G. Bulmer, The Biology of Twinning in Man, Oxford, 1970, Clarendon Press.
[12] G. W. Corner, "An Embryologist's View." In Abortion in a Changing World, op. cit.

divine mercy. If all these early miscarried fetuses possess souls, the majority of "humans" in heaven will have never even reached the stage of being organized into fetal human shape.[13] Without doubt God could largely people heaven with "human" souls in this way, but in that case it is difficult to understand the function of their brief sojourn on this planet: in fact in my view the idea would debase the doctrine of Man. Many centuries ago Aelred of Rievaulx wrote, "the three powers of memory, understanding and will are of the very substance of the soul."[14]

IN VITRO CONCEPTIONS: Human eggs have now been successfully fertilized outside the body, and have gone on to divide at least up to the sixteen-cell stage.[15] As I write I look at the microphotograph of one of these embryos, grown in culture. Does this cell-mass, which is not the result of human intercourse, which has never occupied a human body since fertilization, possess a soul? When the experiment is over and the material is tipped down the sluice, is a soul being destroyed? To think so requires in my judgement a trivialization of the meaning of the soul.

The Soul an Entity?

Bearing these facts in mind I find it impossible to believe that the soul is present in the early embryo – that is if "soul" is to have any real content. Perhaps we have been on the wrong track. Do we *have* a soul? James Barr notes: "The soul is not an entity with a separate nature from the flesh and possessing or capable of a life on its own. Rather it is the life animating the flesh. Soul and flesh do not therefore go separate ways, but the flesh expresses outwardly the life or soul . . . . Man does not have a soul, he is a soul."[16]

Whatever definition we attempt, difficulties face us.[17] A Professor of Biology, advocating easy abortion, writes "People who worry about the moral danger of abortion do so because they think of the fetus as a human being: hence equate feticide with murder. Whether the fetus is or is not a human being is a matter of definition, not fact, and we can

[13] I have here developed an idea from K. Kantzer, "The Origin of the Soul as Related to the Abortion Question," *Birth Control and the Christian* (see ch. 1 fn. 12).

[14] St. Aelred, "On the Soul." Quoted in A. Squire, *Aelred of Rievaulx*, London, 1969, S.P.C.K.

[15] R. G. Edwards, P. C. Steptoe and Jean Purdy. "Fertilization and Cleavage *in vitro* of Preovulator Human Oocytes." *Nature*, 1970, **227**, 1307.

[16] James Barr, Article "Soul" in *Hasting's Dictionary of the Bible*.

[17] D. W. Vere has suggested the definition "*Life* is possessed by those who have personality either present or as a future potential." He goes on to suggest that "we may recognize personality (which is at root the ability to respond to God) by the ability, however slight, to respond to us." (*Why the Preservation of Life?* op. cit). Does this chain of definition still hold now that we know that the fetus can, while still in the womb, respond to us if we make a loud noise or shine a light on the mother's abdomen?

define any way we wish."[18] However, Daniel Callahan has trenchantly criticized that position. "The enunciated principle of defining *as one wishes* provides no philosophical basis for distinguishing between abortion and infanticide. A power group society could by use of the principle define the chronically sick, the senile, the elderly as non-human, and thus justify the taking of their lives on grounds of the social good to be obtained."[19] We would do better to heed the opinion of a Professor of Obstetrics "whatever web of words you like to weave to describe an unborn baby, the real case at issue is whether or not that unborn baby is important."[20]

No manner of skilful definition will evade the fact that there is the likelihood (assuming the woman has already missed one period), and the very strong probability (assuming she has missed two) that the fetus can be born alive and enter into its inheritance. I am not now thinking of its socio-economic inheritance which I am well aware may be grim, but of God's eternal purposes and offer to it.

It will help us to look at a typical Christian attitude. A Canadian pastor has finely written, "Jesus said 'Let the little children come to Me, and do not hinder them; for to such belongs the kingdom of God.' You see the destiny of every child conceived in the womb is the kingdom of God. In God's eyes children are not conceived to add to Canada's natural resources; they are not conceived for a life of bourgeoise middle-aged selfishness; they are not conceived to play in bed and in cars hurtling to nowhere. The intention of God for every child conceived in the womb is that he grow up into God's kingdom, that he live in Christ and, living in Christ, that he pass one day through the portals of death into life everlasting with God himself. This is why Jesus said 'See that you do not despise one of these little ones.' "[21]

A Tentative Solution

So far as God's purposes for children are concerned, this statement is both wholly admirable and true. So far as it applies to every conceptus, I disagree.

As well as the above scientific grounds for dissenting, there are theological grounds. If the author is right about God's intention, then it is frustrated (even without man's deliberate sin) by miscarriage in a high proportion of cases. Then also this view implies that every conception is God's will. Granted that God can make the wrath of men to praise

[18] G. Hardin, "Abortion or Compulsory Pregnancy," *Journal of Marriage and the Family*, May, 1968.
[19] D. Callahan, *Abortion: Law, Choice and Morality*, New York and London, 1970, Collier-Macmillan.
[20] I. Donald, "An Exercise in Destruction." Quoted by G. A. D. Scott, *op. cit.*
[21] G. A. D. Scott, "Abortion, the Last Resort," 1968, United Church (of Canada) Renewal Fellowship.

Him, and that He sometimes uses ungodly men as His instruments,[22] I find it difficult to believe that God can look in anything but anger on a drunken wretch impregnating a terrified girl, or even his exhausted wife. My own view is that while the fetus is to be cherished increasingly as it develops, we should regard its first breath at birth as the moment when God gives it not only life, but the offer of Life. Now this is not an example of the Christian retreating in the face of a scientific attack. This surely is the original biblical teaching that God took a fully-formed man and breathed into his nostrils the breath of life, and thus the man became a living creature – Adam.[23] It is, moreover, the common feeling of man-kind, certainly of those of us who work in labour-wards: an audible sigh of relief goes round the delivery room when the baby gives that first gasp. When a spontaneous miscarriage occurs parents may grieve, but we do not feel that we have lost a child. From time to time obstetricians have the distress of delivering a stillborn baby. We may have felt this fetus kick under our examining hands, we may have listened to its heart-beat repeatedly over four months, yet when the tragedy occurs we do not feel, "Here is a child who has died," but rather, "Here is a fetus which so nearly made it." Miscarriages are not buried, are not named, are not (except in the Roman communion)[24] baptized. This sense that the un-successful pregnancy is ephemeral is well conveyed by David in one of his psalms:

> May they melt, may they vanish like water,
> may they wither like trodden grass,
>   like an abortive birth that melts away
>   or a still-born child which never sees the sun![25]

There is, however, a theological difficulty here. We read in the Bible of God's interest in this man or that before his birth.[26] Solomon, the Psalmist's son, wrote "You do not know how a pregnant woman comes to have a body and a living spirit in her womb; . . ."[27] The matter cannot be settled by pushing His interest back to conception, for to Jeremiah the Lord said, "Before I formed you in the womb I knew you for my own."[28]

It seems we can approach a solution by using a legal analogy. A live-born child (or his representative) can sue for damages suffered *in utero*, suffered even as far back as the first month of intra-uterine life. Being a person he is seen in retrospect to have been a person from conception. But the stillborn cannot have such a claim made in his name. He has never been a person, and even in retrospect therefore had no legal rights.[29]

[22] Ps. 76: 10. Isa. 44: 28.
[23] Gen. 2: 7.
[24] T. J. O'Donnell, In discussion reported in *Abortion in a Changing World, op. cit.*
[25] Ps. 58: 7-8, NEB.
[26] King David and the Apostle Paul are examples.
[27] Eccl. 11: 5, NEB.
[28] Jer. 1: 5.
[29] D. Granfield, A Catholic Lawyer's View. In *Abortion in a Changing World, op. cit.*

It seems to me that similarly a Christian can look down at her new-born baby and see him as a gift from God, who has overshadowed not only conception and intra-uterine growth, but whose purposes for the child are from eternity.[30] However, the same Christian, suffering a miscarriage or even having submitted to a necessary therapeutic abortion in her next pregnancy, is not to feel that God has let a child slip. He had no plans for such a child. This is not to call in question the wisdom of the conception, for God's purposes for the parents may have required this experience.

The fact that we may deny to the fetus the attribute of a soul, or the full status of life, does not in the least denigrate its worth. The mother will sometimes say "I know I'm only two months gone, but to me it is a person." And this sense is not confined to the religious. A personal friend, an agnostic, wrote to me recently:

> It is, I suppose, an enlightening thought that when, as a non-Christian, I was actually offered an abortion when I became accidentally pregnant some years ago, neither my husband nor I would consider it. This in spite of the fact that we did not want another child and also that, in spite of statistical re-assurances, we worried considerably at the thought of bringing a second mongol into the world. In fact, I aborted spontaneously at 3 months – no indication why, but doubtless providential! The point I am trying to make is that, while I hold liberal views, and think I regard a fetus as a bundle of cells, at least for 5 months, my own was a prospective person at 1 month. Very illogical, but not only female illogicality – my husband agreed.

We may therefore discount the sweeping statement, made by more than one author,[31] that the fetus is not a reality to the mother prior to quickening.

From the moment of conception the couple concerned have not the option whether a proferred gift be accepted, but rather whether an already bestowed gift should be spurned.[32] They have already entered the incalculably momentous role of being parents and ancestors;[33] the mother has already acquired all the rights and duties that belong to motherhood.[34] Among these the overriding one is the care of the growing fetus within her but, with its own genetic makeup, circulation and nervous system, not part of her. Its potentialities are hers to protect and cherish, not to be

[30] The Christian cannot accept the view advanced by Sir Peter Medawar (*Annals of Internal Medicine*, 1967, **67**, Suppl. 7, 61). "A hundred years ago it would have been perfectly reasonable for the married couple to think that the child they conceived on any one occasion was a unique and necessary product of that occasion . . . . One of the things that has changed is the realization from Mendelian principles that the actual child conceived on any one occasion is one of a million possible children who might perfectly well have been conceived on that occasion if the luck of meeting of sperm and egg have been otherwise."
[31] For example J. Howells (as quoted by R. B. White) and Natalie Shainess. Both in "Abortion and Psychiatry." In *Abortion in a Changing World, op. cit.*
[32] H. Thielicke, *The Ethics of Sex*, London, 1964, Jas Clarke.
[33] C. S. Lewis, *The Four Loves*, London, 1960, Bles.
[34] Lord Fisher of Lambeth, *In the Service of Medicine*, April, 1967.

bartered for a colour television or a holiday on the Costa Brava, or for anything where (in Karl Barth's phrase) the calculation and venture cannot take place before God, and in responsibility to Him.[9]

"Where the heart has no reasons surrounding nascent life with sanctity, there will always be 'fresh indications' for abortion."[10]

CHAPTER 14

NEW TESTAMENT GUIDANCE

You humans have all kinds of words like pain, and suffering, and unhappiness, and weariness that we robots have to be taught to understand, and they don't seem to us to be useful things to have. I feel very sorry that you must have these things and be so uncertain and so fragile. It disturbs my compassion-circuit.

JOHN WYNDHAM[1]

THE CENTRAL COMMANDMENT OF THE NEW TESTAMENT: TO LOVE the Lord our God utterly, and because of this to love our neighbour, has already been looked at in an earlier chapter. But how does this work out?

The Bible is not, as many suspect, a book the Christian uses to find proof-texts in support of his predetermined action. It is a guide.

Personal Case 14.1. One day in 1968 I had referred to me a girl of 16, who had already had an abortion performed elsewhere at 15. The doctor's letter read "I am sure that termination is necessary for the good of her mental and physical health, but shudder to think what it might do morally." Having examined her and made sure she was pregnant, and not suffering from any disease, I was blunt and brief in my rejection.

Recounting that case to a colleague, shortly after, it suddenly struck me to wonder if that is the manner in which the Lord Jesus would have talked to the girl, had He been the consultant gynaecologist? The next morning my ordinary routine Bible reading reached the passage where Christ says: "Be compassionate as your Father is compassionate. Pass no judgement and you will not be judged. Do not condemn and you will not be condemned. Acquit and you will be acquitted." That was God's word to me about that case. I have never doubted that I was right in rejecting her request; I was wrong in my manner of doing so. Going back over the passage I then noted just before: "You will be a son to the Most High, because He Himself is kind to the ungrateful and wicked."[2]

Compassion, irrespective of desserts: that to me is biblical guidance in abortion. What degree of compassion? Like the Father's. The Greek word (*oiktirmōn*) used in the passage, is spelled out in the Amplified

---

[1] J. Wyndham, *The Seeds of Time*, London, 1956, Michael Joseph.
[2] Lk. 6: 35-37.

version:[3] "So be merciful – sympathetic, tender, responsive and compassionate – even as your Father is (all these)." It is used in only one other place in the New Testament: "You have seen the purpose of the Lord, how the Lord is compassionate and merciful."[4] We have been set a very high standard.

The Meaning of Compassion

An astringent cartoon in *Pulse* showed two gowned and masked doctors leaving a private abortion clinic for the bank, laden down with banknotes. As they pass a poster reading "Crossman worried about 'on demand' abortion," one comments "He simply doesn't appreciate our dedicated compassion."[5] At a slightly more serious level a patient told one of my colleagues, "I sleep with my boy-friends out of compassion."

If we reject these definitions of compassion as inadequate, what do we mean by the word? In the New Testament there are two other Greek words translated by "compassion."

There is *splanchna*, bowels, an anatomical word. "*Splanchna* is a spontaneous, impulsive and emotional word arising out of the depth of human feeling. It always issues in immediate action. It cannot help itself. It sees a need and must act. This is the word used many times of Jesus Christ in His earthly ministry. The sight of individuals in need 'moved Him to compassion.' "[6]

Then there is *eleos*, occasionally translated "compassion" but more often "mercy." "Two important points must be made here. First mercy never stands by itself (as compassion does). It is linked with truth and right, justice and judgement. It is in balance with these. Secondly mercy is constructive and positive. It is concerned to lift the recipient to right living and true relationships."[6]

The Greek word (*oiktirmōn*) in our basic command is in most New Testament versions translated by "mercy" rather than by "compassion."

We can best get to the heart of these words by seeing how it worked out in our Lord's own ministry. The most useful illustration was in His dealings with the woman taken in adultery.[7] First note what Christ did not do: He did not decry the law as old-fashioned, He did not make light of her sin, He did not say, "That's all right, forget it." He did save her from her accusers, He did remind them that they too, as sinners, were under the same judgement, He did not even look her in the face, presumably because of sorrow for her sin (which one day He would bear)

[3] The Amplified New Testament, Marshall, Morgan and Scott.
[4] Jas. 5: 11.
[5] Cartoon by "Lyons" in *Pulse*, May 3, 1969. It will be found reproduced in R. F. R. Gardner, "Abortion in England Today: Confronting the Patient." *Soteria*, May, 1971.
[6] Anon. "A Compassionate Society," *In the Service of Medicine*, July, 1970.
[7] Jn. 7: 53–8:11. For a masterly discussion of the whole episode see G. Campbell Morgan, *The Great Physician*, London, 1937, Marshall Morgan and Scott.

and embarrassment, until all other had gone. Then He spoke those marvellous words discharging her from the tribunal which she had expected to condemn her, adding the words: "Do not sin again." The Christ who dealt so tenderly with this woman is the one who in His teaching demanded consecration: a man looking lustfully at a woman had, Jesus said, already committed adultery with her in his heart.[8]

When Christ healed a person's immediate physical need, He changed that person's character. There was no return to the old ways.

We have seen then that compassion is not a softness leading to the line of least resistance,[9] it is not a way of concession,[10] it is a loving hand in need leading them to a new life.

Now we see the tensions on the doctor in an abortion request. Although many humanists feel entitled to push their religious views (e.g. "every woman has the right to decide whether to bear her child or not") in the patient–doctor relationship, the Christian feels unable to raise the matter lest he be accused of abusing his office. (In the private-patient relationship this, of course, is different, for the patient has chosen this doctor, whose personality includes and is moulded by his faith.) This is frustrating because he is well aware, in these days of psychosomatic medicine, that internal disharmony is often the root of the patient's troubles. As a psychiatrist recently put it, "One reason why more pregnancies are unwanted is that there are more and earlier sexual relations . . . . There are also perhaps more unhappy people about."[11]

We must do what we can. To abort a pregnancy because it is extramarital may sound compassionate, but if it does nothing about the underlying problem it has no resemblance to true compassion.

Medical Case 14.2. A 25-year-old woman with two illegitimate children and the history of a termination a few months earlier, requested a further termination on the grounds that she could not afford another child. This was readily understandable. There were men willing to marry her, but unprepared to take over her existing children. Mere abortion here would postpone the problem but do nothing to get to the root of it, she would be back again in four or five months. The gynaecologist here (who is not a Christian) showed real compassion by setting the wheels in motion to contact the social workers in the patient's distant home town with a view to seeing what could be done about her basic situation.

Real compassion involves taking into consideration the factors to be discussed in part three of this book, in order that one's decision will help not only the woman's short term problems, but her future life.

We must not forget that there is to be compassion too for the fetus.

[8] Matt. 5: 28.
[9] H. Thielicke, *The Ethics of Sex*, London, 1964, Jas Clarke.
[10] Sir Arnold Lunn and G. Lean, *The New Morality*, London, 1964, Blandford Press.
[11] R. Tredgold, "Abortion: Whose Responsibility to Decide?" In *The Abortion Act, op. cit.*

Professor Kalland has said "Are we sure, on biblical grounds, that it is always the just and loving thing to bring into this demanding, complex world a badly deformed, perhaps even mentally incomplete individual? . . . . While the Scriptures establish the sanctity of life, the stress of Scripture is on the quality of life. Such being the case, and with the accompanying advancement in medical science, could not the decision to stop the growth of a terribly deformed fetus be viewed as an advancement in the Christian's moral stature rather than as an expression of depravity?"[12]

Canon Douglas Rhymes has put it well: "Let us be quite clear that compassion is not sentimentality. Nor is it without judgement . . . it is the identification which we can make in suffering with those who are themselves lonely, frustrated, sinful, weary and hopeless. Compassion does not sit in judgement from above and without, it sits in judgement with the beloved, and then suffers."[13] Now, as we have seen, it is not confined to Christians: "It becomes necessary for us in medicine with the rapid advances of our technology to safeguard our humanistic tradition . . . . What are the human values? Bronowski lists them as tenderness, kindliness, human intimacy and love. For medicine these characteristics may be comprised in the one quality of compassion. Compassion is not a characteristic of primitive societies nor of young children. It has to be acquired."[14] But how to acquire it? Jean Pochin, the medical social worker whose work I quote more than once states in her book: "The writer is convinced that Christianity offers by far the most perceptive approach to the mysteries of good and evil: moreover it identifies the source of the compassion which motivates the counsellors of today."[15]

Suffering as Character Builder

That God allows suffering, for the building up of the believer's character is a common biblical concept. The Church early learned to praise "The Father of mercies and God of all comfort,"[16] and to accept suffering from God's hands.

On this basis much has been written of the moral value in character-building of adverse circumstances. This is true when a person accepts suffering, either by her own strength of character, or in the strength God gives her.[17] Is it true when the suffering is unwillingly accepted, and unavoidable only because of the decision of some other human being? The attitude is still found, chiefly in Roman Catholic arguments on the

[12] L. Kalland, in "Abortion, can an Evangelical Consensus be Found?" in *Eternity* magazine (Philadelphia), February, 1971.
[13] Canon D. Rhymes, *No New Morality*, London, 1964, Constable.
[14] D. Hubble, "Medical Science, Science and Human Values," *BMJ*, 1966, **I**, 474.
[15] Jean Pochin, *Without a Wedding Ring: Casework with Unmarried Parents*, London, 1969, Constable.
[16] 2 Cor. 1: 3.
[17] 2 Cor. 12: 7–10.

pregnant woman whose life could only be saved by an abortion, that suffering and sacrifice are meritorious.

As this is an important argument let us take two examples. Many Christians martyred for their faith have had a rich experience of God's presence with them: from Stephen, who in Jerusalem about AD 33, cried "Look there is a rift in the sky; I can see the Son of Man standing at God's right hand!"[18] to Yona Kanamuseyi, who in Rwanda in 1964 sang

> Worthy is our Saviour King!
> Loud let His praises ring . . .

as they tied his hands prior to shooting him.[19] Are we then to bewail the present liberties which deny us such an experience?

Are we to regret our modern low infant mortality rates because in seventeenth-century Scotland bereaved parents got rich consolation from the letters of Samuel Rutherford? "You have lost a child; nay, she is not lost to you who is found to Christ . . . and you have to rejoice that you have now some treasure laid up in heaven . . . . The child hath but changed a bed in the garden and is planted up higher, nearer the sun, where he shall thrive better than in this out-field moor-ground."[20] Would anyone seriously suggest that we should allow more children to die in order that their parents could learn spiritual blessings? Or to put it in another way, are we wrong to rob people of the spiritual benefits of adversity by interfering with the "normal" course of nature?

Freely and willingly accepted, suffering has doubtless been an enabling experience; but in the context of the average abortion patient that is an irrelevant consideration.

Making Ethical Decisions

The New Testament does not contain clear instructions about every relationship of life, and this is quite intentional. The Christian life is a walk. Oscar Cullmann writes: "This walk Paul nowhere defines in the form of new commandments. Rather the working of the Holy Spirit shows itself chiefly in 'testing,' that is, in the capacity of forming the correct Christian ethical judgement at each given moment . . . . Certainty of moral judgement in the concrete case is in the last analysis the one great fruit that the Holy Spirit, this factor in redemptive history, produces in the individual man."[21]

This guidance is specific. Vague platitudes have no place. God has a

[18] Acts 7: 56.
[19] J. E. Church and colleagues. Forgive Them: The Story of an African Martyr, London, 1966, Hodder and Stoughton.
[20] S. Rutherford, Letters, Rotterdam, 1664, Edinburgh, 1891, Oliphant and Ferrier.
[21] O. Cullmann, Christ and Time, London, 1962, S.C.M. Press.

will for this particular problem;[22] and sometimes gives a word to be spoken boldly. This is exemplified well in Ronald Wallace's words, "When the prophet John the Baptist was sent by God to speak to King Herod about his evil way of life, John did not preach to Herod a sermon about some 'absolute ideal of Chastity.' He did not speak generally about the evil of the times, making vague references to the eternal law of God. He did not even say, 'It is wrong to commit adultery.' He rather said flatly and decidedly in the name of God, 'It is not lawful for you to have her.' "[23]

The guidance is specific, and it is for today. There is a real danger among Christians of adopting as their own the norms of secular society one generation after that secular society has moved on to different standards,[24] and in the name of the faith many scientific advances have been resisted. The introduction of anaesthesia in midwifery is a case to point: James Young Simpson wrote: "One day, on meeting the Rev. Dr. H–, he stopped me to say that he was just returning from absolving a patient's conscience on the subject, for she had taken chloroform during labour, and so avoided suffering, but she had felt unhappy ever since, under the idea that she had done something very wrong and very sinful."[25]

Such definite guidance is individual. It may lead a doctor to perform an abortion against the religious standards of his immediate society[24] or even against the laws of the state where these are rigid.[26] He will, of course, be often misunderstood by his contemporaries.

The judgement that matters, however, is not that of one's fellows but of God. Early Christian writers were all agreed that abortion was a violation of the love owed to one's neighbour, and that it was always loveless.[27] It would be terrible were they right. We must go on to search our consciences in the next chapter.

[22] This is a vital point. Daniel Callahan (*Abortion: Law, Choice and Morality*, New York 1970, Collier–Macmillan) bases his ethical approach on a different foundation. "Man is responsible for everything to do with man, including control over life and death . . . contraception, abortion, euthanasia . . . medical experimentation and the prolongation of life are all problems that fall totally within the sphere of human rules and human judgement . . . God Himself does not 'play God' as that phrase is usually understood. God does not directly and miraculously intervene in natural processes." (For evidence that God does, in fact, so interfere see e.g. Basilea Schlink, *Realities: The Miracles of God Experienced Today*, London, 1968, Oliphants.)

[23] R. S. Wallace, *The Ten Commandments: A Study in Ethical Freedom*, Edinburgh, 1965, Oliver and Boyd.

[24] R. P. Meye, "New Testament Texts Bearing on the Issue." In *Birth Control and the Christian*, *op. cit.*

[25] Sir James Y. Simpson. Letter to Dr Brothero Smith in *Obstetric Memoirs*. See also his pamphlet *Answers to the Religious Objections Advanced Against the Employment of Anaesthetic Agents in Midwifery and Surgery*, Edinburgh, 1847, Sutherland and Knox.

[26] K. Barth, *Church Dogmatics* Part III, vol. 4, Edinburgh, 1961, T. & T. Clark.

[27] J. Noonan, "The Catholic Church and Abortion." *Dublin Review*, Winter, 1967–8, **241**, 300.

CHAPTER 15

THE LESSER EVIL?

"May you live to be a pillar of the Kirk," said Mr. Muirhead.
"Keep a Gospel walk," said Mr. Proudfoot, "on the narrow rigging of the truth."
But Mr. Fordyce took the young man's hand, after saluting him, and held it with
a kind of wistful affection. "I pray," he said, "that your windows may be ever
open towards Jerusalem."   JOHN BUCHAN[1]

IN A SINLESS WORLD THERE WOULD BE NO SICKNESS, NO SUFFERING, NO
patients, no doctors and no need for abortion. In this present age,
however, these exist, and in this situation our study of Scripture has
led us to see that abortion, on at least some occasions, can be right. On
such an occasion, what is to be the attitude of the Christian, whether
doctor, adviser, or patient? This is a crucial matter, with implications
not only in abortion, but in other ethical problems which we face today.
To reach an answer involves an apparent detour.

The Christian Walk

We have noted that God made man to have fellowship with Himself,
and that, following man's rebellion, the restitution of this relationship
was so important to God that He was willing to come into the world as
a man, and pay the price of Gethsemane and Calvary in order that it
might be achieved.

The earliest Christians experienced this restored relationship. Paul
wrote, "I have been crucified with Christ: the life I now live is not my
life, but the life which Christ lives in me; and my present bodily life is
lived by faith in the Son of God, who loved me and sacrificed himself for
me."[2] Peter commanded his readers, "The One who called you is holy;
like him, be holy in all your behaviour."[3] Jude reminded the Church of
the "One who can keep you from falling and set you in the presence of
his glory, jubilant and above reproach."[4] It must be realized that this is
no mere rhetoric. When Paul wanted to exemplify the Christian life of
holiness he pointed to himself, and we need not doubt there would be
many willing to give him the lie, were that possible. We should remember

[1] J. Buchan, *Witchwood*, London, 1927, Hodder and Stoughton.
[2] Gal. 2: 20.
[3] 1 Pet. 1: 15.
[4] Jude 24.

too that the early Christians, who outloved their opponents, were living in a robust, alert, civilization not unlike our own.

Down through the centuries there have always been men who have lived Christ-like lives.[5] A missionary doctor in a vivid letter to his sister describes his awakening to the possibility of union with Christ. Reading Christ's statement that He is the vine and we disciples are the branches,[6] Hudson Taylor awoke to realize that the branches are not mere attachments to the vine, they are partakers of its life.[7] In our own day an American Trappist monk has recorded, "There is only one service to please Him, only one sorrow to be displeasing to Him, to refuse Him something, to turn away from Him, even in the slightest thing, even in thought, in a half-willed moment of appetite. In these things, and these alone, is sorrow, in so far as they imply separation, or the beginning, the possibility of separation from Him who is our life and all our joy."[8]

At the other end of the theological spectrum his daughter wrote of Harold St. John (a Bible teacher among the Christian Brethren): "There is no doubt that at this time he underwent some experience too sacred to speak about that elevated him into a radiance and freedom he had never known before. A rather solemn selfconscious holiness gave way to a sort of uncalculating joy as if he no longer had to watch his step in the heavenlies; he was at home there, self-forgetful; absorbed in Christ."[9]

As it cannot be denied that some such experience does exist, one is tempted to limit it to the "professionals:" the men and women whose whole time is given up to the work of the Church. Fortunately this is not true. While in Uganda one had the privilege of meeting many Baganda Christians, and some Europeans, of the *Balokole* – the "saved ones." These are orthodox Church folk (in Uganda they are Anglicans) who by the thousand have found their lives transformed in the forty years since the Ruanda Revival broke out.[10] It was a humbling experience to listen to Christians from many walks of life – postmaster, hospital washer woman, doctor – sharing their experiences of "walking in the light."[11]

All this may seem theologically naïve: those who think so must show comparable results in the lives of their followers before their criticisms can be considered. It may seem to smack of pietism: but those who imagine it implies a withdrawal from the world should recall that at one

[5] For a scholarly record of saints and sanctity in the Catholic, Orthodox, and Protestant communions see W. E. Sangster, *The Pure in Heart*, London, Epworth Press.
[6] Jn. 15: 5.
[7] J. Hudson Taylor, Letter dated Sept. 6, 1869, in *Hudson Taylor and the China Inland Mission*, London, 1918, Morgan and Scott.
[8] T. Merton, *Elected Silence*, London, 1949, Hollis and Carter.
[9] Patricia St. John, *Harold St. John*, Glasgow, Pickering and Inglis.
[10] A. C. S. Smith, *Road to Revival*, London, 1951, Ruanda Mission (CMS).
[11] 1 Jn. 1: 7.

stage after the second war, three of the four Ugandan kingdoms had a member of the Balokole in charge of the treasury.

Here in the industrialized West a new understanding of the mission and power of the Holy Spirit is to be found among all the orthodox denominations, including the Roman Catholic.[12] Christians, ordained and lay, meet in each others houses to share the experience of His power in their medical practices, their colleges, their homes.

This is what Christianity is all about. That union with Christ is the core of the faith has been maintained by James Stewart, a former Moderator of the General Assembly of the Church of Scotland: "Union with the divine (Paul knew) need be no transient splendour, flashing for a moment across life's greyness and then gone; it could be the steady radiance of a light unsetting, filling the commonest ways of earth with a gladness that was new every morning."[13]

Must the Doctor be a Second-rate Christian?

I have laboured this matter because, once having really understood what Christ offers in a life of constant touch with Him, nothing else will satisfy. This is the life we are meant to live, not just in Church on Sunday, but in the gynaecological out-patient clinic, and in the operating theatre. But how is our involvement in abortion usually seen by Christian writers? A British physician has expressed thus his view of sterilization and abortion: "To me, both are always wrongs, justifiable only when balanced against greater wrongs which they are aimed to avert. The alternatives are not right or wrong but rather more or less wrong. The old problem of 'tragic choice.' "[14] He was speaking at a symposium in America which included in its Affirmation[15] the conclusion: "As to whether or not the performance of an induced abortion is always sinful we are not agreed, but about the necessity and permissibility for it under certain circumstances we are in accord." In other words, to some of these Christian scholars abortion was necessary, permissible and sinful.

The Christian doctor, then, seems caught in a dilemma. "Sometimes we feel like withdrawing from the controversy, just opting out as our Catholic colleagues are able to do, and refusing to see patients requesting abortion, but would this be right? Surely it is essential for Christians to face up to their problems, not to escape from them."[16] But as Miss Sib-

---

[12] M. Harper, *Renewal* Magazine (London), Feb./Mar. 1970.

[13] J. S. Stewart, *A Man in Christ*, London, 1935, Hodder and Stoughton. This is an outstanding study of the doctrine as central to the Christian Faith. I have discussed its relevance to practical church issues (R. F. R. Gardner, "Union With Christ," *The Reformed Journal* (Grand Rapids) July/Aug., 1959).

[14] D. W. Vere, "Therapeutic Abortion and Sterilization as ethical problems." In *Birth Control and the Christian, op. cit.*

[15] See ch. 10 for fuller quotation.

[16] Elsie Sibthorpe, "A Definition of Life and Problems of Abortion." *In the Service of Medicine*, April, 1969.

thorpe has implied we cannot yield to that temptation, although to do so would be easy. H. Waddams carried the argument a stage further: "There are some who would like to evade the moral struggle, and therefore find it an easy way out to make a hard and fast rule that avoids the need to wrestle with ethical problems. But this is in itself a form of immorality because it is an evasion of the responsibility which has been placed upon us by the power and the freedom with which we are endowed."[17]

Is it then our lot to press on with an uneasy conscience? A Japanese colleague has said that the Christian doctors act according to their conscience, sometimes compelled to make the choice between two evils. "We perform the abortions with some reluctance."[18] This attitude has the support of some theologians e.g., Helmut Thielicke, who writes: "We can decide only subject to forgiveness. For we know there are no 'slick' solutions either theoretical or practical. We know that whatever we do we incur guilt ... sin is not confined to one particular decision, and that the choice of another alternative would mean the avoidance of sin. Rather here it becomes clear that we are moving in a world saturated with sin, and that no one can pass through it without incurring guilt."[19]

Does this mean that the real Christian life is not for us? Must we reconcile ourselves to being spiritually second-class citizens? When others sing:

> Take my hands and let them move
> At the impulse of Thy love[20]

must our lips remain sealed? We may watch others walk through life hand-in-hand with Jesus Christ, but for our part are we to drop that hand if we are to pick up the curette? Feelingly we acknowledge Paul's dilemma when he cries "I discover this principle, then: that when I want to do the right, only the wrong is within my reach .... Miserable creature that I am, who is there to rescue me ...?"[21] Are we twentieth century doctors never to be allowed to follow Paul in his subsequent words "No condemnation now hangs over the head of those who are in Christ Jesus. For the new spiritual principle of life in Christ Jesus lifts me out of the old vicious circle of sin and death."[22]

I cannot bring myself to believe that we must accept this situation. Paul instructed Titus to see that "those who have come to believe in God should see that they engage in honourable occupations, which are not

[17] H. Waddams, "Termination of Pregnancies: A Dialogue." Crucible, Jan. 1966.
[18] M. Ishihara, The Challenge and Control of the Population Explosion, op. cit.
[19] H. Thielicke, The Ethics of Sex, London, 1964, Jas Clarke.
[20] F. R. Havergal, Take My Life and Let it Be.
[21] Rom. 7: 21 (NEB).
[22] Rom. 8: 1 (Phillips).

only honourable in themselves, but also useful to their fellow-men."[23] Is medicine to be listed as a dishonourable occupation?

Doing the Will of God

We get real light on our problem from Archbishop William Temple's remark: "The rightness of an act then, nearly always, and perhaps always, depends on the way in which the act is related to circumstance: this is what is meant by calling it relatively right; but this does not in the least imply that it is only doubtfully right. It may be, in the circumstances, certainly and absolutely right."[24] I am not slipping back into "situational ethics" here, for the foremost of the circumstances must be a sense of acting for the Lord. The guidance Paul gave to Colossian Christians surely points to the answer "Let Christ's peace be arbiter" (someone has translated this "umpire") "in your hearts . . . . Whatever you are doing, whether you speak or act, do everything in the name of the Lord Jesus, giving thanks to God the Father through Him . . . . Whatever you are doing, put your whole heart into it, as if you were doing it for the Lord and not for men, knowing that there is a Master who will give you your heritage as a reward for your service."[25]

A Hausa of Nigeria, when happy at a decision, will use the idiom "My heart lies down about it." This is the picture: a heart at peace. It seems to me therefore, that the Christian must so consider each case that he can see his abortions, as he sees his caesarean sections, as among "those good deeds which God hath before ordained that we should walk in them."[26] Deeds done, in Christ's name, for Christ's sake. These are daunting words to write, but having once agreed that some abortions are right I can see no other attitude which does not deny the central meaning of the Christian life.

Now this conclusion will not commend itself to some Christians. There are problems facing other Christians to which I can see no answer of peace, but then I am not in their shoes. I do not claim to be able to see the answers to problems which may face me tomorrow. The whole point is that we are called to a Christian *walk*, to a life with Christ. The early believers, before the name "Christian" was coined, were called "the people of The Way." We are not battery-powered, but mains-powered: the contact has to be continuous. The answers I get to my problem today may not even be the answer another Christian in a similar situation will receive; no matter, the principle is identical – that at this unique point of space and time Christ has His hands.

[23] Tit. 3:8.
[24] Abp. W. Temple, quoted by J. Fletcher, *Moral Responsibility*, London, 1967, S.C.M. Press.
[25] Col. 3:15,17,23.
[26] Eph. 2:10.

In the field of abortion the Christian is called upon to do God's will, to be compassionate. Before he can decide what, in this particular instance, is the compassionate decision, he must weigh up all the factors. The remainder of this volume provides data towards making such a judgement, and thus to such an obedience. Surely the Christian attitude must be that expressed by an American gynaecologist: "When a pregnancy threatens the well-being of a patient and her family I will explore the threat just as thoroughly as I would a fever, a fibroid uterus, or an ovarian cyst. Then it becomes a matter of seeking the Lord's will in each particular case. I am confident that He can guide me in these decisions as He does in other areas of life."[27]

In our problems as Christians our prayer for each other should be "Now may the God of peace" (and note well that particular title of God) "make you perfect in every good work to do His will, working in you that which is well pleasing in His sight, through Jesus Christ; to whom be glory for ever and ever."[28]

[27] A. Beer in "Abortion, Can an Evangelical Consensus be Found?" *Eternity Magazine* (Philadelphia) Feb. 1971.
[28] Heb. 13: 20-21.

PART III

THE MEDICAL AND SOCIAL QUESTION: IS ABORTION JUSTIFIED IN THIS CASE?

CHAPTER 16

TYPICAL PROBLEMS AND OPINIONS

As medicine recognizes physiologically ectopic pregnancies which must be terminated for the sake of the life of the mother, perhaps ethics, with a combined genetic-social definition of the human person, and the state, with its recognition of the shifting roles of state and progenitors in a unique condominium, could argue with restraint that there are also some instances of socially or psychologically ectopic pregnancies, namely, those issuing from felonious, unwitting, or adulterous intercourse, or those warranting the removal of the unformed or unviable fetus either out of concern for the progenitors or society at large and in a few cases of extreme deformation out of a humane concern for the still unsocialized or perhaps unsocializable fetus itself.

GEORGE HUNTSTON WILLIAMS[1]

WE MUST NOW SET OUT TO ANSWER OUR SECOND QUESTION: Granted that some abortions are justified, is abortion *in this case* justified? For once the principle is granted it is only too easy to lengthen the list of indications to include the trivial. In the following chapters the various factors involved in abortion requests are considered.

Ideally it should be possible to quantify the risks in each problem, and thus reach a decision on statistical grounds. Unfortunately this ideal eludes us. Take, for instance, the woman who develops German measles in the eighth week of pregnancy. One day we may be able to assess accurately the risk of this woman's fetus being malformed. In the event, however, it turns out that the major problem is quite different; it is the fear this girl has of the outcome. Figures mean little to her. She lies in bed and pictures a baby crippled by blindness or deafness, or by even grosser malformations which are not, in fact, associated with German measles. The cold recital of statistics does nothing to comfort her.

If in such a clear-cut instance the problem turns out to be more complex than we had expected, how much more true is this of most cases which present themselves. For they are not cases – they are women and wives or lovers, perhaps mothers of other children. They are daughters and daughters-in-law. They are the neighbours of families warped by, or triumphant over, the care of malformed children. They are buyers of children's clothes, and payers of rent. And much more.

---

[1] G. H. Williams, "The Sacred Condominium." In *The Morality of Abortion: Legal and Historical Perspectives* (Ed. J. T. Noonan), 1970, Harvard University Press.

In order, therefore, to set the scene for our later studies in the various factors to be weighed, I prepared a series of "mock" cases. In contrast to the *Medical Cases* of other chapters, I have here followed Dr. H. Rosen's[2] example of distorting parts of individual cases, and combining cases to avoid identification. The individual cases cited are no more complex or bizarre than those which present themselves at every out-patient clinic.

The reader should stop after each case and make up his or her mind on the case. It may be of interest to come back and review these decisions after finishing the book.

MRS. A. is a woman of 28 years, with two children, a boy aged 10 and a girl aged 8 years. She is happily married. Her husband is a clerk who is having to spend an increasing amount of time helping his wife with the housework. Three years ago she was diagnosed as suffering from cardiac disease, which is causing increasing limitations in activities so that now she gets breathless on carrying out normal household duties. Cardiac surgery is being contemplated but she is told that any improvement may not be lasting. Despite the fact that she has been using a vaginal cap and contraceptive jelly she has missed two periods. On examination she is found to be an intelligent woman, rather underweight, with evidence of valvular heart disease, ten weeks pregnant.

MRS. B. is a 27-year-old woman who has had four pregnancies. The first baby was stillborn, being grossly abnormal: a hydrocephalic. The second child, now aged 6 years, suffers from a blood disease and has to go into hospital at frequent intervals for blood transfusion. Her third child has a spina bifida and the fourth child is a spastic, now aged 18 months who is unable to control his bowels. Her husband is a clerk and has been preparing for professional examinations, but has had to abandon these in order to help his wife with the family. It is now 5 weeks since her last period and she finds she cannot face the 8 months of waiting, wondering if the child is going to be normal. In addition she fears that she will be unable to cope with another baby in view of her present commitments.

MRS. C. is 40 years of age. She has had 6 children, the youngest of whom is now 9 years. Her husband is a skilled craftsman. She herself has recently started work in a shop. This she claims is largely for the sake of companionship and for the pleasure of at least being able to get out of the home. She is at present complaining of not having had a period for 4 months, and wondering whether, or not, she is at the 'change.' On examination she proves to be 16 weeks pregnant. On being told this she appears indignant stating that she cannot be bothered to start again at her age.

MRS. D. is aged 35 years; the mother of three children aged 13, 10 and 7 years. Her husband is a Trade Union Official. They are happily married, but live in a rather depressed and derelict area, although their own house is well kept. As a

---

[2] H. Rosen, *Therapeutic Abortion: Medical, Psychiatric, Legal, Anthropological and Religious Considerations.* New York, 1954, The Julian Press.

girl she had done well at school but had to leave at 15 because of the death of her mother. She had to run the home and help with the upbringing of her four younger brothers and sisters. She had always bitterly resented the fact that she had been unable to continue with her education. Having completed her family and sent the youngest child into school she was at last able to enter teacher training college. This satisfied her life-long ambition to use her brains and also provided her with intellectual companionship, which she was unable to find in her mining village. She has a further four terms to complete her course and now finds herself to be pregnant. On examination she proves to be an intelligent, co-operative woman. Since finding herself to be pregnant she has been sleeping badly and knows that her work is falling off. She is pathetically anxious for an abortion.

MRS. E. is aged 19 years. She has been married for 18 months and has one 15-month-old child. Her husband is a labourer earning £15 per week. In order to get together a home she goes out to work, full time, bringing a further £8 into the home. This is made possible by the fact that her mother looks after the baby. The patient has missed two periods. She is greatly distressed as a further pregnancy will be a financial catastrophe; almost all of their furniture is being paid for by hire purchase, and could not be continued. Furthermore, her mother who was unhappy about the marriage in the first place will be very annoyed, and may well refuse to help with the children in the future. She and her husband have been practising *coitus interruptus*, not being aware that there were any other methods obtainable apart from 'The Pill' which she felt she could not afford. She herself would like to have another child when the economic situation permits. On examination she is a woman of limited education, obviously sincere and anxious to do the best for the family. It is confirmed that she is 8 weeks pregnant.

MRS. F. is aged 35 years. She has four children, ages 12, 10, 8 and 6 years. Her husband is a schoolmaster. She herself is a housewife. They have a nice home which is normally happy. She admits to a single act of folly, resulting in adultery with the husband of a friend. He is of another race. He has two children. It is now 6 weeks since her last period. She does not know whether her neighbour, or her husband, is the father of the baby, but if the former, the fact will be unmistakable after delivery. On examination she is a likeable woman, in great distress with full insight into the problem and her own responsibility for it.

MRS. G., aged 30 years, has been a widow for the last 6 years, her husband having been killed in a motor accident. In the month after her husband had been killed she had an endogenous depression and required electric convulsive therapy in a mental hospital. She was an in-patient for two months. She has not required treatment since. She has two children, aged 9 and 7 years. For the last three years she has been keeping company with a bachelor. Marriage has occasionally been suggested, but he has never been prepared to discuss a date. Recently they have started to have intercourse. She has not taken precautions, and now finds herself to be 10 weeks pregnant. On questioning she admits that subconsciously she may have hoped to be pregnant in order to persuade him into marriage. In actual fact, he has dropped the courtship completely since she told him of her pregnancy. On examination the pregnancy is confirmed. It is difficult to elicit her history, and she appears rather withdrawn. She burst into tears on several occasions during the interview.

MRS. H. is 32 years. She divorced her husband some 3 years ago on the grounds of adultery, and now lives with her two children aged 6 and 4 years. She has taken a part-time shorthand typist's job to keep the family together, and to provide enough money to be able to send her younger child to a nursery school. After a party recently she had intercourse with a friend, who is himself married. Marriage to him is therefore not possible. She herself has a history of pulmonary tuberculosis, requiring 6 months in hospital at the age of 19 years, but she was finally discharged from the Chest Hospital three years ago. She attended the Chest Hospital for two years for check up – these have been clear for a long time now. On examination there is no abnormality detected in the chest. She proves to be 8 weeks pregnant.

MISS I. aged 20 years has two brothers and a sister older than herself and one younger brother. All of them have been to a school for the educationally subnormal. None of them is married.   She works in a fish and chip shop. Her sister had an illegitimate baby recently of unknown parentage. The patient denies that she has a boy friend and claims that she was 'raped' by her younger brother, aged 18 years. Her mother goes out to clean offices; her father has been dead for some years. The medical social worker confirms the mental status of the family and describes the home as a slum. The patient does not remember the date of the alleged offence, nor can give any details of her menstrual history. On examination she is a well-built, unkempt woman some 10 weeks pregnant.

MISS J. is aged 18 years. Her mother is dead. She has two younger teenage brothers and has been keeping house for the family. She has been going steady with her boy friend for years. She is due to sit her A-levels in three months' time and provided she does satisfactorily has been offered a vacancy at Edinburgh University to read Medicine. Her boy friend is due to go up to Oxford at the same time to read History. They plan to be engaged in 2/3 years time and marry when she qualifies. She is a practising Roman Catholic. They had never had intercourse until a few weeks previously when petting went too far and she states 'we couldn't stop.' It has occurred twice since, without precautions being taken. On examination she is pale, anxious and straightforward and makes no attempt to give excuses for her behaviour. She is obviously perturbed in her conscience. She proves to be 8 weeks pregnant.

MISS K. aged 18 years is a pupil mental nurse. She has a married brother and younger sister who is still at home. The home is a very unhappy one, due to outbursts of bad temper on the part of her father. So much is this so that although the nursing authorities would allow her to live at home she elected to live in the Nurses' Home, going home on occasional week-ends. There have been several episodes of her father's using physical violence against his wife and children. Miss K. says that she has occasionally had intercourse with her boy friend. They have not used any contraceptive measure, but have been 'careful'. They are not engaged and she is by no means sure that she wishes to marry him. Examination reveals that she is physically fit, rather over alert and pregnant some 15 weeks. She states that 'my father will thrash me and put me out of the house.'

The general practitioner's comment is that the girl had no idea of the parental storm that would break over her.

MISS L. is a well-built, well-groomed young lady and looks considerably older than her 16 years. She is an only child living with her mother; her parents are separated. She denies ever having had sexual intercourse previously. She claims she went to a party with several friends. She claims that she was very careful and moderate with her drinking, but believes that the drinks had been 'laced' with vodka, unknown to her. She has no clear recollection of the party, but became aware that one of the boys, in the dark (she does not know which one) had 'raped' her. Her boy friend drove her home. She was too terrified to tell her mother, or anybody else, until she had missed four periods. Examination confirmed that she was 16 weeks pregnant, but no disease was detected. Her mother, who accompanied her, firmly demands an abortion on the grounds of 'rape'.

The suggestion has been made by Dr. D. W. Vere[3] that a graph should be drawn of definite opinions in favour of abortion against known factors. This in the absence of "pure" factors as discussed above, is probably impracticable. However, I have made an attempt to obtain some statistics of opinions along the lines suggested by Vere.

It was decided to send the twelve "mock" histories printed above to groups, each of twenty-four persons, in the following categories: consultant obstetricians and gynaecologists, general practitioners, ministers of religion, well educated lay people and clinical medical students. As the aim was to see how these categories varied in their approach, it was obviously essential to make them as similar as possible in all other respects. Ethical stance being central to opinions on abortion it seemed important to select people known to hold a common viewpoint on life. All those consulted in this experiment are Christians who, although of at least seven different denominations, adopt the conservative evangelical position. This was done to achieve a homogeneous group. A control group of Christians of a wide variety of viewpoints was obtained by sending the same questionnaire to the ministers and clergy whose churches are in south Sunderland. This included Anglicans, Methodists, Presbyterians, "Free Church" and Lutheran, and all degrees of churchmanship from High Church to Evangelical. It will be noted that the opinion of the control group did not vary from that of the ministers in the main experiment. It seems, therefore, that bias due to a particular theological viewpoint can be discounted.

Not all the questionnaires were returned, but enough in each group to give a statistically useful result.[4] The figures, expressed in percentages, are recorded, the lower figure in each case being the percentage of respondents

[3] D. W. Vere, "Therapeutic Abortion and Sterilization as Ethical Problems." In "Birth Control and the Christian" (see p. 15, fn. 5).

[4] R. A. McNay, Medical Statistician to the Newcastle Regional Hospital Board. Personal communication.

Percentage of respondents who would approve (top lines), or would approve under certain circumstances (lower lines), to abortion in the instances given.

	Consultants	GPs	Ministers	Laymen	Laywomen	Students	Control
MRS A.	100	100	85	82	88	57	76
	—	—	14	6	6	—	—
MRS B.	86	76	78	89	77	57	88
	7	13	14	—	6	—	12
MRS C.	—	—	—	6	6	—	—
	7	—	—	—	—	—	—
MRS D.	21	13	—	12	11	7	6
	7	—	7	—	—	—	6
MRS E.	—	13	—	30	11	21	—
	—	—	7	—	—	—	—
MRS F.	36	38	14	30	28	14	19
	7	6	—	—	—	—	—
MRS G.	36	44	21	24	55	14	13
	21	6	14	—	6	—	—
MRS H.	28	26	—	12	17	7	—
	7	—	—	—	—	—	—
MISS I.	50	82	71	59	72	36	63
	14	—	—	12	6	—	13
MISS J.	7	6	—	18	16	7	—
	7	6	7	—	—	—	—
MISS K.	—	32	7	18	11	14	—
	7	—	—	—	—	—	—
MISS L.	28	38	21	24	16	14	19
	—	—	—	12	—	—	—

who gave an equivocal or conditional approval in the particular case. The only statistically significant difference is that of the clinical medical students. These were noticeably less willing to grant abortion than the others. Three points should be made: few of these students had reached obstetrics and gynaecology in the curriculum, and therefore had had no didactic teaching on the question, they were probably all in the age group 20–23, and among them the women students were particularly firm. (The number of women students was far too small for statistical significance, but of the five, not all from the same university, three would grant no abortion at all, one would grant abortion to Mrs. A, and the other to Mrs A., Mrs. B., Mrs. G., and Miss L.) Perhaps we should rethink our judgement of the permissiveness of the younger generation, and of students in particular. Could it be that they see too much of the results of permissiveness among their friends?

Sixteen months later an attempt was made to identify any shift of opinion. The same consultants, general practitioners and ministers were sent the same case histories. It was assumed that by this time they would have forgotten their original decisions. Their replies were compared with those sent in earlier. In a less formal way a number of the original laymen and laywomen present at a gathering had the case histories read to them and were asked to note their opinions which were similarly compared. With the exception of one general practitioner who was now more than twice as liberal as before, there was no evidence of change of standpoint whatever.

This differs from the liberalization of opinion which has been shown by several workers. In an American questionnaire those favouring abortion for unmarried women rose from 14% in 1965 to 28% in 1967; and those who would allow abortion to any woman who wanted it from 8% to 21% over the same period.[5]

The influence of religious persuasion was well demonstrated by a very large group of women in Indiana who replied to a questionnaire circulated by their gynaecologist, in 1968. Asked if they would agree to being aborted were their life to be endangered by the pregnancy, 84% of Protestants, but only 56% of Catholics agreed; in the case of danger to their mental health the figures were 81% and 48%. A similar differential between Protestants and Catholics was shown on all questions; for instance, 33% of Protestants but only 12% of Catholics would grant abortion for a working mother with school-age children, and 16% (4%) to a single college girl.[6]

Several public opinion polls have been conducted in Britain during the past three years on similar lines. All in all figures vary so widely, and so

[5] C. Tietze and Sarah Lewit, "Abortion," *Scientific American*, Jan. 1969, **220**, 21.
[6] F. W. Peyton, A. R. Starry and T. R. Leidy, "Women's Attitudes Concerning Abortion." *Obstetrics and Gynecology*, 1969, **34**, 182.

often appear to confirm the views of those who planned the survey, that little weight can be given to them. This chapter will have failed in its object if it does not underline the fact that only as each case is judged separately, privately, and in such depth as circumstances permit, can a conscientious decision be reached.

CHAPTER 17

THE DISEASED MOTHER

One's basic perceptives toward life might be altered, and one's ordering of values might be different if the first-order affirmations dealt with God's will not only to preserve his creation, but to redeem it. One's attitude toward the persons involved might well be more tolerant, patient, loving, and forgiving, rather than judgmental.
JAMES M. GUSTAFSON[1]

THE DREAD DILEMMA, "SAVE THE MOTHER OR THE BABY," HAPPILY DOES not often confront the obstetrician. If that type of problem were to arise late in pregnancy a Caesarean section would usually be possible. Were it to occur early the state of the fetus would probably be so endangered by its mother's condition that the possibility of its being born alive would not arise. If the dilemma were to arise we should follow Professor Jewett's line of reasoning: "While we may question the humanity of the fetus we cannot question the humanity of the mother who conceives it. Furthermore her life is not (ordinarily) as solitary as that of the life she carries. She is a daughter, a wife, and perhaps a mother. Her life has been wrought into the lives of others, who also have claims upon her, which are more clearly human in their 'I–thou' nature, than the claims of the fetus. Recognition of these facts has led to the near unanimity of opinion that in case of life and death, the mother has the more fundamental claim."[2]

The issue which does confront the obstetrician on occasion is save the mother by an abortion, or lose both mother and fetus. I have not called this a dilemma – for the medical man the problem is unreal, there is no choice. As he cannot save the babe he must at least save the mother. Even Roman Catholic doctors, or those whom I have met, feel it incumbent on them to pass such cases over to a colleague able to perform the abortion. To do otherwise might indeed be criminal, for we have already noted Mr. Justice Macnaughten's comment: "If a case arose where the life of the woman could be saved by performing the operation and the doctor refused to perform it because of his religious opinions and the

---

[1] J. M. Gustafson, "A Protestant Ethical Approach." In *The Morality of Abortion: Legal and Historical Perspectives* (Ed. J. T. Noonan), 1970, Harvard University Press.
[2] P. K. Jewett, "The Relationship of the Soul to the Fetus." In *Birth Control and the Christian op. cit.*

151

woman died he would be in grave peril of being brought before this
Court on a charge of manslaughter by negligence."[3]

It will be moreover, recollected that under the Abortion Act (1967)
Section 4 (2) the right to opt out on conscientious grounds is specifically
withdrawn in lifesaving proceedings.

The number of conditions which might be so aggravated by a pregnancy as to become fatal is small, and constantly becoming smaller. For
instance pulmonary tuberculosis used to be such a condition, but with
modern methods of management it is very rarely necessary to consider
abortion. An American writer sympathetic to liberal abortion writes:
"Today the life of the mother is almost never jeopardized by pregnancy."[4]

A committee of the British Medical Association reported in 1968 on
medical indications for termination of pregnancy, and its list with comments runs to ten columns of print.[5] The main conditions that arise are
certain diseases of the heart and kidney failure.

Medical Case 17.1. A 26-year-old mother of two children was referred for
abortion because of renal disease. The consultant urologist confirmed that one
kidney had already been removed, and that the other was grossly damaged.
Already her life hung on a thread due to poor renal function. Although the
mother would have liked a third child she understood that the extra strain on her
remaining kidney during the pregnancy might well be fatal. "I have my two
children to think of, too." She agreed to termination and sterilization.

Cancer may have a better prognosis if a pregnancy is removed.[6]

Medical Case 17.2. A 35-year-old woman with three children had had a breast
removed for what proved to be cancer which had already spread beyond the
breast. At follow-up she was found to be pregnant. The surgeon requested
that abortion be performed and the ovaries also removed, in an endeavour to
reduce the hormone stimulation to the secondary cancerous growths.

Women with diabetes at one time rarely became pregnant. With the
improvement in their care the problem of maternal diabetes is a frequent
one, but only in the most severe degrees is abortion strongly advised. In
one series of patients with the severe condition of diabetic neuropathy it
was found that of those who insisted on going through with the pregnancy
fewer than half had a surviving baby. This series was reported by workers
in Copenhagen. In view of the widely-held view that Scandinavians are
won over to liberal abortion policies it is interesting to note their comment: "From an ethical, emotional, and surgical point of view therapeutic

[3] Mr. Justice Macnaughten (see p. 30).
[4] R. E. Hall, "Abortion, Sterilization and Contraception." American Journal of Obstetrics
and Gynecology, 1965, 91, 518.
[5] B.M.A. Committee on Therapeutic Abortion. "Indications for termination of Pregnancy." BMJ, 1968, I, 171.
[6] B. Cloeren and M. Mall-Haefeli, "The Prognosis of Patients with Malignant Tumours
in Pregnancy in Relation to the Indications for Termination." Gynaecologia (Basel), 1965,
159, 3.

abortion is an evil. If the treating doctors" (in diabetic cases) "more often and more energetically would recommend contraception in the right cases, much suffering could be avoided."[7]

Contraception in cases where an improvement in the mother's condition may be hoped for (or sterilization where no such improvement can be foreseen, or where her family is completed) is obviously to be recommended in all women whose health would not stand up to a further pregnancy, from whatever cause.

On the other hand there are cases when, on the same principle of saving one life if one cannot save both, abortion is contra-indicated.

Medical Case 17.3. A girl in her twenties, in her first pregnancy was noted to have an ovarian swelling. In accordance with routine practice it was decided to remove it at a stage of pregnancy when the operation was least likely to disturb the fetus. The operation was performed at 22 weeks, when both ovaries were found to be involved by malignant growth which had already spread to the pelvic wall. The larger one was removed and the pregnancy left undisturbed on the view that it was too late to save the mother, but that she had enough time left to get the baby to viability. Caesarean section was performed at 32 weeks.

When during an operation on a cancerous growth a pregnancy happens to be in the way of the complete removal of the mass, it is almost universally agreed that the uterus and its contents can be sacrificed. This practice has the sanction of Roman Catholic dogma.

Advances in medical knowledge have made it possible to keep alive throughout pregnancy an increasing number of diseased women. We must always bear in mind Dr. R. E. Hall's warning lest permitting the pregnancy to proceed to term becomes an academic challenge.[8] It seems to many of us to be important to consider the effect on the mother's health not merely of her pregnancy but of the years to follow. It may be perfectly feasible to keep the woman flat on her back throughout pregnancy and ensure a safe delivery, but what is to happen to her when she crosses her own threshold and has to buckle down to caring for the baby? Who else will lift him every time he cries, break their sleep to feed him during the early months, and care for him unendingly through the early years? A heart which can cope when it is at rest in the ante-natal ward, will have a great deal more work to do in the home, and may then fail. In judging a case the maternal strain to be weighed is not merely that of the pregnancy but of motherhood in its widest sense. Anyone who imagines this can be bridged by professional "mother's helps" should look into the availability, and the cost, of such care.

When considering medical indications for abortion, and here at least the adjective "therapeutic" is justified, it will be helpful to adopt Dr.

[7] E. Barandstrup, M. Osler and J. Pedersen, "Therapeutic Abortion and Sterilization in Diabetic Patients." *Acta obstetricia et Gynecologica Scandinavica*, 1964, **43**, 11.

[8] R. E. Hall, in *Advances in Obstetrics and Gynecology* (vol. 1) (Ed. S. L. Marcus and C. C. Marcus), Baltimore, 1967, Williams and Wilkins.

A. F. Guttmacher's viewpoint: "The physician who performs a therapeutic abortion is motivated by only one desire, that of correcting the pathological status of a particular pregnancy. The one way to accomplish this in his judgement is by removing the cause of that pathological status: the trophoblast." (This is part of the afterbirth.) "The fetus is not his primary target, its death therefore is a by-product of the removal of the trophoblast. The uterus is evacuated to correct disease . . ."[9]

Although the life of the mother is by far the most important – and in the view of many the only – indication for abortion it need not detain us. In the first eighteen months of the Abortion Act of 1967 being in operation, of the 65,241 abortions reported only 2,664 (a mere 4%) were certified under this clause; plus another twenty as "life-saving emergencies;"[10] all others were performed for more debatable reasons. To these we must now turn, but in doing so bear in mind Vere's dictum that it is futile to try to force an antithesis between "clinical" and "social" indications.[11]

[9] A. F. Guttmacher, "The Shrinking Non-Psychiatric Indications for Therapeutic Abortion." In *Therapeutic Abortion* (Ed. H. Rosen, *op. cit.*).

[10] P. Diggory, J. Peel and M. Potts, "Preliminary Assessment of the 1967 Abortion Act in Practice, "*Lancet*, 1970, I, 287.

[11] D. W. Vere, "Therapeutic Abortion and Sterilization as Ethical Problems." In *Birth Control and the Christian*, *op. cit.*

CHAPTER 18

THE SOCIO-ECONOMIC FACTOR

The mother is not a physical reality merely, not even a psycho-physical reality, but a socio-psycho-physical reality. She exists as a person only in community or society. The quality of her existence depends not simply on her physical or psychic well-being. She cannot, in fact, be isolated from her social well-being. And our obligations to her are to this socio-psycho-somatic entity.

PROFESSOR ENDA MCDONAGH[1]

BY THE TERMS OF THE ABORTION ACT 1967 IT IS NOT ILLEGAL TO ABORT a woman where "continuance of the pregnancy would involve risk of injury to the physical or mental health of the pregnant woman or any existing children of her family, greater than if the pregnancy were terminated." This covers, among others, the socio-economic indications for termination, much the most controversial of all grounds.

The title of this chapter was unavoidable, but what an inappropriate phrase it is! To have called it "The woman who can't cope" would have been immediately to give rise to the wrong impression. One doctor has said "Since the introduction of the Act, I have discovered in myself prejudices of which I was unaware. I find, for example, my innate tendency is to despise mothers who feel they cannot cope with a further child. This I must confess is a very damaging and unhelpful attitude in a family doctor."[2] Yet we must consider the woman who feels she cannot cope with a further child if she is to be true to her present children, to her husband, or to herself as a mother and a person. This because finance, accommodation, physical strength, mental stamina, or affection are already near to breaking point. Most women who are referred to National Health Service hospitals as abortion patients are married and legitimately pregnant. Very few of these have any physical disease, or any history of psychiatric treatment. They are, however, daunted by the prospect of this new pregnancy and, in their own eyes, their condition is such that they feel termination to be the best way out. One has to look at them within the context of "the total family constellation."[3]

[1] Professor Enda McDonach is a Roman Catholic Professor of Moral Theology. "Ethical Problems in Abortion," *Theology*, 1968, **71**, 393.
[2] I. G. Lennox, "Problems of the Abortion Act in General Practice." In *The Abortion Act, op. cit.*
[3] The phrase is used by A. A. Baker in *Psychiatric Disorders in Obstetrics*, Oxford, 1967, Blackwell.

The Woman as a Person

The first group consists of intelligent, thoughtful women who want to do the best for their family and to give their children every advantage within their power. The advent of another child would inevitably involve the lowering of their standards and their ambitions for the family. "If they are responsible women who value highly the well being of their existing children, they are horrified and appalled if they find they are having more children than they believe they can look after properly and bring up decently. The reason then that they would seek out an abortion is precisely because they are so deeply conscious of their responsibilities towards their husband and family, and because their maternal instinct arouses within them deeply protective feelings about their existing children."[4] Such women rightly see themselves as the linch-pin of the family and realize that the strain of pregnancy and of caring for another child during its early years may place too great a burden on the other members of the family.

Medical Case 18.1. A man whose health prevented him from carrying out his arduous manual occupation was fortunate to obtain a full-time trade union post. This involved a considerable amount of clerical work which was quite beyond his skill, and an amount of entertaining of visiting officials. Fortunately his wife was able to deal with both these. They had two children in their early teens who had expectations of passing examinations and going for further training. The wife then found herself pregnant. It appeared that this would prevent her from helping her husband in his job, as a result of which he was likely to lose his appointment. Being medically unfit, and alternative employment not being available in the depressed area in which they live, he would be unemployed. The ensuing financial burden would make it impossible for the two children to remain at school and therefore debar them from their hoped for careers. Alternative satisfying occupations were almost unobtainable in that particular area.

Medical Case 18.2. A working-class woman of 38 had 4 children aged 15–5. Immediately after her last delivery, at home, she had been rushed into the Maternity Hospital with life-threatening eclamptic fits. She was now pregnant again and terrified of a recurrence. Her two oldest children were academically bright, and the 15-yr old was already setting his sights on a profession. Her financial situation was precarious. On being fully gone into with the Medical Social Worker it was confirmed that the advent of a new baby would involve the 15 year old boy having to leave school and obtain work, to bolster the family income. The woman gave the impression of being a straightforward, conscientious mother with a real concern for the children's future.

In both these cases it was the opinion of the patients, and of their general practitioners, that abortion and sterilization was essential if the children were not to suffer lifelong deprivation through curtailment of their education. There was the additional factor of the effect on the mother of knowing that she had marred her children's chances. Again in later life the

[4] Madelaine Simms, Letter in the Lancet, 1967, I, 384.

offspring might well bear a grudge against their parents for so ruining their opportunities – the ruin being perhaps less important than the antagonism.

For children the family has more importance than as a source of shelter and finance. There is evidence that an unsatisfactory home is the major cause of juvenile delinquency. "Study of the origins of delinquency has suggested to Cowie and his colleagues that, for girls in particular, the greatest need is to prevent children from entering an environment where they will be unwanted, unloved, and unlikely to receive adequate attention. Overburdening of the mother was a frequent cause of unsatisfactory upbringing among the girls (14–18) admitted in 1958 to the Magdalen Classifying Approved School in London. Family planning as a national policy would probably bring about a large reduction in delinquency."[5] One's sympathies are therefore aroused to those who are trying to keep a happy home together.

A Swedish study of a random sample of women who had recently delivered a live baby and who had no mental symptoms prior to conception showed that 45% developed several mental symptoms after delivery. 25% of the patients had seven or more symptoms; 20% had four to six symptoms; the remaining 10% few, or none. For example – irritability was reported by 36.6%, anxiety by 26.1%, depression by more than 25%. It is interesting that there was no correlation with maternal age.[6] Not only is the mother aware of the positive effect of such symptoms on her family, but there is also the sense of falling short of what she wants to be to them, and for them.

A writer in *The Guardian* describes how, in the treatment of her cancer of the breast, she had very unwillingly, and tearfully, agreed to be sterilized. She then describes her mental outlook after convalescence. "To live abundantly does not mean necessarily to have an abundance of babies. All fertility is not below the waist. I think I have found more meaning in my marriage since further children have become an impossibility, for we have more scope to share our mutual interest in the arts and in ideas which – apart from the usual youth, beauty, hope and hormones – were the things that drew us together in the first place. When the tide of nappie water finally subsided I was filled with an unexpected happiness. Now, I felt, I could discover who I was and what I wanted of life. I was no longer under contract to multiplication. To be a full-time woman and to put all one's talents into procreation, child-rearing and husband-cosseting is, in a sense, to pass the buck. And one's own fulfilment is a buck that cannot be passed. Our gifts are only offered to us, it is a lifetime's work accepting them and if one is denied the opportunity to work at

[5] J. Cowie, Valeria Cowie and E. Slater, "Delinquency in Girls" quoted in *Lancet* Editorial, 1968, **I**, 713.
[6] L. Jacobson, L. Kaji and A. Nilsson, "Postpartum Mental Disorders in an Unselected Sample: Frequency of Symptoms and Predisposing Factors." *BMJ*, 1965, **I**, 1640.

this, one may become a power-mad Puppet-manipulator, living through other people."[7] For the woman who has re-established herself in professional life an unexpected pregnancy may mean the collapse of her dreams. In a complex profession (such as medicine) it is very difficult for a woman to pick up the threads after being at home for a decade while the children are small. The subject has moved swiftly, she has a great deal of catching-up on advances to do. Then she has to break in to the professional situation – not an easy task. Having succeeded at last, and then having had to give up once more because of an unexpected pregnancy, she is unlikely ever to get back in again. This is a loss to the community, but even more to her self-respect. Sir Dugald Baird has pointed out that because of this a professional woman can break down under a new pregnancy.[8]

The Worn-Out Mother

So far we have been discussing the woman who is fit and well. There is, however, another group which the Scandinavians class as "The worn-out Mother." Writing of a group in Norway, Kolstad states "All women within the group of medico-social indications were mentally or physically impaired beforehand; the pregnancy was merely the drop that caused the cup to overflow. Characteristic of their reaction are statements to the effect that they 'cannot bear the thought of pregnancy and another child to tend.' The state of impairment visible in the patient has, on the whole, been caused by social or economic factors. The housewife has, during a number of years, been worn down by chores, by bad living conditions, unhappy conjugal relations, heavy labour, many children, abuse of alcohol, etc. She has thus grown nervous and exhausted, she has lost her physical and mental resources, and is afraid of the future, of what will happen to the husband, the children and herself."[9] This type of patient has sometimes in fact been offered sterilization during a previous pregnancy but has felt unable to afford the extra week away from her family which this would involve. While such women are mostly found among the lower income groups, one knows of the wife of a professional man whose children have so dragged her down that she has abandoned all efforts of keeping a tidy home, thus causing embarrassment to her husband and colleagues.

Not only may the home become a slum, but the woman's mental state often suffers. Dr. H. Rosen points out that psychotherapy may be used on some women, but continues, "This brings up the question of whether we should have helped make it possible, by the means of these techniques for

---

[7] Anna Adams, "Not All Fertility is Below the Waist." *The Guardian* (Manchester).
[8] Sir Dugald Baird, "Sterilization and Therapeutic Abortion in Aberdeen." *British Journal of Psychiatry*, 1967, 113, 701.
[9] P. Kolstad, "Therapeutic Abortion."*Acta Obstetrica et Gynecologica Scandinavica*, 1957, 36 sup. 6.

her to bear a child to be raised in the same noxious environment as that in which her own neurotic symptoms were generated."[10]

Weighing these various circumstances the protagonists of liberal abortion policy would say, with Evelyn Fisher: "Often the mother who seeks an abortion has a truer conception of the dignity and sanctity of human life than those who preach that doctrine to her while rating the quality of her mental and physical life and her value to her family below that of a fetus less than 13 weeks old."[11]

However, in considering the family there is another side to the coin. What is the effect of the abortion going to be on the children in the family? In Hemphill's opinion, "It is impossible to estimate the effect on the mind of a young girl who learns that her mother has been to hospital to have a baby 'taken away.' Many people who have had the opportunity of hearing discussions amongst schoolgirls have told me their anxiety about this. Daughters regret the loss of a baby brother or sister, and children must feel unsure about the strength of the maternal instincts of an active mother who has asked for an abortion."[12]

The Husband's Attitude

The question of the wife's relationship to her husband is, of course, crucial. In a Swedish series of abortion applications, forty-six were single or divorced, fifty-two had a stable marriage, but in another fifty-four cases marriage was unharmonious to the extent of there being real serious conflicts. A number of Scandinavian writers mention the high percentage of unsatisfactory husbands. In two series, 22%[13] and 28%[14] of husbands were alcoholics or had criminal records. A further 13%[13] and 10%[14] were, at the time of their wives' application for abortion, suffering from physical illness affecting their working capacity. While alcoholic, criminal and sick husbands are in the minority, many husbands through failure to understand their wives' problems greatly aggravate the situation.

Medical Case 18.3. A woman suffered a severe phobia which prevented her from leaving the house, following each of her first two deliveries. She felt herself to be at fault, and regarded herself as a weakling, and therefore did not consider medical attention indicated. In her third pregnancy her husband requested termination on the grounds that his wife's health suffered following childbirth, and (though he did not put it quite so frankly) that he was considerably inconvenienced when she could not run the household and do the shopping as efficiently as he wished. He was a rather domineering man with high standards.

[10] H. Rosen, *Therapeutic Abortion: Medical, Psychiatric, Legal, Anthropological and Religious Considerations*, New York, 1954, Julian Press.
[11] Evelyn Fisher, Letter in the *Lancet*, 1966, **2**, 1077.
[12] R. E. Hemphill, Letter in the *Lancet*, 1966, **1**, 324.
[13] P. Arén and C. Amark, "Outcome of Pregnancies Where Abortion was Granted but not Carried Out." *Acta Psychiatrica et Neurologica Scandinavica*, 1961, **36**, 203.
[14] M. Ekblad, "Induced Abortion on Psychiatric Grounds." *Acta Psychiatrica et Neurologica Scandinavica*, 1955, sup. 99.

Termination was refused and psychotherapy given. She had the same phobias after delivery. The psychiatrist discussed the matter with the husband who for the first time was able to understand that in her attempts to please him and maintain standards which he expected she suffered, and this, in some part, precipitated her symptoms. A change in his attitude helped her recovery and future mutual happiness.

It is probably no exaggeration to say that in most cases the degree of the husband's support makes all the difference in enabling his wife to cope with another pregnancy. There are a few cases where the husband is physically disabled and not able to do much, but even here his help in the home can be decisive. When the man will really rally round: help, encourage, take the major share of the burden, then they can usually manage. There are an encouraging number of women in every stratum of society who say proudly "I've got a good man."

It is, however, those who have to confess "No one knows what I've had to put up with from my man" who usually make the abortion request. Perhaps the husband is selfish and refuses to use a condom. Perhaps he comes in drunk on a Saturday night and demands "his rights" without thought of the consequences. Perhaps he merely laughs when his wife tells him she is pregnant again; that is not his problem.

It may be that he co-operates contraceptively, but when the baby does come leaves it, and the rest of the family and house, to his wife's care. He gives her an ungenerous "house-keeping allowance" which he forgets to increase with his own increasing pay, or to keep in step with the rising cost of living.

And so the woman battles on, alone. There comes the moment when even the most dedicated says "I can no longer." There are some, however, who are no longer dedicated. The marriage may be in danger.

Medical Case 18.4. A professional woman age 35 consulted the gynaecologist about a menstrual disorder, and in passing mentioned that although her two daughters were now teenaged, she still longed to have a son. Two years later she came, 15 weeks pregnant, requesting an abortion. "But what if this is your longed for son?" she was asked. "It is too late now." was her reply. Too late, not because she was 37, but because, since conceiving she had discovered that her husband had another woman, and the marriage might therefore soon be over. Because of her well-paid position she had the option of setting up her own home with her daughters. To have to give up work because of a new baby would destroy her financial independence which made this course a possibility.

Things may be even worse. All love between husband and wife may long since have gone. The marriage is a burden which the woman has borne for the sake of the children. She has counted the weary years until the youngest could go out into the world and she herself could follow to make a new life. Such a woman, becoming pregnant, realizes that all hope of escape from entanglement with this detested man is gone. If she is to bear and rear this child she is incarcerated for at least another 15 years, and the prospect is too much for her.

Poverty

Housing, clothing and food are necessities which no one can do without. Even today there are still many families living in meagre housing, often without any indoor sanitation and sometimes with no bath or hot water supply. Some of one's patients have clothing of a very poor quality which is obviously incapable of protecting them from wind and rain.

It is true that there is in Britain a family allowance for each child after the first and there is also provision from the Department of Health and Social Security by unemployment pay and supplementary allowance for those in need. Despite these excellent arrangements they may be inadequate for a large family. It is not therefore to be wondered at that the conscientious mother tries to increase her income by part-time work. Having obtained this she then endeavours to improve the home by purchasing the necessary furniture or clothing by hire purchase. Under these circumstances unexpected pregnancy can mean not only that there will be another child to clothe and feed but also that the amount of money already available for the present family will be greatly reduced and as a result that items of furniture, partly paid for, will have to be returned.

Any assessment of the financial position is, of course, complicated by the fact that sometimes the wife does not know her husband's total earnings. The husband may use the major portion of his wage packet for his own amusement in the public house or the betting shop. In some cases his expenditure on this is kept within bounds of which his wife approves, her feeling being that to deny him these relaxations would be to make him a laughing-stock among his friends. A man who has spent an exhausting shift underground mining coal and who perhaps has few interior resources for relaxation cannot be expected to spend the rest of the day in a two-roomed house full of squabbling children. His presence indeed, may prove to be the last straw. It may even be that the strains of the family and the strains of motherhood are so great that his wife is glad to have her husband out of the house. Alternatively her husband may be of such a temperament that she is far too terrified of him to ask for any extra money, knowing well that he will thrash her were she to make the request. Bruises from a husband's beatings are seen in my patients from time to time. Short term financial grants from benevolent bodies do not appear to be of any great help in meeting these problems.

The problem is the woman who has no obvious mental strain, and makes her request on the grounds of financial inadequacy, pure and simple. How can any judgement be arrived at? One is often aware of very genuine financial need; as one husband put it "a new pair of shoes for one of the eight bairns is a financial catastrophe." It is here that social in-equalities rear their ugly head. The law makes allowance for cases where "other children of the family will suffer." What quantitative meaning can we give to "suffer"? None of us would countenance the request of a woman whose pregnancy would reduce a promised holiday in the Bahamas to one in Blackpool; but could not the children, literally, be said to suffer at least a bitter disappointment? On the other hand, one knows of Ugandan families existing on a total income less than the U.K. children's allowance. If in our different conditions it would be unreasonable for us to expect our people to depress their standard to that degree, are we not introducing class distinctions repugnant to modern opinion? What living standards are unreasonable? I have been in homes where the family had to sit on the floor, in the absence of sufficient chairs, to watch television. Is a TV set essential? Would it be reasonable to tell a mother to dispose of hers? At first sight, yes. But in a tiny crowded home with no other amusements, in the absence of TV the family would spend the evenings on the streets; only TV keeps them in and, to some measure, maintains a family unit. Should it not then be considered an essential to those families lacking the amenities and inner resources to maintain a family life without it?

These women almost invariably smoke. As a non-smoker it is easy for me to chide them for this: however, I am told that many of them skimp on their meals to allow themselves this little luxury.

More than once a woman has complained that financial stringency makes feeding another mouth impossible, when I am aware that, after rent has been paid, they are left with more than the "minimum stipend" of many of our British ministers of religion. If the latter can cope and keep up appearances, why not them? But if motive and competence are at a lesser level, is this comparison valid?

Suppose we could agree on a basic level of need. A computer could be programmed to assess each case, allowing points for maternal age, educa-tion, details of the children, housing, needs and wants. At the end a figure would be produced. Could I then say to this woman, as I look at the computer's print-off, "I'm sorry, you have a weekly income five new pence above the limit for abortion: you'll have to bear the baby," or perhaps, "Congratulations, you are just below the limit, come into the ward for your abortion tomorrow"?

Can the fetus be weighed like this? Its extinction or survival measured in coppers? Of course not! But, having said that, what is the doctor to do? If pounds and pence are not to be the measure, what is? The degree of pressure the woman can exert? Her ability to weep in the consulting room?

Medical Case 18.5. A 30-year-old woman requested abortion solely on grounds of financial stringency. She had four children. Since marriage they had 'lived in' with her 'in laws' until four months ago when they had managed to rent a council house. The move and the extra furniture had been a great financial burden, but had left all concerned happier.

Although her husband was now employed he had been unemployed throughout the previous year. During this he had done, surreptitiously, the odd bit of work but had been found out. His fine, and the bill to repay social security benefit amounted to a considerable sum. Money was owed to relatives, none of whom were well off. The patient's engagement ring was in pawn, and she had had to borrow the bus fare to hospital, but refused the proffered refund. Her pram and cot had been disposed of.

Should the gynaecologist arrange abortion? Alternatively should he promise sterilization, and meanwhile personally get into touch with the various authorities with the aim of mitigating their claims for repayment, arrange the provision of a cot and a pram, and generally wrap the woman in support?

Housing

On average the people of England and Wales have the most ample housing of any nation in the world; with five times as much room per person as the worst off – the citizens of Mexico City.[15] Despite this, housing is often a very difficult problem, sufficiently so to drive the mother to request an abortion rather than try to fit another child in.

Medical Case. 18.6. A woman, 37 years of age, was referred for abortion. She had borne 8 children in 10 years; thereafter she was on 'The Pill' for 5 years until her general practitioner felt it was necessary to give her a break from it. Other measures were taken but these proved unsatisfactory and she became pregnant for the 9th time. Her accommodation consisted of a three-roomed council house, the 5 daughters slept in one room, the 3 boys in another and she and her husband shared what amounted to little more than a box-room. The Medical Officer of Health's opinion, when contacted, was 'it is not a case of being unable to swing a cat, you couldn't swing a mouse.' This patient's husband had become redundant, on the closing of his factory, and had only been able to find his present job recently. A further move was therefore economically impracticable. The Council in question owned no larger council house whatever. This woman's request was for termination solely on the grounds of inadequate housing. The obstetrician personally took the matter up with the appropriate authorities and found re-housing to be impossible.

Medical Case 18.7. A mother of two requested abortion early in her third pregnancy. She would be glad to have another child but she felt her home made this impossible. The ground floor of the house was very well cared for, the upper floor was uninhabitable as the roof had fallen in. The gynaecologist personally investigated this with the authorities. The position proved to be that the house belonged to the National Coal Board, and had been allotted to the patient's husband while he was a miner. He was no longer in the employ of the NCB, but was permitted to remain as the house was of no use to them. He had therefore, no grounds to complain. In fact complaint would merely result in ejection. Alternative accommodation was not obtainable.

[15] United Nations Statistical Year Book quoted in *The Guardian* (Manchester), July 6, 1970.

The problem facing the young couple who are still "living in" with the parents of one of them is no easier, yet "living in" is often the only choice available in the early years of marriage. This is never a placid emotional situation. It is worse when, as so often is the case, the couple had to get married in the first place to legitimize a pregnancy, and the husband has started off in his mother-in-law's black books. Soon the time comes when mother, or mother-in-law, makes it quite clear that no extra child will be acceptable. They will have to get out. This news, plus the scorn which the older woman pours upon the girl for her carelessness in conceiving, is an added strain. It is part of the culture pattern in the North-East of England for "Nanna" (the grandmother) to look after her daughter's child, to enable her to go out to work full time. This is often necessary if the young couple are going to set up their own home. Grandmother may be quite happy to do this for one child, but when the second, or third comes along she goes on strike. The girl finding herself in this predicament turns to the gynaecologist to solve her problem.

Weighing the Social Factors

Where these various problems produce physical or mental symptoms in the mother, the doctor can judge the problem from a medical viewpoint. He decides whether or not abortion is justified under the clause of the Act relative to the woman's health. Frequently it proves that the present pregnancy is merely the last straw that broke the camel's back. Prior to this conception the woman has been tired, irritable, moody. She had been a frequent visitor to her doctor and had had many prescriptions for tranquillizers. Here the decision to terminate is relatively easy. Sterilization at the same time is almost always offered.

Decision is more difficult when the practitioner tells one that the patient is rarely, if ever, seen by him. She is a fit woman who has apparently coped without difficulty. Her recent visit to him for confirmation of pregnancy, and with her request for termination is the first time she has mentioned depression. True, she now says she has had this on and off for years, but this tale is obviously suspect.

The question of her contraceptive history is also taken into account. The woman who "has never used anything," whose husband is usually "careful" finds her request less well received. True, there may be good reasons for her not having used the pill. The story, quite often heard, that "I couldn't afford it that month" is difficult to accept. Without exception those who have told me this admit to smoking ten cigarettes or more a day: a single pill costs less than two cigarettes. Every practitioner with whom I have discussed this has told me that he is always ready to "find" a month's supply for anyone in financial want; but this may not be well known. A surprising number of women maintain that they have never thought of alternative methods of contraception. In these days sexual topics appear almost to monopolize the media. I have been repeatedly and credibly informed by patients and nurses that it is discussed in a wealth of detail, ad nauseam, by the patients in gynaecological wards. One therefore finds one's credulity stretched in most, although not all, cases where ignorance of contraception is pleaded.

Where the request for termination is solely on socio-economic grounds one is in a real dilemma. The easiest step is to say that one never operates on these grounds. But on a visit to the house the threadbare furniture, the crust-strewn table, tell their own tale of poverty. The haggard, anaemic woman with two or three infants hanging whimpering on to her patched skirt long past bedtime, is a woman at the point of despair.

Faced as one is with these problems, sooner or later the question forces itself into one's conscience: In making the woman go on with this pregnancy when she has had a miserable life up till now, what are we trying to achieve? This woman's life has been hell. Her accommodation is inadequate beyond description. Her life has been a burden with almost continuous childbearing. She has never known how she is going to face the rent collector, and how the larder is to be replenished. She is still in this state, which is made even more unbearable by another cot to be squeezed in, another mouth to be fed. Perhaps her previous children are now old enough to allow her to do some part-time work in an endeavour to augment a pitiably small income. A new pregnancy will require her to give this up. Perhaps after fifteen or twenty years of being tied at home by the children she has, at last, had an opportunity of starting to establish her personality, instead of being a mere drudge at the sink. Is it now for me to say "you must go back to your penury" – or should I relieve her of this burden and take steps to ensure that it will never, either in actuality or in dread expectation, trouble her again?

If the baby is allowed to be delivered it will no doubt receive a large measure of affection, however poor the material circumstances, and may well in years to come overcome these early trials and do some great work. But if we follow the latter argument to its conclusion the only logical plan is to produce as many children as is physically possible. It can be argued that so far this child does not exist. Are we right in insisting that it should be brought into being despite the miseries which must inevitably result, because of the paucity of the financial resources?

In this type of case one must lean heavily on the advice of the woman's general practitioner with his long knowledge of the family, and on that of the interested medical social worker with her unrivalled knowledge of the resources which can be made available. In my cases it is my hope that as I consult these separately I will find that all three of us come to the same conclusion as to the best management of this case in the interests of the patient. This hope is very frequently fulfilled.

To the eyes of some readers the problem will seem easy, the doctor's dilemma artificial. Of course these women are in a tight spot: get on with the operation! Unfortunately, however, the gynaecologist knows of the women who wake up night after night hearing their baby crying: *but there is no baby*. Of those who find themselves laying an extra place at table for their child, only to remember with a start that she had him "taken away." These cases are not fictional.

To the eyes of other readers the problem will seem easy: never operate on non-medical grounds. Is "health" adequately manifest merely because the physical functions, somehow and surprisingly, still keep ticking over?

No problem in abortion is so intractable as this. The day must surely come when the legislature will suggest better guide-lines for abortion in this field.

CHAPTER 19

ILLEGITIMATE PREGNANCY

To eliminate the scourge of illegitimate children more self-discipline to prevent their conception is required, not more freedom to destroy them in the womb. For each illegitimate child born because the abortion laws are strict, there may be ten or more such children not conceived because these laws are strict.

RABBI DR. IMMANUEL JAKOBOVITS[1]

IN INTERVIEWING AN UNMARRIED PREGNANT WOMAN THE FIRST ESSENTIAL is to rid oneself of any feeling of antagonism. There are good grounds, even at a non-Christian level, for thinking chastity to give the happiest results: these will be discussed in a later chapter. I am no more required to condone extra-marital sex than I am required to condone opium-smoking: the fact that in other societies both these practices are accepted does not prove them harmless. It makes, however, for a better rapport with the patient if we remind ourselves "There, but for the grace of God, go I." When dealing with such a case a matron remarked, "Perhaps we have never been there because no-one asked us." There is no place for the attitude of one abortion-committee member who said with ill-concealed irritation: "Now that she has had her fun, she wants us to launder her dirty underwear. From my standpoint she can sweat this one out."[2] Josephine Butler drove home the point that there would be no immoral women if there were no immoral men. Jean Pochin, an experienced social worker reminding us of that, goes on to remark that some now see unmarried pregnancy not as a deadly sin but as a grave symptom.[3]

Now here we have to be careful. Recent Canadian work makes this point: "In caring for these girls we perhaps must not lean so heavily on the certainty that only those with abnormal psychodynamics get pregnant. It is often pointed out that these patients go to great lengths to conceal or deny the pregnancy, but this is probably not from a psychodynamic aberration but because of parental or societal reaction. The fascinating pastime of probing into the emotional background of these young people, discovering some repressed anxiety or upset in parent–child relationship, and without any more evidence labelling this as the cause of the illegitimate

[1] I. Jakobovits, "Jewish Views on Abortion." In *Abortion and the Law* (Ed. D. Smith), Cleveland, 1967, Press of Western Reserve University.
[2] Quoted by A. J. Mandy in *Therapeutic Abortion, op. cit.*
[3] Jean Pochin, *Without a Wedding Ring: Casework with Unmarried Parents*, London, 1969, Constable.

pregnancy may be an example of the 'self-fulfilling prophecy', a definite hazard of the retrospective study."[4]

Having straightened out our attitudes we can now meet the patient. We will immediately note that she will fall into one of a number of categories, which must now be looked at separately.

Pregnancies Arising From Unwilling Intercourse

The circumstance in which this most commonly arises is rape, which is defined as "the carnal knowledge of a woman by force and against her will."[5] The essence of rape is that it is without consent of the woman, and herein lies the difficulty. Not infrequently a girl is brought to the gynaecological clinic by her mother with the story that she was raped, usually some two to three months previously, but that only now has she told her mother the story. In one such case in my own practice the girl later made it quite clear to the nursing staff that she had in fact been a willing lover.

During debates on abortion law reform it has been frequently pointed out that the doctor here is put in the place of a judge. At this distance in time he has not the slightest medical evidence to go on and his opinion on this point is therefore of no more value than that of anyone else. To include rape, therefore, in any statutory regulations would require some other machinery of proof. Where rape has occurred and the girl concerned greatly distressed in mind, dishevelled in clothing, scratched and stained in the struggle, runs for help, the police are normally immediately informed and they seek medical opinion. At this stage, then, within an hour or so of the offence having been committed there is evidence to be found in forensic medical tests. It is noteworthy that in some laws, e.g. those of Denmark, for termination to be perfomed on the grounds of rape it is a prerequisite that the offence has been reported to the police, and that they have not dismissed it as false.[6] Certain of the United States which permit abortion on out-of-State residents on other grounds, restrict abortions for rape to state residents for reasons of police co-operation.[7] In the District of Columbia, where Public Health nurses follow up claims of sexual assault of women, they found that of 668 complainants only 322 had probably been victims, and they identified seven imagined cases, and eleven fabricated cases.[8]

Where there is no doubt that rape has occurred concensus of opinion is that termination should be performed, both to save the mother the long

[4] R. A. H. Kinch, M. P. Wearing, E. J. Love and Dianne McMahon, "Some Aspects of Pediatric Illegitimacy." *American Journal of Obstetrics and Gynecology*, 1969, **105**, 20.

[5] Sir Sydney Smith, *Forensic Medicine* (9th ed. with F. S. Fiddes), London, 1949, Churchill.

[6] Vera Skalts and M. Norgaard, "Abortion Legislation in Denmark." In *Abortion and the Law, op. cit.*

[7] J. M. Ingram, "Changing Aspects of Abortion Law." *American Journal of Obstetrics and Gynecology*, 1969, **105**, 35.

[8] C. R. Hayman, F. R. Lewis, W. G. Stewart and M. Grant, "A Public Health Program for Sexually Assaulted Females." *Public Health Reports*, 1967, **82**, 497.

months of animosity to her growing fetus, and to save the baby from being born only to find itself abhorrent as a constant reminder of its conception and of its father. It might well be best to carry out a thorough uterine curettage about seven to ten days after the assault, to avoid the knowledge and memory that conception had ever occurred. This procedure has the sanction of Roman Catholic Canon Law.[9] Rape is rare. Out of more than 54,000 abortions in Britain in 1969 only 80 were performed for this reason.[10]

Incest

Incest is defined as "carnal intercourse between persons who stand within certain degrees of kinship."[5] For our present purpose brother–sister and father–daughter relationships are the only two likely to be involved. Here again the question of the lack of consent is important and cannot always be assumed. A case has been recounted where a girl forbidden all outside liaisons by her mother's vigilance became an equally willing partner in incestuous intercourse with her father. Drs. Adams and Neel report eighteen incestuous pregnancies. Of the twelve brother–sister matings, seven of the sisters were aged twelve to fifteen; intelligence and socio-economic conditions were average. In the six father–daughter matings the girl was older (seventeen, on average), and of very widely varying intelligence, but the fathers were generally poorly educated and held jobs requiring low to average ability. The poor outlook for their children is reported in chapter 22.

In the classical Bourne Case described in an earlier chapter, Dr. Rees, a psychiatrist, laid emphasis on the enormous importance of mental breakdown or deep and lasting neurosis following a sexual experience of terror and horror, in undermining physical health. Not the least of the legacies of incest and rape in the young is the lifelong revulsion against a sex life and even marriage. He describes two cases of girls below sixteen who had suffered incest or rape, and who in adult life were unable to make a successful marriage. They were terrified by all matters connected with sex, and were mentally unstable. They had both been refused abortion.[12]

Before we leave the topic of pregnancy arising from unwilling intercourse we should recall that by far the most frequent occurrence of this is within the marriage bond. Philosophers and theologians, often celibate, paint a roseate picture of happy conception in marriage. This can be true, but it is only too often caricatured in the impregnation by selfish or drunken husbands of their worn-out, unwilling wives. In my practice not infrequently women, now separated from their husbands, tell me that they

[9] R. F. Drinan, "The Inviolability of the Right to be Born." In *Abortion and the Law, op. cit.*
[10] Registrar General's *Statistical Review of England and Wales for 1969*, London, 1971, H.M.S.O.
[11] M. S. Adams and J. V. Neel, "Children of Incest." *Pediatrics*, 1967, **40**, 55.
[12] A. Bourne, *A Doctor's Creed: The Memoirs of a Gynaecologist*, London, 1963, Gollancz.

were deliberately impregnated as an act of malice. "He threw my diaphragm and cream into the fire."

Pregnancy Arising From Willing Intercourse Outside Marriage

Single women make up the greatest number of these patients but do not form a homogeneous group.

i) *The Unchurched.* These women have never been through a church or civil wedding ceremony but have been living in a stable union with their man for a number of years, and plan to continue to do so. In the eyes of their neighbours, and often in the eyes of some government agencies, they are married. It is difficult to see why requests for abortion from among such should be considered on different grounds from those from their sisters who have been through a marriage ceremony.

ii) *The Premarital.* Girls who are engaged, officially or unofficially, make up the largest percentage of the illegitimately pregnant. In a Manchester series of unmarried mothers attending ante-natal clinic, there were 36% "casual pregnancies" to 64% "pre-marital."[13] In November 1969 I reviewed the notes of all patients who were then under my ante-natal care in their first pregnancy, or in a subsequent pregnancy for whom records of the first pregnancy were available. It proved that 40.5% had been pregnant on their wedding day. Dr. Shirley Nathan's figure for a Greater London Housing Estate of 54% for babies conceived out of wedlock is even higher.[14] The phenomenon is not new. The kirk session records of earlier centuries in Scotland are full of discipline cases arising out of the inconveniently early arrival of the first babe in a marriage. In Colonial America "during a period marked by a 'moral awakening' one-third of the couples in one church who were admitted to communion made a confession of sexual intercourse before or outside wedlock."[15] As the great majority of such couples marry prior to delivery, the question of abortion should not arise on these particular grounds. If abortion is carried out the couple in later married life may well regret the lost child. "Regret" is too superficial a word to describe the emotion if they fail to conceive again.

iii) *The Permissive.* These are the girls who have regular intercourse with their boy friend on a long-term basis. In some cases they meet and sleep together several times a week, in others they actually live together. They differ, however, from the earlier groups in that they do not make the pretence of being married, they do not claim that their liaison will be lifelong, and they certainly do not intend to produce a family. They both understand that they may well change partners at a later stage. This group of young people who have elected to act as though married should be

---

[13] D. A. Thomson, "The Unmarried Mother." *In the Service of Medicine,* April, 1963.

[14] Shirley E. Nathan, "Pregnancies Conceived Extra-Maritally." *Journal of the Royal College of General Practitioners,* 1969, 18, 72.

[15] T. P. Monahan, "Premarital Pregnancy in the United States." *Eugenics Quarterly,* 1960 7, 133.

granted the dignity of being treated as such. Their abortion requests should be assessed accordingly.

iv) *The Promiscuous*. My own impression, for which I have no statistical backing, is that this is the smallest group. In Jean Pochin's view it is clearly linked with poverty, squalor, low intelligence, and the almost complete absence of a positive family life. The parents are usually divorced, in hospital, in prison, or dead. If there is a home it is usually overcrowded and often in condemned property. Of the eighteen cases she discusses, seventeen had such low I.Q.s that "they had dragged through school as an incomprehensible boredom which had to be endured." To such girls sex experience provides a relief and release readily available and seldom frowned on.[3] In Michael Schofield's series two girls gave "boredom" as the reason for their first sexual experience.[16]

Whatever their I.Q. most promiscuous girls are able to avoid pregnancy, or if they do become pregnant have long had their contacts with an abortionist. Assuming they are not mentally subnormal there is no obvious reason why these girls should be assessed for abortion on criteria different from those applicable to a married woman.

v) *The Curious*. In these days when one's eyes and ears are being bombarded by titillating stimuli it would be a matter of surprise if teenagers were not curious in sexual matters. Such a large number manage to control the temptation that it is nonsense to suggest one must yield, but a good number do yield. In Britain, Michael Schofield estimated that in the early 1960s by the age of eighteen 34% of the boys and 17% of the girls were sexually experienced. He reports that the first experience was often unpremeditated and unplanned. In actual fact only 25% of the boys and 13% of the girls gave "curiosity" as the reason for their first experience of intercourse; the boys were more likely (46%) to reply that they were impelled by sexual desire and the girls (42%) by being in love.[16] The factor of group pressure, the frequent tirades by the older generation, the persuasion of the media, all lead young people to believe that here is something they are missing.

The girl who has been curious or caught up in a wave of emotion, and becomes pregnant, perhaps on the first occasion, has to be given lengthy consideration. Factors worth weighing include the following:

Was intercourse premeditated, or at any rate knowingly risked? Schofield[16] states that only 3% of boys and 9% of girls were under the influence of drink on the first occasion. On the other hand, Dr. Nathan found that of her eight patients who had had intercourse once only with the putative father, five had been drinking before coitus.[14] Most teenagers are so well aware of the facts of life that in some pregnancy can almost be considered as a "self-inflicted injury." In this category I include the

[16] M. Schofield, *The Sexual Behaviour of Young People*, Revised Edition, London, 1968, Penguin.

modern miss, well made-up when she comes to the clinic, who tells me that she conceived while drunk, or at an all-night party. Some time ago there was a stir when an Australian professional man, in issuing invitations for his daughter's party, added the words "Girls should come prepared"; the implication was objected to by some recipients. Wise young people go home before, in the words of one of them, "it reaches the horizontal stage"; those who remain can hardly expect the doctor to lend an indulgent ear.

Whereas with married women one tends to be more sympathetic to those who are trying to practise efficient contraception and fail, the opposite is true here. In fact the single girl who used contraceptives is in the minority, even among those having fairly regular intercourse. Michael Schofield found that eight out of ten girls having intercourse were at risk,[16] which agrees with a Canadian figure of 75% unprotected despite the fact that they all had some knowledge of contraception but "were not in a planning mood at the time of the 'accident'." The Canadian workers go on: "It is our impression that they became caught up in an emotional upheaval and made the mistake of not 'applying the brakes'."[4] Such a girl is more to be pitied than the girl who has gone into the adventure open-eyed.

The age of the girl is obviously an important factor. There can be few sights more heart-rending than the little, flat-breasted schoolgirl with her gym-slip tense over a distended abdomen, bewildered at what has happened when with her childhood's playmate they began exploring. Such girls, if seen early enough, present few problems in decision-making.[17]

The fifteen-year-old especially is the real problem. As intercourse at this age is technically a misdemeanour,[18] pressure has been made to make age alone a ground for abortion. Opponents of this suggestion point out that this might well encourage sexual activities at that age, if these carried a carte blanche. The incidence of early sexual activity is undoubtedly rising. Professor Russell has produced some frightening figures. Using the standard 100 for the number of illegitimate births in 1950, he found that by 1967 it had reached 200, but that there was little, if any, increase in illegitimacies over twenty-five years of age. However, as one comes down the age groups the numbers rise steeply. By 1967 these rates were 240 between twenty and twenty-four; 270 between sixteen and nineteen; and 560 at fifteen years of age. This fifteen-year-old rate had, in fact, risen from 100 in the previous twelve years only: truly an "explosion of illegitimate births affecting especially the youngest age group." It seems to me that for this the avant-garde members of the older generations must take a large share of the blame, for as Russell comments, "The apparent

[17] In 1969 abortions were performed on 326 girls aged fourteen or younger. Two of the girls were aged eleven. Two of the fourteen year olds were aborted for the second time. (p. 169, fn. 10).
[18] Criminal Law Amendment Act 1885.

advantages of this permissive attitude are freely and repeatedly presented in current novels, in the cinema, in the theatre and on the television screen. The personal and family tragedies that may flow from these relationships, especially in young teenagers, are seldom portrayed."[19]

On the other hand it is generally believed that the girl is too immature to take on the responsibilities of motherhood.

Medical Case 19.1. A girl of 15 years and 8 months was referred at her mother's request, by a G.P. who did not support the request for termination. The girl stated to the gynaecologist that she wished to keep the child, and that her boyfriend (who was about 3 years older) also wished to keep it. They hoped to get married. Her mother maintained that this was being used as a lever to persuade her and her husband to permit this marriage in a few months: this they had no intention of doing as the girl was too young, and they had educational plans for her. The mother also maintained that, as her daughter was under 16 the latter had no say in the matter, and could be compelled to submit to a termination at her mother's wish. Both doctors felt that it would be unforgiveable to force a girl to have her womb emptied against her will, such a course being likely to lead to severe mental trauma both now and in the future.

As at any ages the physical risk of the operation had also to be considered.

Medical Case 19.2. A 24-year old woman was referred to an infertility clinic because of two miscarriages at 14 and 16 weeks of pregnancy. She was found to have a badly damaged cervix (neck of the womb). It turned out that she had had a pregnancy terminated when aged 15. Shortly after marriage, and before the first miscarriage, she had told her husband this story, and she did not think it had altered his affection for her. The damaged cervix was repaired but a third miscarriage occurred a few months later. Soon she became increasingly aware of her husband's resentment that she was unable to have a child. He was openly blaming this failure on her prenuptial therapeutic abortion. She was deeply concerned about the future of her marriage.

The problem of management is not, therefore, quite as straightforward as it may at first seem.[20]

vi) *The Mentally Subnormal.* This group again can be subdivided many times. For our purposes we need only consider the two extremes. There are the girls who at first sight appear quite normal.

Medical Case 19.3. An attractive looking girl of 20 years was seen with her 62 year old mother. She conversed normally and gave a history of being 8 weeks pregnant. Her mother then explained that the girl could not read nor write, had a vicious temper, and could not be left alone for any length of time. She could not, for instance, be left in the house with children lest she harmed them, or at

---

[19] J. K. Russell, "Pregnancy in the Young Teenager," *Practitioner*, 1970, **204**, 401.

[20] In June 1971 in England there was a furore because a N.H.S. woman gynaecologist refused to abort a twelve year old girl (*Sunday Times*, June 20, 1971). It excited wide television and newspaper coverage, much of it highly critical of the gynaecologist. Interestingly the media almost completely ignored, the very next week, the report of a coroner's inquest into the death of another twelve year old, following a legal termination of pregnancy. (*BMJ*, 1971, **3**, 125.)

least fail to care for them. Her only friends were men, a series of whom took her up until her deficiencies became apparent. She would never be able to marry, rear a family, care for a home. Any man who wished would, without difficulty, be able to persuade her to yield to his advances.

Such cases are in some ways more difficult to deal with than the gravely sub-normal.

Medical Case 19.4. A 16 year old girl, physically well developed and apparently normal, could not speak, could not keep herself clean. Her periods had been absent for four months. On examination the uterus was found to be the size of a sixteen week pregnancy. There was, of course, no question of her ever being marriageable. Her periods would continue to be a burden to her parents (while she had parents). She was available to any boy who could catch her out of sight of her mother. The gynaecologist performed a hysterectomy.

The Options Open

There are five options open in the management of single girls with an illegitimate pregnancy.

a) *Quick marriage.* This has usually being regarded as being the obvious course. Where the couple were already planning marriage it should be encouraged. Frequently courting girls are sent to me for confirmation of pregnancy, and the only advice that needs to be given is that they should bring forward the date of their wedding. However, on two recent occasions the girl has turned and said: "But how do I know he will marry me? We have never discussed the matter."

For girls who had not planned to marry the putative father, is a wedding the best answer? The figures from America give pause for thought. In USA, where the normal divorce rate is 25%, it has been shown that teenage shotgun marriages carry a divorce rate three to four times as high as that in marriage over the age of twenty.[21] Dr. T. P. Monahan described a series of cases in Philadelphia which although from the municipal courts he believed to be typical of the city as a whole. Of whites 20.1% and of Negroes 45.6% had pre-marital pregnancies; interestingly among whites the figures for those who had a religious wedding ceremony (17%) were only half those for the couples who had been married by a civil ceremony. White couples with a premarital pregnancy came to separation at 3.3 years and to divorce at 5.4 years; while those who did not have a premarital pregnancy took considerably longer to come to separation (5.5 years) and divorce (9.2 years). He comments ". . . they separate or come to court sooner if they have conceived children before marriage. The quickening of family crisis and separation is considerable. Persons who enter marriage under such circumstances, it seems, have special liabilities and difficulties facing them. Undoubtedly this is to some extent also a result of couples being forced into marriage to protect the mother, or to give the child a name; with youthfulness of the partners, and concomitant difficulties adding further to the adjustment problems."[15]

Medical Case 19.5. A nineteen-year-old girl was referred for abortion largely because of her mother's health. It turned out that the mother had had herself to get married because of a premarital conception. Her married life had been a misery and her husband had eventually deserted her. She had now taken a dislike to her daughter's fiancé and was afraid that history would repeat itself.

b) *Adoption*. If the pregnancy is to continue the arguments in favour of adoption appear to be threefold. First, once the adoption has taken place and the scars have healed, the record can be closed, and the episode forgotten. The girl will be a free agent, can behave as any other single girl, and eventually enter at some future date into marriage, with a clean slate. Secondly, the child will receive a suitable emotional background, which requires a permanent unconditional relationship of love with someone who mothers him, and with a father and other family figures. It also requires a daily life and a dwelling place to ensure him a reasonable continuity of experience; thus finance and housing are factors to be considered. At the best, room has to be made for the illegitimate child in a family which was already complete without him, whereas the adopted one steps into a place prepared for him in a family which was not complete until his arrival.[3] This welcome is the third factor: he will complete the joy of the childless couple.

Whilst those arguments may seem convincing to the adviser what is the girl's attitude? An American psychiatrist, Dr. Rosen, is clear on this: "No one in the technical literature has stressed the heartlessness, the cruelty and the sadism that the pregnant woman so frequently senses – perhaps correctly, perhaps mistakenly – when the physician, minister, or lawyer suggests to her that she carry the child to term and then hand it over, never to see it again, to someone else to rear. They object to 'farming the child out for adoption' and maintain 'I'm not an animal. Do you think I could give away my baby after carrying it for nine months? . . . A hundred years ago you could take the babies away from slaves . . . . You can't do that now! And you can't turn me into the kind of animal that would give my baby away'." Rosen continues that during the past eighteen years he had seen only three patients for whom "farming out" of a child for adoption would not have been emotionally exceedingly traumatic and psychiatrically contra-indicated. For some twenty-nine patients who came into psychiatric treatment within one to four years after they had accepted this kind of recommendation (which they considered to be the abandoning of their infants), all but seven required extensive therapeutic management. A woman does not lightly leave a baby on someone else's doorstep, or in a hospital nursery.[22]

[22] H. Rosen, "Psychiatric Implications of Abortion. A Case Study in Social Hypocrisy." In *Abortion and the Law, op. cit.*

Medical Case 19.6. A nineteen-year-old girl became pregnant to her boy-friend who then broke off the relationship. She had been adopted as a child and had had every affection and luxury provided. Despite this her request for termination was mainly based on the fact that, in view of her own experience, she was not prepared even to contemplate adoption for her child. She became so mentally distraught that abortion was performed.

If adoption is to be carried out I am sure that the child should be handed over immediately, preferably without the mother handling it at all, or even seeing it. However because of nursing staff shortage it is often necessary for the mother to care for the baby, just as married women in the lying-in ward do, for the first ten days. Unless there is the likelihood that the girl may change her mind and keep the child, I think this should be avoided. More than once I have heard such a mother, in her middle teens, say, "The worst moment hasn't come yet." It is heartbreaking to see the loving care with which they check through the baby's layette, the garments often beautiful, prior to wrapping them up for handing over with their child. As Jean Pochin has finely said, "Society blames her for shuffling off her responsibilities, but she undergoes the pangs of real bereavement, without the sympathy and understanding that would have been hers if the babe had died. She is left with the memory of a demanding helpless infant, and a constant unfulfilled desire to know how he is getting on."[3]

c) *Fostering.* This has all the disadvantages of adoption, plus two others: the physical mother has to make a regular financial contribution to the child's upkeep; and as there is always the option of claiming him back neither physical nor foster mother has any real peace of mind.

Fostering in an institution has the advantage of trained staff and the companionship of other children, but what is possibly a greater disadvantage: the lack of a normal home life.

d) *Keeping the Baby.* One surprising fact we must notice is that some girls (30% in one series of pregnant unmarried students)[24] have a desire to be pregnant. Jean Pochin states that in her experience there may be a strangely detached attitude of the girl towards the actual begetting of the child, the girl often insisting that she had a blackout and remembers nothing. "It is almost as though intercourse and conception were two different and unrelated things . . . many potential unmarried mothers seem to be unconsciously looking for conception without intercourse."[3] Many others, no doubt, enjoy both the intercourse and its fruit.

The trouble arises when, as Dr. M. D. Enoch describes it, such girls "as a result of pressure from society, family, 'friends' and their own moral conscience demand termination, believing that this will put everything

---

[23] "In cases where there is a 'love child,' the moment of parting with the one link with a man whom they loved and who has abandoned them is the bleakest hour in many women's lives." (Mary Ellison, *The Adopted Child*, London, 1958, Gollancz).

[24] P. W. W. Gifford, quoted in Editorial, *BMJ*, 1967, **I**, 711.

right. On close questioning it is often obvious that most of these women are deeply motivated towards a successful pregnancy. They want the baby, firstly, as part of their maturing process; secondly as a way of reinforcing their relationship with this man, and thirdly as a way of asserting their own independence.... These cases therefore should *not* be terminated since there is a greater threat to health, e.g. from severe depressive reaction following a termination – than if the pregnancy is allowed to proceed normally."[25]

Medical Case 19.7. A nineteen-year-old girl admitted that she wanted this baby despite the extraordinary degree of family opposition. Her only question was "If I succeed in having this baby will they be able to take it away from me?"

Even in the young age group the question of the actual delivery need give rise to little alarm. In a series of English girls under the age of sixteen it was found that pregnancy and labour were usually without difficulty, the only increased incidence being the common one of pre-eclamptic toxaemia.[26] Dr. W. H. Utian found that although in his series there was some increase in loss of babies around the time of delivery "from the standpoint of pure physical ability the young primigravida does very well."[27]

Where the girl is keen to go on with the pregnancy, and her parents are willing to assimilate the new baby into their family as their child, this may be the best solution. It is not, however, altogether an easy one. Is the new baby to be brought up thinking that its grandparents are its parents, and its mother is its sister? The truth will come out sooner or later. When the girl eventually leaves home, will she take her child with her, or leave it permanently, as though a younger sib, in her parental home?

At times of tension in the home, especially when the new baby is fractious or requiring heavy expense for clothes, it will take a good deal of understanding and grace for its behaviour not to be thrown in the girl's face.

Where the girl has already left home, or where she takes the baby with her on leaving home, unmarried, things get much more difficult. Can she be both father and mother to her child – and breadwinner? Again Pochin has reminded us of the difficulties of such a situation – psychological, economic and practical. Some men make it plain that they expect her to be "obliging." There is the loneliness of her state; she is not a girl, being a mother, yet not eligible for "Young·Wives" because not married: she belongs nowhere.[3]

In Denmark, where only 3% of illegitimate babies are adopted outside the family circle, there are special houses containing flats for the single mother and her child, with communal facilities. These are let for a limited

[25] M. D. Enoch, Letter in the *Lancet*, 1966, **2**, 1316.

[26] B. V. Lewis and P. J. Nash, "Pregnancy in Patients under 16 Years." *BMJ*, 1967, **2**, 733.

[27] W. H. Utian, "Obstetric Implications of Pregnancy in Primigravidae Aged 16 Years or Less." *BMJ*, 1967, **2**, 734.

period only, usually two years, to help the girl get over the first difficult time until she can become adjusted.[6] These must be a great help, as must the companionship with other girls in a like plight.[28] "Half-way Houses" are being set up in England by Church welfare bodies.

e) *Abortion.* In view of the difficulties implicit in each of the other courses this often is the first possibility considered. For the very young, Mary Romm has no doubt that it is the correct management: "She is by no means ready for the emotional experience of either the pregnancy or the childbirth. The traumatic experience of an abortion appears to be less dangerous to her welfare than the vicissitudes involved in pregnancy, childbirth and maternity before she is capable of weathering them."[29] On the other hand Dr. Kinch and his colleagues point out that while the older teenager applies for abortion, the younger girl rarely considers it, but "paradoxically the younger age group appears to experience more emotional pain on giving up the baby, which compounds the guilt of allowing the pregnancy to continue."[4]

In those girls who basically wanted to get pregnant, this desire may be associated with resentment at the need for delay in marriage and the establishment of a home of their own.[24] In such cases it is foolish to consider abortion, for even if that were performed the basic problem is left unsolved.[30]

A further point to which I, at any rate, give considerable weight is the foreseeable post-abortion behaviour of the girl. The young girl who became pregnant in a first act of curiosity has had a very bad fright. One cannot imagine that her memories of the episode are such as to encourage her to repeat it. Her parents often insist that the relationship with the boy is broken off. She frequently realises for the first time how valuable her opportunities for study are, having so nearly lost them. This girl is likely to make a fresh start. In contrast there is the girl who for many months, perhaps years, has been having intercourse frequently, often two or three times a week with one man. It seems to me to be unrealistic to expect her to abandon this life and suddenly become chaste. In all but name she has been married to her partner. Abortion is going to achieve nothing. She will be back at risk in three weeks' time. The same probably applies to the girl who has been "sleeping around" with a number of partners. Here, however, there is no tight bond to one. Occasionally I believe the shock of the pregnancy and abortion may be enough to make them change their ways. For this book I am using a pen which arrived from one such – the accompanying note said: "Thank you for enabling me to make a fresh start."

[28] "If a girl really loves her child and wants to keep it, society should either help her whole heartedly, or, in the best interests of herself and her child, discourage her from making the attempt. No other lines of treatment are fair to her." Mary Ellison, *op. cit.*
[29] Mary Romm, "Psychoanalytical Considerations." In *Therapeutic Abortion, op. cit.*
[30] E. H. J. Cotter, letter in the *BMJ*, 1967, **2**, 177.

How often should one be prepared to abort the same woman? How many times does one need to learn the same lesson?

Medical Case 19.8. A 24 year old girl had to give up nursing because of an illegitimate pregnancy. When the child was born grandmother cared for it and the girl restarted nursing elsewhere until she became pregnant again. She was offered an abortion but refused it, whereupon her boy friend abandoned her. Grandmother refused to help further, the girl had to take a flat, in a new town, with her two children. Finances did not run to two nursery school fees. It was her aim, when the older was five and able to go to school, to send the younger to nursery school and start nursing for a third time. A year before this became possible a relative called on her, befriended her at a time when she saw very few folk, and made her pregnant once more. She requested abortion. A third child would make impossible for at least another four years any chance of her getting out of her solitary seclusion. The impression given was of a lonely young woman, tied day in day out to her small flat and her two fatherless children.

In such a case it can be argued that she should previously have learnt her lesson; on the other hand it can be argued that her mental health will suffer. Decision would depend on one's impression of the woman.

The Widowed, Divorced and Separated

These women usually tell the story of having had a liaison for some considerable time with a man, on the understanding that marriage is in the offing. Usually he has to wait for his own divorce proceedings to be completed; in the case of the separated it may be her situation which is causing the delay. Often both these circumstances are found together. The request for abortion is usually made on the grounds that the man, on being told of the pregnancy, disappeared. Her hopes are dashed, her reputation is going to be publicly ruined, and her financial pittance is going to be stretched even further. In addition the long term future is hopeless. Whereas a widow with a small family may have some hope of remarriage and making a new home, the chances for such a woman with an additional illegitimate child are completely different. It can be argued that she should go away, have the baby quietly, and have it adopted. Pochin has shown that for a woman with her own home and her own children the chances of her giving up a child for adoption are negligible. Even if she sets out to do this, she soon reclaims the baby.[3]

For the separated there is an additional complication.

Medical Case 19.9. A 35-year-old woman had initiated divorce proceedings against her husband on the grounds of his adultery. They were already legally separated and he was making a financial contribution towards the care of the children who had been put in her custody. The family doctor stated that she cared for them very well, and ran a good home. She became pregnant by the man she hoped later to marry. She was referred for abortion, and found to be very distressed at the prospect that she might lose the custody of her children when her pregnancy became known. Legal opinion was that this was unlikely, but that her husband's financial contributions were in jeopardy.

One difficulty, of course, as in all abortion requests, is in knowing whether the patient is telling the truth.

Medical Case 19.10. A divorced woman with three children requested abortion on the grounds of desertion by the man who had promised to marry her. She pointed to scars on both wrists; these proved to be exceedingly superficial scratches, made with some sharp instrument; they did not extend beneath the skin. A psychiatric appointment was made – which, incidentally, she failed to keep. On her leaving the consulting room one of the clinic nurses took Sister aside and said, "I know that woman well, I hope Mr. X realises that he is dealing with a whore."

In considering these cases a series of separate factors runs through one's mind: anger at the woman's betrayal, frustration at her foolishness, impatience with her having walked into trouble, sometimes even a sense that she is experiencing the just retribution for her actions, nevertheless, the principal emotion is that of sympathy for her in distress.

At this stage one must remind oneself that matrimonial irregularity is not a ground for abortion in law. An abortion performed for the kindest of motives, if not according to the Act, is a criminal abortion. On seeking legal advice about a tricky problem in a young teenager I received a reply which started: "The first point, and one which you are doubtless well aware of, is that the particular circumstances surrounding this 15 year old girl may well not permit her to be aborted within the terms of the Abortion Act."[31]

The British Medical Association Annual Representative Meeting in July 1970 was asked to affirm that abortion solely on social grounds, if supported by two doctors acting in good faith, and performed within the meaning of the Abortion Act 1967, was indeed ethical. It refused to do so.[32]

Sympathy for the girl, therefore, is not sufficient grounds for abortion. The larger problem of her baby we will consider in a later chapter.

[31] Medical Protection Society. Personal communication, July, 1970.
[32] Report in the *BMJ*, 1970, 3 (supp.) 52.

CHAPTER 20

THE PREGNANT STUDENT

The teaching profession clings automatically to the old view that spiritual beliefs and morality are so different from the other enquiries of men – so disreputable academically – that they can't be considered freely in the ordinary classroom in relation to the issues of today . . . . But surely the search for a morality that accords with man's nature and man's predicament is as much a search for the truth as the search, for example, for the essential nutrients in his diet. DR. BENJAMIN SPOCK[1]

THIS ADDENDUM TO OUR LAST TWO CHAPTERS IS NECESSARY BECAUSE of the frequency with which the problem is met. It can be argued that the fact that the woman, married or single, is a student is irrelevant to the problem. Certainly in the eyes of the law it does not entitle her to any special consideration. In terms of the Abortion Act 1967 in Britain her status as a pregnant student is relevant only when it has implications for the welfare of the other children in her family, or has a bearing on her mental health.

A woman with a completed family takes up studies usually for one of two reasons. It may be that her husband has been disabled by an accident or that his health is failing. In either case she will have to become the breadwinner. In this difficult situation a woman may decide to train for a career, usually teaching, which will bring in a reasonable income, yet leave her free to be with her children when they are at home. Such a woman, unexpectedly becoming pregnant, is in a dilemma. Were she already qualified it would be possible to take time off for the latter part of the pregnancy, and make arrangements for baby-care while she returned soon after to work. Being, however, a student this will probably be impossible to arrange. Her training will stop, once more she will be bound to the home, and the financial provision for the family will fail to materialize. The strain of all this may, in addition, produce mental symptoms. Consideration can, therefore, be given to her request under either of these clauses in the Act.

On the other hand she may have taken up training, not because of financial need, but because of her desire at last to use her intellect, and to bolster up her self-respect. For perhaps fifteen years she has been tied to the round of cooking meals, washing up, making beds and doing the

[1] B. Spock, *Decent and Indecent*, London, 1970, The Bodley Head.

laundry. Some women find this emotionally rewarding, but few would claim it is intellectually satisfying. The woman with a good brain often feels it is fast deteriorating for want of use. Now, the family safely settled, is the time to find herself. In this high moment of fresh endeavour, with her mind stirring out of its long slumber, the discovery that she is pregnant is a dreadful blow. Gone are her hopes; it's back to the kitchen. Despite our sympathy, only if her despondency becomes black depression can her request be considered at all. Such a case is exemplified in "Mrs. D" in chapter 16.

A much commoner problem is that of the single girl about to embark on a university career. Despite everything that is said about equality of opportunity men tend to be more equal than girls in obtaining vacancies; certainly it appears so in medical schools. If, therefore, a girl has managed to obtain the offer of a place in one of the more sought after faculties this is an unrepeatable chance. I have more than once had such a girl come with the request for an abortion. It is here that one recalls the clause in the act which says that "account may be taken of the pregnant woman's actual or reasonably foreseeable environment." If this opportunity is missed it is eminently reasonable to foresee the years of mental strain from self-reproach. The same remarks apply, of course, to the girl already up at university. They are much less applicable for the girl in one of the "easy" courses, or in teacher training college, where a year's delay in admission would be of less consequence.

The incidence of extra-marital intercourse among students is increasing. Among American students Benjamin Spock reports that whereas in Kinsey's report 51% of the men and 27% of the girls were sexually experienced, a generation later Vance Packard has shown that the figures are 58% and 43%, a small change among the men, but a large increase among the women.

In one English university known pregnancies among unmarried female students rose from 0.7% (of the total student body) in 1962–3, to 2.6% in 1964–5;[2] in another, students attending the venereal disease clinics rose from 2.5 per thousand in 1961 to 5.5 per thousand in 1965.[3] Commenting on these figures the editor of the *British Medical Journal* wrote: "In spite of denials from some quarters most people who stop to think would agree that sexual promiscuity is debasing to the personalities of those who practise it, fraught with serious dangers especially for women, and damaging to the interest of society."[4]

Protagonists of the permissive society are fond of talking about the responsible behaviour of young people in their extra-marital affairs. I have no doubt there are such. I have no doubt there are young men and

[2] P. W. W. Gifford, quoted in fn. 4.
[3] R. S. Morton, quoted in fn. 4.
[4] Editorial: "Sexual Promiscuity Among Students," *BMJ*, 1967, I, 711.

girls spending long hours persuading themselves and their tutors of the profound philosophical reasons why they wish to do what young people from the dawn of time have wished to do, although more often without such parade of scholarship. However, I don't meet these responsible young people in my clinics, and I wonder if they form any perceptible percentage of the population. The girls I meet have acted from emotional not philosophical motives. The motives behind intercourse have come, not from their heads, but from their hormones and their hearts. I have the suspicion that the coal-fields of Durham are more typical than are the cloisters of Oxbridge.

In our endeavours to understand young people, one factor to be re-called arises from the generation gap. Older folk tend to emphasize the importance of security. The girl must have security. It is important to understand that the eighteen-year-old student with her own flat, her own grant, her own life, doesn't see it this way. For her security, which means marriage, implies a subtle lessening of status. She would no longer be in standing and in independence the equal of her fiancé. She would share his flat, her money would probably come as part of his married-man's grant. From inside marriage we can see that the gains outweigh these disadvantages. We must not expect the girls automatically to agree.

Those who deal with abortion problems are almost all graduates. As such we have a special affinity for the student which we cannot feel for her sister who is mentally less well endowed. Despite this, in the end we have to apply the rules of judgement laid down in our last chapter.

CHAPTER 21

THE CHILD EMOTIONALLY AT RISK

"You haven't got no da'. . ." The others took it up. No one unless he has been through a similar experience and has had the security of parents wrenched from him, can have any idea as to the force of this impact. How it shatters for always the whole world of childhood, and reverberates through the rest of life.

CATHERINE COOKSON[1]

IN CONSIDERING THIS SUBJECT IT WOULD BE WISE TO START BY REMINDING ourselves that it is not only the illegitimate child who is in risk of emotional deprivation:

Medical Case 21.1. A woman aged 24 was referred for termination early in her third pregnancy. The general practitioner stated that the husband was a psychopath who was intensely jealous of his children. He had been so upset following the birth of the second child that he remained off work for many months. He was an exceedingly strict parent and beat both his daughter and his son frequently. The home was bizarre, to say the least. While the mother was a nice stable woman, the risks both to the next babe – if born – and the added risks to the existing children were thought to be too great to permit the pregnancy to continue.

Medical Case 21.2. A woman in her mid-thirties was referred for termination early in her fifth pregnancy. This was her second marriage, the first three children being to her first husband. Her second husband's business required him being away from home frequently for long periods, but when at home he made life hell, especially for the children. So much was this so that the 14-year-old girl was under the care of the pediatrician. The latter told the gynaecologist that the girl appeared almost well while her father was away, but broke down as soon as he came home, and required constant medical care. There was no evidence that the father cared for the fourth child – his own – more than the others. It was, therefore, suggested that as the mother was at the end of her tether, and as any further addition to the family was likely to exacerbate matters, termination and sterilization be performed.

If this kind of situation can arise in a home where the child is legitimate, the position of the illegitimate child within a family can be far worse. It is quite common for a man to marry a girl who already has an illegitimate child prior to marriage. Such a child is an understood factor in the marriage, and has a chance, particularly if young at the time of the wedding, of winning a place in its stepfather's affections. Whether that

[1] Catherine Cookson, *Our Kate*, London, 1969, Macdonald.

place will remain secure when his own children come along is less certain.[2] However, when there is an episode of adultery within the marriage the position must be far more grave. Our fictional case Mrs. F. in chapter 16 exemplifies the problem. To expect a child, unwelcome and illegitimate, to take in a family a normal place sandwiched between legitimate brothers and sisters, is unrealistic. The husband's forgiveness may be completely genuine, and may in fact manifest itself in his attempts to accept this infant. Children, however, are cruel. Sooner or later the child will become aware of its difference. If there is any racial difference this awareness will come sooner rather than later, and will not be transitory.

There are, of course, exceptions. Joseph Fletcher records what he calls a case of "sacrificial adultery," in which a German woman captured by the Russians could only achieve repatriation to her family by being pregnant. She persuaded a friendly prison guard to impregnate her. "Her condition being medically verified she was sent back to Berlin and to her family. They welcomed her with open arms, even when she told them how she had managed it. When the child was born, they loved him more than all the rest, on the view that little Dietrich had done more for them than anybody."[3] The unusualness of that story emphasises the hurdles which normally confront such a child.

Illegitimacy carries a stigma that sears itself into the soul of a child. The novelist Catherine Cookson recorded her own childhood's experience in the passage quoted as our chapter heading. It may well be that this fact has played a crucial part in the story of the English speaking peoples. Winston Churchill, discussing the Conqueror, writes, "The taint of bastardy clung, and sank deep into William's nature. It embittered and hardened him."[4]

This bitterness is not inevitable. It may be obliterated by the love of adopting parents. It may be overcome by grace. That prince of the pulpit, Alexander Whyte, was brought up in conditions of real poverty by his unmarried mother.[5] It cannot be doubted that his sermons (which more than half a century later are still being reprinted) owe much of their tenderness to this background.[6]

---

[2] Mary Ellison (*The Adopted Child:* London, 1958, Gollancz) notes: "Again and again maladjusted, unhappy children have proved to be those who, while living in their mother's home, were born not to her marriage, but were offered shelter by a stepfather acting on an impulse which he has later had reason to regret. The presence of such a child in the home is a living daily reminder of something both husband and wife would wish to forget. If children are subsequently born to them, there is frequently a pitiful contrast—which the unwanted child is quick to sense and take to heart—between the cherished little ones of the marriage and the older child, unloved through no fault of his own."

[3] J. Fletcher, *Situation Ethics*, London, 1966, S.C.M. Press.

[4] Sir Winston Churchill, *History of the English Speaking Peoples*, London, 1956, Cassell.

[5] G. F. Barbour, *The Life of Alexander Whyte D.D.*, London, 1923, Hodder and Stoughton.

[6] Just prior to going to press I was fascinated to discover that the first chairman of the A.L.R.A., in 1936, was Mrs Janet Chance, second daughter of Dr Alexander Whyte (K. Hindell and Madelaine Simms: *Abortion Law Reformed*. London, 1971, Peter Owen).

The child who has been kept by his unmarried mother does not have an easy lot. It has been pointed out by a psychiatrist that it is the "unstable or emotionally disturbed mothers who are more likely to keep their children, despite the presence of characteristics which would ordinarily tend towards adoption."[7] The problems from the mother's side have been discussed in chapter 19; they are equally grave from the child's angle. Few mothers even in the most favourable circumstances find it easy to maintain an equable temper at all times. This child, whose very existence wrecked its mother's hopes and aspirations, is likely to find that mother swings between moods of excessive affection when she cuddles it as the only loving person left to her, and moods of anger as she recalls her bitter lot. Landladies of such tenants are frequently critical, neighbours are disapproving. At the earliest possible moment the child must be dumped in a nursery for the maximum number of hours to allow mother to earn their keep. During the long evening hours the mother is torn between her natural desires to be out with folk of her own age, and the unending demands of her fractious child who is poor company. All this must make a child early aware of its difference from other children, aware perhaps of its deprivation of father and siblings, prone either to retreat into itself, or to develop a chip on its shoulder.

As the child grows up the absence of a home into which to bring its friends, the absence of brother or sister, must make the streets its playground. All information shows that these children have a much greater likelihood than children of normal homes of becoming delinquent in later years.

A study of ninety-two illegitimate children aged fourteen–fifteen who had remained with their mothers or relatives in Toronto has shown that 52% had changed their mother-figures – usually two, three or more times. Signs of maladjustment were found in 47% of the children, and in 22% this took the form of delinquency, mostly stealing and truancy.[8] The child who is fostered has the advantage of a home situation. Yet the disadvantage of this relationship was highlighted in July 1970. On a High Court order a nine-year-old girl was removed from the home in which she had been fostered since the age of six months. In front of TV and newspaper cameras she was dragged, crying "Don't let them take me" from the arms of her foster mother to be returned to the care of her natural mother.[9] *The Times* in its leading editorial remarked: "A child is not a piece of property to be disposed of according to some iron law of the right of possession. Wherever a child had his home for any length of time, ties of affection and of habit are established. They cannot be broken without some shock and obviously the longer they have been established

[7] Margaret Yelloly, quoted by Jean Pochin, *op. cit.*
[8] J. Bowlby, *Child Care and the Growth of Love* (2nd ed.1965), London, Penguin.
[9] *The Times*, July 17, 1970.

the greater the suffering is likely to be. Where the foster home has provided stability, both material and emotional, and where the natural parents are feckless or show only an intermittent interest, it is clearly too facile to assume that the child will be better off with his natural parents."[10]

Fortunately this episode has caused so much indignation that it is likely to result in an improvement in the law, with hopefully less of the uncertainty which must be an underlying cause of strain in the fostering relationship.

Particularly in the last century the obvious place for the illegitimate child was seen to be in an institution. The disadvantages of institutional upbringing are becoming increasingly recognized, although only the ignorant would scorn the great work done, for example, in the Orphan Homes founded by Müller, Barnardo and Quarrier, in Britain, or for Anglo-Indian children by Graham in Bengal. The child psychiatrist John Bowlby has remarked: "Even for good organizations the rate at which children have to be shifted from foster-home to foster-home is deplorably high; even in good institutions the turnover of staff is a constant problem. However devoted foster-parents or house-mothers may be, they have not the same sense of absolute obligation to a child which all but the worst of parents possess." He sums the situation up with the startling statement, "Young children thrive better in bad homes than in good institutions."[8] In one follow-up study, comparing the social adjustment in adult life of children who spent five years or more of their childhood in institutions, with others who had spent the same years at home (in 80% of cases, bad homes), the results were clearly in favour of the bad homes, those growing up to be socially incapable numbering only half (18%) of those from institutions (35%).[8]

It seems therefore that the child who lives alone with its unmarried mother and the child fostered privately or in an institution, is likely to be deprived. "Just as a baby needs to feel that he belongs to his mother, a mother needs to feel that she belongs to her child, and it is only when she has the satisfaction of this feeling that it is easy for her to devote herself to him. The provision of constant attention night and day, seven days a week and 365 days in the year is possible only for a woman who derives profound satisfaction from seeing her child grow from babyhood, through the many phases of childhood, to become an independent man or woman, and knows that it is her care which has made this possible. It is for these reasons that the mother-love which a young child needs is so easily provided within the family, and is so very very difficult to provide outside it."[8]

The results of the absence of such love from a mother or an equivalent mother-figure lead to deprivation. Hilda Lewis differentiates several types

[10] *The Times*, July 18, 1970.

of deprivation; rejection by parents seems to lead to unsocialized aggression, neglect by parents precedes socialized delinquency; and a repressive regimen is associated with later neurosis.[11] Where a series of people, perhaps in an institution, looks after the child each for a few days, the child delays forming attachment to specific figures. According to Mary Ainsworth if the discontinuity persists long enough he may be expected to develop an affectionless character, incapable of attachment – a picture seen where an illegitimate child passes successively from mother to granny and on to a series of foster-mothers.[12] Unfortunately the warping of this child's character is not the end of the story. Socially incapable adults they may become, but they are unlikely to be childless, and many of their children are in their turn likely to be neglected and deprived. In a series of 100 unmarried mothers no fewer than forty-three had been brought up in broken homes; while a study of 255 promiscuous men showed that 60% came from homes which had been broken by death, separation, or divorce. Quoting these studies Bowlby comments that it is emotionally disturbed men and women who produce illegitimate children of a socially unacceptable kind.[8] This vicious cycle starts in one generation with a home that may have been accidentally broken by death or illness. As a result the children of the next generation grow up to have difficulties in interpersonal relations and are unable to provide an affectionate, secure environment for their children. As a consequence the third generation develops conduct disorders.[12]

Medical Case 21.3. A 17-year-old girl was seen with her adoptive mother. The girl had been born illegitimate when her mother was 17 years of age, and had been brought up in an institution until the age of 9 when she had been taken over for fostering, and later adoption by the lady who accompanied her. Since then the patient had been given the best opportunities, including private schooling, but remained rather "slow." However she later started a job which she was holding down satisfactorily. She was very carefully and closely cared for by her adoptive parents, so much so that they were able to pinpoint to the hour the only time when conception could have occurred "It's history repeating itself," said the adoptive mother. A year later it was repeated yet again.

With the arrival of an illegitimate child, how is Bowlby's vicious circle to be prevented? He implies that only if at least four of the following conditions are present is the unmarried mother wise to take her baby home: that she is a stable personality, that she takes a sensible attitude towards the problem, is loving and accepting of the child, that she really cared for the supposed father, and that she has a family which does not insist on the child being disposed of. Social workers, he goes on, "now conceive it to be their duty to help the unmarried mother to face the real situation before her, which so often is that of an immature girl, on bad

[11] Hilda Lewis, quoted by Mary Ainsworth, *op. cit.*
[12] Mary D. S. Ainsworth, "Further Research into the Adverse Effects of Maternal Deprivation." In Bowlby, *op. cit.*

terms with her family, with no financial security, having to undertake with little or no help the care of an infant for whom she has mixed feelings, over a period of many years. If this is in fact the real situation, and it is put before her in a sympathetic way by someone whom she has learned to trust, many girls recognize that it is in the interest of neither themselves nor the baby to attempt to care for him, and are prepared to release him for adoption.... Moreover, it is in the mother's interest to make the decision to keep or part with her baby early rather than late. Unless it is reasonably clear that she will be able to care for the child, it is no kindness to permit her to become attached to him; parting is then all the more heart-breaking. Some unmarried mothers decide, after reflection, that they would prefer not to see their babies, a decision which should be respected. Rigid policies that all unmarried mothers must care for their babies ... can have no place in a service designed to help illegitimate babies and their unmarried mothers to live happy and useful lives."[8]

"From the child's point of view there is no doubt that, in general, adoption offers much the best prospect of a happy and permanent home with the love of two parents," remarks Jean Pochin adding "but it demands of the mother the ability to surrender her child completely."[13]

Adoption does not, unfortunately, guarantee that for the child all will be well. That the child born out of wedlock has no more than a 50% chance of growing up into a well-adjusted adult, whether he is adopted or brought up by his mother, is the judgement of Alexina McWhinnie who has done a retrospective study of fifty-two adults in South-East Scotland who were adopted as children.[14] She found it essential for a good result that the child was adopted where there was a stable essentially happy and mutually satisfying marriage relationship between the adoptive parents. The child must be accepted because of a love of children, of concern for this child, and not to fulfil the needs of the adoptive parents. The child must not be expected to be grateful for having been adopted. The attitude towards him must be kept up if a biological child is later born. The whole family group must approve of the adoption. She identified several possible sources of failure to provide the best for the child. The adoptive parents, especially the wife, often feel inadequate because of their own infertility, and therefore avoid telling the child of its own relationship until an age when this news is very traumatic. The parents may adopt because there is some incompatibility in their marriage. Later the mother may become jealous of the relationship between her husband and his non-biological daughter. Parents who are of good academic standard may be frustrated and critical of a child who is less well endowed

[13] Jean Pochin, *Without a Wedding Ring: Casework With Unmarried Parents*, London, 1969, Constable.
[14] Alexina McWhinnie, *Adopted Children: How They Grow Up*, London, 1967, Routledge and Kegan Paul.

mentally. Strict parents may be so determined that the child will not fall into the moral delinquencies of its natural parents that they may make its life unhappy by rigid discipline.[14]

It is possible to paint the picture in too sombre colours. There are many illegitimate children, principally among those adopted in the earliest months of life, who have a happy secure childhood and grow up with a love for their parents undimmed by the knowledge that they are not theirs biologically. One friend of our own was so saddened by the death of her adoptive mother that she persuaded her husband that they should go abroad to work rather than to live in England where the sense of bereavement was so strong.

Generally there is no doubt that the lot of the unwanted child is hard. It is not that the mothers necessarily feel antipathetic. As Jean Pochin remarks: "There is no doubt that many girls who keep their babies are sincerely devoted to their children, make excellent mothers. The trouble is that society often loads the dice against them so heavily that they have no chance of bringing up their children happily and successfully."[13] In a German study it was noted that whereas 10% of its 350 unmarried mothers had a negative attitude towards the child immediately after delivery, later this had risen to 23%.[15]

It appears that there is no emotional deprivation more severe than the rejection of a young child by the mother or mother-person.[16] If this be so then we can no longer avoid criticizing those who, in the words of a Roman Catholic Professor of Moral Theology, "irresponsibly burden society with children whom they have no intention of caring for – and what is infinitely worse, burden their children with a life in which there is no love."[17] There may be mitigating circumstances. The girl or her lover may themselves be caught up in the vicious circle having been deprived of affection in their own childhood. When allowance is made for all this the blame for their child's plight must lie with those who conceived it, and those who talk about "responsible" extra-marital sexual relationships. True responsibility might well start with a perusal of Bowlby's *Child Care and the Growth of Love*. It is significant that there have been, although not yet in Britain, a series of legal actions on account of wrongful life, including those in which a child (or someone on his behalf) sues a parent for bringing him into the world illegitimate.[18]

To most the obvious answer is to avoid the tragedy of the unwanted child by ensuring that he is not born. And with this we would all agree.

[15] Binder (1941). Quoted by P. Arén and Amark, *op. cit.*

[16] R. L. Jenkins, "The Significance of Maternal Rejection of Pregnancy on the Future Development of the Child." In *Therapeutic Abortion, op. cit.*

[17] S. E. Kutz, "Conscience and Contraception." In *Contraception and Holiness* (Ed. Abp T.D. Roberts), London, 1965, Collins.

[18] D. Daube, "The Sanctity of Life." *Proceedings of the Royal Society of Medicine*, 1967, 60, 1235.

And agree too that the ideal is that he should not be conceived. While many would say this can best be achieved by the more adequate dissemination of contraceptive information and supplies, the Christian would make his plea for chastity.

When, however, an illegitimate child is conceived, and we foresee the inevitable train of events, what is to be done? The easy answer is abortion. It is true that illegitimate conception is not a ground for action under the 1967 Act, but many would press into service the clause: "there is a substantial risk that if the child were born it would suffer from such physical or *mental* abnormalities as to be seriously handicapped." Before doing so however, we must carefully consider the alternative of adoption.[19] A woman recently wrote: "My sister and I are both adopted, having been placed with wonderful parents as small babies. Although no-one in this family unit is related by blood, my sister and I feel just as much part of a family as anyone else. We do not refer to the people who produced us as 'real' parents, for we feel that our real parents are the ones who adopted us, the others being merely the instruments used to give us life. I think these two arguments do a lot to negate the contention of pro-abortionists who say that the child, if born, would be unwanted. This need not be the case . . ."[20]

Assuming then that there is a local policy to encourage adoption, the risk of emotional harm to the innocent illegitimate baby need not persuade us towards abortion. As it has been shown[13] that widowed, divorced and separated women with their own house and children rarely give up a child to adoption, in these cases further thought must be given. In these cases, however, we know that the child would not be bereft of a permanent home and the affection of its own mother.

Having said all this we must remember that a plea for abortion on the grounds that the child is unwanted is made most often by married women caught in a time of panic. The *pregnancy* may have been unplanned and therefore unwanted, but the *child* from the very moment of birth, will not be unwanted. Rabbi Jakobovitz may have been a little sweeping in asserting that there are no unwanted children of five years old,[21] but the percentage of such must be trivial by comparison to those unwanted in the second month of intra-uterine life, which is when the woman pounds on her doctor's door. An attempt has been made to correlate unwanted conceptions with undesirable effects in pregnancy, with miscarriage, toxaemia, premature labour and difficulty in delivery, but no data to support

[19] L. Nelson Bell, "An Alternative to Abortion." *Christianity Today* (Washington), June 18, 1971.

[20] Member of the Society for Protection of the Unborn Child, quoted in its *Bulletin* no. 5, 1970.

[21] I. Jakobovitz, "Jewish Views on Abortion." In *Abortion and the Law* (Ed. D. Smith), Cleveland, 1967, Press of Western Reserve University.

such a correlation could be found.[22] This is not to claim that no such data may be found, or to suggest that there are no disadvantages following unwanted pregnancy, but within a normal family the difficulties can be overcome. Certainly any quick decision in favour of abortion should be resisted.

The Half-Caste Child

The problem of the child illegitimately conceived by parents of different races and skin pigmentation deserves special consideration.

For a single girl to keep a half-caste child carries all the disadvantages outlined above, plus the hallmark of immorality obvious to every passer-by. There is no chance of her escaping into anonymity. For a married woman, with a family of ordinary children, to have a single one among them of different colour would be in most cases to so placard her adultery as almost inevitably to cause the break up of her family, with emotional trauma to everyone, not least to her legitimate offspring.

For the child itself the future can never be easy. It is usually thought that these children are unadoptable, and therefore must inevitably be brought up in an institution, with all the disadvantages we have noted.[23] In fact there are an increasing number of couples who, out of a sense of compassion for these children, ask the adoption societies for them. However, the child can never be assimilated into the family, at least in the eyes of its playmates and neighbours, in the same way that a baby of the same race could be. Even when he grows up into independent life his problems are not over. He is truly at home in no country, he is at a disadvantage in competition for jobs. When his age-mates start courting he will be odd man out, few girls will be willing to take him seriously as a suitor, and fewer prospective parents-in-law approve of him. At the back of his mind, remembering his own bitter experiences, will be an unwillingness to have children of his own doomed in their turn to a similar future.

It is difficult not to be angered at the utter folly of girls who get into this position. They usually do not know even the home address of the boy, who has almost always gone abroad on learning of the pregnancy. Nevertheless if the story can be substantiated it seems to me that this situation is one in which abortion may well be the wisest management for the sake of the fetus.

[22] E. Pohlman, "Unwanted Conceptions: Research on Undesirable Consequences." *Eugenics Quarterly*, 1967, **14**, 143.

[23] However, a four-year study of 50 children of coloured or mixed race has shown that "Children who are of minority race in Britain today *can* find adoptive parents who will love and cherish them." Lois Raynor, *Adoption of Non-White Children*, London, 1970, Allen & Unwin.

CHAPTER 22

THE MALFORMED FETUS

Our baby came into the world with an appalling handicap . . . I believe with all my heart that God sent her on a two-year mission to our household, to strengthen us spiritually and to draw us closer together in the knowledge and love and fellowship of God. It has been said that tragedy and sorrow never leave us where they find us. In this instance both Roy and I are grateful to God for the privilege of learning some great lessons through His tiny messenger, Robin Elizabeth Rogers.
DALE EVANS ROGERS[1]

"AMONG THE RIGHTS OF THE UNBORN CHILD MUST BE INCLUDED THE right of being well-born."[2] That fundamental belief underlies the legislation which permits abortion where there is a substantial risk that the child, if born, would suffer from such physical abnormality as to be seriously affected.

Before accepting its validity we should remind ourselves that periodically during the abortion debate letters appeared in the press from deformed adults or children, a group of thalidomide victims among them, stating that they are glad to be alive and grateful that no-one had had them aborted. At a philosophical level Albert Schweitzer claimed: "A man is truly ethical only when he obeys the compulsion to help all life which he is able to assist, and shrinks from injuring anything that lives. He does not ask how far this or that life deserves one's sympathy as being valuable, nor, beyond that, whether and to what degree it is capable of feeling. Life as such is sacred to him. He tears no leaf from a tree, plucks no flower, and takes care to crush no insect."[3]

Despite this it is widely held that if the birth of a child, doomed to deformity and forever prevented from enjoying a full life, can be prevented, this should be done. It has always been one of the principal arguments for a liberal abortion policy that it would prevent the birth of such children. Professor Hill has estimated that there are about 15,000 defective babies born each year in the United Kingdom. "While for the less severely defective, who are the more numerous, the outlook is

---

[1] Dale E. Rogers, *Angel Unawares*, London, 1953, Marshall Morgan & Scott.
[2] K. F. Russell and J. G. Moore, "Maternal Medical Indications for Therapeutic Abortion." *Clinical Obstetrics and Gynecology*, 1964, **I**, 43.
[3] A. Schweitzer, *Civilization and Ethics*, London, 1961, Allan & Unwin.

increasingly encouraging; for the severely defective, mentally and physically, the outlook has changed very little. We cannot anticipate that from the time of birth there will ever be any reprieve for these."[4]

Unfortunately any steps we can take at the present stage of medicine to prevent such births will merely nibble at the problem. Where an abnormal child has already occurred in a family, and the abnormality is known to be due to a single genetic cause, the risk of recurrence can be calculated. For instance, in the central nervous system (one in twenty) and the heart (one in fifty). Even if recurrence of an abnormality in the same family is eliminated by avoidance of later pregnancy this would have little effect on their incidence. "The large majority of malformations are unpredictable, and are likely to remain so because they result mainly from accidents associated with fertilization, implantation and early development . . . . Few malformations are recognized during pregnancy, and none at the early stage when abortion is technically easy."[5]

The proof of this can be seen in figures from Japan, where in 1947 there were 2,679,000 live births. Following the introduction of a very liberal abortion policy in 1948, abortion became popular, and in 1953 there were only 1,868,000 live births. Yet the infant death rate from congenital malformations had *risen* from the 1947 figure of 14.7 to 21.1 per ten thousand births. That this was no chance poor result is shown by the fact that the 1960 figures were little improved (an even higher percentage of abortions, and 19.0 infant deaths due to congenital malformations per ten thousand live births).[6]

However disappointing this is, we must still try to spot pregnancies with particular risks and see what can be done to eliminate those few of the malformed fetuses we can identify.

Inherited Abnormalities

Human genetics is a complex study. Sufficient to remind ourselves here that every human cell contains twenty-three pairs of chromosomes. One of these pairs controls sex differences being XX in the case of a female and XY in the case of a male. The end-products of the reproductive cells contain only a single set of chromosomes 22 plus X (in the ova) or 22 plus X or Y (in the sperm). Thus their union at conception provides the first cell of the new fetus with its full complement of a double set of chromosomes, and fixes its sex. Each chromosome carries on it many separate genes which are the substance determining the inherited characteristics of the individual.

[4] Sir Denis Hill, "Economic and Ethical Considerations Arising from Modern Care of the Defective Child and the Very Old." *Proceedings of the Royal Society of Medicine*, 1967, **60,** 1232.
[5] T. McKeown, "The Community's Responsibility for the Malformed Child." *Proceedings of the Royal Society of Medicine*, 1967, **60,** 1219.
[6] E. Matsunaga, "Some Genetic Consequences of Family Planning." *Journal of the American Medical Association*, 1966, **198,** 533.

Congenital disorders may be due to a damaged chromosome. Others are caused by a harmful gene, which can be transmitted to the next generation in one of three ways. If it is *dominant*, any children who inherit it will be affected. However, as only one of each pair of chromosomes is passed on at each conception, it follows that in any four children two may be expected to be affected and two normal.

Then there is *recessive* inheritance where the gene only reproduces the disability provided it is present in both chromosomes of the pair; i.e. it has inherited the damaged gene from both parents. Therefore if both parents carry this damaged gene in any four children one will have the disability and one will be quite normal. The other two will carry the gene on only one of the pair of chromosomes, and therefore will not themselves be diseased but will be "carriers" able to pass it on to their offspring in turn.

In *sex-linked inheritance* if the damaged gene is carried on the X chromosome of one parent, one son in two will be a patient, one daughter in two a carrier, and the other two children should be unaffected.

It will immediately be obvious that where both parents are close blood relatives the risks of any inheritable abnormality being passed on, and becoming evident, are much increased. The closer the relationship the greater the risk. In a study of eighteen incestuous pregnancies Drs Adams and Neel found that by six months only seven of the children of incest were normal and able to be adopted, of the eleven others three were dead, two were severely mentally retarded and were institutionalized, three were less severely mentally retarded having estimated I.Q.'s of about 70, while one had a bilateral cleft lip but was otherwise normal. After reviewing the literature they feel that although not all the abnormalities in their own series were genetically induced the risks of death-plus-defect in children in incest is about 16–20% higher, and in children of first-cousin marriage 4–5% higher, than with non-related parents.[7]

This sounds very formidable. When, however, a list of inherited diseases[8] is consulted it will be found that each condition mentioned is excessively rare; few of them would be met in even several years of obstetric practice. Normally the first that is known of either parent carrying a defective gene is when a child exhibiting one of these rare conditions is born. It is then possible, in many cases, to seek help from a genetic advisory centre, identify the trouble, and put a figure to the risk of a further abnormal child being born.

A large number of these deformed children, as the first such in the family, are unexpected. A still larger group can never be foreseen being born to unaffected parents, the condition having arisen due to a fresh mutation in the cells.[8]

[7] S. Adams and J. V. Neel, "Children of Incest." *Pediatrics*, 1967, **40**, 55.
[8] Standing Medical Advisory Committee for the Central Health Services Council and the Ministry of Health. *Human Genetics*, 1967.

Mongolism – Down's Syndrome

This is probably the most important genetically-caused disease for us to consider, both because of its comparative frequency and because of the interest aroused in it recently. After birth the child has a very low mentality, and may need care in an institution. It may be due to there being an extra chromosome, so that the patient has a total of forty-seven; or it may be due to an interchange (translocation) between two chromosomes.

Down's syndrome occurs once in 600 births, but the incidence varies with the maternal age from 1:2,000 for women under the age of twenty-nine, to 1:50 over the age of forty-five.[9] (In the rarer group, due to the mother's having the chromosomal translocation, the risk of an affected child is 1:5.)[10]

Now it is obvious that in the case of parents who have already had a mongoloid child it is essential to find out their chromosomal make-up before further advice can be given. For the woman who has never had such an affected child the statistical risks are those given above: even at 45 years of age they are 50:1 against a baby's being affected. It is important to realize this. In June 1970 the pro-abortion lobby mounted a campaign implying that the risks of an older woman having a mongoloid baby are so great that older women should be granted abortion on request. The Abortion Law Reform Association reported to the then Secretary of State for Social Services the cases of three older women whose applications for abortion had been turned down, and who later delivered mongoloid babies. There appear to have been other grounds for an abortion to be considered, but the implication was that in some way the consultants had failed in allowing a mongol to be born. The Secretary of the ALRA was quoted as saying, "now that the department has asked questions I feel sure this consultant will be careful about turning down such cases again."[11] The same month in the religious press a columnist wrote of a "pregnant middle-aged woman, who has suffered a serious injury in a car accident. She was held up by unnecessary delays until it was too late and now she has to face the probability that she is going to have a mongoloid baby."[12] In view of the incidence of this condition – dread as it is – it is difficult to see such statements as other than part of the constant campaign to pressurize gynaecologists into unthinking acquiescence to every demand.

Damage to the Fetus

Broadly speaking the fetus is organized and developed during the first

[9] F. Fuchs and L. L. Cederqvist, "Recent Advances in Antenatal Diagnosis by Amniotic Fluid Analysis." *Clinical Obstetrics and Gynecology*, 1970, I, 170.

[10] C. O. Carter, "The Genetics of Congenital Malformations." In *Scientific Foundations of Obstetrics and Gynaecology* (Ed. E. E. Phillips, Josephine Barnes and M. Newton), London, 1970, Heinemann.

[11] *News of the World*, June 7, 1970.

[12] Ruth Adams, *Church of England Newspaper* and *Christian Record*, June 19, 1970.

thirteen weeks, after which it merely grows. During these first three months any noxious insult to the fetus can cause its development to be upset, with the result (if the damage is severe) that a miscarriage ensues; if less severe, that a malformed child is delivered. These insults take three forms.

Radiation Damage occurs when the early fetus is subjected to a sufficiently high dosage of radiation. Experimental work quoted by Dr. R. E. Hall suggests that the maximum dose tolerated by the human fetus during the first 6 weeks is 10r; and thereafter 25r.[13] In Denmark therapeutic abortion is permissible throughout the first trimester if the pelvis of the mother has been exposed to 10r.[14] On the other hand at Hiroshima it was only those women who had acute radiation sickness (estimated to demand 200–600r) who delivered defective babies.[15]

Medical Case 22.1. A 30-year-old-woman had been married 8 years and after a spontaneous miscarriage had never again conceived. She had irregular periods and was ordered XR treatment to her pituitary gland (at the base of the brain) and to her ovaries. Unfortunately this was not started for 7 weeks. On the third weekly treatment she was found to be 8 weeks pregnant. The radiologist said there was no choice but to perform an abortion; all the obstetricians agreed. The patient however, insisted that the pregnancy was something of a miracle and that "with God's will" it would proceed to term. It did. At 6 years the child's physical and mental growth were above normal.

Drug damage. Although many drugs have been inculpated as causing fetal malformation the classical one is thalidomide. The deformities resulting from the taking of this, especially during the fifth to seventh week of pregnancy, consist principally of an absence, or gross stunting to, the bones of the limbs. Since this incident in the early 1960s very stringent rules have been introduced on the testing of new drugs, and it is profoundly to be hoped that a similar tragedy will not recur. Despite this it is wise to abstain from all avoidable medication during pregnancy, especially during the first three months.

Women who are at risk of falling pregnant must bear this question of drugs in mind. It is important to note that the drug LSD, popular among certain groups of young people, has in more than one case been blamed for fetal abnormalities, when taken by the mother in the early weeks of her pregnancy.[9]

Infection. The invasion of the developing fetus by viruses can cause malformation. A number have been blamed but the only one we need to notice here is German Measles (Rubella). Rubella is a trivial infection of no importance to the mother, but for her fetus it can have the most severe

[13] r (roentgen) is the international unit used in measuring exposure dosage to radiation.

[14] R. E. Hall, In *Advances in Obstetrics and Gynecology* (vol. 1) (Ed. S. L. Marcus and C. C. Marcus), Baltimore, 1967, Williams and Wilkins.

[15] R. E. Moloshok, "Fetal Considerations for Therapeutic Abortion and Sterilization." *Clinical Obstetrics and Gynecology*, 1964, I, 82.

consequences. Prospective studies have shown that after maternal rubella in the first four weeks of pregnancy, 47% of liveborn children were defective; after rubella in the second four weeks 22%, in the third four weeks 7% and in the fourth four weeks 6%. In addition, rubella in the first eight weeks is associated with up to 57% of fetal deaths, as well as with many premature deliveries. The classical triad of defects is deafness, cataracts in the eyes, and cardiac abnormalities, but other anomalies may occur.[16]

Fortunately rubella is not highly infectious, and trivial contact unlikely to be important. It is the pregnant mother who nurses one of her own children suffering from the disease who is principally at risk. In these cases an attempt may be made to prevent the woman's developing the condition by giving her an injection of gamma-globulin: this is material from the blood of a person who having had the disease has built up a resistance to it.

Prophylaxis against rubella in pregnancy is achieved either by making sure all young girls have an infection in childhood, thus manufacturing their own immunity, or recently by the inoculation of girls with live attenuated rubella virus vaccine. As 15–20% of women of child-bearing age in urban communities have not had rubella and are therefore at risk, and as following the USA epidemic of 1964 some 10–20,000 babies were born with one or more congenital abnormalities (quite apart from those stillborn[17]), it is obviously a major problem which must be tackled.

Clinical Management

When a mother has already had a malformed child the risks of a further one being born have been divided by Dr. C. O. Carter into three groups:

Random risk. These are the cases where the abnormality was due to an environmental cause unlikely to recur, such as rubella or toxoplasmosis.

Near-random risk to a later child when the affected child has an anomaly which although genetically determined, arose from a fresh mutation, the parents being genetically normal, such as Down's syndrome when the affected child has the extra chromosome but the parents do not.

High risk where the parents have abnormal chromosomal make-up; such as translocation of chromosomes causing Down's syndrome.[18]

What steps then are we to take? We can identify the cause and let the parents know the statistical risks of a further abnormality. Recently techniques have become available in research centres for amniotic fluid, or even placental tissue, to be removed from the mother's uterus at an early stage of pregnancy, usually in the fourth month, and examined for

[16] K. McCarthy and C. H. Taylor-Robinson (1967), quoted by Rosalinde Hurley in *Scientific Foundations, op. cit.*
[17] "Vaccination against Rubella." Editorial in the *BMJ*, 1970, **1**, 318.
[18] C. O. Carter, "Genetic Counselling." *Lancet*, 1969, **1**, 1303.

the presence of abnormal cells, and for biochemical studies.[19,9] This is a tremendous advance because in these cases the genetic counsellor may be able to say categorically that the baby is affected, or not.

If these techniques are linked with the offer of abortion it is no longer necessary for parents to deny themselves their right to their own children. They can go ahead and achieve conception knowing that if the child proves to be affected it will be removed and they can try again.[20,21]

This attitude has been strongly condemned by a Canadian pediatrician who wrote: "One cannot question the value of scientific studies of the amniotic fluid and cells to further our knowledge of some of the inherited metabolic diseases. When, however, the main object of these studies is to encourage therapeutic abortions, one can certainly question this from the point of view of the unborn baby. One can understand how some parents, alarmed by information about a possible defective pregnancy, would consider this form of antenatal euthanasia a logical solution . . . . Surely these small human beings have some right to life despite the mental stress placed on their parents. When parents are faced with the possibility of a defective baby, should they not either be strongly encouraged to prevent pregnancy, or else be prepared to accept a defective child?"[22]

Such a view, however, does not commend itself widely, and most would agree with Lederberg: "Far from limiting efforts to have children the availability of voluntary abortion should go a long way to encourage the gamble in risky matings, by putting the stakes under more effective anticipation. Such a policy represents the only humane reconciliation of the individual's rights of parenthood and social concern for the containment of genetic disease."[23]

In the case of rubella it is possible to perform blood tests of the mother to see whether or not she has been affected.

Medical Case 22.2. A woman of 35 was referred in her fifth pregnancy. Although this was unplanned she had had no thought of abortion, to which both she and her husband were opposed in principle. Her fourth child, then aged 4, developed German measles when the woman was eight weeks pregnant. The family doctor took a maternal blood sample a week later which was reported as showing evidence of recent rubella infection in the titre of 1:8. Four weeks later a similar test was taken which was now positive in a dilution of 1:128. The increasing strength of the reaction revealed that the woman had indeed, had an infection, although she had not been aware of it. It was strongly advised by the public

[19] H. L. Nadler, "Prenatal Detection of Genetic Defects." (Review Article) *Journal of Pediatrics*, 1960, **74**, 132.

[20] L. I. Gardner, Letter in the *Lancet*, 1969, **2**, 1067.

[21] There is a rare, fatal, hereditary condition known as Tay-Sacks disease. By the use of amniocentesis and selective abortion women with a high risk of producing affected children have been able to take the risk, and in 50% of cases deliver normal children. (J. S. O'Brien, quoted by Nature-Times News Service, *The Times*, April 15, 1971.)

[22] L. L. De Veber, Letter in the *Lancet*, 1969, **2**, 845.

[23] J. Lederberg, "A Geneticist Looks at Contraception and Abortion." *Annals of Internal Medicine*, 1967, **67**, supplement 7, 25.

health bacteriologists that abortion be performed. Abortion was performed; examination of the fetus showed that it had been affected.

This new technique is very important, for up to now abortion has usually been done in rubella contacts merely because the fear the woman has that she may have been infected, and that, if so, the babe may have been affected.

A few years ago Dr. Hall commented on how ludicrous the situation had become in the U.S. "In California, revocation-of-licence proceedings resulting from the concern of prominent Catholic physicians, have been instituted against doctors for having *done* abortions for German Measles whereas in New Jersey lawsuits brought by parents of a child deformed during pregnancy by the German Measles virus have been instituted against doctors for *not* having done an abortion."[24]

The tests on the fetal amniolic fluid, or placental tissue, mentioned above are not without some risk.[9] They would probably only be justified in the case of a woman who had already had an affected baby, or who is known to be the carrier of a diseased gene, or perhaps for the normal woman pregnant in her mid-forties. The vast majority of abnormalities will not be discovered by this policy. Until some safe technique of screening the early fetus for abnormality has been developed, and until facilities are available to use such a technique in every case, we can make only modest headway.

The importance of doing all we can to prevent the birth of deformed children, can best be understood by those who have delivered a woman of a grossly abnormal child. They wonder firstly what to tell her, and secondly how to ensure that the child does not survive overlong in view of the inevitable mental strain. A strain felt not least by the young nurses in whose care it will be placed.

Even with the less severely deformed there is the black moment when one has to break the news to the mother. It is only relieved by the tremendous fortitude and love which so many such mothers summon up. Putting away their glad hopes, they gird themselves to the months and years of unwearying care for their unfortunate babe. That such a task is not without its rewards has been noted in the testimony of Dale and Roy Rogers which heads our chapter; to which testimony the present writer and his wife would add their own in thanksgiving for their son Alistair.

[24] R. E. Hall, Final Commentary to *Abortion and the Law* (Ed. D. Smith), Cleveland, 1967, Press of Western Reserve University.

CHAPTER 23

MENTAL AND SPIRITUAL RESULTS OF ABORTION

My baby would have been beautiful with tiny waving hands. He would have been a comfort and joy to hold and love. But there was no future for him. As I'm still very young, and unmarried, it was decided I should have an abortion. Last week I lost my baby and now plead with you not to condemn girls like me. No-one who has not been through the experience can know the unendurable heartache this causes.[1]

THE PICTURE PAINTED BY PROTAGONISTS OF ABORTION CAN BE SUM-marized somewhat like this: A woman as the result of a "mistake" finds herself pregnant, and realizes that she does not wish to bear the baby. She goes to her general practitioner who lends his sympathetic ear and – whatever the grounds – agrees to arrange the abortion, as the woman surely has the right to decide. She is sent to a further doctor who, feeling that the general practitioner is the person to know best, adds his signature to the statutory form. This is presented to a gynaecologist who recognizes that he is cast in the role of technician and carries out an easy, safe, swift, uncomplicated operation under excellent conditions. This patient spends a further one to twenty-four hours in hospital and then returns to the bosom of her family. There may be a momentary phase of mild depression lasting a day or two, but within the week she is back into her previous life: not unchanged, but matured by this unfortunate but none-the-less useful growth experience. "A lot of moral shackles are gone. I have an increased awareness of myself as a human being and not just in the eyes of the Church or of my husband. The abortion turned out well, so I now know I can trust what I feel."[2]

There is no doubt that in many cases things do appear to go smoothly, the patient does not admit to any regrets, the post-operative period is uncomplicated, and the patient is discharged from one's medical care apparently little affected by the episode. The observant will have noted that that statement includes the words "many" and "apparently:" they demand that we look into the matter with care.

[1] Miss R. A., Letter in *Woman's Own*, March 15, 1969.
[2] S. L. Patt, R. G. Rappaport and F. Barglow, "Follow-up of Therapeutic Abortion." *Archives of General Psychiatry*, 1969, **20**, 408.

Maternal Uncertainty

First: how sure is the woman of her own mind? A psychiatric social worker from University College Hospital, London, comments: ". . . at this time of panic and despair women are apt to deny strongly their feelings of guilt and ambivalence, in their determination to obtain an abortion. To 'wipe out' the situation appears to them the only possible solution."[3] This opinion is echoed by a Yale psychiatrist: "At the time of the (pre-abortion psychiatric) interview, most of the women were adamant as to what they thought they wanted. However, once the interviewer allowed the patient to discuss and display feelings, ambivalence would appear – accompanied by tears, recriminations, and other indications of guilt."[4]

Having been granted abortion, not all women will in fact present themselves for operation. From the Stockholm area, Drs. Arén and Åmark were able to find 142 women who, although officially granted abortions in the period 1950–1952, had not had the operation, but had given birth. In half (seventy-one) of the cases the women had refrained voluntarily: seventeen because in their cases sterilization was insisted on, seven on the persuasion of relatives, but the remaining forty-seven because they had changed their minds, without persuasion.[5] The Swedish workers think that this change of mind is often due to the women passing out of the first trimester of pregnancy with its physiological depression, before permission for abortion comes through. In Britain our natural eagerness to avoid the difficulties of the late abortion means that we operate earlier, and therefore see fewer of these pre-operative changes of mind. However, they do occur:

> *Medical Case* 23.1. A separated woman, who lived with a woman friend knew that she would be asked to leave if it were discovered she was pregnant. She had no family. The putative father was married. Abortion was agreed on social grounds. On recovering from the anaesthetic after operation she began to cry, and wept more or less constantly for the remaining 24 hours of her time in hospital. It turned out that while being wheeled to the operating theatre she had told the accompanying nurse that she wasn't sure she wanted the abortion, but the nurse had failed to pass the message on.

Depression, Remorse and Guilt

One of the great causes of our ignorance as to the real effects of abortion arises from the failure to differentiate between these factors. By most writers mental sequelae are judged to be noteworthy only if they require psychiatric treatment,[6] and trivial if they do not. Only workers who

[3] Eva Learner, "The Abortion Act 1967." *Social Work Today*, 1970, **1**, no. 4, 43.

[4] C. F. Kimball, "Some Observations Regarding Unwanted Pregnancies and Therapeutic Abortions." *Obstetrics and Gynecology*, 1970, **35**, 293.

[5] P. Arén and C. Amark, "The Prognosis in Cases on which Legal Abortion has been Granted but not Carried Out." *Acta Psychiatrica et neurologica Scandinavica*, 1961, **36**, 203.

[6] J.-O. Ottosson, "Legal Abortion in Sweden." *Journal of Biosocial Sciences*, 1971, **3**, 173.

understand the apostolic aim to have "a conscience void of offence to-wards God"[7] can appreciate what it may mean to a woman to carry a load of guilt.

Medical Case 23.2. A 40-year-old woman was found to be suffering from a respiratory difficulty while in the fifth month of her fifth pregnancy. She was advised termination, but was not altogether sure whether this was morally permissible. She was strongly reassured, especially in view of the probable organic nature of her disability. Following termination she became greatly depressed, feeling that in view of the great sin she had committed life would never again be worth living. This sense of guilt continued for years, and left its deep mark on the whole family.

Such patients are not in need of tranquillizers, or electro-convulsive therapy, but of the ability to accept forgiveness.

In the heat of the Abortion Act debate a correspondent in the medical press wrote: " 'The distressing postabortal guilt complex' is a myth that ought no longer to be invoked."[8] It is time now to look at the evidence.

In considering the voluminous literature of the psychiatric effects of abortion there are some points to be kept in mind. First, as already indi-cated, where the investigator leaves out of account the spiritual dimension his results must necessarily be seriously incomplete. Then we must bear in mind the personal attitude of the investigator. In any study there is the danger of interpreting results to fit one's own preconceptions; this is particularly difficult to guard against when the data deals with such intangibles as mental sequelae.

Thirdly, there is the difficulty of finding out the woman's true feelings after the event. Eva Learner, a medical social worker, states: "At present social pressures are such that women do not easily report or acknowledge their post-operative depressions and guilt feelings. I have found in a follow-up study we are doing that women will report their unhappiness by tele-phone or letter but will refuse help when it is offered. Women feel they are expected to prove that they will not cope with the pregnancy but that they will cope with the abortion. This is part of the rationalization that the abortion was necessary."[3]

In the fourth place results will depend upon the care taken in the choice and management of cases. Dr. J. H. Friedman has drawn attention to the importance of the patient's religious training being taken into account. He feels that if her religious tenets do not condone a therapeutic abortion, then it should not be considered, as it might lead to secondary guilt feeling with marked suicidal tendency.[9] Guilt feelings may be induced by

[7] Acts 24: 16.
[8] Letter in the BMJ, 1967, I, 236.
[9] J. H. Friedman, "The Vagary of Psychiatric Indications for Therapeutic Abortion." American Journal of Psychiatry, 1962, 16, 251.

unsympathetic or critical comments by the doctor, or by cruel or malicious comments by the neighbours.[10]

A number of workers report that adverse mental after-effects rarely occur. Sir Dugald Baird's experience in Aberdeen is that deterioration in his patient's emotional health as a result of feelings of guilt is practically non-existent.[10] Dr. J. M. Kummer claimed that there is a substantial incidence of psychiatric illness complicating pregnancy and childbirth. He states that of female psychiatric illness causing admission to American mental hospitals approximately 2% were precipitated during pregnancy or the puerperium.[11] (As more than 2% of adult women are at any time pregnant or in the puerperium his figures could be construed as proving that these physiological events protect against psychiatric illness!) He contrasts this with information from Israel, Japan and Denmark suggesting that moderate to severe psychiatric sequelae are rarely, if ever, encountered after induced abortion. He similarly discounts sterility or damage to the capacity for achieving orgasm as after-effects of the operation. "If the ill-effects of induced abortion have been so grossly exaggerated, we must ask ourselves why. Might the answer be that this is part of the means of enforcing the taboo. The taboo concerning abortion goes far back into antiquity. It has deep roots in the Judaeo-Christian ethic . . . . My conclusion from my preliminary investigations would be that abortion, as a precipitating stress towards moderate to severe psychiatric illness, is of only very minor significance, probably similar to any of a number of non-specific factors, such as a disappointment in love, an accident, loss of a job etc. This stands in vivid contrast to pregnancy, birth and child rearing which have found to be substantially significant stresses in susceptible females."[11]

Other writers are equally clear that adverse mental results are common. Dr. S. Bolter states that he has never seen a patient who has not had guilt feelings about a previous therapeutic abortion or illegal abortion.[12]

It would seem likely that the two opposite views so far considered are less typical than a central position.

The patient with genuine psychiatric illness antedating the pregnancy may be comparatively unchanged by the operation.

A study of a group of married, private-patient, mostly Jewish women in New York failed to show any deterioration in the mental status of 25 women aborted for psychiatric reasons, most of which pre-existed the pregnancy and were serious. "There was no change in the basic psychiatric status of these women. Those who were schizophrenic remained so, those

[10] Sir Dugald Baird, "Sterilization and Therapeutic Abortion in Aberdeen." *Journal of Psychiatry*, 1967, **113**, 701.

[11] J. M. Kummer, "Post-Abortion Psychiatric Illness—a Myth?" *American Journal of Psychiatry*, 1963, **119**, 980.

[12] S. Bolter, "The Psychiatrist's Role in Therapeutic Abortion: The 'Unwitting Accomplice'." *American Journal of Psychiatry*, 1962, **119**, 312.

who were neurotic remained so. However, the anxieties and depressions which were the direct consequences of pregnancy at this time in their lives were relieved. With this change those who had, prior to their pregnancy, been able to manage without psychiatric treatment would continue without it. Those who had required treatment prior to the pregnancy still required it."[13]

Most women, however, have no previous psychiatric history of any significance. How do they fare? Flanders Dunbar describes as "post-abortal hangover" the time corresponding closely to the unfulfilled length of the aborted pregnancy, and feels it may represent an unconscious carrying through of the pregnancy. "Whether the abortion has been 'spontaneous' or 'therapeutic' the potential mother thereby deprived of motherhood is likely to behave in a peculiar way. She will feel both relieved and deprived. Just how she behaves will depend on the degree to which she feels herself responsible for the abortion. She may feel inadequate because of a spontaneous abortion, she may feel guilty because she asked for a therapeutic abortion. In either case she will feel herself psychosomatically out of contact with the world around her. In this state of dis-ease she will begin to blame husband or society, for her dilemma."

She summarizes: "Whatever the difference in conscious or unconscious motivation for abortion, the experience of abortion inevitably arouses an unconscious sense of guilt."[14] We should take heed to the words of Aleck Bourne: "Few women realize that if their future baby is killed in the early stages of pregnancy they may, and very often do, suffer from remorse, one of the most eroding emotions. The great majority are so thankful for their relief that they forget the whole hateful episode, but still there are a few of the married ones who suffer from the 'biting back' which is remorse."[15] Enough, however, of opinions. We should now look at some figures. In doing so it should be realized that series are not really comparable. The indications for the abortion, the care with which cases are chosen, the proportion of cases in which sterilization is simultaneously carried out, the length of time before post-abortal assessment, and the philosophical stance of the assessor – these are all factors which vary from series to series.

The most thorough studies so far published come from Scandinavia[6] where there experience goes back three decades. Dr. P. Kolstad reports from Norway a follow-up of 897 women (only 22.3% of whom were aborted on psychiatric grounds), of whom 82.5% were glad without reserve. The remaining were classified as having "late mental effects." 9.8% were satisfied but doubtful; 3.8% not happy but realized the

[13] A. Peck and H. Marcus, "Psychiatric Sequelae of Therapeutic Interruption of Pregnancy." *Journal of Nervous and Mental Diseases*, 1966, **143**, 417.

[14] Flanders Dunbar, "A Psychosomatic Approach to Abortion and the Abortion Habit." In *Therapeutic Abortion, op. cit.*

[15] A. Bourne, *A Doctor's Creed; Memoirs of a Gynaecologist*, London, 1963, Gollancz.

abortion had been necessary; 3.7% were repentant. In all 4.3% had serious mental disturbance.[16]

In Sweden a follow-up of 479 women aborted on psychiatric or socio-psychiatric grounds showed that 65% were satisfied; and together with a further 10% who had found the operation unpleasant, had not felt any self-reproach. In 14% there was mild self-reproach and in 11% serious self-reproach, or the operation was regretted. Reporting this, Dr. M. Ekblad comments of this last group that the subjective sufferings may be severe but the depression only mild:[17] a perceptive distinction.

In the Swedish town of Malmo, women who, having previously had a legal abortion, went to term with a later pregnancy, were studied by Dr. P. Arén. In 100 consecutive cases he found that their reactions to the previous legal abortion in retrospect were as follows: Content 35%; content but with a bad conscience 17%, mild guilt feelings 25%, severe guilt feelings 23%. Commenting on this last group he states that the guilt feelings were so severe that the women had suffered for a varying length of time from nervous disorders, insomnia or decreased working capacity. Many of the women had been troubled by the sight of small children. Some complained of strange feelings of emptiness and longed for the child they had not borne. They often regarded mishaps or diseases in the family as a punishment for the abortion. Sometimes guilt feelings appeared even before the women left hospital, although usually later. In one case self-reproach made its first appearance three years after the abortion and then not until the woman had been delivered of her first child, when she realized what she had missed by having a legal abortion. In most cases however, subsequent birth of a child had the opposite effect: the guilt feelings became less poignant and the memory of the abortion began to fade.[18]

A Danish series reported by Dr. N. Hoffmeyer gave better results: of 126 legally aborted 112 were perfectly happy, 5 regretted it, and 9 had a "complicated view."[19]

Reviewing 61 Swiss women who had been aborted (and most of them simultaneously sterilized) Siegfried felt that the abortion might have been the wrong procedure in two cases. Despite this only 28% had no adverse reaction or were better adjusted. Feelings of guilt or unhappy memories, yet the knowledge that abortion had been right under their circumstances, were felt by 59%. In 13% there were more severe or persistent feelings of

[16] P. Kolstad, "Therapeutic Abortion." Acta Obstetrica et Gynecologica Scandinavica, 1957, 36, Supplement 6.
[17] M. Ekblad, "Induced Abortion on Psychiatric Grounds." Acta Psychiatrica et Neurologica Scandinavica, 1955, Supp. 99.
[18] P. Arén, "On Legal Abortions in Sweden: Tentative Evaluation of Justification of Frequency During the Last Decade." Acta Obstetrica et Gynecologica Scandinavica, 1958, 37, Suppl. 1.
[19] N. Hoffmeyer, "Medical Aspects of the Danish Legislation on Abortion." In Abortion and the Law (Ed. D. Smith), Cleveland, 1967, Press of Western Reserve University.

guilt, or frustrated motherhood and half these regretted the operation.[20]

The difficulties of presenting adequate statistics have been pointed out by the psychiatrists N. M. Simon and Audrey G. Senturia, who have reviewed and criticized the various series published up to 1964.[21] They comment on the frequent confusion between the presence of subjective feelings of guilt and the presence of psychiatric illness, but commend one series where the findings distinguish between guilt feelings and impairment of mental health, suggesting strongly that one may be present without the other. In this series from Stockholm, Karin Malfors visited eighty-four women in their homes two years after their legal abortions. Of these thirty-nine were perfectly happy. Of the remaining forty-five, four were embarrassed and did not like to discuss it; nine were consciously repressing guilt feelings about the experience; twenty-two had open feelings of guilt, and ten suffered impairment of their mental health. Some of these latter had had various complaints before the abortion, and the abortion became an additional psychic trauma that contributed to a fixation or accentuation of the symptoms.[22]

Recent series from both sides of the Atlantic report much less serious consequences. In San Francisco, of forty women who had been aborted on fairly strong psychiatric grounds, 80% returned a questionnaire a few months later. There were no serious psychiatric sequelae. Guilt feelings at two weeks had been absent in eighteen, mild in seven, moderate in three and severe in four. At three to four weeks these feelings had become absent in twenty-nine, mild in two, and severe in one. Asked if they would repeat the same course of action if required 81% were affirmative without reservation.[23] Of 250 patients referred to the Psychiatric Department of St. Bartholomew's Hospital in London, 130 were recommended for abortion. "Mild feelings of guilt were not unusual. These generally lasted one or two weeks and in only 17 cases (13%) for longer than three months"[24]

The interesting observation has been made that single girls who are aborted following conception during promiscuous pleasure-motivated activity rarely show regret. On the other hand the girl who conceives to the man she deeply loves, in an act of self-giving, is much more likely to suffer remorse after abortion.

As a rough approximation it looks therefore as though some 80%[19]

[20] S. Siegfried (In the Swiss literature), quoted p. 208 fn. 25.

[21] N. M. Simon and Audrey G. Senturia, "Psychiatric Sequelae of Abortion." *Archives of General Psychiatry*, 1966, **15**, 378.

[22] Karin Malfors, quoted by B. Brekke in *Abortion in the United States, op. cit.*

[23] H. I. Levene and F. Rigney, quoted by Catherine D. Pike, *California Medicine*, 1969, **III**, 318.

[24] C. M. B. Pare and Hermione Raven, "Follow-up of Patients Referred for Termination of Pregnancy." *Lancet*, 1970, **I**, 635.

to 85%[25] of patients will have little in the way of adverse mental reactions; the remainder will have reproach or mental symptoms which in the majority will gradually fade, but in some be long-lasting.

In our own area my colleague Dr. G. Gillis, giving even better figures, wisely comments "either our judgement is infallible and we have been right every time in deciding which pregnancy shall continue and which pregnancy shall be terminated, or (a more likely conclusion) whether termination is done or not the great majority of women will come to very little harm, or thirdly psychiatric complications may yet occur in some of our cases[26]. A further difficulty in assessment will be noted in a recent London series. When six months after abortion on psychiatric grounds 120 women were reviewed, 108 of them were wholeheartedly satisfied, but only in seventy cases did the G.P. feel that their condition had improved.[27]

A generation must pass before we can see the emotional results of the abortions now being performed. Psychiatrists remind us that of the post-abortal patients who "even after the passage of years, accuse themselves of being murderesses, and who then go into very pronounced depressive reactions"[28] and of others in whom "feelings aroused at the time of an abortion performed many years previously can become reactivated to be the focus of the self-derogation that depresses the aged patient."[29]

Suicide is the ultimate evidence of mental upset. Attempted suicide after abortion has been reported by many authors, while in Britain the Royal College of Gynaecologists report of the first year's workings of the 1967 Act includes mention of two women who indeed committed suicide in these circumstances.[30]

Childbirth after Abortion

"Never again!" is the usual cry of the woman who has become unwillingly pregnant. How does she in fact behave? The most useful information comes from the two Swedish series:

Dr. Ekblad found that 37% of women were pregnant within less than two years of their legal abortion, almost always unintentionally.[31] Of all these women only 27% had a further legal abortion, 61% gave birth and 12% had a "spontaneous" abortion.[17]

[25] D. W. K. Kay and K. Schapira, Letter in the *Lancet*, 1967, 1, 299.

[26] A. Gillis, Letters in the *BMJ*, 1969, 4, 368 and 1970, 1, 506.

[27] M. Clark, L. Forstner, D. A. Pond and R. F. Tredgold, "Sequels of Unwanted pregnancy. A Follow-up of Patients Referred for Psychiatric Opinion." *Lancet*, 1968, 2, 501.

[28] H. Rosen, In *Abortion in the United States:* A Conference Sponsored by the Planned Parenthood Federation of America at Arden House and the New York Academy of Medicine. (Ed. Mary Calderone), New York, 1958, Hoeber-Harper.

[29] L. C. Kolb, in *Abortion in the United States op. cit.*

[30] Royal College of Obstetricians and Gynaecologists. "Findings of an Inquiry into the First Year's Working of the Act." *BMJ*, 1970, 2, 529.

[31] For further pregnancies the figures were as follows. Married women aged under 26: 38% became unintentionally pregnant and 2% intentionally. Aged 26–35 33% and 8%; over 35 years 5% and 0%. For single women the figures of further pregnancies were: Under 26 25% unintentionally and 10% intentionally; 26–35 12% and 5%, over 35 6% and 0%.

Arén's series gave a similar finding: 40% of the women who had been aborted but not sterilized were back at the same hospital with a further pregnancy within three years. When one has to reckon that some others may well have delivered elsewhere the percentage may be even higher. The number who go on to deliver children (61%) is identical with Ekblad's series, but only 17% had a further legal abortion.[18] Of the 21% who went on to miscarry, a fifth were infected, which suggests that some will have had a criminal attempt after being refused a further legal abortion.

The Japanese experience is even more thought provoking: 43% of aborted women pregnant again within six months.[32] Similar Eastern European figures can be found.

Future intentional pregnancies may be due to an improvement in the social situation or the woman's health allowing for a pregnancy to be attempted; or the woman may have had an abortion for a non-recurring cause – e.g. rubella – and now wishes to have a child. In others in Malfors' experience "It sometimes happens that the women want to free themselves from their feeling of guilt for the abortion through a new intentional pregnancy."[33]

The Fathers

Single patients include the whole spectrum from those who have had intercourse only once to the Oxford woman "who had lost count of the number of different men she had slept with but estimated 'over 70.' "[34] How do they react to the man responsible with them for the pregnancy which ended in legal abortion?

In Arén's series of women who delivered in their next pregnancy, fifty-six had been single, divorced or widowed at the abortion; of these thirty-six had given the man up, while 20 had their next pregnancy to the same man (in nine cases without having married him meanwhile).[18] Of the unmarried women in Ekblad's series, 77% had no further contact with the man, 23% continued.[17]

Among married women who are aborted it is not surprising to find a number whose marriages are unsatisfactory. Dr. F. E. Kenyon's investigations show that 73% of the marriages involved were generally unhappy, and in 30% the husband was not the father.[34] In Arén's series, at the abortion of the married women 23% were happily married and 21% unhappily, but when their next pregnancy went to term (and these include the single girls who had married in the meantime) the happy

[32] Y. Koya, A Study of Induced Abortion in Japan, and its Significance. *Milbank Memorial Fund Quarterly*, 1954, **32**, 282.
[33] Karim Malfors, quoted by Ekblad, *op. cit.*
[34] F. E. Kenyon, "Psychiatric Referrals since the Abortion Act 1967." *Postgraduate Medical Journal*, 1969, **45**, 718.

210 ABORTION: THE PERSONAL DILEMMA

marriages had gone up to 51% but the unhappy remained almost unchanged at 24%.[18] Hatred of the spouse or lover is a recognized complication of abortion, although this probably arises only if the woman has
been pressurized into the operation by his wishes for selfish, neurotic, or
childish motives of his own.[35]

It is not infrequent, in my experience, for the putative father to accompany his girl-friend to the gynaecological clinic, or to write or telephone
the consultant on her behalf. More often, however, the girl reports
that from the moment she told him of her condition he broke off all
contact, frequently leaving the town and covering his tracks. Other
despicable tricks include the men who persuade their fiancées to seek
abortion so that they can continue their studies, and – the operation over –
break off the engagement; leaving the girl doubly bereft. On the other
hand in some cases they marry the girl, and the couple then bitterly
regret the child they have lost. From the time of the abortion, sexual
frigidity on the part of the girl or wife, is a recognized, if uncommon,
complication.

The fact of the abortion will affect the whole family circle.

Medical Case 23.3. A 16-year-old girl was, after a good deal of indecision on
the part of herself and her family, aborted. From then on her 34-year-old mother
began to feel increasingly guilty at having agreed to the procedure. Suddenly,
almost exactly on the date that her daughter should have been delivered, she
developed an acute paranoid schizophrenia with very acute aural hallucinations
all centred on her daughter's abortion. She was sure that everyone in the street,
in shops, and later in the ward, was aware of every facet of the case. Electro-
convulsive therapy and drugs were used with complete success. Both before
and after this episode she appeared to be a completely normal individual.

Conclusions

The figures and facts given above leave one with an air of uncertainty.
A wealth of further information will be found as the original papers
listed in the bibliography are consulted, but unfortunately will not lead
to any more firm conclusions. Reviewing the first eighteen months of our
British experience three writers, themselves protagonists of a liberal
policy, make the statement (so much wiser than the pronouncements of
others during the debate): "The psychiatric sequelae of abortion are
virtually unexplored."[36] It seems to the present writer that until the
central bastion – the relationship of a woman to her Creator, Redeemer
and Judge – is included in the exploration, the maps will be ill-drawn and
virtually useless.

One vital statement must not go unnoticed. Speaking of feelings of

[35] R. B. White, "Induced Abortion: A Survey of their Psychiatric Implications, Complications and Indications." *Texas Reports in Biology and Medicine*, 1966, **24**, 531.
[36] P. Diggory, J. Peel and M. Potts, "Preliminary Assessment of the 1967 Abortion Act
in Practice." *Lancet*, 1970, **I**, 287.

guilt or loss two London writers comment "The more mature and motherly the woman, the more likely such feelings were, and the more immature, psychopathic, or unmotherly, the more the patient was unaffected by a termination of pregnancy."[24]

Along with all who have actual care of patients I like to find that at follow-up they are happy and content. It is often suggested that as the operation becomes commoner and more accepted the incidence of emotional reaction will become ever less. If the price of this is to have our womenfolk "immature, psychopathic or unmotherly," it will have been too high. It is clear that in the world of Orwell's 1984[37] no-one would care a scrap about an abortion, nor would the moronic lotus-eaters of Wells' "Golden Age."[38] Surely we want more conscience, more responsibility, more integrity, more *person*, not less. Let us look at the abortion price-ticket very carefully: it may look like "Freedom" but when we get it home will we find it reads "Emotional and spiritual atrophy"?

[37] G. Orwell, *Nineteen Eighty Four*. London, 1949, Secker and Warburg. 1959, Penguin.
[38] H. G. Wells, *The Time Machine*, 1895. (London, 1964, Penguin).

CHAPTER 24

THE PHYSICAL RESULTS OF ABORTION

Thus, when every effort is made to suggest that emotion and feeling are perfectly appropriate to decide the social and personal goals of abortion, but that a clinical language only is appropriate when the actual techniques and medical objective of an abortion is described, then the moral imagination is being misled.

DANIEL CALLAHAN[1]

A N AMERICAN PSYCHOLOGIST IS QUOTED AS SAYING "DORENE IS LIKE most of the girls who come here. She has a family problem, a social problem, a religious problem and a legal problem – when all she should really have is a medical problem. One simple five minute procedure and she has the whole world off her back."[2]

Simple? Opinions on this are at four levels, depending on the involvement of the one expressing the view. First there are the writers, the propagandists whose views and figures are only as good as their sources: these must be verified. Second there are the persons performing abortions, perhaps in great numbers, in a clinic where the patients are discharged within 24 hours or less: the opinion here on immediate results should be valid, but only if they have long-term follow-up arrangements can they form any useful opinion of late results. Third there is the large hospital in a great city using a variety of techniques: the experience of such a unit is excellent and their figures invaluable. The one snag is that there is no guarantee that patients with late complications will turn up at the same unit. Fourth there is the experience of gynaecologists working in a smaller centre where there are no alternative units and no nursing homes: the failures have to be re-admitted, the unsuccessful sterilizations have to be booked for delivery; there is nowhere else for them to go!

I think it would be widely accepted that abortion performed in good hands in good circumstances, within the first eight weeks from the last menstrual period, is not attended by any short-term or long-term physical complication in the vast majority of cases. That during the next four weeks it is increasingly difficult, and after the end of the first trimester the number and severity of complications rises sharply, is the view of many of us

---

[1] D. Callahan, *Abortion: Law, Choice and Morality*, New York and London, 1970, Collier-Macmillan.
[2] Quoted in *Newsweek*, April 13, 1970.

whose opinions rank in the third and fourth categories I have just described.

First let us look at the methods employed.

Techniques of Abortion[3]

Dilatation of the cervix (the neck of the womb) and curettage of its contents has been the classical method in the earlier weeks. It becomes increasingly difficult after 10 weeks, and many of us feel it is rarely wisely employed after 12 weeks. Professor Stallworthy has commented "To evacuate an anteverted uterus after one missed period should be a simple procedure, but to empty the retrogravid uterus of a nulliparous woman after she has missed three periods can tax the skill of the most experienced surgeon even if he does use the suction technique."[4] In one series of 320 D. & C. operations there were 13 complications including perforation of the uterus on five occasions.[5] Perforation is extremely easy to do. It is also under-reported. There can be few of us who in our junior days were not so appalled at this misadventure that we "kept mum," in our senior days we still do it but have the wisdom to be honest.

Medical Case 24.1. A well-qualified gynaecologist performed a D. & C. operation for a 6 weeks pregnancy.* Six hours later at laparotomy for severe abdominal pain the small intestine was found to be perforated in five different places, and 15 cm. of it had to be removed and the ends rejoined. A tear in the top of the uterus had also to be closed. After a stormy post-operative period the patient recovered.

(* the gynaecologist reporting this in the literature said "4 weeks" which presumably was from the time of conception)

Vacuum Aspiration introduced into Eastern Europe from China has been popularized in Britain through the zeal of Miss Dorothea Kerslake.[6] It is gradually replacing D. & C. as the method of choice, being attended with less risks. However fracture of the vacuum curette inside the uterus[7] and perforation of the uterus requiring hysterectomy have been reported.[8]

Medical Case 24.2. A seventeen year old single girl was being aborted of a ten week pregnancy on the grounds of acute anxiety reaction. Due to a poor anaesthetic the patient made a sudden movement as a result of which the suction

[3] For a study of the various methods, including research techniques, see D. M. Potts "Termination of Pregnancy." British Medical Bulletin, 26, no. 1, 56.
[4] J. A. Stallworthy, "Complications of Therapeutic Abortion: Immediate and Remote." In The Abortion Act, op. cit.
[5] K. R. Niswander, M. Klein and C. L. Randall, "Therapeutic Abortion: Indications and Technics." Obstetrics and Gynecology, 1966, 28, 124.
[6] Dorothea Kerslake and D. Casey, "Abortion Induced by Means of the Uterine Aspirator." Obstetrics and Gynecology, 1967, 30, 35.
[7] J. M. McGarry, Letter in the BMJ, 1970, 1, 49.
[8] Anne Boutwood, "The Effect of the Act on Gynaecological Practice." In The Abortion Act. op. cit.

curette perforated the uterus. The abdomen was opened and it was found that the uterine artery on one side had been damaged and was bleeding. The womb had to be removed.

In Eastern Europe this technique has been employed under local anaesthesia thus reducing it to an out-patient procedure.[9] In the medical school in Belgrade eighty are done between eight and eleven o'clock, the whole procedure taking three to four minutes, and the patient going home two hours later.[10] On the other hand Professor Novak, also from Yugoslavia, in whose hospital 12,000 vacuum extractions have been performed, dislikes the out-patient method and prefers general anaesthesia.[11]

In 1970 Harvey Karman introduced a further refinement to vacuum aspiration by designing a very narrow bore disposable plastic curette which can be introduced through the cervix without dilatation. This being so no anaesthetic is necessary and the operative risks are greatly reduced.[12] Already many thousands of terminations using this technique have been performed in the United States.[12a] The patient is welcomed at the clinic and a history taken by a woman who has herself undergone the procedure and can therefore calm the patient, she is escorted to the treatment room, the womb sucked out, and the patient leaves the clinic within an hour of her arrival. No medication other than the soothing conversation of the receptionist is employed.[13] The method is being experimented with in a professorial unit in London.[14] Advocates of a liberal abortion policy are rapturous in their praise of this technique. It has been suggested that four centres would be enough to cope with all the British demands for abortion, allowing each patient a four-hour stay.[15] In that it appears to trivialize the whole procedure, and pregnancy as a state, its emotional effects may be less happy, especially for married women, if the Rumanian experience cited earlier[16] is anything to go on.

The desire for a quick operation – for the sake of secrecy, to save the patient money, to avoid a scar and the risks of a larger operation, as well as the wish for a quick turn-over – has tempted some to use D. & C. and

[9] M. Vojta, "Therapeutic Abortion by Vacuum Aspiration." *Journal of Obstetrics and Gynaecology of the British Commonwealth*, 1967, **74**, 768.

[10] E. M. Gold, In discussion reported in *Abortion in a Changing World*, op. cit.

[11] F. Novak, "Experience with Suction Curettage." In *Abortion in a Changing World*.

[12] H. Karman, *The Non-Traumatic Abortion*. A cyclostyled memorandum issued from 11914 Santa Monica Boulevard, West Los Angeles, California 90025.

[12a] D. Goldsmith and A. J. Margolis, "Aspiration Abortion without Cervical Dilatation," *Amer. Journal of Obstetrics and Gynaecology*, 1971, **110**, 580.

[13] A film showing the whole procedure was screened during the Third International Congress of Psychosomatic Medicine in Relation to Obstetrics and Gynaecology, in London, April 1971.

[14] P. Huntingford, Personal communication. June, 1971. Professor Huntingford kindly provided me with a Karman curette for personal evaluation.

[15] See news report and Editorial, *The Guardian*, July 5, 1971.

[16] See chapter 4, pp. 49f.

vacuum techniques at an increasingly late stage in pregnancy. It is necessary forcibly to stretch the neck of the womb (a seaweed preparation can be used) and, as one operator said to me, "I find it important to have a very heavy pair of forceps to crush the skull." European authors have warned of the increasing difficulties even at 11 and 12 weeks of using the vacuum aspirator.[17] It is interesting that the liberal abortion countries of Eastern Europe restrict termination (except where there is grave danger to life or where serious eugenic reasons exist) to the first three months of pregnancy.[18] With our badly framed British law we have the astonishing situation in which, in 1969, no less than 210 vacuum aspirations and 722 D. & C.s were performed at 17 weeks of pregnancy or beyond.[19]

For women in the second trimester of pregnancy there are two possible techniques. The first is to try to induce labour, persuading the uterus to expel its contents (and afterwards, if necessary, curetting it to ensure it is empty). This avoids any major operation. Unfortunately the uterus is difficult to persuade using presently available methods: it may be different when the prostaglandins are available.[20]

Amniocentesis: the passage into the uterus, through the abdominal wall, of a fine needle, with the aspiration of some of the liquid which surrounds the fetus and its replacement by a toxic fluid, has been widely used. For reasons not fully understood the fetus usually dies and is aborted spontaneously. Various substances have been employed: hypertonic saline,[21] glucose[22] and urea.[23] There are dangers: of maternal death from brain damage by the saline[24] and of infection.[25] An added disadvantage is that the delivery of the fetus often takes up to four days after injection to occur. In a Japanese method using Rivanol[26] the fetus is usually delivered alive.

Perhaps the oldest method is the use of an irritant paste injected through

[17] Z. Dvorak, V. Trnka and R. Vasicek, "Termination of Pregnancy by Vacuum Aspiration." *Lancet*, 1967, 2, 997.

[18] M. Potts, "Legal Abortion in Eastern Europe," *Eugenics Review*, 1967, 59, 232.

[19] Registrar General's *Statistical Review for England and Wales for 1969. Supplement on Abortion*, London, H.M.S.O.

[20] For a discussion on the prospects with the prostaglandins see chapter 30.

[21] M. D. G. Gillmer, J. R. Friend and R. W. Beard, "Termination of Pregnancy with Intra-Amniotic Saline." *BMJ*, 1971, 1, 434.

[22] B. V. Lewis, J. W. G. Smith and D. C. E. Speller, "Penicillin Prophylax During Termination of Pregnancy by Intra-Amniotic Glucose." *Journal of Obstetrics and Gynaecology of the British Commonwealth*, 1969, 76, 1008.

[23] J. O. Greenhalf and P. L. C. Diggory, "Induction of Therapeutic Abortion by Intra-Amniotic Injection of Urea." *BMJ*, 1971, 1, 28.

[24] J. M. Cameron and A. D. Dayan, "Association of Brain Damage with Therapeutic Abortion by Amniotic-fluid Replacement." *BMJ*, 1966, 1, 1010.

[25] H. de Watteville, *Proceedings of the Royal Society of Medicine*, 1969, 62, 828.

[26] Y. Manabe, "Artificial Abortion at Midpregnancy by Mechanical Stimulation of the Uterus." *American Journal of Obstetrics and Gynecology*, 1969, 105, 132.

[27] A. H. C. Walker. "Termination of Pregnancy using Utus Paste." *Proceedings of the Royal Society of Medicine*, 1969, 62, 832.

the neck of the womb. Although still occasionally advocated[27] it has often been found dangerous[23] and a recent fatality has been reported.[28]

As none of the methods so far described have proved really acceptable for late abortions many of these are performed by operation. The usual one is the opening of the uterus (hysterotomy) by what amounts to a Caesarean Section operation. It can be performed by a vaginal approach which has the great advantage of leaving no visible scar. While this must mean a lot to the single girl I have found it technically difficult in a first pregnancy. In 1188 Swedish cases (983 being vaginal hysterotomies) on review a year later there was increased pain in the abdomen, or with a period, or on intercourse, in 16.1%; troubles due to the implantation of menstruating tissue in the scar in 19.8%, and one fatality.[29] The abdominal approach usually employed in Britain has many advantages in that the view is good and bleeding can be readily controlled. However the removal of a perfectly formed, heart beating, chest moving, limb waving fetus is a most repugnant and quite literally nauseating procedure, both for the surgeon and for the theatre nurses. This is one reason for most of us having an upper limit of duration of pregnancy where we say "no" to all but the most desperate cases. If the Eastern European countries, so often held up to us as shining examples, can be allowed to draw the line at 13 weeks, I see no reason why we should be ashamed at copying them in this. This revolting situation cannot by any certainty be avoided by the use of intra-amniotic saline injections, for a colleague who has wide experience of this technique tells me that on occasion the ward nurse is presented by a living fetus "aborted" by its mother, and finds herself in a desperate quandary. Please note I make no apologies whatever for the emotive descriptions of the last paragraph. If we are to keep abortion in perspective the gynaecologist must keep his conscience alert by performing these operations himself. The recent tendency for instance in the London Teaching Hospitals,[30] to pass this work on to junior staff, and to expect them to operate on these cases on the same level as they would other operations (thus making the "conscience clause" largely a mockery) is a retrograde one.

One technique which avoids this mental trauma to the staff is that of hysterectomy, where sterilization was planned in any case. The uterus is removed, unopened, and the twin purposes of the operation achieved. In a review of American hospitals it was found that in 1964-65 hysterectomy was the method of termination in 10% of cases.[31] Perhaps this percentage

[28] S. V. Sood, "Termination of Pregnancy by the Intra-uterine Insertion of Utus Paste." *BMJ*, 1971, **2**, 315.

[29] J. Lindahl, *Somatic Complications Following Legal Abortion*, Stockholm, 1959, Heinemann.

[30] An unpublished survey made in July 1971 showed that in only one of these (St. Bartholomew's) were less than 50% of terminations being done by junior staff, while in four of them more than 75% of cases were handed over for juniors to do.

[31] C. Tietze, "Therapeutic Abortions in the United States." *American Journal of Obstetrics and Gynaecology*, 1968, **101**, 784.

was so large because it is an easy operation to explain when the law does not countenance abortion. In Britain its use in 1968,[32] and again in 1969,[19] was confined to 1.4% of cases; it will no doubt become more common. From Oxford 56 cases (with two post-operative complications) have been reported: "the operation is preferred over all others when the patient is highly parous, needs permanent contraception, and suffers from uterine disease."[33]

> *Medical Case* 24.3. A forty-year old widow conceived during a liaison with a married man. By the time that she had realized that she had not reached the menopause the pregnancy was eighteen weeks advanced. She became genuinely suicidal believing that her teen-aged children would disown her. Total hysterectomy was performed.

Complications of Abortion

As has already been noted the vast majority of abortions, especially if performed early on, are without physical complication. In a minority of cases the results are less fortunate.

How big is this minority? It is very difficult indeed to find out. Figures from Eastern Europe where they have a vast experience suggest that only a tiny number of abortion patients suffer deleterious physical aftereffects.[18] However Sir Norman Jeffcoate has given reasons for believing these figures to be "politically adjusted." He says "If one talks to gynaecologists from Hungary and Czechoslovakia when they are in this country and free to tell the truth they present a different story, one which fits with all other professional experience. They admit that deaths occur, that the uterus is ruptured once in every 250 cases, that significant illnesses follow in 3–15% of cases, and 1–2% of women are subsequently sterile . . ."[34] More recently a paper from the Hungarian Central Statistical Office quotes an immediate harmful effect rate of 2.8%, and states that the deleterious effect of induced abortion on health is sufficient reason to change the present situation.[35]

Similar difficulties arise in a study of the experience in Japan. One follow-up report does not reveal any marked ill-effects within the limits of its survey.[36] This is difficult to reconcile with another paper from the same source reporting 47.4% of women as having some abnormal condition of one kind or another post-abortion.[37] If deaths are included the picture is more sinister, for in one area of Japan there was a mortality

[32] See p. 215 fn. 10, 1968 edition.
[33] A. C. W. Lewis and E. A. Williams, "Termination Hysterectomy." *Journal of Obstetrics and Gynaecology of the British Commonwealth*, 1970, **77,** 743.
[34] T. N. A. Jeffcoate, "Abortion." In *Morals and Medicine*, 1970, London, B.B.C.
[35] A. Klinger, "Demographic Consequences of the Legalization of Induced Abortion in Eastern Europe." *International Journal of Gynaecology and Obstetrics*, 1970, **8,** 680.
[36] Y. Koya (Ed.) *Harmful Effects of Induced Abortion*. Family Planning Association of Japan, 1966.
[37] Y. Koya, "A Study of Induced Abortion in Japan and its Significance." *Milbank Memorial Fund Quarterly*, 1954, **32,** 282.

rate from sepsis alone, in 1955, of 2.3 per ten thousand operations,[36] and it is suggested that not all harmful side-effects, and even deaths, are reported.[38]

The only other area with wide experience is Scandinavia. Work stimulated by the Swedish Medical Research Council suggests that 3.6% of legally aborted women have "relatively serious complications."[29] While in 1966 the Danish experience was of a mortality rate of 0.7 per thousand.[39]

Prior to the introduction of the Abortion Act in Britain the Royal College of Obstetricians and Gynaecologists estimated that serious non-fatal complications occur in not less than 3% of cases induced by experts, and the figure might rise to 15%.[39] Protagonists of a liberal abortion policy pooh-poohed these prognostications, and found support in Mr Peter Diggory's excellent results in a thousand cases in which complications were few and unimportant.[40] He is a highly qualified consultant with a special interest in the subject[41] and managed these cases personally. How does it come about, then, that in 1971 another liberally minded gynaecologist wrote of "the unacceptably high morbidity-rate associated with induced abortion"[42]? The answer will be found in hospital statistics few of which have yet been published. For instance in one London hospital[43] a review of 519 cases terminated in 1969 showed that in no less than 150 morbidity occurred – in other words there was some untoward complication of the operation: the principal ones being infection, bleeding, or the retention of some of the products of conception requiring further operation. The risks were related to the duration of pregnancy. Operations performed before the 14th week carried a morbidity rate of 19.76%; but over 14 weeks the rate was 57.94%.

Sepsis is the greatest danger. In the Samaritan Hospital series it occurred after vacuum aspiration in 10% of cases, after utus paste in 36%, after hysterotomy in 45% and after intra-amniotic saline in 60% of cases.[43] How much more likely is it to occur in less favourable circumstances. One English consultant during the period of six weeks saw three cases of severe septicaemia following abortion in one particular private clinic.[44]

Medical Case 24.4. A twenty-three year old married woman was aborted at seventeen weeks for socio-economic reasons. Labour was induced and then completed by curettage. The next day she became febrile, was treated by antibiotics apparently satisfactorily and discharged. Four days later she developed abdominal pain, more antibiotics were given and the next day a further curettage performed. She deteriorated the following day and was transferred

[38] M. Maramatsu, in *Abortion in a Changing World, op. cit.*

[39] "Legalized Abortion": Report by the Council of the Royal College of Obstetricians and Gynaecologists. *BMJ*, 1966, **1,** 850.

[40] P. L. C. Diggory, "Some Experience of Therapeutic Abortion." *Lancet*, 1969, **1,** 873.

[41] P. L. C. Diggory, in *Abortion in Britain, op. cit.*

[42] P. Huntingford, Letter in the *Lancet*, 1971, **1,** 1012.

[43] Abortion Statistics, 1969, The Samaritan Hospital, London.

[44] Quoted by B. G. Irvine as reported in the *BMJ*, 1970, **1,** 508.

from the private clinic to a hospital. At operation she was found to have gross infection of the pelvic organs and a purulent peritonitis. She died four days later.

Haemorrhage is an ever present risk with abortion and may occur even with an experienced operator. The present writer has been met with profuse haemorrhage on more than one occasion while operating, even with the use of all the accepted techniques to avoid and control this. Similar experience is widespread.

Medical Case 24.5. A 35-year-old mother of six had an abortion by a consultant gynaecologist who thought he might have perforated the uterus, and arranged a special post-operative watch on the patient. She deteriorated and was taken from the clinic to a general hospital where she was transfused with two pints of blood and two of plasma; despite this she died before more blood could be obtained. There had been no facilities at the clinic for blood transfusion.

It must always be remembered that the operation may not achieve its intention.

Medical Case 24.6. A woman, aged 40, with three children, all in their teens, and whose husband had a poor genetic inheritance, was "aborted" at 6 weeks, and sterilized at the same operation, by an experienced consultant gynaecologist. She was seen again months later with an abdominal tumour in which a fetal heart could be heard beating! When delivered at term she was as delighted as a young mother with her first baby. She had either had twins, only one being removed at the operation, or the gestational sac had been missed altogether.

Then it must be recalled that the operation may prove fatal for one of three reasons. All operations carry a certain mortality risk due to anaesthetic.

Case History (reported in the Press) 24.7. The inquest was held in London in May 1969 on an American girl who desired an abortion because her husband had left her. She phoned to the clinic in London from America and arranged the operation. The patient died of a respiratory obstruction during the anaesthetic.

The disease which necessitated the operation may prove fatal – this explains a series with four deaths in eight abortions! Obviously the more strict the indications for abortion, the more ill will be the patients chosen, and therefore the poorer the figures. This is one of the explanations for the wide discrepancy in published figures.

Then as we have seen, the actual operation may prove fatally traumatic. In 1969, the latest year for which government statistics are available, the death rate in Britain from abortion (with or without simultaneous sterilization) was one-and-a-half times as high as the maternal mortality rate.[19]

Effect on Future Childbearing

The risk that the woman aborted may never again be able to conceive is one to be considered carefully. Short of death, this must be the ultimate tragedy for the young girl. Figures range widely – from 27.7% to less than 1% were reported in Lindahl's study.[29] X-ray evidence of post-abortal damage is found in between 1% and 6%.[3] Kolstad's Norwegian experience includes 3.4% post-abortal sterility.[45] The Japanese studies showed very little increase.[36] However in 1971 in our unit my colleague was investigating the infertility of three women who gave a history of previous legal abortion elsewhere.[46]

Sterility may be due to blockage of the fallopian tubes following infection. Whether or not there will be an increased number of pregnancies remaining in the tube (the highly dangerous condition of ectopic pregnancy) is not yet agreed. What is agreed[3,47] is that there is an increase in the number of future babies born prematurely: these have a greatly diminished opportunity of survival. This is due to damage to the neck of the womb during the operation.

Sterility can be due to psychogenic factors. In a textbook on the management of impaired fertility we are reminded: "Sometimes a woman's sense of guilt is extreme because she has not told her husband of a previous conception and termination of the same: sometimes it is the guilt of both husband and wife who have taken steps to terminate a pregnancy for which they were not yet prepared.... Once it has been proved to her that a previous unfortunate experience has not left her with VD, or that an illegally induced abortion has not caused irrevocable damage, conception follows."[48] That, written before the days of legal abortion, will no doubt prove equally true of the guilt the latter will sometimes engender.

A further complication of abortion which affects future child-bearing is that of rhesus-sensitization. Women who themselves have the blood-group Rh-negative may carry in their womb a fetus who has inherited its father's Rh-positive blood group. In these circumstances the mother may destroy her child's red blood cells, causing severe anaemia, or often death. This will occur if previous to this pregnancy she has herself been sensitized against Rh-positive blood, and this most usually happens during an earlier delivery or abortion. It has been found that conditions exist for this sensitization to occur after inter-uterine injection to initiate labour[49] after dilatation and curettage[50] and after termination by the abdominal

[45] P. Kolstad, "Therapeutic Abortion." Acta Obstetrica et Gynecologica Scandinavica, 1957, 36, Supplement 6.

[46] S. Cohen, Personal communication.

[47] Y. Moriyama and O. Hirokawa, "The Relationship Between Artificial Termination of Pregnancy and Abortion of Premature Birth." In The Harmful Effects of Induced Abortion, op. cit.

[48] Margaret White and V. B. Green-Armytage, The Management of Impaired Fertility. 1962, Oxford University Press.

[49] D. N. Menzies and D. F. Hawkins, "Therapeutic Abortion using Intra-Amniotic Hypertonic Solutions." Journal of Obstetrics and Gynaecology of the British Commonwealth, 1968, 75, 215.

[50] J. Gellen, A. Kovacs, F. E. Szontagh and D. Boda, "Surgical Termination of Pregnancy as a Cause of Rhesus Sensitization." BMJ, 1965, 2, 1471.

approach. It is doubtful if the risks after vacuum termination are less than when curettage is used.[51]

If detected within 24 hours or so of the sensitizing procedure it is possible by giving a fairly rare blood constituent (anti-D immune globulin) to prevent sensitization occurring. Not until July 1971 did this material become available in Britain for abortion cases. There is usually an interval of several days between the blood samples being taken from the woman and the results becoming available on which depend whether or not she should receive the protective injection on abortion. In the N.H.S. situation where a number of days normally elapse between the first visit to the out-patient department, and the actual operation, this presents no great problem. In the private sector, however, the patient is usually operated upon on the day on which she is first seen. Under these circumstances it is likely to prove much more difficult to protect Rh-negative girls and their future babies. Meanwhile, as 15% of the population are Rh-negative a considerable number of girls must already have been sensitized during their abortions. This number increases day by day, with all the future train of affected, and possibly stillborn, babies yet to come.

Medical Case 24.8. A woman booked for ante-natal care in her second pregnancy was found at 34 weeks of pregnancy to have a high titre of Rh-antibodies in her bloodstream. The only event which could have caused these to develop was a termination of pregnancy by hysterotomy at fourteen weeks in her first pregnancy. As a result of this Rh-sensitization she was delivered of a stillborn (hydropic) baby the next week.

A number of other complications, such as increased menstrual loss and painful intercourse have been reported following termination of pregnancy, from time to time.

What the true incidence of post-abortal medical complications is time alone will tell. Certainly no method is without its dangers, and maternal death is said to have been recorded with every method of termination.[52] One thing is abundantly clear and that is the claim that the procedure is without risk is quite unfounded, at whatever stage the operation be performed. In any case, unless we think of women as cattle, physical risks are not the most important of our problems in abortion.

[51] Sheilagh Murray, S. L. Barron and R. A. McNay, "Transplacental Haemorrhage after Abortion," *Lancet*, 1970, I, 631.
[52] A. D. Brown, Letter in the *BMJ*, 1971, 2, 590.

CHAPTER 25

THE FUTURE FOR MOTHER AND CHILD
WHEN ABORTION IS REFUSED

... there is one fundamental difference between the sociological conditions in Bible times and our own: that is that then all babies were wanted; now not all babies are ... Hence the totally different situation.[1]

REFUSAL OF A REQUEST FOR ABORTION, WE ARE LED TO BELIEVE, IS the most heinous crime in the calendar. Gynaecologists, as much as other men, like to be popular. Why then do they risk the wrath of their patients, and the vituperations of the propagandists? There are two explanations to be looked at here.

The first is biological principle. In Dr. Galdston's words ". . . abortion must be looked upon as an eventuation that runs counter to the biological stream of life. It is against the grain . . . a logical corollary emerges: if and when a so-called adult woman, a responsible female, seeks an abortion (unless the warrant for it is overriding, as say in rape or incest) we are in effect confronted both with a sick woman and a sick situation. Furthermore, and I want strongly to underscore this point, neither the given person nor the given situation is likely to be remedied by the abortion qua abortion ... I would like to go on record that in numerous instances both the individual and the situation are actively aggravated rather than remedied by the abortion."[2]

The second explanation is that the gynaecologist has looked at the results.

It must be realized that those rejected form a minority. In an unpublished review of the practice of a considerable number of gynaecologists in the North of England it appears that some 72.5% of applicants are granted abortion. Those rejected will first think of trying another gynaecologist, who will probably not be aware that she had been seen elsewhere earlier. In a London series 13% of those refused were accepted elsewhere under the N.H.S.[3] In our own local experience it was fairly common in the first few months of the Act's operation for women and

---

[1] Church Assembly Board for Social Responsibility, *Fatherless by Law*, London, 1965, Church Information Office.
[2] I. Galdston, *In Abortion in the United States* (*op. cit.*).
[3] M. Clark, L. Forstner, A. D. Pond and R. F. Tredfold, "Sequels of Unwanted Pregnancy. A Follow-Up of Patients Referred for Psychiatric Opinion." *Lancet*, 1968, **2**, 501.

the general practitioners to "shop around," but this does not appear now to be happening to any noticeable degree. There is probably little crossing of catchment boundaries: I at any rate have had no requests from doctors who do not routinely send me their gynaecological cases. Details of spill outside the home regions of the women have been published.[4]

The next move may well be to try for a private abortion, usually in London. For those who can afford the fees, there is no evidence to suggest they are likely to be turned away. A technique almost indistinguishable from blackmail is open here:

> *Medical Case* 25.1. A woman was seen by a gynaecologist who did not fee abortion justified. She was then referred by her G.P. to a psychiatrist who recommended abortion and arranged a further appointment with the gynae-cologist. Before this took place the patient's husband turned up at the gynae-cologist's house stating that they were determined on an abortion and had an appointment at a London private clinic at noon next day. To allow for transport arrangements their existing children would have to be farmed out with relatives, and this would have to be done within the next three hours, before their bed-time. As the abortion was going to occur in any case, would the gynaecologist please reconsider his decision then and there: and save the risks and expense of the trip to London?

For the determined patient unable to afford the private clinic there is the back-street abortion.

What, in fact, happens to the women who are refused abortion? The Scandinavian figures are unanimous: of those aborted legally, 84%[5] said they would have gone on to delivery had they been refused. Of those actually refused in Norway[6] and Sweden,[7] 86% did go on to deliver. A more recent London series gives the smaller figure of 59% delivering.[3]

Among those refused the numbers known to have turned to an illegal abortion are 20% in London[3] and 9%[6] and 11%[7] in Scandinavia. It is interesting to note that although in the last-mentioned series 30% had said they would seek illegal abortion if refused, almost two-thirds changed their minds. Many writers use infection following abortion as evidence that an illegal operation has been performed. This is unsatisfactory. Professor Rhodes has pointed out that in spontaneous abortion high fever is not uncommon,[8] while from the opposite approach in Kirstin

[4] Registrar General, *Statistical Review of England and Wales Supplements on Abortion* for *1968 and 1969*, London, H.M.S.O.

[5] P. Arén, "On Legal Abortion in Sweden: Tentative Evaluation of Justification of Frequency During the Last Decade." *Acta Obstetrica et Gynecologica Scandinavica*, 1958, **37**, Supplement 1.

[6] P. Kolstad, "Therapeutic Abortion." *Acta Obstetrica et Gynacologica Scandinavica*, 1957, **36**, supplement 6.

[7] Kirstin Höök, "Refused Abortion." *Acta Psychiatrica Scandinavica*, 1963, **39**, Supplement 168.

[8] P. Rhodes, "A Gynaecologist's View." In *Abortion in Britain, op. cit.*

Höök's series only 23% of the admitted procured abortions developed fever.[7]

Suicide

Suicide is the great threat, and the great fear, in refused abortion. First let us get it into perspective. An American writer has examined all traumatic deaths in pregnant women in Minnesota between 1950 and 1965. The commonest cause of violent death was automobile accident (23 cases), which, as Dr. Barno points out, does not create such a furore as do criminal abortion (21) or suicide (14). Incidentally not a single one of these suicides was illegitimately pregnant, and not one had requested a therapeutic abortion.[9] The next point to remember is that, prior to the liberalization of the law, the threat of suicide was often the only means of procuring an operation.

Just how often is suicide attempted or committed in pregnancy, due to refusal? In New York City the incidence of suicide is eleven times commoner among women in general than among the pregnant.[10] In Brisbane, where at any one time 7% of women are pregnant only 6.2% of attempted suicides are pregnant.[11] In California, among pregnant psychiatric patients where statistically 17.6 pregnant suicides would be expected, only three were found.[12] In Philadelphia in 100 successive suicides in women who were examined post-mortem not one was pregnant, suggesting as in similar studies that pregnancy protects women from taking their own lives.[13]

Suicide in pregnancy does occur. In Sweden before the reform of the abortion law 11–12% of suicides among women of childbearing age were pregnant;[14] in Britain Seager reported six cases (three of them recently delivered) in five years.[15] What we need to know is how many of these were provoked by the pregnancy. Among young women under 21 attempting suicide Otto found that in only 43.6% of those pregnant was the pregnancy "the provoking moment." He compared these girls with non-pregnant girls also attempting to end their lives. He found that among the pregnant, "love problems" were commoner than among the non-pregnant (65.9% to 42%); but that the home and parental situation

[9] A. Barno, "Criminal Deaths, Illegitimate Pregnancy Deaths, and Suicides in Pregnancy." *American Journal of Obstetrics and Gynecology*, 1967, **98**, 356.

[10] C. M. McLane, in *Abortion in the United States, op. cit.*

[11] F. A. Whitlock and J. E. Edwards, "Pregnancy and Attempted Suicide." *Comprehensive Psychiatry*, 1968, **9**, 1.

[12] A. J. Rosenberg and E. Silver, "Suicide, Psychiatrists and Therapeutic Abortion." *California Medicine*, 1965, **102**, 407.

[13] M. J. Daly, "The Unwanted Pregnancy." *Clinical Obstetrics and Gynecology*, 1970, **13**, 713.

[14] L. Bengtsson (in the Swedish literature) quoted by D. W. K. Kay, *Lancet*, 1966, **2**, 1315.

[15] C. P. Seager, in discussion in *Abortion in Britain, op. cit.*

(27.3% to 36.5%) and mental upsets (6.8% to 14.6%) were less important.[16] These latter findings go against most popular opinion.

There is a world of difference between threat of suicide and commission of suicide. In Australia a search of the records in Brisbane failed to discover a pregnant woman who had taken her life.[11] In England in a seven-year period, 119 women below the age of fifty committed suicide in Birmingham, yet there is no record of any woman known to be pregnant doing so.[17] Many American psychiatrists do not know of even one case.[18] Of the 13,500 Swedish women who were refused abortion, between 1938 and 1958 only three committed suicide, a rate of 0.2 per thousand refusals. This surely puts the risk into perspective.[19]

The lesson, surely, is not to exaggerate the risk, but to attempt to pick out circumstances which drive women to desperation. Relationships are an important factor, as is the stability of the situation in which the woman finds herself. Of Dr. L. Bengtsson's nineteen pregnant suicides, only one was married.[14] In the Australian series reported by Whitlock and Edwards, of their pregnant attempted suicides the act was precipitated ten times as often by interpersonal disputes as by the fact of pregnancy. They comment: "Our own study indicates that in the majority of patients the pregnancy is not the only, or even the most important, cause of the suicidal act. Persistent discords of personality and unstable sexual and interpersonal relationships seemed to be more important contributors to the suicidal act by these women. It follows, therefore, that for the majority of pregnant patients making suicidal threats termination of pregnancy will not necessarily deter the patient from putting her threat into action, as the pregnancy is not the most important cause of her emotional distress."[11]

Before leaving the topic of suicide we should notice a comment of Russell Shaw ". . . it is at least worth reflection that the two highest suicide rates in the world for women in the 20–24 age bracket are those of Japan (44.1 per 100,000) and Hungary (17.1 per 100,000) – two countries whose abortion rates are amongst the world's highest. This has led Professor Shiden Inoue of Japan's Nanzan University to suggest a possible 'causal relationship' between abortion and suicide in these two countries."[20]

Outlook for the Mother

How do women who deliver after refusal of abortion feel in retrospect? Although a minority wish the abortion had been performed, more than half even of these would not wish to be without the baby. The vast

[16] U. Otto, "Suicidal Attempts Made by Pregnant Women Under 21 Years." *Acta Paedopsychiatrica*, 1965, **32**, 276.

[17] M. Sim, "Abortion and the Psychiatrists," *BMJ*, 1963, **2**, 145.

[18] S. Bolter, "The Psychiatrist's Role in Therapeutic Abortion: The 'Unwitting Accomplice'." *American Journal of Psychiatry*, 1962, **119**, 312.

[19] J.-O. Ottosson, "Legal Abortion in Sweden." *Journal of Biosocial Sciences*, 1971, **3**, 173.

[20] Russell Shaw, *Abortion on Trial*, London, 1968, Robert Hale.

majority, however (84%[6], 73%[7]) were glad the pregnancy had not been terminated. Some declared that it was inconceivable that they could have thought of such a thing. Much depends on the male. In a Swedish series, among those married to their partner 80% were satisfied at the way things had turned out, but only 58% in those not married to him.[7] Professor Stallworthy has remarked: "I work in a unit where we do terminate pregnancies so I cannot be accused of being bigoted, but I have been at this job long enough to know that some of the most happy people that I know are people who have come, not once but time and time again, and have said: 'You don't remember, but the first time I came wanting an abortion. Thank God you did not agree, because this child has brought the greatest joy into our home that we have ever known.' "[21]

> *Medical Case 25.2.* A thirty-three year old married woman with three children requested abortion on the grounds that the oldest girl, who had a mild degree of physical disability resulting from injury at birth, was "difficult." Abortion was refused. At the post-natal examination the whole family turned up to thank the obstetrician for his refusal. The "difficult" child was so no longer, being busy idolizing the baby. The middle child helped with its care from the moment of awakening until going to school. The family unit had never been so happy.

The point which cannot be emphasized too strongly is that an unwanted pregnancy is not the same thing as an unwanted child. The reader should discuss this with his own parents and his friends' parents. Obviously a thousand illustrations are available, but one must suffice. It concerns the great Confederate General, Robert E. Lee. In his recent biography of him, C. Dowdey writes: "Ann Carter Lee wanted no more offspring to Mr. Lee. This she wrote very candidly to her sister-in-law . . . (nevertheless) in the summer of 1806, Ann, pregnant with a child she did not want, left Stratford . . ." Robert was born in January 1807. "It was about the age of 13 that neighbours observed that the young man was 'the man of the family' . . . his elder brothers had never shown a strong urge to look after their mother, one sister was sickly and the other still a child . . . . As the centre of her life Robert had drifted into his duties gradually and naturally . . . . He did the shopping, carried his mother to her carriage in his arms, waited on her when she was sick . . . . Later, when he left home, his mother said 'How can I live without Robert? He is both son and daughter to me.' "[22] How fortunate for Mrs. Lee and for the American tradition that she lived in the early 19th century! In the late 20th century Robert would probably have been a white blob of tissue being sucked down plastic tubing.

Outlook for the Child

How do the children fare? Is G. Leach correct in asserting that "the higher claims that challenge the right of the fetus are bound to increase

[21] J. A. Stallworthy, "Complications of Therapeutic Abortion: Immediate and Remote." In *The Abortion Act, op. cit.*

[22] C. Dowdey, *Lee: A Biography*, London, 1970, Gollancz.

as our view of human being and society enlarges and we see more of the evil consequences of not aborting?"[23] He supports this from the important study by Professor Hans Forssman and Inga Thuwe.[24] These Swedish workers reviewed cases where abortion had been refused at least 21 years earlier, between 1939 and 1941. They followed up 120 children in all, and for the purposes of statistical control each was matched by a similar child born on the same day. They considered childhood to be insecure when there was an official report from the children's aid bureaux that home conditions were unsatisfactory, or the child was removed from home by authority, or it was placed in a foster home; also where the child was born out of wedlock and never legitimized, or his parents were divorced or dead before the child was fifteen. On these criteria, 54.2% of their series (21.7% controls) had an insecure childhood. Children of unwanted pregnancies were twice as likely as their controls to require psychiatric treatment: or to be registered for delinquency. They were five times as likely to require public assistance between the age of sixteen and twenty-one, but were only half as likely as their controls to stay at school after the obligatory leaving age. These figures quoted by Leach have been much emphasized by reviewers. One point that has escaped notice is that of social grouping. Swedish statistics divide these by father's occupation into three groups. For groups I and II, the children of "unwanted" pregnancies in fact did statistically as well as the control group ("Freedom from inferiority": 76.0% compared to 77.8%); it is only in the children of group III fathers that the problems – and they are very real problems – arise. In this group they had only two chances in five of being free of inferiorities; while group III children in the control group had three chances in five. It must be remembered that the mothers had applied for termination on psychiatric grounds; it was not until 1946 that Swedish law was widened to include consideration of the mother's circumstances. As our British 1967 law permits this, the series is not comparable to present day ones, and certainly should not legitimately be used as a lever towards abortion on request. It does emphasize, however, the importance of taking into account the whole situation in considering an application from an under-privileged woman.

The "battered baby" syndrome is often quoted as an outcome of refused abortion. A recent survey of "battering adults" showed that in most cases they are between twenty and thirty years of age, married and with small families. In most cases the parents have "some defect in character structure."[25] They appear to have long-standing emotional problems aggravated by the demands and responsibilities of parenthood, and their treatment of their children can be seen in many instances as a plea for help.

[23] G. Leach, *The Biocrats*, London, 1970, Cape.

[24] H. Forssman and Inga Thuwe, "120 Children Born after Application for Therapeutic Abortion Refused." *Acta Psychiatrica Scandinavica*, 1966, **42**, 71.

[25] J. M. Cameron, "The Battered Baby." *British Journal of Hospital Medicine*, 1970, **4**, 769.

Pregnancy is an important factor, for of forty "battering females," 42.5% were pregnant at the time of the incident.[26] It will be noted, however, that their families were not large, but small. The significant issue here, surely, is of help to the emotionally inadequate.[27]

What does it mean for a baby to be "wanted"? J. P. Donnelly has pointed out that there would be a considerable discrepancy as to whether a child were wanted if the question were posed one month before conception, on the night of conception, two months later when the mother is vomiting "and the other two kids have the croup," or on the day of delivery when the mother has the child in her arms.[28] Commenting on which T. Lidz adds: "There are women who do not realize how gratifying it can be to mother a baby until they actually have it in their arms, and maternal feelings are aroused by the tangible situation."[29]

Can we quantify the emotional results for the child? In London fifty-five babies were born after refusal of abortion on psychiatric grounds. Of the forty-six women who could be contacted, only three were worse, and twenty-nine were improved mentally following the birth of the child.[3] In a Danish series of 151 women who kept their babies after application for abortion was turned down, only thirteen said they did not feel any affection towards their baby, thirty-one were absolutely happy, the remainder were "moderately happy."[30]

Everything depends on the personality of the mother: in a Swedish series of women with a "normal personality," 85% adjusted satisfactorily to the child, 2% more did so later, and 13% were poorly adjusted. Among women with a "deviating personality," however, her figures were much poorer: 39% adjusted, 15% later, but 46% remained poorly adjusted.[7] Dr. Hook adds the surprising comment that even where the child had died or been given away, women often declared that they were glad they had had it, indicating that the care of the child, and possibly the actual fulfilment of the pregnancy, had proved to be a positive experience.

We can get a little more light on the subject by considering the women who did not go through with their granted abortion – in most cases because they had got past the thirteenth week, and were now feeling better. Of 162 women who gave birth, seven babies died, twelve were adopted, and the remaining 143 women kept the child. They were divided almost equally between those living in stable marriages, those living in inharmonious marriages with really serious conflicts, and those single or divorced. Only 6% of the women had some regrets at the birth. Reporting this, Arén and Åmark comment: "Sometimes we got the impression that

[26] A. E. Skinner and R. L. Castle, quoted in *Health Trends,* 1970, **2**, no. 1, 24.
[27] D. M. Douglas, Judith M. Brearley and Sula Wolff, "Battered Babies, A Symposium." *Contact*, Feb., 1971.
[28] J. P. Donnelly, in *Abortion in the United States, op. cit.*
[29] T. Lidz, in *Abortion in the United States, op. cit.*
[30] H. Hoffmeyer, "Medical Aspects of the Danish Legislation on Abortion." In *Abortion and the Law* (Ed. D. Smith). Cleveland, 1967, Press of Western Reserve University.

the child was made the object of somewhat exaggerated care on account of self-reproaches on the mother's part from having applied for abortion, and the fear that something might happen to the child . . . . In the majority of cases the women had not encountered the great difficulties they had themselves imagined would arise with the advent of the child. Nor had their health been impaired or their marriage been rendered unhappy . . . . Several women saw a direct connection between the improvement of their marital situation and the advent of the child in question: especially when elderly and the child had drawn parents together." They found that adjustment was facilitated by the following factors: a stable marriage, normal level of intelligence, and the absence of marked mental abnormality. Sexual relationships were not affected by the pregnancy, but depended rather on the psychological relation to the husband.[31]

We should note Arén and Åmark's conclusion: "At the time of our follow-up 79% of the women had improved, or were unchanged with respect to their psychic state. Our investigations have afforded evidence of the fact that even severe psychic symptoms tend to disappear as soon as the woman has decided to go on with the pregnancy . . . . Statistically our material represents a socially "worse" selection than the average case upon whom abortion has been performed in Sweden, and would thus rather be calculated to give deteriorated results with respect to sequel and adjustment than improved results . . . . The results of our investigation on the whole seem to support the assumption that one gets fewer somatic and psychic complications in connection with a completion of the pregnancy than in connection with a termination of the same with legal abortion."[31]

[31] P. Arén and C. Amark, "The Prognosis in Case on which Legal Abortion has been Granted but not Carried Out." *Acta Psychiatrica et Neurologica Scandinavica*, 1961, **36**, 203.

CHAPTER 26

PSYCHIATRIC ASPECTS

The scientific study of man is a myth, perhaps the most dangerous of all the myths of modern civilization. Ultimately the psychologist, the psychiatrist, the sociologist must each confess that his work must be prefaced by "I believe" and not by "I have proved scientifically". PROF. DAVID HORROBIN.[1]

A DECADE OR MORE AGO IN ONE OF THE SEMINAL BOOKS ON ABORTION Glanville Williams, a lawyer, wrote: "A few (hospitals and surgeons) regard themselves as entitled to accept the report of a psychiatrist without question . . . a larger number control or usurp the discretion of the psychiatrist. Thus many obstetricians refuse to act upon psychiatric advice unless they themselves – though not psychiatrists – think there is 'something in it.' "[2]

How does it come about that obstetricians bring themselves to act in such a way, for is it not widely accepted that "Doctors Know Best (and Psychiatrists even better)"?[3]

The Status of Psychiatric Recommendations

There appear to be four reasons why the obstetrician finds psychiatric opinions difficult to evaluate.

First the whole field of psychiatry is ill-defined, and some practitioners appear to consider it has no bounds.

No doubt with his tongue in his cheek Professor Henry Miller, a neurologist, recently propounded some home-truths to a meeting of the World Psychiatric Association. "The Oxford Dictionary's definition of a psychiatrist," he said, "is 'one who treats mental illness'. Not, you will observe, one who prevents wars, cures anti-semitism, or is the ultimate authority in bringing up children. There are many quite well-educated people who believe that psychiatrists have special and mysterious methods of finding out what is going on in their patients' minds that are denied to the rest of the profession and to the rest of humanity . . . . Of course, all human behaviour can be described in the psychiatrist's terminology.

[1] D. F. Horrobin, *Science is God*, Aylesbury, 1970, Medical and Technical Publishing Co.
[2] G. Williams, *The Sanctity of Life and the Criminal Law*, London, 1958, Faber.
[3] Quoted by Alice D. Rossi in "A Behavioural Scientist's View." In *Abortion in a Changing World* (op. cit.).

Equally it can be described in the terms and concepts of the anthropologist, the historian, the sociologist, the economist or psychologist – or even the practical politician."[4] Were Henry Miller not a "fervent atheist"[5] he would doubtless have added "the theologian" to that list.

It would perhaps have been more fair to quote a psychiatrist, and one discussing abortion. One such writes "In deciding whether to destroy a nascent life in order to enhance the existing life of the mother, the psychiatrist is confronted by a clear limitation in his art. He has no actuarial or probability estimates on which to base his recommendations. While struggling to couch his findings in phrases that resound with scientific certainty he is most aware that he is, after all, only a practising moralist striving to temper as best he can the rigours of the human condition."[6]

Secondly, unlike specialists in other disciplines whose views vary only within narrow limits, psychiatrists appear to have no agreed view on the cause, diagnosis and treatment of many mental conditions.[7] "Psychiatrists belong to a number of different schools of thought roundly and sometimes violently contradicting one another's basic principles, so that none of them can speak with the authority of established scientific doctrine."[8]

A few years ago, after making enquiries among Californian psychiatrists, Rosenberg and Silver comment: "The extreme range of opinion represented among the psychiatrists is a far cry from the scientific objectivity that one hopes would apply to determinations affecting the life and health of patients. The range was from those who essentially never recommend therapeutic abortion to those who seem always to do so, from those who regard pregnancy as definitely increasing the incidence of mental illness to those who feel that pregnancy represents virtually no

[4] H. Miller, "Psychiatry—Medicine or Magic?" *British Journal of Hospital Medicine*, 1970, **3**, 122.

[5] H. Miller (see p. 49, fn. 35).

[6] H. G. Whittington, "Evaluation of Therapeutic Abortion as an Element of Preventive Psychiatry." *American Journal of Psychiatry*, 1970, **126**, 1224.

[7] The practical outworking of the personal viewpoints of psychiatrists was well demonstrated by J. H. Friedman (in "The Vagarity of Psychiatric Indications for Therapeutic Abortion." *American Journal of Psychotherapy*, 1962, **16**, 251). At a psychiatric staff conference he recounted the case history of a schizophrenic woman in her third pregnancy. "It was interesting to note the discussion of the group. Their viewpoint varied in relation to their training, social outlook and religion. All of them knew of the legal psychiatric indications for therapeutic abortion. After an hour of heated discussion a vote was taken: five were in favour, five were opposed. When the group were then told that the woman had, in fact, delivered successfully the psychiatrists who had favoured therapeutic abortion were not dismayed. They argued cogently that those who had argued against the abortion could not have predicted with accuracy that this woman would not commit suicide. However, they themselves could not give any definite reason why this woman would commit suicide. Each group cited examples of their own or other's experience to bolster up their position. Faced with such problems the obstetricians and the general practitioner will also be swayed by humanitarian consideration, economic factors or social reasons."

[8] C. H. Whiteley and Winifred M. Whiteley, *The Permissive Morality*, London, 1964, Methuen.

additional stress."[9] Similarly in Britain, forty-five psychiatrists were contacted in the hope of finding some general measure of agreement on the criteria on which decisions to abort are based. Such agreement was largely lacking.[10]

The problem was well summed up by Dr. A. A. Baker: "There is not available sufficient evidence of a reliable kind in any series of cases (including control groups) to show whether termination does more good than harm."[11]

The third cause for distrust of psychiatric opinion arises from the fact that during times when abortion laws were stringent psychiatrists allowed themselves to be manipulated. One is quoted as saying: "Our response is not dictated by psychiatric conditions, for these are rare. Our response is a response to the appeal of a woman anguished at the thought of an experience distasteful to her, and so we find medical, psychiatric or social rationalization to circumvent the law and bring her relief."[12] Writing in 1962, Dr. S. Bolter commented that in a recent ten-year period the percentage of therapeutic abortions performed for psychiatric reasons in New York State had risen from 8.2% to 40%. "It is possible that instead of being flooded with new insight into the unconscious, doctors are recognizing an 'easy out' when under pressure to stop a pregnancy? Is it possible that the psychiatrist has become the unwitting accomplice?"[13]

This possibility is reinforced when one considers that back in 1953 while there were 125 psychiatrists attached to the Columbia Presbyterian Medical Centre only twenty-five abortions were performed for psychiatric indications.[14]

With the enactment of more liberal abortion legislation this policy has continued. It is interesting to notice that even supporters of easy abortion are disturbed by this subterfuge. Recently in Alaska those pressing for repeal of all abortion laws, made the following comment ". . . Many psychiatrists maintain that there are almost no valid psychiatric reasons for abortion. Pregnant women, for example, rarely commit suicide. Yet in California 86% of the indications for abortion under the new law are psychiatric. This suggests considerable psychiatric casuistry or games-playing."[15]

The fourth reason is that the gynaecologist quite frankly cannot credit

[9] A. J. Rosenberg and E. Silver, "Suicide, Psychiatrists and Therapeutic Abortion." *California Medicine*, 1965, **102**, 407.

[10] J. W. D. Pearce, *Proceedings of the Royal Society of Medicine*, 1957, **50**, 321.

[11] A. A. Baker, *Psychiatric Disorders in Obstetrics*, Oxford, 1967, Blackwell.

[12] Unnamed psychiatrist quoted by M. O. Vincent in *Birth Control and the Christian, op. cit.*

[13] S. Bolter, "The Psychiatrist's Role in Therapeutic Abortion: The Unwitting Accomplice." *American Journal of Psychiatry*, 1962, **119**, 313.

[14] H. C. Taylor, in *Abortion in the United States:* "Proceedings of a Conference Sponsored by the Planned Parenthood Federation of America at Arden House and the New York Academy of Medicine." (Ed. Mary Calderone), New York, 1958, Hoeber-Harper.

[15] Alaska State Medical Association. "Abortion—Repeal of Alaska Laws." *Alaska Medicine*, 1969, **11**, 105.

some of the things he is told by psychiatrists. One reform-oriented psychiatrist has stated that "being caught in an unprepared-for pregnancy is prima facie evidence of immaturity or neurotic conflict, therefore emotional fitness for parenthood should be questioned."[16] That is not merely abortion on demand, it is abortion on demand legitimatized by a psychiatric diagnosis.

The obstetrician's bewilderment is increased when he is told, by a psychiatrist: "The woman requesting an abortion confronts us with our deeply buried murderous feelings, making us feel extremely uncomfortable, enough so as to cause us to retaliate against her."[17]

A professor of obstetrics has well summed it up: "Very often it seems we are asking the psychiatrist to be a soothsayer rather than a medical scientist . . . it seems high time that we stopped the game of psychological blind-man's bluff."[18]

The Problems of the Doctor's Philosophy

The problems inherent in any therapeutic relationship are especially great when there is no physical ailment to give objective grounds for measurement. The personality and mental outlook of the doctor is an unavoidable factor. "In judging this man to be healthy and that man diseased the psychologist is bound to make some use of his own standards of good or evil, and some reference to those of his society."[8]

And here we come to the crux of the matter. M. Keeling has pointed out that "we cannot define terms like 'mental health' or 'normal personality' or 'happiness' without recourse to some assumptions about the nature of man and of the world we live in; and try as we may we cannot logically give such assumptions any status other than that of 'beliefs'. The Christian belief about 'normal' mental health is that it is not primarily a state of integration with oneself, or with society, but with God."[19] The tension between psychiatry and philosophy was clearly pointed out by C. S. Lewis in a letter to a friend: "Keep clear of psychiatrists unless you know that they are also Christians. Otherwise they start with the assumption that your religion is an illusion and try and 'cure' it: and this assumption they make not as professional psychologists but as amateur philosophers. Often they have never given the question any serious thought."[20]

We have already noted in our chapter heading some remarks of Professor David Horrobin, who occupies the Chair of Medical Physiology at Nairobi. Some further comments of his are apposite: "In human psychology, psychiatry and psychoanalysis the attitude of the observer and

[16] Z. A. Aarons, quoted by E. M. Schur in *Abortion in a Changing World, op. cit.*
[17] J. M. Kummer, "A Psychiatrist's View." In *Abortion in a Changing World, op. cit.*
[18] N. Morris, in *Abortion in Britain, op. cit.*
[19] M. Keeling, *Morals in a Free Society*, London, 1967, S.C.M.
[20] *The Letters of C. S. Lewis* (Ed. W. H. Lewis). London, 1966, Bles.

the motives which lie behind the questions he asks are just as important in determining the results as is the mind of the human being being observed ... The interaction between the two is a unique unrepeatable event. ... The intellectual basis for what the scientist says of man is no stronger than that for what the theologian says. By means of a gigantic confidence trick, by pretending that the study of man is science, by hanging on to the coat tails of solid, successful, reliable physics and engineering, an army of atheists and agnostics has forced many theologians to turn and flee."[1]

The Difficulty in Forecasting the Outcome

It is now time to notice that the psychiatrist has not only to combat the suspicions of his colleagues but has difficulties other doctors do not often face.

First there is the question of frankness on the part of his patients. It is true that patients sometimes quote false dates to their gynaecologists, but by and large we have objective findings to work on. When dealing with the psychiatrist, patients often hide their true feelings lest they do not achieve their desired result.[21,22]

Then there is the uncertainty of the patient's emotional reactions to continuation of the pregnancy, or to having a termination. To consider only patients with definite mental disease, Dr. A. Simon makes the point that the patient who has had a postpartum psychosis after two or more successive pregnancies will not necessarily have one after the next delivery, nor is it, however, certain that she will recover from another episode.[23]

Medical Case 26.1. A woman was in a mental hospital for 18 months with a schizophrenic psychosis after childbirth. At her husband's request she was discharged. She became pregnant, and was offered termination which she refused. After delivery of the child she improved and went on to full remission of symptoms. She had a further child without deterioration.

The psychically abnormal find it more difficult to stand the stress of a legal abortion. This means that the greater the psychiatric indications for a legal abortion are, the greater is also the risk of unfavourable psychic sequelae after the operation.[24]

Medical Case 26.2. A single 16-year-old girl in her first pregnancy was found to be functioning at a psychotic level not due primarily to the pregnancy. She appeared calm and content with the decision while in hospital for the abortion, and on discharge. Three days after discharge she returned to the hospital searching for her baby. "I didn't know they were going to take it away from me." She displayed evidence of psychotic depression and required further hospitalization.

[21] P. Arén and A. Amark, "Outcome of Pregnancies Where Abortion was Granted but not Carried Out." *Acta Psychiatrica et Neurologica Scandinavica*, 1961, **36**, 203.

[22] S. L. Patt, R. G. Rappaport and P. Barlow, "Follow-Up of Therapeutic Abortion." *Archives of General Psychiatry*, 1969, **20**, 408.

[23] A. Simon, "Psychiatric Indications for Therapeutic Abortion and Sterilization." *Clinical Obstetrics and Gynecology*, 1964, **7**, 67.

[24] See e.g. the paper by M. Ekblad, *op. cit.*

The difficulty in foretelling the outcome can perhaps best be seen from an account of women who abstained from their officially-granted abortion: "In some of our cases psychiatrically vital indication for abortion was considered to exist, and at follow-up examination it was possible to confirm that the situation had really appeared to be as serious as the documents showed. And yet the actual course taken by the case had not at all been that which had been feared."[21]

This confirms a point made by Professor Rhodes: "In all the debate about abortion we may be in danger of losing sight of the fact that there are other solutions than termination of pregnancy in the psychiatrically ill pregnant woman."[25]

One problem which must be remembered is the effect which may be expected on the child, if he is allowed to be born. While it is well-known that children of psychotic mothers run no greater risk of becoming psychotic than do children of normal mothers,[23] there is the danger inherent in the prolonged, close influence of such a sick person on the child particularly during its formative years. Dr. H. M. Murdock's suggestion that this influence can be prevented by placement in a foster home[26] is doubtless valid, but the idea will not commend itself to everyone.

The Treatment of the Woman with Mental Symptoms

What then is to be done about pregnant women seeking abortion on account of mental symptoms? The following rough-and-ready division of cases and responsibilities is tentatively advanced as a rule-of-thumb at the present time, until psychiatry has become a unified discipline speaking with a united voice.

Group I. A woman with organic mental disease, or mentally subnormal, or with a history of psychiatric treatment prior to this pregnancy, should certainly be referred to the psychiatrist, and the pregnancy managed according to his advice. Steps should be taken to ensure that if she is aborted she is thereafter returned to the psychiatrist's care for continued surveillance.

Group II. The woman who has never needed referral to a psychiatrist, but has – prior to the pregnancy – been treated by her general practitioner for nervous upsets or depression, should be thoroughly discussed with the general practitioner from this point of view. My own feeling is that where there has been endogenous depression, or even reactive depression of frequent or long-standing occurrence, the woman, and more particularly the family, have had enough, and abortion is probably indicated. On the other hand, when the doctor reports that he gave her a barbiturate for

[25] P. Rhodes, letter in the BMJ, 1966, I, 1168.
[26] M. H. Murdock, "Experiences in a Psychiatric Hospital." In Therapeutic Abortion, op. cit.

a few days some years ago, and has not seen her since, her complaints of mental upset require a lot more substantiation.

Group III. The woman most often considered on mental grounds is the one with no previous history of mental complaint whatever, but who is upset by the occurrence of an unwanted pregnancy.[27] In fact, in Britain in 1968 no less than 82% of the abortions performed had as their principal reported cause either "neurosis" or "transient situational disturbance," while in 1969 of abortions performed in the private sector 91% were under these headings.[28] The crucial question is whether her request should be decided by the psychiatrist. To return to Professor Miller: "You will observe that the real issue concerns the use of the term *mental illness*. As in the case of physical illness the definition has a social as well as a semantic importance. All of us have physical and mental disabilities . . . . All of us occasionally magnify disabilities of both kinds to obtain our own ends. Such exaggerations range from fabricating a sick headache or pleading normal fatigue to avoid an unattractive social engagement, to simulating more serious disability for more serious purposes – madness to escape imprisonment. The practitioner of internal medicine or neurologist is fallible, but probably more sparing than the psychiatrist in bestowing the accolade of illness with its consequent privileges. This, I believe, is where he is most abused."[4]

On this question of abortion a consultant psychiatrist friend of mine wrote: "To include the wide range of social distress, anger, resentment etc. which make up the bulk of 'psychiatric' referrals as truly psychiatric I feel is quite wrong and is quite unwarranted. I do not think we have sufficient wisdom or expertise to assess this large group any more ably than lay people."

It might well be that a committee of general practitioner, social worker, psychiatrist and gynaecologist would be best to decide on these cases.[29]

---

[27] Mr Hugh Arthur feels these cases can be subdivided and recognizes (1) Those with a stress situation prior to pregnancy as a result of which the sex act may be judged to be an abnormal behaviour response. The pressures towards cohabiting here are over and above those which might be considered to be within the patient's own control and therefore amenable to self-discipline. In this group he instances the loneliness of the widow or divorcee long accustomed to marital relations, the breaking marriage with attempted reconciliation, the woman under mental or physical duress, and the grande multipara with a demanding and irresponsible husband. (2) Other women in whom the stress situation arises only as a result of pregnancy, and where there is a pathological degree of stress due e.g. to extramarital pregnancy with racial differences, the inadequate or financially precarious woman with contraceptive failure, the single woman supporting dependants, and the final year student after an alcoholic party. He feels that in some stress situations abortion should be performed as an exercise in preventive medicine. (Unpublished.)

[28] Registrar-General's *Statistical Review of England and Wales. Supplement on Abortion.* 1968 and 1969 volumes, London, H.M.S.O.

[29] In deciding which cases come into this grouping it might be useful to accept the definition suggested by L. Marder ("Psychiatric Experience with a Liberalized Therapeutic Abortion Law."*American Journal of Psychiatry*, 1970, **126,**1230). Mental illness: "A disorder of thinking, feeling or behaviour producing a breakdown in living so that the individual cannot deal with reality or cannot function in dealing with daily problems of living."

Few, if any, of these appear to have been set up in Britain. Failing this some one person has to decide. As he is the one professional person whose life is spent dealing with pregnant women, and as he is the one who will actually have to *do* something if abortion is approved, it seems that the decision must be taken by the obstetrician. However he is more than grateful for all help possible in reaching the difficult decision. One consultant psychiatrist has stated that he does not wish to be asked to decide for or against abortion, but to express an opinion as to the future situation for the woman if the pregnancy continues or is terminated.[30] If this approach were to be universally accepted it would make the gynaecologist's task far lighter.

There are other workers, too, whose advice could be invaluable: general practitioner, medical social worker, the patient's spouse, even her pastor. Even with every help it would be naïve to imagine we yet know enough to make a decision with any certainty as to the mental outcome.

[30] A. West, Personal communication, July 1971. See also his paper "Termination of Pregnancy—A Psychiatrist's View." *In the Service of Medicine*, July, 1970.

CHAPTER 27

THE DECISION

Having to act as a finite god is painful.   FRANCIS SCHAEFFER[1]

The Decision Makers

WHO IS TO DECIDE? A RABBI HAS POINTED OUT THAT MEDICAL training does not equip the doctor to reach capital verdicts, and that as such judgements are not medical, but moral, they should be made by specialists in morals.[2]

A lawyer has suggested that as the law has the ultimate concern for the rightness and wrongness of actions it should determine priorities in this field.[3] There is a widespread belief that the woman should decide.[4]

In practice, at the moment, a number of people take part in decision making.

The Pregnant Woman. I have already argued that the patient, drugged as she is with hormones, is in no fit state to decide objectively. The very existence of the abortion option has magnified her difficulties. As Scandinavian workers have put it, "For many women the knowledge that the possibility of legal abortion exists implies that they find themselves confronted with a choice which they cannot cope with. Through this they become anxious, depressed, emotionally labile and in some cases aggressive and desperate. One said 'Going about wondering whether I should apply for abortion or not just made me more nervous. When it was decided that there was to be no operation I became a different person.'"[5] However, it would be wise for the married woman to give this question a long cool look when not pregnant. If then she feels that her situation is such that were she to conceive she would seek an abortion, now is the time for her to ensure that conception does not occur. The woman's right to decision lies prior to conception.

[1] F. Schaeffer, *The God Who is There*, London, 1968, Hodder and Stoughton.
[2] I. Jakovobits, in *Abortion and the Law* (Ed. D. Smith), Cleveland, 1967, Press of Western Reserve University.
[3] D. Smith, in preface to *Abortion and the Law, op. cit.*
[4] R. F. Tredgold, "Abortion. Whose Responsibility to Decide?" In *The Abortion Act, op. cit.*
[5] P. Arén and C. Amark, "The Prognosis in Cases in which Legal Abortion has been Granted but not Carried Out." *Acta Psychiatrica et Neurologica Scandinavica*, 1961, **36**, 203.

The Woman's Family. They know her best, they should love her most. They should be in a position to support, not to criticize her, and by surrounding her with their affectionate understanding reduce the number of problems she faces.

The Pastor. This word best describes the relationship which is appropriate between the woman in need and her spiritual adviser. He must be in a position not merely to point out moral principles, but guide her into living touch with the God who waits to be gracious to her. But he must remember there are profound medical issues to be thought of, and would be wise to adopt Bishop John Robinson's attitude: "I speak . . . as a concerned Christian man – and, in this field, very much a layman."[6]

The General Practitioner. He is the key man. He is the last in this chain of decision-makers really to know the woman and her situation, not just as it now is, but as it has been down the long years. Few will go against his advice if given in detail. It has been suggested that in fact his is the decision, for by his choice of specialist he can, if he wishes, often ensure what action will be taken.

The Medical Social Worker. The patient needs to have an opportunity to talk out her difficulties in an atmosphere of complete and unconditional acceptance. "It is a caseworker's task and privilege to offer them, if they will accept it, a relationship of this kind."[7] She has a diagnostic contribution to make.[8] It is a comfort to the doctor to know that his patient's account is confirmed: as we shall see, fictions are not unknown.[9]

The Abortion Committee. These have been popular in America: since complex systems are often arranged to preserve the anonymity of those taking the decision, they ensure that decisions can be made objectively, and protect the obstetrician from being pressurized by patient or relatives.[10] In Scandinavia, social workers take part in government-appointed committees. In Britain committees do not appear to have found favour, although verbal consultation with one or more colleagues is very frequently used. However locally, after four years of making our own decisions, we set up in May 1971 a small unofficial committee consisting of the two gynaecologists and the principal medical social worker. Prior to our weekly meeting the latter has interviewed the applicants for abortion. We sit round with our case notes and invariably come to a unanimous decision

---

[6] Bp J. A. T. Robinson (see p.42, fn 5).

[7] Jean Pochin, *Without a Wedding Ring: Casework with Unmarried Parents.* London, 1969, Constable.

[8] Norah M. Cogan, "Account of the Environment. A Medical Social Worker Looks at the new Abortion Law." *BMJ*, 1968, **2**, 235.

[9] J. L. D. Fairfield, letter in the *BMJ*, 1967, **1**, 173.

[10] A. F. Guttmacher, "The Shrinking Non-Psychiatric Indications for Therapeutic Abortion." In *Therapeutic Abortion, op. cit.*

T. W. McElin, *American Journal of Obstetrics and Gynecology,* 1969, **103**, 694.

L. E. Savel, "Adjudication of Therapeutic Abortion and Sterilization." *Clinical Obstetrics and Gynecology*, 1964, **7**, 14.

as to the action to be taken. The patient is notified of our decision the same afternoon and if abortion has been agreed she is usually admitted the next day. Since the introduction of this system we have found the mental strain considerably less. It is, however, only practicable in that we all have a similar approach to the question.

Unless some other specialist has to be involved due to a particular medical problem, the final decision maker is *the gynaecologist*. This is inevitable. To quote a scientist: "I see no way at all of relieving this burden on the clinician. The clinician will simply have to face the fact that his task is indeed getting much tougher, much more exacting, much further removed from technicalities of professional practice itself . . . . I see no way of getting round it."[11] A psychiatrist has said: "The real problem is that the gynaecologist has some skill which the patient needs and the patient wants to persuade him to use it at her discretion . . . . Yet the fact that they have the skill forces gynaecologists to impose their moral views on others;"[4] and another: "We must never forget that the gynaecologists are the final arbiters and must have the last word."[12] That this right includes that of refusal was agreed by 93% of women in an American poll,[13] and the official advice of the Medical Protection Society notes: "Although abortion may be recommended by two practitioners, a gynaecologist cannot act contrary to what he believes to be in the patient's best interest."[14] Inevitably then he is left in the position of being judge, jury and executioner.[15]

The Approach to the Patient

What attitudes should inform the mind of a person who has to take a decision on a request for abortion?

The first need is to establish a personal relationship, the need to be honest with each other, to establish empathy.[16] A French surgeon has maintained that surgery is not only a technical discipline, but also an encounter between human beings, a mutual relationship and understanding between two persons in the full sense of the term – at physical, psychical and spiritual level.[17] In no branch of surgery is this more important than in gynaecology.

[11] Sir Peter Medawar, in discussion on "The Cost of Life." *Proceedings of the Royal Society of Medicine*, 1967, 60, 1242.

[12] P. H. Tooley, "If All Abortions are Legal, Which are Desirable?" In *The Abortion Act*, op. cit.

[13] F. W. Peyton, A. R. Starry and T. R. Leidy, "Women's Attitudes concerning Abortion." *Obstetrics and Gynecology*, 1969, 34, 182.

[14] Medical Protection Society. *Abortion Act 1967. Comment and Advice*.

[15] The phrase is Wallace Barr's in debate "That the Abortion Act of 1967 was a Disastrous Mistake." *Scottish Medical Journal*, 1968, 13, 396.

[16] J. M. Gustafson, "A Christian Approach to the Ethics of Abortion." *Dublin Review*, Winter, 1967–8, 241, 346.

[17] J. Dor, *Surgery of the Person*. Quoted by P. Tournier, *The Healing of Persons*, London, 1966, Collins.

One does not have to be a Christian to realize that is is useless trying to think merely as a scientist. Bronowski has referred to the importance of those values which are not generated by the practice of science, the values of tenderness, of kindliness, of human intimacy and love.[18] It was Kinsey who remarked that if one wants to define the function of an embryo or the function of reproduction, one must identify the definition as philosophic. This he maintains was perfectly justifiable, and perhaps the best approach to the problem.[19] While among the questions which one must ask oneself, in the view of Lord Cohen, is not only, "Is my recommendation based on the best scientific probabilities?" but "Is my proposed course of action the one I would advise for someone I love, and if I were similarly circumstanced would I wish this done for me?"[20]

We must remind ourselves that there are varying value estimations. After reviewing abortion practice in 350 primitive or pre-industrial societies G. Devereux stated: "From a strictly sociological and anthropological point of view, social criteria based on existing systems of value determine what *kinds* and *degrees* of stress are accepted as constituting 'socially legitimate' motivation of, or 'therapeutic indication' for abortion."[21] Our values may not be those of our patient; where they are, the problems are much easier.

The doctor who for religious reasons cannot have anything to do with abortion in practice refers such cases to a colleague. This despite the charge that "in referring patients to other physicians for abortion Roman Catholic physicians give scandal in a serious degree both to the patient and to the physicians to whom he refers the patients, since he gives other human beings an opportunity to do the wrong which he knows he cannot in conscience do himself."[22] The Declaration of Geneva includes the oath: "I will not permit considerations of religion ... to intervene between my duty and my patients." It does, however, go on, "I will maintain the utmost respect for human life from the time of conception."[23] A self-proclaimed atheist has said: "We try to reach a decision on abortion on rational grounds, without predetermined ethical considerations. When I say predetermined, I mean predetermined by faith of any kind that is not relevant to this problem."[24] We can all agree with such a

[18] J. Bronowski, *Science and Human Values*. Quoted by J. Hubble, *British Medical Journal*, 1966, **I**, 474.

[19] A. C. Kinsey, *In Abortion in the United States, op. cit.*

[20] Lord Cohen, Summing up Symposium: "The Cost of Life." *Proceedings of the Royal Society of Medicine*, 1967, **60**, 1243.

[21] G. Devereux, "A Typological Study of Abortion in 350 Primitive, Ancient and Pre-Industrial Societies." In *Therapeutic Abortion, op. cit.*

[22] F. Curran, "Religious Implications." In *Therapeutic Abortion, op. cit.* He quotes St. Thomas Aquinas' definition of "Scandal" as anything, word or deed, of lesser worthlessness which presents to another an occasion of spiritual ruin.

[23] *Declaration of Geneva:* Adopted by the General Assembly of the World Medical Association 1948.

[24] P. O. Hubinot, in discussion in *Abortion in a Changing World, op. cit.*

statement, the Christian considering that as his faith is strictly relevant to the problem, it is therefore not excluded.

It is, of course, impossible to have an absolutely impartial standpoint, as one's attitude to any ethical problem is related to one's view of the meaning of life. We will be accused of being "judgemental",[25] but the whole of medicine must be judgemental: diagnosis and therapy are founded on it, so the accusation is ill-chosen. In particular the Christian may be accused of arrogance; but as it was one of themselves who admitted that the besetting sin of the agnostic is arrogance,[26] it is a little difficult to see who can cast the first stone.

An eminent American lawyer has said: "The great traditional safeguard of medicine is the disciplined fidelity of the physician to his patient, guided by his dominant therapeutic aim and responsibility, considering the patient as an end and not as a means."[27]

Factors Influencing Decision

The background to decision has occupied our thinking throughout this book; there are one or two specific points to be clarified in the interview.

How serious is the problem to the patient? The woman who took no precautions during regular intercourse, or who cannot manage to keep an appointment with the social worker, or whose face brightens up at the offer of sterilization after delivery, is probably not a serious candidate.

Medical Case 27.1. A thirty-two year old woman with three children was referred when 14 weeks pregnant by her practitioner who wrote "She is very depressed, weeps all the time, and feels she cannot carry on." She was given an urgent appointment with the gynaecologist for six days later. However she telephoned to say that she could not attend as she was going on holiday! When seen after that she readily accepted that there were no grounds for termination and agreed to being booked for confinement and sterilization.

The truthfulness of the story has to be weighed. One doctor wrote: "I have personally known women invent heartrending stories of brutal husbands or landlords or rape by mental defectives, even of the risk of hereditary transmission of disease, and get away with their fictions."[9] Both in the illegal[28] and legal abortion[5] fields it is not uncommon to find patients untruthful about the duration of their pregnancies.

It is important to take the social problems seriously. A government study of the effect of closing a coal mine says of the redundant men: "they have been stranded by the tide of industrial change, technological advances and discoveries, and they confront the nation with a social, economic and

[25] Bp I. T. Ramsey, "On Not Being Judgemental." Contact, March, 1970.
[26] Marghanita Laski, in discussion with Abp Bloom on B.B.C. T.V. July 12, 1970.
[27] T. Lambert, "Legal Rights of the Fetus." In Birth Control and the Christian, op. cit.
[28] Moya Woodside, "Attitudes of Women Abortionists." Howard Journal, 1963, 11, 93.

moral problem."[29] Such moral problems cannot be discounted, especially by those of us who work within a mile of this derelict mine, and are responsible for the medical care of the wives. Similar problems abound.

The long-term future must be discussed to ensure that the woman does not have the same problem in a few months' time. To many married women sterilization should be offered, although it is doubtful if it should ever be a condition of termination. Although usually performed at the same time as abortion, the combined operation has a higher risk than if sterilization were postponed to a later date.[30]

The patient who comes back a second time requires special attention, otherwise one could emulate the American doctor who, operating on non-legal grounds, aborted a single woman on no less than thirteen occasions.[31] There can be few reasons to justify a second abortion, although there are some:

> Medical Case 27.2. A 20-year-old married woman in her second pregnancy was aborted because a chronic disability made it impracticable for her to cope with two small children. At follow-up she rejected "the pill" as she was now separated from her husband. He returned to her, for what proved to be one night only, a year later, and left her pregnant once again. In this case sterilization did not appear indicated as when her first child was older another one might not be too great a burden, there was the hope that a cure might be found for her disability, and after divorce, remarriage is not unlikely.

An attempt should be made to ensure that the patient understands all that is involved, and has faced up to the risk of regret later. Her usual reaction is to say, "It won't happen to me." That, however, is what she said a few weeks earlier: she was wrong then and is quite as likely to be wrong now.

It is vital to identify the woman who is ambivalent. Sometimes she is being pushed: perhaps by a husband who is rejecting the child, or by parents whose selfish ambitions for their daughter may outweigh their considerations for her feelings. With these there is a great risk of serious self-reproach.[32]

> Medical Case 27.3. An unmarried girl made it clear to the gynaecologist that she would have liked to keep the baby. However, her parents kept up such pressure on her that she broke down mentally and had to be aborted because of this factor. On leaving hospital post-operatively she was sobbing.

Where the woman is not convinced about an abortion this should not be done; or in cases where, for genuine medical reasons, pressure has to be

[29] Department of Employment and Productivity. *Ryhope: A Pit Closes*, London, 1970 H.M.S.O.

[30] P. Huntingford, letter in the *Lancet*, 1971, I, 1012.

[31] R. D. Spencer, "The Performance of Non-Hospital Abortions." In *Abortion in a Changing World, op. cit.*

[32] M. Ekblad, "Induced Abortion on Psychiatric Grounds." *Acta Psychiatrica et Neurologica Scandinavica*, 1955, Supplement 99.

brought to bear towards an abortion, it must be remembered that she will need extra psychological and spiritual preparation. Even so, bitter and lasting regret cannot always be avoided. There are few indications so urgent that one is entitled to run this risk. My own rule is that if there is the slightest suspicion of doubt decision must be postponed, unless abortion can be immediately ruled out.

I have talked so far of "the patient," but one must constantly remind oneself that there are two patients under one's care: mother and fetus. Of the latter Miss Shotton has reminded us "If while it is part of the mother, its existence threatens her life or health, it must be excised, the incomplete personality sacrificed for the sake of the complete. *It must be emphasized that this is indeed a sacrifice*, only to be undertaken in the interest of the mother's health, for the doctor's calling is to preserve life, not to destroy it."[33]

Diagnosis

It is often difficult, even in cases where abortion seems to be clearly indicated, to know how to classify cases as required for government returns.

Medical Case 27.4. A single girl was referred for abortion with the story that her mother had recently died. The patient was the only child. Her father was suffering from a malignant condition (the general practitioner's letter added that the girl did not know this) and although at present apparently well, would be expected to become bedridden shortly. The patient would then have not only to run the home but cope with a good deal of nursing.

A case like that seems clearly to warrant termination as the added problems of a pregnancy at such a time would be great, even without a baby to care for as well as a dying parent. But where does it fit into the Act's neat categories? It is usually squeezed into clause II, with the knowledge that this is bending the law.

Bearing in mind the long sessions of Parliament devoted to the exact wording of the Act, it is amusing to note how readily a widening of the indications is accepted. The official governmental report records, without comment, paternal indications such as "Drug Addict," "Young; immature" and "Husband away from home."[34] I do not criticize these indications, but note must be taken of this tendency by all involved in drafting legislation. The Swedish experience is that "we no longer see clear-cut diseases so much as ill people."[35]

It is useful to try to define to oneself the actual problem. The Scandinavians who have had wide experience, recognize that a large number of

[33] Margaret D. Shotton, "Some Problems of a Christian Obstetrician." *In the Service of Medicine*, Oct., 1960.
[34] Registrar General, *Statistical Review of England and Wales: Supplement on Abortion* (1968, 1969), Table 12.
[35] Ottossod, J. O. Legal Abortion in Sweden. *Journal of Biosocial Sciences*, 1971 3, 173.

applicants are experiencing a "convention conflict," as the pregnancy provokes a conflict between the woman and the conventions of her group. A reactive depressive state may be produced, but this is rarely deep, being a panic reaction. "As a defence she is apt to repress completely the factors favouring continuation of the pregnancy in order to be able to carry through her strong one-sided advocacy for legal abortion. Seen against this background it is quite clear that the strength of the indication for legal abortion cannot be determined by the strength of the emotional reaction."[36]

On the other hand the principal Scandinavian ground for termination has been "worn-out housewife's neurasthenia" (which Dr. Brekke likens to that seen in concentration camp victims[37]). The poor conditions obtaining before the pregnancy include many apparently unconnected factors – poor housing, economic difficulties, marital problems, illness, maladjusted children, the husband a poor breadwinner. Physically she is in poor shape, probably with varicose veins and piles, and there are psycho-matic symptoms such as muscle tensions and chronic headache. She is always tired, irritable, sleeps poorly and has an anxiety state. All these get progressively worse with each new burden placed on the woman until what has been termed "insufficiency" develops.[36] Such women are legion, especially (although not solely) among the working class community. Termination and sterilization may be the first steps on the road to recovery, but additional help from the social services should be initiated at the same time.

However carefully the case has been weighted the outcome may be unexpected:

Medical Case 27.5. A twenty-eight year old woman with three children was deserted by her husband after he had made her pregnant in a desperate re-conciliation attempt. Her pregnancies were usually complicated involving long periods in hospital. Abortion was performed, definite fetal material being obtained.

At follow-up she still felt pregnant and a 22 week pregnancy was discovered. She refused proffered hysterotomy. Her husband got into touch with her, and hearing that she was still pregnant, returned. She was delivered by Caesarean section of the second twin, evidence of the first twin's earlier removal being found at operation.

Her main joy in having the pregnancy continue is her feeling that the marriage is reasonably stable again.

Granted that abortion is performed: have we solved the problem? At an American symposium Dr. Sarrel, a gynaecologist, remarked that he was concerned about the practice of abortion in that it tends to become de-personalized and places too little value on the deep-seated human prob-

[36] H. Hoffmeyer, "Medical Aspects of the Danish Legislation on Abortion." In *Abortion and the Law* (Ed. D. Smith), Cleveland, 1967, Press of Western Reserve University.
[37] B. Brekke, in *Abortion in the United States, op. cit.*

lems involved. He was concerned with people leading better lives. The doing of abortions should not be a substitute for responding to the needs of human life. To this Professor Hardin, a biologist, replied "That sort of argument disturbs me . . . it seems to me the issue here is that it is much easier to perform abortions than to remake the lives of all the women who want them. Granted, the remaking of many of these lives would be admirable, but it is hardly practicable. There is not enough time to follow your suggestion. Today we must do abortions. Tomorrow we can work on the more basic problems."[38]

Now it seems to me that Professor Hardin, perhaps unwittingly, has hit upon the central issue of the whole problem of abortion. In some cases the question arises due to poor circumstances and we can and must work to improve these. In other cases, the majority it would seem, it is not so much the remaking of the environment but the remaking of lives that is needed. A larger task, but not an impossible one. Fortunately Professor Hardin is in error in saying the task is "hardly practicable". Today, more than perhaps for a long time, there are great numbers of Christians of a wide variety of churchmanship who are happy to proclaim out of their own experience that God remakes lives. There is no need to wait for tomorrow to work on the basic problem. Tomorrow never comes, we have only today.

Decision

While at the back of one's mind are all the issues dealt with in this book one comes to decision with only two, perhaps three, questions in mind.

First: What is this woman's total situation? This requires an estimation of her environment, family, and hopes in the light of her personality. Although one makes up one's mind from the patient's story, filled out by the practitioner's and medical social worker's assessments one is constantly aware of how little one can fully enter into her world, a disadvantage counterbalanced by one's ability to see the issue "in the round."

Second: What are the risks of an abortion to this woman? The physical risks, especially to her future ability to bear children, in view of the procedure which will be necessary at this duration of pregnancy; and the mental risks in the light of her personality.

The third question: What of the fetus? does not occur in every case to most of us. That it is there in the background is obvious from the bias against abortion which increases very sharply from twelve weeks when the fetus has become organized into human shape. This bias is sufficient to ensure that all of us have an upper limit to approval: the more seriously we take the fetal "potential life" the lower we draw the line. The fetus is considered specifically when the question of possible abnormality occurs, and in the cases, not infrequent, when a doctor who knows the family well

[38] Discussion, "Abortion and Poverty." In *Abortion in a Changing World, op. cit.*

says "I am convinced for the baby's sake that it were better not to be born. Its life would be hell."

If there is a doubt in one's mind decision should be postponed and the patient told to see her practitioner in 48 hours for the result of her application.

Whatever decision is reached, every effort should be made to ensure that the patient realizes the concern of the medical staff for her problem and their genuine desire to come to the right conclusion. In the case of a refusal, the offer of a hospital booking, of sterilization in the postnatal period, of the help of the almoners, must be made. That it is sometimes rejected curtly is only a part of the cost of providing this service. There are few doctors involved with this problem who do not return home from a clinic in a state of mental and spiritual exhaustion almost unknown prior to the introduction of the Act. This is a price which must be paid, for "it has been acutely observed that the freedom of competent physicians to treat their patients as total persons (a woman carries a child not only in her uterus but suffused and implanted in her psyche as well) is probably the strongest interest that can be advanced in favour of therapeutic abortion."[27]

CHAPTER 28

THE BETTER WAY: PREVENTION OF EXTRA-MARITAL CONCEPTION

Every induced abortion whether legal or criminal, is an expression of failure of one form or another – failed contraceptive technique, irresponsibility by one or both partners, ignorance, betrayal of trust or denial of human dignity.

PROF. JOHN STALLWORTHY[1]

Filling the Moral Vacuum

SOCIAL STUDIES HAVE SHOWN THAT ILLEGITIMATE PREGNANCIES MOST commonly arise against an unsatisfactory family background,[2] and rarely occur in those brought up in an atmosphere of frankness and mutual trust by two parents who love each other and their children. "It follows from this that the prevention of unmarried parenthood begins at the nursery stage, where the foundation of every quality of character is laid."[3] A happy home is therefore one of the greatest safeguards we can provide for our children.

If we are going to alter the incidence of illegitimate pregnancies, with the consequent pressure for termination, we will have to tackle the whole climate in which our youngsters are brought up. Dr. Benjamin Spock admits to having come full circle: "Recently I've come to realize that the worst problems of America . . . are caused not by lack of knowledge or means but by moral blindness or confusion . . . Many youths are left in a vacuum. They are offered no set of values either to subscribe to or argue about. This situation amounts to a serious deficiency disease for a species designed to live by the spirit."[4] Sir Dugald Baird has remarked that it is no use blaming the modern teenagers. They are the casualties, not the cause.[5]

The distinguished anthropologist Margaret Mead is more specific: "We permit and even encourage situations in which young people can indulge in any sort of sex behaviour they elect . . . . We bring up girls to be free and easy and unafraid, without the protection given by shyness and

---

[1] J. A. Stallworthy, letter to *The Times*, Jan. 3, 1969.
[2] J. Bowlby, *Child Care and the Growth of Love*, London, 1965, Penguin. Barbara Thompson, *Social Studies of Illegitimate Pregnancies*. Quoted by Jean Pochin, *op. cit.*
[3] Jean Pochin, *Without a Wedding Ring: Casework with Unmarried Parents*, London, 1969, Constable.
[4] B. Spock, *Decent and Indecent*, London, 1970, Bodley Head.
[5] Sir Dugald Baird, in Interview with *The Times*, June 18, 1969.

fear to girls of many other societies. We bring our boys up to be just as free and easy, used to girls, demanding towards girls. We actually place our young people in a virtually intolerable situation, giving them the entire setting for behaviour for which we then punish them whenever it occurs."[6]

Medical Case 28.1. A girl, under 15 years of age, was most carefully supervised by her parents. Her boy friend had to collect her from her home and escort her straight to his house, and bring her directly home. The parents were always at home at such times. When she came requesting abortion she admitted to having had intercourse, more than once, on the lounge sofa, and that it had not occurred to her to take precautions.

Nineteenth century chaperonage apart, control by supervision is useless.[7] There are only two real choices. We can further loosen sanctions. This policy has been actively pursued for the past decades. I know of not the slightest evidence that it has brought real joy (I did not say momentary pleasure) or contentment or satisfaction with it.[8] On the other hand I have seen a good deal of sadness and emptiness and despair and threatened suicide as a result. Alternatively we can teach our youngsters the real meaning of love, and point them to the real source of joy: to the God who uses the metaphors of sexual love to describe His love for us.[9] This will have to be tackled at two levels: an attempt to awaken society to moral issues,[10] and a teaching of moral standards to our own children.

The Case Against Extra-Marital Intercourse

It was God who made male and female. This is one of the aspects of His creation upon which He looked and "it was very good"[11]. C. S. Lewis has said "Christianity is almost the only one of the great religions which thoroughly approves of the body – which believes that matter is good, that God Himself once took on a human body, that some kind of body is going to be given to us even in Heaven and is going to be an essential part of our happiness, our beauty, and our energy. Christianity has glorified marriage more than any other religion; and nearly all the greatest love poetry in the world has been produced by Christians. If anyone says that

[6] Margaret Mead, *Male and Female*, London, 1962, Penguin.

[7] M. Schofield, *The Sexual Behaviour of Young People* (Rev. Ed.), London, 1968, Penguin. "The first experience of sexual intercourse took place in the parental home of one or other of the young people concerned in more than half of all the cases. So parents who worry about their sons and daughters coming home late at night should, perhaps, start wondering what is happening in their own front room when they go out in the evening."

[8] C. H. Whiteley and Winifred Whitely, *The Permissive Morality*, London, 1964, Methuen. "There is no reliable evidence . . . to show that a looser sexual morality is more conducive to human happiness than a stricter one."

[9] Cant.; Isa. 62: 5; Rev. 21: 2.

[10] An organization "The Responsible Society," dedicated to achieving this in Britain, was announced in June, 1971. (1/39 Portland Place, London W.1).

[11] Gen. 1: 31.

sex in itself is bad, Christianity contradicts him at once." He points out that the contemporary propaganda for lust which makes us feel that the desires we are resisting are so "natural," so "healthy" and so reasonable, that it is almost perverse and abnormal to resist them is a lie, the lie consisting in the suggestion that any sexual act to which you are tempted at the moment is also healthy and normal. This, on any conceivable view, and quite apart from Christianity, must be nonsense, for the surrender to all our desires obviously leads to impotence, disease, jealousies, lies, concealment and everything that is the reverse of health, good humour and frankness.[12]

In fact everyone is agreed that there are duties and responsibilities which take precedence over sexual desire. During four years overseas service during the Second World War, one heard many bitter complaints about separation from wives and family, but never once did I hear the comment that the country had no right to enforce this separation with its attendant sexual abstinence. To maintain that regular sexual activity is essential even in war time would require approval of rapine and a provision of a Corps of Prostitutes! Surprisingly neither of these suggestions has been made even in our liberal day.

In deciding on one's actions it is common to start with enlightened self-interest. What may this cost? Extra-marital sexual activities may cost a pregnancy with mental turmoil and recriminations at the least. It has been shown that the student may find that studies suffer.[13] Those who suggest that medical advances in contraception have ruled out the physical risks of promiscuity[14] do not appear to have noticed that the incidence of venereal disease has reached epidemic proportions,[15] nor that recent work suggests that youthful intercourse, and the number of male partners may be related to the later onset of cancer of the neck of the womb.[16]

But, it may be said, the rewards are so rich as to make the possible risks insignificant. The major expectation is of physical satisfaction. That this does not automatically follow can be seen in the analogy of a kiss. On a physical level a nerve impulse goes up to the brain from the membranes of the lip as the result of every kiss: the kiss of the repugnant old relative who must be placated with an eye to her Will; the happy kiss for one's mother

[12] C. S. Lewis, *Mere Christianity*, London, 1952, Bles.
[13] At Reading University in 1968 12% of freshmen women were taking oral contraceptives by the end of their second term. It is of interest that no less than 45% of those failing their first year examinations were using oral contraceptives. (J. D. Cumming, "Contraceptive Advice in an Academic Community." *Syntex Bulletin of Family Planning*, May, 1970).
[14] e.g. J. Fletcher, *Moral Responsibility*, London, 1967, S.C.M. Press.
[15] It should be noted that in Britain there were 300,000 new cases of venereal disease in 1969. In Sweden in the fifteen years up to 1966 there had been an increase in Gonorrhoea of 167% in boys and more than 300% in girls (C. Malmas, "The Medical Implications of Promiscuity." In *The Christian Physician, op. cit.*).
[16] Margaret Hennigan, "Clinical Observations on the Aetiology of Cervical Cancer." *Journal of Obstetrics and Gynaecology of the British Commonwealth*, 1968, **75**, 479.

on returning home after a long absence; the marvellous kiss when one's lover has accepted an offer of marriage. Why is it then that these identical impulses do not achieve identical responses? A moment's thought will show that there is a second factor, an emotional one, which is in fact the major agent in making that same physical stimulus appear objectionable, casual or marvellous. Even if one loves the other person the value of the kiss is different should she be a fiancée proudly displayed to the world, or should she be the wife of a friend who may butt in at any moment.

If this is true of a kiss it is equally true of sexual intercourse. The response must be totally different in clients of a certain prostitute who is reputed to peel and eat oranges while entertaining her visitors, from that experienced with a wife one has taken "in the sight of God and this congregation."

I have described the difference as being an emotional factor. In reality there is a cluster of factors including the aesthetic factor, the response factor, and that moral factor which can be called conscience. We must weigh this moral factor. It will be well to ask what is this doing to ME. I am not yet a fully formed complete person; no one ever is. Granted that these few minutes may be pleasurable. I am my future child's Daddy. I am my future wife's Husband. After this half hour I will never be the same again.

What is this doing to the girl? She too is a person in the process of formation; or is she merely a substitute? Gore Vidal is quoted as stressing exactly this point of anonymity by telling the story of a man who after coitus said to his partner "if you tell me who you were thinking of, I'll tell you who I was thinking of."

Perhaps some man is contemplating intercourse with the girl who will one day become one's wife. What will he do with her? More important, what will he do to her?

There is another factor to consider here. To a man intercourse is an entity, an end in itself, but not for a girl. For her it is an integral part of a relationship within which she fulfils herself as lover and mother. Mr Hugh Arthur, drawing attention to the basic provisos of the permissive society, has made the point that these have been largely promulgated by males with no knowledge of female psychology and physiology. "It is the man's responsibility to consider whether he is simply arousing these emotions in the woman with intent to use her for his own satisfaction and pleasure, and perhaps incidentally to give her some pleasure *in the male sense* . . . . There is no doubt physiologically and psychologically speaking that whereas for men intercourse is a pleasure and an end in itself – it is a pleasure and a beginning for a woman . . . . The first proviso of the permissive society is that the rights and dignities of neither party should be ignored or injured in sexual intercourse, but I have been repeatedly given to understand, explicitly and implicitly by girls and women that the basic feminine sexual need really is security. The first proviso of the New Morality is therefore contravened and the normal instinct and desires of young women debased and prostituted rather than developed and matured by permissive patterns of sex."[17]

At the level of satisfaction the results cannot be foreseen with certainty. In a survey of illegitimate pregnancies among nurses and medical students, Dr. Kenneth Moynagh has reported a girl writing in despair: "Tell my friends it is not worth it. I had satisfying intercourse with my fiancé before marriage but all desire disappeared during the honeymoon and has not returned."[18] Dr. Geraldine Howard states: "I always remember one girl who came saying that she had no friends, no contacts, but her young man came to see her once a week for intercourse. He stayed half an hour. 'And he doesn't even speak to me' she said."[19] An American woman gynaecologist has reported that most teenage girls she has worked among did not find coitus particularly pleasurable.[20]

In fact it has been said that the most common problem now is not social taboos on sexual activity or guilt feeling about sex in itself, but the fact that sex for so many people is an empty, mechanical and vacuous experience.[21]

There is an even graver risk, exemplified in the story of Amnon, who after premeditated subterfuge seduced his half-sister Tamar: "He would not listen, but overpowered her, dishonoured her and raped her. Then Amnon was filled with utter hatred for her; his hatred was stronger than the love he had felt, and he said to her, 'Get up and go.' She answered, 'No. It is wicked to send me away. This is harder to bear than all you have done to me.' He would not listen to her, but summoned the boy who attended him and said, 'Get rid of this woman, put her out and bolt the door after her.' "[22] This sorry episode resulted in Amnon's murder and set in motion the chain of events leading to civil war. The risk of a like swing: from love to hate, from longing to repugnance, still needs to be weighed.

Suppose, however, that none of these undesirable results occur. Suppose the episode is entirely pleasurable. There is still a hostage in the memory. There will always be that little cloud in later marriage: the desperate hope that in the moment of climax the wrong name will not be uttered; the nagging wonder whether at some stage down the long years the truth will out.

[17] H. Arthur, *Sex and Society*. A Report of the Church and Community Committee of the Presbyterian Church of England, 1969.
[18] K. D. Moynagh, Personal communication. Nov. 1969. A similar case has been reported by Shirley E. Nathan, "Pregnancies Conceived Extra-maritally." *Journal of the Royal College of General Practitioners*, 1969, **18**, 72.
[19] Geraldine Howard, "Problems over Abortion in Birth Control Clinics." In *The Abortion Act*, *op. cit.*
[20] Mary A. Friedrich, "Motivations for Coitus." *Clinical Obstetrics and Gynecology*, 1970, **13**, 691.
[21] R. May. Quoted by O. S. Walters in *The Christian Physician*, *op. cit.*
[22] 2 Sam. 13: 14–17

However, despite all this reasoning, one's own situation is always unique. Canon Streeter has put it perceptively; "When passion is the arbiter, my own case is always recognized to be exceptional. There never were in history lovers like we two, never were any kept apart by a fate as hard as ours. When Aphrodite whispers in my ear, a principle which admits no exception may nerve me to resist; but if any exception is admitted, my case is certain to be the one."[23]

We are wise then, to admit no exceptions.

Contraception for the Unmarried

It is universally agreed that it is better to prevent a pregnancy rather than abort it. This being so, many leaders of opinion, clerical[14] as well as medical,[24] consider not only that contraceptives should be offered to unmarried young people, but that it is quite wrong not to do so.

A number of clinics have been set up to provide contraceptive advice for the unmarried. Very divergent interpretations can be placed on their statistics. Workers at the King's College Hospital Youth Advisory Clinic in London paint a cheerful picture of stable couples proceeding to matrimony. Within a year of so of their first visit to the clinic 22% of the girls had married their boy-friends, a further 66% continued to go steady with the same boy: some of these having become officially engaged. Only 6.5% of their clients had changed partners. These figures, the workers maintain, refute the suggestion that such a clinic aids and abets a promiscuous society. Furthermore as 97.5% of the girls were already having intercourse prior to their first visit to the clinic its existence could not be held responsible for their behaviour.[25] Similarly at the Brook Advisory Clinic in Birmingham 96% of their first nine thousand patients were already sleeping with their boys.[26]

However at a similar clinic in Edinburgh 26% of the single girls attending stated that they would "definitely stop" having sexual intercourse if no contraceptive advice were available as a result of their clinic visit. Further, fully two-thirds of the girls said there was no view to marriage or "other permanency" in their sexual liaison.[27] In view of these Scottish figures the activities of such contraceptive clinics for the unmarried cannot be considered morally neutral. Paul Ferris has made some illuminating observations: "Nothing illustrates the confusion of middle-aged liberals, faced with the sexual life of the young, more clearly than the

[23] B. H. Streeter, quoted by Sir Arnold Lunn and G. Lean, *The New Morality*, London, 1964, Blandford Press.

[24] P. J. Huntingford, *op. cit.*

[25] J. Newton, J. Elias and Patricia Newton, "Hospital Family Planning A Youth Advisory Clinic," *BMJ*, 1971, **2**, 642.

[26] J. A. Jordan, Paper read at the Third International Congress on Psychosomatic Medicine in Obstetrics and Gynaecology, London, April, 1971.

[27] M. Wadsworth, Nancy Loudon, Margaret Rankin and Isabel Herbert, "Attenders at a Contraceptive Clinic for Single Women." *Journal of Biosocial Sciences*, 1971, **3**, 133.

anxiety of those doctors at Brook clinics who prescribe the pill for teenage girls, but groan inwardly at the same time . . . If anyone takes teenage sex in his stride one would expect it to be these volunteers in the cause of sexual freedom. Instead some of them are unhappy about their work. . . . 'I go to conferences where there's vague talk of liberality,' says Dr A., a middle-aged woman, 'but no one ever says, *What does the wise parent advise the child? . . .*' "[28]

For the Christian doctor this poses a more serious moral problem than abortion. For abortion, as we have seen, there is no clear-cut Scriptural guidance; we have had to build up our position on inferences. The Bible, however, is absolutely clear that fornication is wrong.[29] However we may define fornication, without doubt it includes "sleeping around," which is the purpose behind many requests from unmarried people for contraceptives.[30] Fornication, unrepented and unforgiven, is listed among those sins which debar a person from welcome into God's presence.[31] How can a Christian aid and abet it? With a Christian patient there is no problem: no compromise. But how right is the Christian doctor to force his moral views on a non-Christian patient? No more right than the patient is to coerce the doctor's conscience to fit her own desires. My own feeling is that the problem can usually be got round. The doctor should see the patient ("a patient not seen is a patient not counselled"[30]) make his position clear, and decline to prescribe what he feels is not in the patient's best interests (medical best interests as well as spiritual). He should then point out that she can readily obtain the supplies she desires by attending the family planning clinic; or even from another doctor.

There are, however, cases where these alternatives are not appropriate, either because there is no clinic and no other doctor who will help, or because the patient is such that the doctor has had to spend long careful years building up a relationship of trust. The matter has been given careful thought over many months by a study-group of medical Christians whose findings have been presented by Jacqueline Keighley, herself a general practitioner. They comment that there is no real evidence to prove that prescribing the pill will reduce illegitimacy or abortion; on the contrary, this may produce a permissive climate in which the incidence of extra-marital sexual activity will increase and include both protected and unprotected intercourse. They see the Christian as being called to be involved in situations, however reprehensible or complicated, which already exist, and, recalling our Lord's parable of the Good Samaritan, remind us how easy it is for the religious to pass by on the other side. They list both the good and the harm that may be done in prescribing

[28] P. Ferris, "Teenage Sex/The New Dilemma." *The Observer*, July 18, 1971.
[29] 1 Cor. 6: 18 and Eph. 5: 13.
[30] R. J. Pion, "Prescribing Contraceptives for Teenagers—A Moral Compromise?" *Obstetrics and Gynecology*, 1967, **30**, 752.
[31] Rev. 22: 15.

contraceptives under these circumstances, and conclude that no hard and
fast rules can be laid down, but that the Christian doctor must rely on the
Holy Spirit to guide in each individual decision.[32]

That there are many who will not agree with that point of view was
evident in the heated debate in the General Assembly of the Church of
Scotland in May 1970 on the question of whether the pill should be
available for promiscuous unmarried women. The view of the Church's
committee was that while the evil of having brought an unwanted child
into the world could not be retrieved, a promiscuous girl might be
brought to see the folly of her behaviour.[33] The debate continues. Before
taking sides it is worth pondering Dr. Keighley's remark that in their
group it was interesting to note that those who took a rigid view were
those who were not meeting the problem in the consulting room whereas
those who were facing it daily tended to be more permissive, or perhaps
more compassionate is a better term. On the other hand those who were
rigid about contraception were more liberal with regard to abortion
because they were more involved in that problem.[32]

The Case for Chastity

So far we have been looking at the matter negatively: there is a much
more positive approach. The delight of chastity. The knowledge that one
is keeping something very precious in trust till the great day when un-
ashamed and in thankfulness, one can give oneself to one's beloved, and
have an intimacy which puts one's spouse in a relationship utterly different
from all other people. "The marriage ceremony is the step in the relationship that creates the complete intimacy which it is the function of sexual
intercourse to express."[34] J. W. Bowker has well put it: "Intercourse is
also part of the creation of what you are becoming as a person .... The
continuity of relationship makes possible a whole range of relationship
which cannot – simply cannot – exist in a casual or single encounter, or in
a relationship from which one or other participant may withdraw at any
moment. There is, in other words, a quite different responsibility and
potentiality in a relationship which is directed towards an undefined
future 'For better for worse, for richer for poorer, in sickness and in
health.' Equally there are quite different returns from such a relationship."[35]

With this high picture of the purpose and rewards of marriage before
one, the price of waiting is not high.

In a letter to his brother, C. S. Lewis recorded: "On Monday Charles
Williams lectured, nominally on *Comus* but really on Chastity. Simply as

[32] Jacqueline V. Keighley, "Contraceptives and the Unmarried—The Present Position."
In the Service of Medicine, Jan., 1970.
[33] Church of Scotland: Committee on Moral Welfare. *Why Marriage? A Report on Personal Relationships*, Edinburgh, 1970, St. Andrew Press.
[34] M. Keeling, *Morals in a Free Society*, London, 1967, S.C.M. Press.
[35] J. W. Bowker, "The Morality of Personal Relationships." In *Making Moral Decisions*
(Ed. D. M. MacKinnon), London, 1969, S.P.C.K.

criticism it was superb – because here was a man who really cared with every fibre of his being about 'The sage and serious doctrine of virginity' which it would never occur to the ordinary modern critic to take seriously. But it was more important still as a sermon. It was a beautiful sight to see a whole roomful of modern young men and women sitting in that absolute silence which can *not* be faked, very puzzled, but spell-bound .... What a wonderful power is in the direct appeal which disregards the temporary climate . . ."[36]

There are those who point out, correctly, that other societies have different patterns of relationships between the sexes, patterns which often approve of pre-marital intercourse, and sometimes permit multiple partners. What they do not go on to point out is that the quality of family life in these societies is inferior, both so far as the status of women is concerned, and in romantic love to our ideals. I write from experience of having worked among both polygamous and polyandrous peoples. Our traditional ideal of virginity before marriage and chastity within marriage can only be replaced by practices which are not only lower on an ethical standard, but yield less satisfaction to their practitioners.

[36] *The Letters of C. S. Lewis* (Ed. W. H. Lewis), London, 1968, Bles.

CHAPTER 29

THE BETTER WAY: PREVENTION OF
UNWANTED PREGNANCIES WITHIN
MARRIAGE

*There are many situations where precisely in obedience to the primary end of
marriage, husband and wife are morally obliged to prevent a new pregnancy.*
FR. GREGORY BAUM[1]

T HE MARRIED WOMAN WHO REQUESTS TERMINATION OF A PREGNANCY
which she took no steps to prevent is liable to find her request
falling on unsympathetic ears. There may be extenuating circumstances, such as those cases where the unco-operative husband forbids
his wife to take precautions. Only too often the doctor suspects that he is
being used as a contraceptive agent[2] and rightly refuses this role.

Married women can be divided into three classes: those who desire a
pregnancy; those who are quite willing to accept one if it comes along;
and those who would be most upset were they to conceive at this time,
or have been advised on medical grounds not to do so. The last group
should face facts and take active steps to prevent conception.

Is Contraception Against Nature?

Some are unhappy at using contraceptive techniques because these are
"unnatural." Of course they are – but all of us are constantly manipulating
and thwarting nature in everyday life.

It is not "natural" to drink purified water, to treat disease by medicines,
to take even an aspirin, to shave or to visit a dentist.

Is there any one of us who would agree, who even would think it
morally right, to go back to nature? Consider the safety of childbirth for
mother and child. Would any of us accept for our wife the maternal
mortality rate of earlier centuries, or for our children the present infant
mortality rates of under-developed countries? My wife and I have studied
infant mortality rates in Northern Nigeria and produced figures of death
rates ranging from 202 to 825 deaths in every thousand births.[3] These

---

[1] G. Baum, "Can the Church change her position?" In *Contraception and Holiness, op. cit.*
[2] See ch. 7 Case 7.1.
[3] R. F. R. Gardner and Elizabeth S. Gardner, "Infant Mortality in Northern Nigeria with
Especial Reference to the Birom Tribe." *Journal of Obstetrics and Gynaecology of the British
Empire,* 1958, **65,** 749.

figures improve markedly year by year,[4] in no small measure through the activities of mission hospitals. Are these efforts, using the unnatural means of anti-malarial drugs, chemotherapy, anaesthesia and surgery to be disapproved or despised?

In subduing nature in these, and a thousand other ways, we are being obedient to the biblical command.[5] In life some risks are inherent in our situation and here we must use our God-given brains to minimize them. If the missionary is to live and work fruitfully in the tropics then he must accept inoculation against smallpox and cholera and typhoid, and must regularly swallow his antimalarial drug.[6] And these unnatural activities he does not only with a clear conscience but with a thankful heart to the God who has given man the skill to discover how to manipulate nature. Among these modifications, in my view, are contraceptives.

Abstinence

It may be argued that pregnancy is not a necessary risk of marriage and that the obvious answer is to abstain from intercourse except at non-fertile times. There are three arguments against this course.

First we do not know when a woman is non-fertile. It is possible to acquire a large family by experimenting with "the safe period." One sees many patients in ante-natal clinics who shake their heads saying "I don't know how I got pregnant at that time in the month, Doctor."

Secondly the results of trying to follow this course lead to more sorrow, distress, and the break-up of family life than possibly any other factor. The effects of the resulting unhappy home on the children are too well known to spell out. As Archbishop Roberts, a Jesuit, has commented, "methods of abstention often threaten the very marriage itself and the good of children already existing."[7]

Almost the commonest syndrome one sees in gynaecological clinics is the woman presenting with one or more of a wide variety of symptoms, who turns out to be in dread of a further pregnancy at this moment in time. In order to prevent this she may take a late-night job to make sure her husband is asleep before she comes in; one of my patients not only worked in the day but went on to serve in a chip shop reaching home after midnight. Or she may go to bed very early and fake sleep when her husband comes upstairs. Or she develops prolonged menstrual losses which prevent intercourse. Or she has such pain during it that it has to be abandoned.

[4] J. R. Lang, "A Further Study of Fetal Loss and Child Mortality in the North of Nigeria." *Journal of Obstetrics and Gynaecology of the British Commonwealth*, 1970, **77**, 427. It is shown that whereas twelve years earlier we found that of every thousand children born 490 would be dead by the age of four, now only 266 will die.
[5] Gen. 1: 28.
[6] Those who either through ignorance, bravado, or for other reasons failed to take these precautions rarely survived: see e.g. the biography of Fenton Hall.
[7] Abp R. D. Roberts (Ed.) *Contraception and Holiness*, London, 1965, Collins.

The end result in each case is strain in the home. The husband may react, according to temperament, in different ways. The bad husbands are merely unfaithful. The better ones become irritable and quarrels develop. They take up other pursuits and develop a world closed to their wives. When in desperation they force their attentions on their wives they are thereafter filled with remorse. The wives at first inwardly feel how unfair they are being, but their fear of pregnancy drives them on to appear completely devoid of affection. This barrier is built up to such a degree that I know women who long after all risk of pregnancy is past, still hold their husbands at arm's length, and are unable to display their very real affection, so deep has the habit become ingrained.

In no other field have some ages and some sections of the Church wandered further from biblical teaching than on this point. There is biblical approval for those who are called for some particular purpose to a life of celibacy, but nowhere is it implied that abstinence in marriage is spiritually superior to regular intercourse.[8] The burden laid by some clerics upon men and women is harder than they can bear, and there is no reason why they should bear it. "Let everyone be fully convinced in his own mind."[9] Recent Roman Catholic authors have pointed this out from their own bitter experience. One greatly admires those who take upon themselves deprivation in this sphere,[10] but their resulting ignorance of the real tension makes their judgement on such matters of very limited value. Dr. Anne Biezanek, a devout Roman Catholic doctor, has pointed out that it is one thing for a priest to control his desires, but this is quite unlike the strain on a married man who spends every night in bed with his desirable lawful wife.[11]

Another Roman Catholic woman tells how "over and over in my reflection I have come back to the question, why do we call secondary the ends of the sexual act which have been accorded in fullness only to us, and why do we call primary the end that we share with the lower animals . . . . It is not actually more proper to control or suppress the function of conception after this function has been fulfilled in the bringing forth of children, than it is to control or suppress the function of the sexual act which is meant to be permanent."[12]

[8] I Cor. 7: 3–5; Heb. 13: 4.
[9] Rom. 14: 5.
[10] See e.g. *The Priest: A Prayer on Sunday Night*
Lord, I'm 35 years old,
A body made like others,
    ready for work,
A heart meant for love,
But I've given you all . . .
M. Quoist, *Prayers of Life*, Dublin, 1963, Gill.
[11] Anne Biezanek, *All Things New*, 1964, Peter Smith. 1965, Pan Books.
[12] Elizabeth A. Daugherty, "The Lessons of Zoology." In *Contraception and Holiness, op. cit*

The third reason is that any attempt to organize married life on the basis of thermometers, temperature charts and calendars largely frustrates one of the central purposes of marriage, which is the spontaneous expression of intimate love between husband and wife. As the "safe-period" fails again and again the despairing couple lengthen their times of abstinence until it becomes for all practical purposes continuous. They move into separate bedrooms, thus missing also those times of uninhibited conversation and gentle affection which mean so much to a marriage. In this way they destroy marriage as it was meant to be.

The intimate physical union of intercourse is meant to be an expression of, and a means of enriching the unique relationship of marriage: it is the cement which bonds husband and wife into "one flesh." The release of tensions and the deepening of love spill over to enrich the relationship between parents and their children. Now if this coming together is to fulfil these aims it must be free from the tensions which are inevitable if an unacceptable pregnancy is being risked. As one Roman Catholic woman scholar has noted, "We come to the ironic fact that in our present situation man is only able fully to say 'yes' to procreation if he is also able to say 'no' ".[13] Another remarks "The great advantage of the human marital union, freed from physiological domination, is that it permits a sharing of personalities, a psychic union, and a growth of love. This is to the great advantage first of all to the couple so united, and secondly to the new individual, born not necessarily of one specific act, but of that union."[12]

Only if pregnancy is desired or acceptable, or if a method of contraception in which they have confidence is in use, can this good gift of God be fully enjoyed. Not otherwise.

Contraception

It does not lie within the scope of this book to discuss contraceptive measures.[14] In deciding on the method to employ, one point is often overlooked. The risks in any method are found by adding up two factors: the risk to the mother of the method itself, and the normal statistical risks of childbirth in those cases where the method fails. For example, the pill has risks to the woman who takes it, but there is for all practical purposes no failure rate when properly used. It has, therefore, an overall safety rate better than that of the male condom, which carries no risk to the woman, but whose failure rate involves the risks involved in the resulting pregnancies.

New contraceptive techniques are constantly being introduced. General practitioners and family planning clinics are at present the best sources of information.

[13] Rosemary Ruether, "Birth Control and Sexuality." In *Contraception and Holiness, op. cit.*
[14] There are many excellent books. At the professional level e.g. J. Peel and M. Potts. *Textbook of Contraceptive Practice*, 1969, Cambridge University Press.

Sterilization[15]

Where the family is complete it is usually thought to be the sensible thing to sterilize either wife or husband, and thus obviate the nuisance and risks of contraception. With a woman in her upper 30s or older, happily married, with a healthy husband and three or more healthy children, I agree. However, even here there are snags: we must look at these.

The first possibility is that the woman will lose one, or even more of her children. Especially if she loses the only son she may wish to try to produce another boy.

Then it is possible that the woman's marriage may come to an end perhaps through divorce, perhaps by the husband's death.

Medical Case 29.1 A 28-year-old woman with three children was booked for sterilization two days after delivery. On the day after delivery, word was received that her husband was in hospital and thought to be dying. It appeared wisest to discharge her almost at once to be in time to see her husband. There was obviously no risk of her conceiving in the near future. If he recovered, the operation could be done in a few months time, if he did not there was no need of it until remarriage when it might not be desired.

In these days of accidents both on the road and in industry, it is unwise to assume that a young woman is not going to remarry. Under such circumstances she may well be anxious to give her second husband a child of his own. I have already had to attempt to unsterilize a woman of thirty-four under these circumstances.

A further and to my mind more important risk is that of the woman who, while not desirous of having another child, feels herself to be no longer a woman in the full sense, after sterilization. "My feelings on sterilization are impossible to express. No man can possibly know what it is like to be left a mere shell of a woman."[16]

Follow-up studies of women who have been sterilized give widely varying results. Three-quarters of women are satisfied with the effects of the operation; many are much happier, feel fitter, have improved sexual relationships with their husbands. On the other hand one-quarter of the women are regretful, feel less well, their relationships with their husbands are worse, and in some cases (8 to 10%) the regret is bitter and has a disastrous effect on their sex lives.[16,17] In one series, four marriages which had definitely been at risk before operation because the wives refused intercourse, became settled and happy; on the other hand, in three marriages the result of the operation was marital unfaithfulness and probable divorce.[17]

[15] See Church Assembly Board for Social Responsibility. *Sterilization An Ethical Enquiry.* London, 1962, Church Information Office.

[16] D. R. McCoy, "The Emotional Reaction of Women to Therapeutic Abortion and Sterilization." *Journal of Obstetrics and Gynaecology of the British Commonwealth,* 1968, **75,** 1054.

[17] D. B. Whitehouse, "Tubal Ligation. A Follow-Up Study." *Advances in Fertility Control,* 1969, **4,** 22.

It will be seen that the results are by no means as certain as the women evidently think who beg (sometimes as early as at the age of twenty-two) for sterilization. A useful criterion in my opinion is to consider two factors: If this woman were to become pregnant would she have a good case for abortion? Is this marriage coming under strain as a result of dread of a further pregnancy? If the answer to either of these is 'Yes', then sterilization must be seriously considered. The question which is often overlooked is whether it should be the wife or husband who should be sterilized.[14] In favour of the operation being performed on the wife is the fact that she is the one who has to bear the results of another pregnancy – not only for nine months before delivery but in most cases full-time for five years afterwards, and part-time for another decade and more. Against this is the fact that there may be some disease present which makes any additional strain by way of operation risky. Moreover, female sterilization involves an abdominal operation usually similar in degree to a non-urgent appendicectomy, and with a stay in hospital of up to ten days. There is a technique by which it may be done by electro-coagulation through a tube inserted through the abdominal wall[18] or the vaginal vault, but this requires special skills and equipment not commonly available, and carries its own risks, as well as having a higher failure rate.

The arguments in favour of male sterilization by division of the *vas deferens*, a tube running up from the scrotum into the groin, are that it is technically a minor procedure, can if desired be done without a general anaesthetic and as an out-patient, and the man need lose little if any time off work.[19] It is, moreover, said that the operation is reversible if required – e.g. on remarriage. While this has been successfully performed in India, where surgeons have a vast experience of the operation there seems little experience of reversal procedures so far in Britain. It has recently been suggested that spermatozoa could be obtained from the husband, prior to his being sterilized, and stored in a sperm bank, so that if due to unforeseen circumstances a further pregnancy were desired, these sperms could be used for artificial insemination of his wife.[20]

The fact needs to be weighed that in a couple aged around thirty-five, by sterilization the woman would surrender ten years of fertility, but the man twenty-five years or more. Operative complications of vasectomy are uncommon. The main ones are psychological; these, it is claimed, can be avoided by careful pre-operative vetting.[21]

[18] J. A. Jordan, R. L. Edwards, J. Pearson and P. J. K. Maskery, "Laparoscopic Sterilization and Follow-Up Hysterosalpingogram." *Journal of Obstetrics and Gynaecology of the British Commonwealth*, 1971, **78**, 460.
[19] Pauline Jackson, B. Phillips, Elizabeth Prosser, H. O. Jones, V. R. Tindall, D. L. Crosby, I. D. Cooke, J. M. McGarry and R. W. Rees, "A Male Sterilization Clinic." *BMJ*, 1970, **4**, 295.
[20] Brenda Herzberg, letter in the *Lancet*, 1970, **I**, 90.
[21] Helen Wolfers, "Psychological Aspects of Vasectomy." *BMJ*, 1970, **4**, 297.

CHAPTER 30

THE FUTURE: THE HIND-SIGHT PILLS

When a fetus is aborted no one asks for whom the bell tolls. No bell is tolled. But do not feel indifferent and secure. The fetus symbolizes you and me and our tenuous hold upon a future here at the mercy of our fellow men. RALPH POTTER[1]

A METHOD OF PREVENTING PREGNANCY, AFTER THE RISK HAS BEEN taken, has long been searched for. On theoretical grounds there are three schemes to consider.

The "Morning-After" Pill

Sperm and ova do not unite for some hours after intercourse, and another four to five days normally elapse before implantation into the womb. It might be possible chemically to alter the sperm so that it cannot reach the ovum, or not at least while in a state in which fertile union could occur. It should also be possible to affect the fertilized egg in some way, perhaps by speeding its passage down the tube, so that it is not ripe for implantation.

To achieve these aims there has been the search for a pill which could be taken the morning after risk, or perhaps in marriage regularly every few days.[2] In view of the progress with the prostaglandins this particular aim is not likely to be followed up at the moment.

The Monthly Pill

Very recent work on the prostaglandins suggests that it should be possible to develop a pill which, taken once a month, will produce a loss similar to an ordinary period. So far the method has been used only where the period is a few days overdue and it is suspected that the woman is pregnant, terminating what must presumably be regarded as an early pregnancy. Most of these cases had no more than a heavy period.[3]

---

[1] R. Potter, quoted by G. A. D. Scott, *op. cit.*

[2] For research prior to the prostaglandins see: D. M. Potts, "Termination of Pregnancy," *British Medical Bulletin*, **26**, no. 1, 65. L. E. Engstrom, "Experience with the M Pill." In *Abortion in a Changing World, op. cit.* B. N. Nathanson, "Drugs for the Production of Abortion: A Review." *Obstetric and Gynecological Survey*, 1970, **25**, 727.

[3] Much of the work on prostaglandins has been done in Uganda at Makerere University by Karim and Trussell. I am grateful to Prof. R. R. Trussell for much of the information in this section. Personal communication, Oct., 1970. See S. M. M. Karim and G. M. Filshie,

When the pill is perfected and available it is to be expected that its normal use would be just before the period was due, rather than just after it had been missed. It would only need to be used in months where the risk of pregnancy had occurred.

Embrey has warned that much time-consuming work remains to be done to establish the efficiency and safety of the prostaglandins before they can be passed by the Committee on Drug Safety in Britain, and of the even longer time for the corresponding process in America.[11] Despite this it seems that, medically speaking, the prospects are bright for the introduction within the next few years of such a pill. As with all other new methods the disadvantages and dangers will become obvious later. It seems that the prostaglandins do not carry the risk of fetal abnormality if pregnancy continues.[3] This is a most important matter. Several of the pills tried experimentally up till now have had the overwhelming disadvantage that where abortion has not occurred the baby when born has in a high percentage of cases shown multiple deformities.[2] If no marked unfortunate sequelae occur it seems not unlikely that a monthly pill "to bring the period on" may quickly replace other methods as the standard means of family limitation.

The Abortion Pill

Prostaglandins will induce abortion at any stage.[3] At the moment they cannot be used orally for therapeutic abortion as the side effects at the necessary dose level are too marked.[3] This will be overcome. It is likely that their use as a vaginal tampon will be practicable.[4]

Whether or not they are made officially available on prescription it can be assumed that they will somehow come into the hands of those who wish them. It has been suggested[5] that the black market in them could make that in heroin look like child's play.

Although the advantages of such a pill are obvious the cries of delight already uttered by some of the protagonists of liberal abortion are premature. Careful thought will show that the problems attendant on the self-administration of such a pill will be formidable, leaving aside all ethical considerations.

Which married woman has not, even if only for a few hours, regretted her pregnancy? A passing fit of depression, muscle ache, constipation, a

"Therapeutic Abortion using Prostaglandin F2α" Lancet, 1970, 1, 157. S. M. M. Karim, letter in the Lancet, 1970, 2, 610. J. J. Spindal and R. T. Ravenholt, letter in the Lancet, 1970, 1, 565. S. M. M. Karim, letter in the Lancet, 1970, 1, 1115. N. Wiqvist and M. Bygdeman, letter in the Lancet, 2, 717.

4 S. M. M. Karim and S. D. Sharma, "Therapeutic Abortion and Induction of Labour by the Intravaginal Administration of Prostaglandin E2 and F2α. Journal of Obstetrics and Gynaecology of the British Commonwealth, 1971, 78, 294. M. P. Embrey and K. Hillier, "Therapeutic Abortion by Intra-Uterine Installation of Prostaglandin." BMJ, 1971, 1, 588.

5 The phrase, I believe, is that of the Secretary of the Abortion Law Reform Association, Mrs Diane Munday.

tiff with her husband, a fleeting illness of one of her children, a bank statement "in the red", a tempting job advertized, a long-sought house now on the market. Normally in a few hours the mood passes. Her husband is attentive, the child is better by next day, the bank statement was an error, the job proves to have been already promised, the envied house has dry rot. And she is once more happy at the thought of the coming child. If, however, every woman has a packet of prostaglandins in her medicine cupboard, the pill – or the first of the course – may have been taken in those dark hours, later to be regretted. Are these weeks or months of pregnancy – and the earliest ones are the most tedious – to have been wasted? Get the doctor! Try anything! If abortion occurs – regret. If not there will be the further months of waiting to know whether the degree of damage to the fetal implantation has been such as to cause peri-natal death.

Or, whatever her emotions, her bleeding may go on and on. In the work so far done it has been found that in a number of cases, curettage of the womb in hospital is necessary where prostaglandin-induced abortion has been performed between the sixth and fourteenth weeks of pregnancy.[3]

Or the pill will be taken very late, say at the twenty-fourth week or after. Although this will be uncommon, it must be recalled that in the first twenty months of the Act no less than 366 terminations were done at this period of pregnancy.[6] And some of these fetusus are born alive. The mother will be faced with a breathing, limb-waving, whimpering child of perhaps two pounds or less.[7] Now what? Get a portable incubator! Get the doctor! Why doesn't he hurry?

This may sound dramatic but I have not the slightest doubt that these sequences will occur times without number if and when abortions can be self-induced at home.

Professor Richard Trussell, one of the very few as yet experienced in the use of prostaglandins, writes "Abortion . . . will continue to need the supervision of a suitably qualified doctor."[3]

The Changed Medical Scene

Self-administered abortion would lift the great burden of decision off the gynaecologist's shoulders. Only in the case where the medical pros and cons of continued pregnancy have to be weighed would he be involved. For him it would be back to the halcyon days before 1967. There would, of course, be the increased problem of incomplete abortions, and the despairing cries for help of those who change their minds. Presumably before long we will know if it is medically feasible to do anything to

---

[6] Registrar General, *Statistical Review of England and Wales: Supplement on Abortion*, 1968 and 1969 issues, London, H.M.S.O.

[7] See case reported in ch. 8 (p. 84).

help such. If not, they can be left at home with their consciences. But such will be for the doctor straightforward medical problems without moral overtones.

There is still the chance, then, that obstetrics and gynaecology will be able in the future to recruit men and women of first-rate calibre, which it may not do if the present situation continues.[8] This can only be for the good of motherhood.

The paediatricians will have their problems, and no doubt will have to start up flying-squads equipped to deal with tiny premature babies; again these will be medical problems only.

If the pill is, however, to be available only on prescription it will be the family doctor who will have the moral problems to face. The general practitioner who is known not to prescribe these pills on demand is going to risk losing a great number of patients, as not only the patient but the whole of the family usually change doctors together.

On the other hand, if the pills are available over the counter without prescription, it is the minister who will have the weeping women to care for, especially where the babe has survived briefly. I do not envy the minister who has to explain to the parent why he cannot at the graveside say "Forasmuch as it hath pleased Almighty God to take to Himself the soul of this little one . . ."[9]

These problems are coming. We would do well to give them thought now.

Moral Problems in Retrospective Contraception

The problems are different for each of the three types of pill suggested. Let us consider the married woman.

If in fact a morning-after pill acts by preventing a sperm making a fertile union with an ovum, then morally it is no different from the present hormonal pills.

If it acts by preventing the fertilized ovum from implanting, those who believe that a human being starts when the nuclei fuse will find this method unacceptable, while those who consider the inception of life to be at the moment of implantation will find nothing objectionable in it. While the exact mode of action of the intra-uterine contraceptive device (IUCD) is not understood, it appears to work after fertilization and before implantation,[10] and thus has identical moral overtones. I have not noticed any theological outcry against the IUCD by those accepting the principle of contraception.

The monthly pill, presumably taken in the fourth week of the cycle,

[8] R.C.O.G. Report (see p. 76 fn. 7).

[9] Book of Common Order of The Church of Scotland: "Burial of a Child." Oxford, University Press, 1952.

[10] J. A. Loraine and E. T. Bell, *Fertility and Contraception in the Human Female*, Edinburgh, 1968, Livingstone.

brings us into more difficulty. Those few women who are aware they have conceived even before a period is missed will be aware of their state and face a moral issue. The great majority of women, however, do not suspect pregnancy until a period has failed to arrive. Such will be able to take such a pill with equanimity, persuading themselves that they have merely brought on a period which would have occurred in any case. One knows of many women who have used contraceptives for years, and only later, when a wished-for pregnancy fails to materialize, discover that they have never been able to conceive and all their earlier precautions have been wasted. I imagine that most women will rationalize in this way.

When the pill is taken, a period having been missed and the symptoms of pregnancy being present, the women will know, and the prescriber of the pill will know, that an abortion is being procured. When challenged on the morality of this procedure the ready answer will be, "But we have been doing this for months – for surely some months there must have been an unrecognized implanted ovum dislodged – and up to now nobody has censured us. What is the moral difference?"

Going back over our argument it will be found that, granted prostaglandins are to be used, there is no clear-cut place where a line can readily be drawn. As in the whole abortion issue the problems and situations merge imperceptibly until one is in danger of finding oneself with all ethical barriers down.

Of course single women will get hold of these tablets and use them. It is a jibe of non-believers that Christians like to ensure that girls have their waywardness exposed. Little do such critics realize that we Christians are far too well aware of our own sins, just as great in God's sight, to point the finger at anyone else.

A heroin preparation has twice saved the life of one of my own family: the fact therefore that a chemical can be used wrongly says nothing about its value. To ban prostaglandins is no answer: they will prove a very real boon in the induction of overdue labour,[11] in the getting rid of a "missed abortion," and in other straightforward gynaecological problems.

In view of these prospects it is a matter of supreme urgency for Christians to reconsider their attitude to contraception and abortion. Especially must we beware of taking up positions from which the very genuine needs of women, as well as logic, may make us later retreat.

[11] S. M. M. Karim, R. R. Trussell, K. Hillier and R. C. Patel, "Induction of Labour with Prostaglandin F2a." *Journal of Obstetrics and Gynecology of the British Commonwealth*, 1969, **76**, 769.

EPILOGUE: CHAPTER 31

THE CHRISTIAN AS PATIENT AND CONFIDANT

There are two kings and two kingdoms in Scotland. There is Christ Jesus the King, and His Kingdom the Kirk, whose subject King James the Sixth is, and of whose kingdom, not a king, nor a lord, nor a head, but a member.

ANDREW MELVILLE TO KING JAMES VI.[1]

Why a Separate Code for Christians?

AFTER TALKING TO A GROUP OF UNDERGRADUATES ON CHRISTIANITY and Abortion, one of them said to me, "You talk as though it were possible to be a fully paid-up, card-carrying Christian." It is. All fees paid, by Christ, that first Good Friday; and if not physically card-carrying, at least with the assurance of membership of The Family.[2] It has been said of Oliver Cromwell that where he parted company from the radicals theologically was in his distinction between "the people" and "the people of God."[3] No one reading the history of the early Church in the pages of the Acts of the Apostles can have any doubt that the Christians knew themselves to be different from other men: they were no longer their own, they had a new allegiance. A failure to make this unpopular distinction clear lies at the root of the Church's equivocal statements on moral issues. Letha Scanzoni, in an excellent presentation of the Christian philosophy of sex,[4] starts her book with a diary-entry of Jim Elliot who was to be martyred seven years later by the Auca Indians. A mid-twentieth-century American, at twenty-one he wrote: "One treasure, a single eye, and a sole Master." A sole Master. That is the Christian standard, and within this allegiance one can consider the problems of abortion by appeal to the King.

Contrast with this the picture of our age, painted by the Whiteleyes. "This indefiniteness of contemporary standards is reflected in the quality of the discontent expressed in some of the literature of our day... Kafka, Sartre, Camus, Colin Wilson. Its characteristic complaint is that

---

[1] A. Melville, "Autobiography and Diary:" Quoted by J. H. Burleigh, *A Church History of Scotland*, 1960, Oxford University Press.

[2] Col. 2, 13,14. John 5, 24.

[3] C. Hill, *God's Englishman: Oliver Cromwell and the English Revolution*, London, 1970, Weidenfeld and Nicolson.

[4] Letha Scanzoni, *Sex and the Single Eye*, Grand Rapids, 1968, Zondervan.

the world is 'absurd,' lacking 'meaning,' point or purpose .... The difficulty of the people who lodge this complaint is 'commitment,' to use the existentialist term. They want a faith to live by, a cause to serve, a star to hitch their wagons to: without it they suffer from a sense of not being at home in the world, of being all dressed up with nowhere to go."[5]

The results of this, in the field of our present interest, can be seen in a review by Dr. H. Balint in the *British Medical Journal*, of the book *Sex and Society in Sweden*. "It is fair to say," he comments, "that of all the countries in the world Sweden probably has the most 'enlightened' and most 'liberal' social institutions regulating sexual behaviour. Teenage girls may get contraceptive advice openly in various Government-supported clinics without any questions asked .... Treatment for venereal diseases is free and confidential. Moreover at school from the age of 14 on systematic instruction is given about them and about how to avoid the dangers of infection. It is surprising then to learn that the incidence of syphilis and gonorrhoea is steadily increasing in Sweden and especially in the 15 to 19 age groups. There are parallel increases in illegitimate births and requests for abortion. Some sort of devil must be at work there, wrecking the good and persistent efforts of several generations of honest people who tried their best to clear society from hypocrisy and narrowminded prejudice, and to create in their place a world of self-respecting freedom and equality . . ."[6]

In drawing a sharp distinction between the Christian family and non-Christian society, I am not for a moment suggesting that high moral standards are the prerogative of Christians only. We applaud the efforts made by those of any faith and none to call all men to a life controlled by ethical ideals. However, because the reasons for such a call to the committed Christian are different from those to the rest of mankind, it is evident that the frequently made attempts to produce a common religious, even Christian,[7] approach applicable to everyone are foredoomed to failure. This chapter then is addressed to Christians, using the word in its New Testament meaning.[8]

Avoiding the Need for Abortion

In marriage the principles laid down in chapter 29 apply. There are occasions when a Christian couple just do not know whether they should have a further pregnancy. Here I feel it is reasonable to live a normal

[5] C. H. Whiteley and Winifred Whiteley. *The Permissive Morality*, London, 1964, Methuen.
[6] H. Balint, Review in the *BMJ*, 1969, **2**, 564. The Christian would agree with this assessment perhaps even more fully than the reviewer intended.
[7] e.g. *Sex and Morality*, *op. cit.* and I. M. Fraser, *Sex as Gift*, London, 1967, S.C.M. Press.
[8] For the use of the name "Christian" see C. S. Lewis. Introduction to *Mere Christianity*, London, 1952, Bles.

regular sexual life, and pray that God will overrule so far as pregnancy is concerned. Where, however, a further pregnancy is not desired, my personal view is that adequate contraceptive precautions should be taken. The unhappy strained home due to fear of pregnancy is not unknown among Christians. I do not see how one can expect God to take care of some facet of life (in this case conception) when one is not prepared to use the means available: we do not normally expect His care to excuse us from having good brakes on our car, or to absolve us from taking care of our health.

For the single girl and boy all the arguments for chastity in chapter 28 are valid. But there are other arguments – and more vital ones. These have been discussed by a number of writers.[9] We should note two. First, the succinct comments of Valerie Pitt: "Chastity is a small virtue, but it is part of the obligation a Christian owes his Lord. Deliberate breach of it has the defining property of sin: it breaks covenant . . . . The Christian has, in his love, surrendered all rights in himself. His life is hid with Christ in God. He is no longer his own man, and together with his other powers his sexuality is not his own to use as he pleases . . . . The covenant of our redemption is life for life – sexual activity is not exempt from the conditions of the contract."[10]

Second a statement made, on television, by the popular Scots theologian Professor William Barclay: "There is no way of making Jesus a supporter of a permissive society. If we support sexual intercourse before marriage or outside marriage, then I do not see how we can continue to call ourselves Christian, for a man cannot be a Christian and flatly contradict the teaching of Jesus Christ. It is one thing honestly to say that we will abandon the demands of Christian morality; it is quite another to abandon them and to deceive ourselves into thinking that we are still keeping them."[11]

Facing an Unwelcome Pregnancy

Legal abortion amongst committed Christians appears to be very uncommon.[12] Naturally the Christian applicant for an abortion will be reviewed in hospital on exactly the same criteria as everyone else. Here we have to discuss an earlier stage, the decision on what to do when an unwelcome pregnancy occurs.

[9] e.g. C. G. Scorer, *The Bible and Sex Ethics Today*, London, 1967, Tyndale Press. O. R. Barclay (Ec.) *A Time to Embrace*, Inter-Varsity Press.

[10] Valerie Pitt, *op. cit.*

[11] W. Barclay, *Ethics in a Permissive Society*, "The Baird Lectures." London, 1971, Collins.

[12] I made an attempt through the British monthly *Crusade* and the American fortnightly *Christianity Today* to contact any Christian woman who had had an abortion, or any pastor who has counselled such a woman. Some replies were received, but no cases unearthed. The Rev. Dr. Martyn Lloyd-Jones, probably the doyen of evangelical confidants writes "It is literally the truth to say that I have never in over 40 years of pastoral experience heard anyone make a confession with regard to this subject." Another well-known medically-qualified minister, the Rev. Dr. Hugh Trowell, knows of one case. (Personal communications, 1969.)

In the anonymous replies to Dr. Jacqueline Keighley's questionnaire on sexual views and behaviour, sent to various youth groups with a religious affiliation, extra-marital intercourse was reported not infrequently; but only rarely by committed Christians. Among this last group the incident had occurred either prior to conversion, or during a time of backsliding.[13] In such cases pregnancy will occasionally occur. It is interesting to note that among those reporting intercourse during a time of spiritual drifting, in each case coitus occurred only once. No doubt conscience spoke. How much more troubled must it be when a pregnancy has resulted. In such an hour it must be easy to feel that this has been the ultimate betrayal: that all hope must be gone of reconciliation with a Christ one has so blatantly dishonoured. But God's promise of forgiveness makes no distinction between sin and sin. "If we confess our sins, He is faithful and just to forgive us our sins, and to cleanse us from all unrighteousness."[14] "It is not sinning that ruins men, but sinning and not repenting."[15] J. S. Stewart has reminded us that forgiveness is the restoration of a relationship. He also makes a point important in the climate of today: "Who can say how many demons are being exorcized, how many potentialities of mental trouble, neurasthenia and even organic disease are being rooted out by the assurance of pardon and renewal? 'I always send my patients,' said a distinguished psychiatrist, 'to hear Dr. So-and-so preach: he preaches the forgiveness of sins.' "[16]

The relationship with one's Lord re-established, the question as to the best course must be faced in obedience to His will. An article appeared in the evangelical press by a girl who had an abortion. "I regret what happened more and more," she wrote, "and I wish now that I had gone through with having our child. I'm sure that real life had begun in me and I deeply regret my actions."[17] Shortly after, a letter[18] was printed from another girl who had decided to go through with her pre-marital pregnancy: "From the moment when I really gave my life, problems and all, over to God things changed amazingly. We did suffer in many ways from friends. However, God provided us with very many more and very loving Christian friends. We were desperately poor but never went without necessities. We missed out very much on the activities of our

[13] Jacqueline V. Keighley, "Contraceptives and the Unmarried—The Present Position." *In the Service of Medicine*, June, 1970.

[14] 1 Jn. **1,** 9. M. Lloyd-Jones, commenting on that text, writes "That is a categorical statement made by God the Holy Spirit through His servant. There is no limit to it. I cannot see any qualification to it. Whatever your sin—it is as wide as that—it does not matter what it is, it does not matter what it was. If you do not believe (that text), and if you go on dwelling on your sin, I say that you are not taking God at His word, you do not believe what He tells you, and that is your real sin." *Spiritual Depression*, Glasgow, 1965, Pickering and Inglis.

[15] Unnamed writer quoted by H. R. Mackintosh, *The Christian Experience of Forgiveness*, London, 1927, Nisbet. 1961 Fontana Books.

[16] J. S. Stewart, *A Faith to Proclaim*, London, 1953, Hodder and Stoughton.

[17] *Crusade*, Jan., 1970.　　　　[18] *Crusade*, March, 1970.

contemporaries but it didn't seem to hurt... our eldest daughter is undoubtedly our greatest blessing, a fine, healthy, intelligent girl and a Christian."

Although in the cases I have quoted abortion was judged to have been wrong, I am sure there are other cases in which it will be judged to be right. The point is that first the relationship with the Lord must be re-established, and then the matter must be prayed through, perhaps alone, but better with an understanding confidant. This is not a subjective method. Throughout the history of the Church it has been found to be the way to know the will of God.

If the problem is rare among the unmarried, it is commonplace among Christian wives. So much so that Marjorie Holmes, in her book subtitled "A woman's conversation with God," has a special prayer "For an unexpected child."

"Dear God, it's true, we're going
to have another child. And I am
aghast, I am stunned. I didn't
expect this, I didn't want it, and
there's no use pretending – to you
or to myself – I don't want it now.
With so many childless women longing
for babies, why have you chosen me?
You, who are the Author and Giver of
Life, as the prayer book says – why
not one of them? Why me, why me?
I don't need or want this gift. I
am not grateful for it. I don't
understand you ways.
'Some day it will be a great comfort
to you,' the doctor says. And some
deep abiding instinct assured me he
is right. But that is small comfort *now*.
Then there is that other cliché,
'The Lord will provide,' And
you will, financially you will,
you always have.
Yet I don't want to have to wait
for that proof either. Provide
for me *now*. Provide for this
child. Provide me with love and
joy and a feeling of welcome for
this little new unexpected life."[19]

[19] Marjorie Holmes, *I've Got to Talk to Somebody, God*, London, 1969, Hodder and Stoughton. Copyright © 1968, 1969 by Marjorie Holmes Mighel. Reprinted by permission.

There will be cases, although not perhaps commonly, where the right thing is to seek an abortion. The point which cannot be underlined too heavily or too often is that the decision must be made after careful thought and prayer alone and together as a Christian couple. The story is recorded by a woman who had an abortion and then went through anguish: "My husband was aghast at the result and tried to pray with me. But I could not look God in the face. After two years I felt a driving need to pray with someone (my husband can't any more) – yet no one I met could or would. God, in his mercy, sent a Christian woman across my path, and after her wondering if I was a Christian, I poured out the secret abortion story, and its torment. Calmly she said, 'You'd better tell the Lord.' It took me about four days to gather up the courage, and I knew his presence as never before. He's real. He forgives in such a way no-one can know or understand who has not experienced it. I'm glad I've no 'number five' in the sense that I know I could not have coped at the time. But sometimes, laying a meal or dishing up, I get a quick panic that one of them is not here – but a prayer of thanks, and knowing all is well, now, calms me."[20]

Now it appears probable, from the end of her account, that an abortion was the right course here. What was wrong, and led to the years of anguish, is that the operation was requested without prior peace of heart about it. If the Christian couple can arrive at the hospital, and thank God for this provision in their need, then the outcome will be well. That is provided they have earlier learned the basic lesson of never looking back and doubting past guidance.

The Christian Father

It takes two to start a baby. The Christian young man is called, no less than his girl, to pre-marital chastity. The Christian husband as much as his wife is responsible for any child conceived. The temptations,[21] the problems and doubts are ones which should be discussed and prayed about jointly.

From her experience as a family planning doctor Elizabeth Gardner[22] considers that a great deal of the problem associated with contraception, and its failure, is due to lack of communication between husband and wife. The man all too often leaves that side of sexual activity to his wife, giving thought only to his own pleasure. Now here is a place where Christian marriage scores (as it does on many other counts). Within it

---

[20] *Crusade*, May, 1970.
[21] They would do well to heed Dietrich Bonhoeffer's remarks on desire. "The Bible teaches us in times of temptation in the flesh to flee. Flee fornication (1 Cor. 6:18) and youthful lusts (2 Tim. 2:22)." He goes on "Flee to that place where you find protection and help, flee to the Crucified." (*Temptation*, London, 1955, S.C.M. Press).
[22] Elizabeth S. Gardner. Personal communication.

every facet of the home and family, including sex, is a matter for mutual discussion and prayer, with a sense of mutual responsibility. Decisions on abortion must be joint decisions: and "joint" means all three who together make up the Christian couple!

The Christian Confidant

It will be obvious that there is a vital role for the mature, understanding, Christian adviser. Margaret Wardle, having discussed with Christian girls their sexual temptations and yearnings, was saddened to find how many could not talk these problems over with their parents. When these are prepared to be involved, what a tower of strength they can be! "I talked to a young married woman who told me that her parents had warned her about the force of sex for as long as she could remember. When she started 'going steady' with her husband they all four had a heart to heart talk about the temptations. 'My parents told us that in their courting days they had made a deliberate agreement together that they would not allow themselves to get into any compromising situation. They prayed about the matter regularly and always found that when one of them was weak the other remained strong.' "[23]

Only too often, however, more experienced Christians turn disapprovingly away, or imply that the very existence of the problem implies that the enquirer is not a committed Christian. Such attitudes are not only useless but harmful, in that the enquirer is less likely to pluck up courage to ask for help elsewhere.

The experienced Christian counsellor can be of help, not only in advising young people how to avoid calamity, but in lovingly and tenderly counselling those who are in distress. If the question of abortion is raised it must not be brushed aside but the pros and cons thoughtfully and prayerfully discussed, and the help of an informed minister or believing doctor obtained. The scope for Christian laymen and laywomen to help in this field is not limited to advising fellow-believers in distress. Daniel Callahan has commented "Conservative Christian opponents of abortion ... speak vividly of the alternatives conceivably open to a woman but do all too little to press for those reforms which will make the alternatives actually available."[24] We can become involved with people, but in doing so must heed the warning of Mary Ellison: "Another far-reaching result of harsh treatment at such a time goes deeply into the roots of an unstable personality: it is the fixed conviction that religion and unkindness are synonymous. 'I've no use for good people!' How many times has this been said to probation officers who feel the bitter implications in a sincere statement based on personal suffering. What an insult to One

[23] Margaret Wardle, *Crusade*, May, 1970.
[24] D. Callahan, *Abortion: Law, Choice and Morality*, New York and London, 1970, Collier-Macmillan.

who never spoke a harsh word to a delinquent, but was the 'friend of sinners'!"[25]

In the matter of providing a home for a girl during the later months of her illegitimate pregnancy, or by fostering, or even adopting, an unwanted child, there is an opening for concerned Christian help. If, however, such help is given in a judgemental spirit it will do little good.[26] But the Christian family whose members know themselves to be forgiven, and who out of love will proffer help, can make a real contribution to the problem.

A Practical Example: "Birthright"

A group of Canadian Christians, Roman Catholic and Protestant, have set up the organization Birthright.[27] Analagous to the Samaritans telephone-answering service for those contemplating suicide,[28] Birthright invites women in despair at pregnancy to telephone in the first place for advice. It defines itself as "An emergency pregnancy service, a private, non-sectarian organization, operating a Crisis Centre, where any girl or woman, distressed by an unwanted pregnancy, can find help as near as the nearest telephone." Its creed is "It is the right of every pregnant woman to give birth, and the right of every child to be born." Help consists of arranging medical or psychiatric care; accommodation, emergency or long term employment, or advice in obtaining it; referral to community service such as children's aid societies, family services and maternity homes. Help and advice are given concerning medical and hospital insurance, welfare, immigration, financial problems, spiritual counselling.

The office is staffed by voluntary workers; at most hours a woman is standing by to listen sympathetically and compassionately to the caller. At other times a tape-recorded message is played, ending, "Have courage; Have this baby: Remember, this human being you carry within you may some day thank you for the gift of life. Even if you are unmarried, do not forget that you are a person of worth and dignity, and more especially so when bringing new life into the world. Why not let 'Birthright' share the burden of this pregnancy with you. The essence of *our* service is Love. We can help you find a place to stay, inside or outside Toronto, or do you

---

[25] Mary Ellison, *The Adopted Child*, London, 1958, Gollancz.

[26] See Bishop Ian Ramsey's remarks "We have not to choose between denunciation on the one hand which oppresses and imperils the spirit of man, and toleration on the other, if that is supposed to be, as it often is, a just-couldn't-care-less attitude. For Christians at least there is a third possibility: redemption and loving concern—the conviction that by the love of God shown forth in Christ, and reflected at least in true Christians, there is no evil which cannot in measure be already redeemed and have its part in a creative development." *Contact*, March, 1970.

[27] Birthright, 21 Donegal Drive, Toronto 17.

[28] The Samaritans, according to Chad Varah (personal communication June, 1971) have 1–2% of their clients in distress with problems of unwanted pregnancy: not all of them wish abortion. "As Samaritans we naturally have no views on the rightness or wrongness of a girl having an abortion." Their approach is therefore different from that of Birthright.

need employment, or medical care – or just someone with whom you can talk over your problems and yet remain anonymous? If you need us please call us again when our office is open."

"Birthright" opened in Toronto in October 1968 and in the first two and a half years gave help of one kind or another to 5000 girls and women. By June 1971 there were fifty centres at work in the United States. The New York centre opened in April 1971 and within three weeks had helped 168 girls to decide to have their babies, despite the availability of abortion.[29]

It is worthy of our attention here as exemplifying something practical that Christian concerned people can actually do. In addressing its workers Graham Scott made these points: "Birthright is of course more a first-aid centre than a hospital. You women, as women, cannot offer the medical and social care that the distressed mother may very often need. But you can offer that one essential ingredient: compassionate love. And your compassion and love will not only be valuable for the distressed woman herself, but will also be valuable in going the second mile and getting her the specialized help she may need. In this sense, you will be brokers between distressed mothers needing professional help and the help that may seem to them so far off and unapproachable."[30]

The founder and director, Louise Summerhill,[31] writes: "All of us who work in Birthright office are acutely aware of the Spirit of God in our midst. And we know from these miracles of grace and rebirth that we encounter daily in the lives of those who come to us that the Creator and Sanctifier of human life is guiding and inspiring us. Again and again He shows us that there are practical solutions to unwanted pregnancies; and that these are found in a positive and loving reaction to mothers in distress."[32] "In Birthright we help rather than abort, we believe in making a better world for babies to come into, rather than killing them. If we value our own existence we must not deny it to another."[33]

The present writer, while convinced that there is a real place for abortion in some cases, nevertheless is sure that the approach of Birthright is essentially the right one, and would be applicable to the majority of women seeking abortion today.

Already in Britain the evangelical Shaftesbury Project[34] is, among other things, looking into problems of the family, and abortion. Is it too much to hope that Christians will feel impelled to take practical steps, to help terrified and bewildered pregnant women?

[29] Louise Summerhill, Personal communication, June, 1971.
[30] G. A. D. Scott, *A Christian View of Birthright*: duplicated notes of a talk given at a Teach-In, June 14, 1968.
[31] R. Keene, "The Woman Who Tells Girls in Trouble: 'Have Your Baby'." *Maclean's Magazine*, May, 1970.
[32] Louise Summerhill, "Helping Girls in Trouble." *Our Family*, May, 1970.
[33] Louise Summerhill, Personal communication, July, 1970.
[34] See p. 94 fn. 30.

READING LIST

In the following lists I have included only papers and volumes which I consider to be important, the most significant being printed in heavy type. At the end will be found fuller details of a few outstanding works which have appeared since this manuscript went to press. For papers up to 1968 the basic tool is:

An Annotated Bibliography of Induced Abortion. Edited by G. K. af Geijerstam. University of Michigan, 1969.

This lists and gives a brief résumé, of 1175 papers in the world literature. Due to the very rapid changes in abortion laws and practice it must be supplemented by more recent works.

GENERAL SURVEYS OF ABORTION

Abortion: Law, Choice and Morality. D. Callahan. New York and London, 1970, Macmillan.

This is the only single-author work, known to me, which endeavours to cover the whole field. The author is a professional writer who therefore looks at the issues from outside. Regrettably it came to hand too late for me to quote it adequately in the present work. There are excellent bibliographies.

Abortion in a Changing World: The Proceedings of an International Conference on Abortion convened by the Association for the Study of Abortion, at Hot Springs, Virginia, November 1968. Ed. R. E. Hall, 1970, Columbia University Press.

Vol. 1 Papers from various countries reporting the situation in 1968.

Vol. 2 Reports from discussion groups on the relevance of Abortion to Animation, Constitutionality, Morality, Obstetrics, Poverty, Progeny, Psychiatry, Public Health, and Womankind.

(There was no clinician in the groups discussing animation, nor in that on morality).

Spontaneous and Induced Abortion. Report of a W.H.O. Scientific Group. Geneva, 1970, World Health Organisation Technical Report 461.

WORKS WRITTEN UNDER STRICT ABORTION LAWS

The Sanctity of Life and the Criminal Law. Glanville Williams. London, 1958, Faber.

Abortion and the Law. B. M. Dickens. London, 1966, MacGibbon and Kee.

"A Fifth Freedom?" Sir Dugald Baird. *BMJ,* 1965, **2,** 1141.

Abortion in Britain. Proceedings of a Conference held by the Family Planning Association, London, April, 1966. London, 1966, Pitman.

The Nameless: Abortion in Britain Today. P. Ferris. Revised ed. London, 1967, Penguin.

"Attitudes of Women Abortionists." Moya Woodside. *Howard Journal of Penal Reform,* 1963, **11,** 93.

Abortion in the United States: A Conference sponsored by the Planned Parenthood Federation of America at Arden House and the New York Academy of Medicine. Ed. Mary Calderone. New York, 1958, Hoeber-Harper.

The Abortionist: Dr. X. London, 1962, Gollancz.

Abortion and the Law: A Symposium. Ed. D. Smith. Cleveland, 1967, Press of Western Reserve University.

ABORTION PRACTICE UNDER LIBERAL LAWS

BRITAIN

The Abortion Act 1967: Proceedings of a Symposium held by the Medical Protection Society in collaboration with the Royal College of General Practitioners, London, February, 1969. London, 1969, Pitman.

"The Abortion Act 1967: Findings of an Enquiry into the First Year's Working of the Act." Royal College of Obstetricians and Gynaecologists. *BMJ*, 1970, 2, 529.

Supplement on Abortion to the Registrar General's Statistical Review of England and Wales: 1968 (1970) 1969 (1971). London, H.M.S.O.

Annual Reports of the Chief Medical Officer of the Department of Health and Social Security: 1968 (1969) 1969 (1970) 1970 (1971). London, H.M.S.O.

EASTERN EUROPE

"Legal Abortion in Eastern Europe." M. Potts. *Eugenics Review,* 1967, **59**, 232.

Abortion in Eastern Europe. K.-H. Mehlan. (In Abortion in a Changing World. *op. cit.*).

"Demographic Consequences of the Legalization of Induced Abortion in Eastern Europe." A. Klinger. *International Journal of Gynaecology and Obstetrics,* 1970, **8**, 680.

SCANDINAVIA

"Legal Abortion in Sweden." J.-O. Ottosson. *Journal of the Biosocial Sciences,* 1971, **3**, 173.

MEDICAL ETHICAL WRITINGS BEARING ON ABORTION

"Medical Ethics." Sir Roger Ormrod. *BMJ,* 1968, **2**, 7.

"Symposium on The Cost of Life:" held by the Royal Society of Medicine. *Proceedings of the RSM,* 1967, **60**, 121.

"Colloquium on Ethical Dilemmas from Medical Advances: at the American College of Physicians." *Annals of Internal Medicine,* 1967, **67**, Sup. 7.

MENTAL AND EMOTIONAL ASPECTS

"Induced Abortion on Psychiatric Grounds: A Follow-up Study of 479 Women." M. Ekblad. *Acta Psychiatrica et Neurologica Scandinavica,* 1955, Sup. 99.

"Outcome of Pregnancies Where Abortion was Granted but not carried out." P. Arén and C. Åmark. *Acta Psychiatrica et Neurologica Scandinavica,* 1961, **36**, 203.

"Refused Abortion: A Follow-up Study of 249 Women whose Applications were Refused." Kirstin Höök. *Acta Psychiatrica et Neurologica Scandinavica,* 1963, Sup. 168.

"Mental Disorders After Abortion." B. Jansson. *Acta Psychiatrica et Neurologica Scandinavica,* 1965, **41**, 87.

Psychiatric Disorders in Obstetrics. A. A. Baker. Oxford, 1967, Blackwell. In shorter form this will be found in *Medical Disorders in Obstetric Practice,* ed. C. G. Barnes. 3rd ed., 1971, Blackwell.

"Psychiatric Indications or Psychiatric Justification of Therapeutic Abortion?" E. Pfeiffer. *Archives of General Psychiatry,* 1970, **23**, 402.

SOCIOLOGICAL WORKS

The Sexual Behaviour of Young People. M. Schofield. London, 1968, Penguin.

Without a Wedding Ring: Casework with Unmarried Parents. Jean Pochin, London, 1969, Constable.

Child Care and the Growth of Love. J. Bowlby, 2nd ed. London, 1965, Penguin.

Children Under Stress. Sula Wolff. London, 1969, Allen Lane.

The Adopted Child. Mary Ellison. London, 1958, Gollancz.

"120 Children Born after Application for Therapeutic Abortion Refused." H. Forrseman and Inga Thuwe. *Acta Psychiatrica et Neurologica Scandinavica*, 1966, **42**, 71.

RELIGIOUS STUDIES ON, OR RELEVANT TO, ABORTION

Birth Control and the Christian: A Protestant Symposium on the Control of Human Reproduction: Held at Portsmouth, New Hampshire, August, 1968. Ed. W. O. Spitzer and C. L. Saylor. 1969, Wheaton, Tyndale House.

Twenty-six theologians, geneticists, sociologists, lawyers and medical men discussed the fundamental issues of contraception, sterilization and abortion. This is the basic background volume for Christian studies. I am grateful to the British publishers, Coverdale House, London, for permission to quote at length from this work.

Abortion: An Ethical Discussion. Church Assembly Board for Social Responsibility. London, 1965, Church Information Office.

This document, produced by a committee of theologians and doctors in the Anglican Church, was very influential during the parliamentary debates of 1966–7. There are companion booklets on "Sterilization", and on Illegitimate Children "Fatherless by Law".

The Morality of Abortion: Legal and Historical Perspectives. Ed. J. T. Noonan. A series of papers by Catholic and Protestant theologians. 1970, Harvard University Press and Oxford. (Much of this material will be found in the *Dublin Review* issue dated Winter, 1967–68.)

Abortion on Trial. R. Shaw. London, 1969, Robert Hale.

A popular account of the abortion struggle from the orthodox Roman Catholic standpoint.

"Ethical Problems in Abortion." E. McDonagh. *Theology*, 1968. **71**, pp. 393, 443, 501.

Church Dogmatics. Part III, Vol. 4. K. Barth. Edinburgh, 1961, T. & T. Clark.

The Ethics of Sex. H. Thielicke. London, 1964, Jas. Clarke.

"Deeds and Rules in Christian Ethics." P. Ramsey. *Scottish Journal of Theology*, Occasional Paper, No. 11, 1965.

The Sanctity of Life. D. M. Jackson. London, 1962, Christian Medical Fellowship. (His booklet "Human Life and Human Worth," C.M.F., 1968, should also be consulted.)

Ethical Responsibility in Medicine: A Christian Approach. A symposium edited by V. Edmunds and C. G. Scorer. Edinburgh, 1967, Livingstone.

Contraception and Holiness: The Catholic Predicament. A Symposium introduced by Abp T. D. Roberts S.J. London, 1965, Collins.

The Agonising Choice: Birth Control, Religion and the Law. N. St. John Stevas. London, 1971, Eyre and Spotiswoode.

A Study of the problems for Roman Catholics, associated with the publication of the encyclical *Humanae Vitae*. In this connection *"Infallible?"* by the German Roman Catholic theologian H. Kung, London, 1971, Collins, should also be consulted.

STUDIES BY CHRISTIANS INVOLVED IN ABORTION

"Abortion: Can an Evangelical Consensus be Found?" A Symposium in *Eternity Magazine*, February, 1971, issue.

"Christian Choices in a Liberal Abortion Climate." R. F. R. Gardner. *Christianity Today*, May 22nd, 1970, issue.

"A Definition of Life and Problems of Abortion." Elsie M. Sibthorpe. "The Doctor in a Permissive Society." W. Y. Sinclair. *In the Service of Medicine*, April, 1969.

"Termination of Pregnancy: A Psychiatrist's View." A. West. *In the Service of Medicine*, July, 1970.

RECENT PUBLICATIONS

An increasing spate of articles on abortion has appeared since this manuscript was completed. Only a few of the more significant can be noted here.

"Artificial Termination of Pregnancy in Czechoslovakia." A. Kotasek. *Internat. Journal of Gynecology and Obstetrics*, 1971, **9**, 118.

> In Czechoslovakia more than 100,000 abortions were performed in the previous 12 months, more than 80 per cent for social indications, therefore in the first 12 weeks (when abortion is safest). Immediate complications due to infection occurred in 5 per cent, permanent complications in 20–30 per cent. There was a striking increase in later ectopic pregnancies, and a high incidence of damage to the cervix increasing spontaneous miscarriage in later pregnancies to 30–40 per cent. "We realise the necessity of altering our law."

"Abortion Games: An Inquiry into the Working of the Act." I. M. Ingram. *Lancet*, 1971, **2**, 969.

> Examines the working of the British act in terms of games theory. He sees the doctor faced with a meaningless Act, and obliged to give opinions on matters he considers to be non-medical, finding himself in a situation of doubt and conflict, unwittingly involved in games playing.

"The Abortion Decision." D. W. Millard. *British Journal of Social Work*, 1971, **1**, 131.

> He discusses the psychology of the decision process. A "tough-minded" decision—whether to terminate or not, admitting of no middle way—has to be made on the basis of a series of "tender-minded" judgments (e.g. on the extent of a woman's depression, or the degree of adversity of her housing) to which there are scarcely any unequivocal answers, the answers being distributed along some imagined scale.

Legal Abortion: The English Experience. A. Horder. London, 1971, Pergamon.

> In this volume a Psychiatrist recounts the British situation to 1970. A final chapter gives an account of the U.S. situation, and that in Canada, Australia, New Zealand and elsewhere. There is appendix with six very detailed case-histories of women aborted on psychiatric grounds.

"Survey of 3000 Unwanted Pregnancies." J. Lambert. *B.M.J.*,1971, **4**, 156.

> An account of 3000 consecutive patients seen at the London Pregnancy Advisory Service. Only 87 were turned down as having no legal grounds, 2258 were aborted, only 124 in N.H.S. hospitals.

THE AMERICAN SCENE

The new situation following on liberal legislation in many of the States is recorded, e.g., in:

"Legal Abortion in the U.S.A.: A Preliminary Assessment." M. Potts and B. N. Branch. *Lancet*, 1971, **2**, 651.

Legal Abortion in New York State: Medical, Legal, Nursing, Social Aspects. Ed. G. Schaefer.

This is a 320 pp issue of *Clinical Obstetrics and Gynecology*, 1971, **14**, 1. See especially *"Nursing Care in an Abortion Unit."* Beverly Yoloff, MargotWade, and Mildred Burlingame. (p. 67) "It is not unusual for some patients to cry and even ask their doctor how long it takes for the fetus to die" (this for saline installation techniques). In *"Out-patient Intra-amniotic Injection of Hypertonic Saline,"* T. D. Kerenyi makes the same point—so abhorrent to an obstetrician—by a graph (p. 137) of the time taken for the fetal heart to stop. *"Social Aspects of Abortion Counseling for Patients Undergoing Elective Abortion,"* Elizabeth D. Smith, Mary Veolitze and Ruth Markatz (p. 204) is most interesting in its discussion of group therapy for the pre-operative woman.

GENERAL INDEX

An asterisk indicates additional relevant material in the Reading List

Abortifacent drugs, 26
Abortion Committees, 239
Abortion Law Reform Association, 54ff, 64
Abortion on Demand, 36, 39, 59, 62, 65, 67, 77, 80, 108
Abortionists, illegal, 25, 35, 171
Abortoria, 39, 84
Adjustment to refusal of abortion, 226ff
Adoption, 175, 179, 189ff, 275*
Adverse sequelae of legal abortion, 60, 79, 85, 173, 204, 210, 212ff, 229, 246*
Agnostic views, 55–7, 89, 127, 131
Amniocentesis, 198, 200, 215
Anaesthetic misadventures, 214, 219
Animation of the soul, 98, 122, 126
Assimilation of babe into family, 177
Association for the Study of Abortion, 11
'Battered Baby' syndrome, 227

Birthright, 275
Bourne case, 22, 29, 62, 151, 169
Breadwinner, mother as, 181
British Medical Association, 60, 152
Cancer, 152, 250
Certification, 67, 69, 83
Cervical incompetence, 173, 280
Chastity, 167, 191, 255ff, 270
Child's right to be wanted, 44, 45
Children: deprived, 184ff, 227, 247
Children: unwanted, 21, 85, 86, 185, 191, 226, 228
Christ, 92, 95, 96, 117, 129ff, 135, 268, 271, 275
Christianity and Sex, 249
Christian Medical Societies, 11, 106
Chronic Ill-health: after illegal abortion, 22
Climate of opinion, 71, 248, 254
Compassion, 100, 107, 129ff, 192, 241, 255
Committee of Inquiry, 86

Confidentiality, 46, 69, 70, 214
Congenital abnormality, 21, 32, 44, 68, 100, 117, 132, 143, 193ff, 264
Conscience: personal, 17, 53, 203, 251, 271
Conscience: of hospital personnel, 14, 30, 51, 66, 68, 81, 83, 91, 100, 101, 106, 138, 216, 241
Contraception, 23, 44, 52, 71, 153, 172, 238, 257ff, 266, 270, 273
Contraception as alternative to abortion, 37, 38, 52
Contraceptives and the unmarried, 253ff
Declaration of Geneva, 241
Depression as indication for abortion, 235
Desire to be pregnant, 176
Destiny of man, 57, 92, 100, 125, 127, 210, 233.
Diabetes, 152
Dilatation and curettage, 14, 213
Disposable persons/pregnancies, 49, 50

Peace of heart, 139, 140.
Perforation of Uterus, 26, 213
Permissive nature of Abortion Act 1967, 53, 64, 81
Personality, 116, 211, 255
Population pressures, 37, 47
'Post-abortal hangover', 205
Poverty, 161, 271
Pregnancy:
after abortion, 208
continued despite abortion granted, 228
premarital, 170
Premature delivery, 220
Pretexts for abortion, 14, 31, 35, 66, 168, 196, 232, 242
Priest: see Pastor, also see Roman Catholic viewpoints
Private sector, 30, 42, 77, 78, 103, 223
Proffered abortion rejected, 202
Professional women, 24, 158
Promiscuity, 171, 207, 253, 255
Prostaglandins, 215, 263ff
Prostitutes, 180
'Protestant Affirmation', 106
Psychiatrists, 14, 59, 31, 65, 66, 230ff
Psychoses, 204, 234, 235
Quality of woman's life, 15, 24, 48, 49, 72, 89, 155ff, 181
Quickening, 127
Racial factors, 185, 192
Radiation damage to fetus, 197
Rape, 68, 168
Recruitment to gynaecology, 84, 266
to nursing, 83
Refusal to perform abortion, 42, 74, 222ff
Regret, 44, 92, 101, 182, 201ff, 243, 271

Religious involvement, 17, 89ff
Renal failure after abortion, 26
Repeat abortions, 49, 53, 179, 188, 209, 243
Research use of fetal material, 85
Responsibility in sexual behaviour, 182
Retained products of conception, 218
Rhesus sensitisation, 220
Risks to health—degree of, 60, 64
Risk to maternal life, 151
Roman Catholic viewpoints, 30, 56, 58, 65, 82, 89, 98ff, 108, 122, 132, 151, 241, 259
Royal College of Obstetricians and Gynaecologists, 60, 63, 85, 218
Royal College of Nursing, 83
Rubella, 143, 197ff
'Safe period', 258
Saline method of termination, 215
Sanctity of Life, 15, 22, 45, 61, 89, 100, 106, 124, 132, 193, 246
Sanctity of Unborn Life (S.O.U.L.), 91, 105
Scandinavian experience, 36, 41, 42, 52, 153, 159, 168, 202, 205, 208, 218, 220, 223, 224, 226, 227, 228, 239, 244, 269
Scars, operative, 82
Schizophrenia, 204, 210, 231
Screening for fetal abnormalities, 199, 200
Self reproach by women, 229
Separated women, 179, 191
Sex education, 269
Sexual frigidity, 210
Sexual permissiveness, 57, 170ff, 182, 190, 250ff.
Shot-gun marriages, 174

'Shopping-around' for abortion, 223
Socio-economic factors, 46, 47, 60, 65, 67, 155ff (see also poverty, housing)
Society for the Protection of the Unborn Child (S.P.U.C.), 58, 62
Soul of the fetus, 15, 124
Sperm banks, 57, 194, 262
Stable unions, 170
Step-fathers, 185
Sterilization,
female, 69, 72, 153, 157, 158, 164, 205, 216, 243, 247, 261ff
male, 262
Students, 13, 176, 181ff, 250
Suicide, 21, 31, 42, 57, 85, 208, 224ff
Teenage sexuality, 171
Temptation, sexual, 171
Thalidomide, 49, 54, 197
Transient Situational Disturbance, 236, 245
Tuberculosis, 152
Twins, 123, 219
United States of America, 35, 39, 168, 200, 207, 231, 232*
Unmarried fathers, 209
Unmarried mothers, 177, 186ff
Unwanted pregnancies, 23, 47, 73, 86, 191, 226 272
Unwilling coitus, 168ff
Utus paste, 215
Vacuum aspirat.on, 213
Veneral diseases, 182, 220, 250, 269
Virus infection, 197ff
'West-End abortions', 23, 32, 42, 72
Widening indications for abortion, 244
Widows, 179, 191
Women's right to choose whether to give birth, 13, 17, 42, 43, 78, 105 131, 201, 238ff

INDEX OF AUTHORS CITED

An asterisk indicates authors whose work(s) appear(s) in the Reading List

INDEX OF SCRIPTURE REFERENCES